EARLY AMERICAN PRESSED GLASS

MAGNET AND GRAPE WINE JUG, INSCRIBED IN GILDED
LETTERS, "TRY ME"

EARLY AMERICAN PRESSED GLASS

Enlarged and Revised

A Classification of Patterns Collectible
in Sets Together with Individual
Pieces for Table Decorations

By

RUTH WEBB LEE

CHARLES E. TUTTLE COMPANY
Rutland, Vermont & Tokyo, Japan

REPRESENTATIVES

For Continental Europe:
BOXERBOOKS, INC., Zurich

For the British Isles:
PRENTICE-HALL INTERNATIONAL, INC., London

For Austrlasia:
BOOK WISE Beverly, South Australia

Published by the Charles E. Tuttle Company, Inc.
of Rutland, Vermont and Tokyo, Japan
with editorial offices at
Suido 1-chome, 2-6, Bunkyo-ku, Tokyo

Library of Congress Card No. 85-050502

International Standard Book No. 0-8048-7004-7

First Tuttle edition 1985

Printed in USA

ACKNOWLEDGMENTS

This book could not have been completed without the whole-hearted cooperation of scores of friends. I feel especially indebted to Mr. Harold Rugg of Hanover, New Hampshire, and Mr. Thomas C. Pears, Jr., of Pittsburgh, Pennsylvania, who unhesitatingly entrusted to me valuable old trade catalogues in their possession and enabled me to learn the old trade names, the approximate date of manufacture and the factory where many popular patterns were produced. As a matter of historical interest, to show what trade literature our grandfathers were favored with, I have reproduced many of these pages for the benefit of collectors. My grateful thanks are due Mr. Frank H. Wheaton of Millville, New Jersey, for the time spent showing me over his glass works, where I was able to watch all the fascinating processes of glass-making, including old-fashioned methods of blowing and finishing by hand; and to Mr. Marshal Fry for his helpful suggestions about the decorative possibilities of old pattern glass.

My acknowledgments are due to friends and acquaintances for specimens and information I needed. While I cannot mention them all by name, I sincerely hope they will accept with this acknowledgment the assurance of the gratitude I feel. I wish to express my thanks to those who loaned me so many pieces for my illustrations that without their help this book could not have been completed in so short a time: Mrs. George Hanagan, Mrs. Myrta Olmsted, Mrs. Carolyn Hager, Mr. Herbert Smith, Mrs. John Murdock, Mrs. Lester Garson, Mrs. L. E. Bird, Mrs. Ellis Gay, Mrs. William Strom, Mrs. Henry Freeman, Mrs. Elsa Sampson, Mrs. Emma Goldsmith, Mrs. Sarah Benham, Mr. George McKearin, Miss Ella Kegerreis, Mrs. Ola Sutherland Ahrens, Mrs. S. H. Knox, Miss Susan Hawks, Mr. Frank Schwarz, Mrs. L. B. Tuttle, Mrs. W. H. Wierman, Mrs. A. H. Barnhart.

FOREWORD

Had the number and magnitude of the obstacles that stand in the way of writing the ideal book on early American pressed glass been made plain to me at the start, I never would have undertaken the work. I knew that, being pioneer work, I could not hope to make it the final book on the subject. Of the scores of collectors and dealers that I have met not a single one remotely suspected that nearly three hundred patterns could be treated as being "collectible in sets." And when it came to securing historical information about the patterns themselves, I found that no library or private person had data that would shed light on one-tenth of the known patterns.

I can count on the fingers of one hand the known available illustrated catalogues and price-lists issued during or previous to the Civil War period that will show when and where certain patterns of early pressed glass were produced. I have examined what records I could and you will find references to them scattered throughout the book.

The reason for the appalling dearth of historical material is obvious. Do not forget that pressed glass, after it began to be manufactured in large quantities, or, say, from the late 1840's on, was never what you would call an aristocratic product with a pedigree worth preserving. There was not the slightest suspicion on the part of a single glassmaker of that period that a day would dawn when the six-inch plates they were glad to sell at less than three dollars a dozen would readily bring thirty times more from collectors nearly one hundred years later. They saw no reason why they should put themselves out to preserve, for an antique-collecting posterity, books of designs or statistics of their business any more than a toothpaste manufacturer to-day would think of sending specimens of his various tubes to the Smithsonian Institution for the benefit of future historians.

I have travelled, literally, thousands of miles, visited hundreds of antique shops and interviewed scores of collectors and dealers in search of specimens and data. Out of my natural desire to have as complete a list as possible, certain problems developed that had to be met. Unfortunately, I cannot say I think I have solved them successfully, for, whatever my decision may be, I am certain criticism will descend upon me in generous measure. For example, nothing can be more valuable to collectors and the antique trade than to know exactly how many "forms" or different articles come in each pattern. From the very outset I was confronted with the question of whether I should take the testimony of others as to their existence or set down only those that I myself had seen. After much consideration I decided to give, as positively existing, only those forms or items that I had seen with my own eyes and personally examined for design, size, etc.

Too many books on glass have been published the authors of which depended upon hearsay evidence and were thereby led to make assertions which they could not substantiate. The memory of dealers and even of veteran collectors is not always reliable. I realize as clearly as anyone that my lists are necessarily bound to be incomplete. No single person, however industrious, can hope to encounter every specimen of the many thousands that were made in the first half century of the American pressed glass industry.

It is a perverse habit misinformation has of spreading more widely than the truth and of persisting more obstinately. There are antique dealers who actually resent being set right in the matter of early American pressed glass. Doubtless, the average customer's demand for attributions is responsible for some of the misleading answers returned by certain dealers. The majority appear to think that it is not only safe but proper to call nearly everything in the pressed glass line "Sandwich." If you tell them the particular piece in question was made by the New England Glass Company and offer to show them an early catalogue to prove it, they may smile or they may frown; but in either case they stick to the old story. Magazine writers have not succeeded in exploding the Sandwich myth, though they have tried hard to do so of late years, nor have the small antique dealers in America learned to discard obviously impossible explanations about the origin, meaning, age and name of certain patterns, especially those which happen to be most popular at the moment. The quality of the glass itself, the character or lines of the design, the number and purpose of the articles that come in a particular pattern, the diagnostic value of its characteristics, all are blithely ignored. Now, the differences in pressed glass pieces may not tell the period to which they belong as certainly as the differences in costumes; but there is the same necessity to consider material and design if you wish to determine their age. I am convinced that many stories were evolved after some dealer or collector gave a name to a pattern and the need arose to justify the christening. Glaring anachronisms do not deter the myth-makers though, as a matter of fact, most of the mistakes are in the nature of claiming, on general principles, greater antiquity for the pieces than they are entitled to. Altogether it is to be hoped that dealers hereafter will not feel called upon to supply romances to glass collectors. The buyer of antiques usually knows exactly what he wants and why. There is no need to sell him fiction.

The need of establishing a standardized nomenclature for Early American Pressed Glass, was another strong factor in deciding me to undertake this work. It has been a source of annoyance and expense to both collectors and dealers to find that different sections of the country have different names for the same pattern. No collector could be certain that if he ordered Inverted Fern from Ohio he would receive what Pennsylvania or Connecticut dealers knew by that name. But even worse was the fact that many attractive patterns were practically uncollectible by mail because they had no name at all. Descriptions and rubbings did not always prove successful in obtaining matched specimens for the amateur who wanted to complete a set of the pattern of which the trade name had been lost and no substitute agreed upon.

The course I have followed in trying to bring order out of chaos is doubtless open to criticism but no one has suggested a better plan to me. Whenever I have found in old catalogues the original trade name of a certain pattern, I have used it in preference to others, except in the cases of very popular patterns which have come to be widely known by later names of their own. For example, the name given by the New England Glass Company to one of its patterns was Palace, but to-day it is generally known as "Waffle and Thumbprint." I have kept this ungraceful but popular later name in preference to the other. The old Lawrence pattern of the New England Glass Company has been known for some years now as Bull's Eye. The Blaze pattern of the same company was made with slight variations by the M'Kee Brothers of Pittsburgh, Pa., and by them called Stedman. I have thought it proper to call these by their old trade names since few collectors know the patterns by any name at all. What to-day is known as Ribbed Palm among Northern collectors was once called Acanthus in the South and Oak in some Western states. The old trade name of the M'Kee Brothers was Sprig. I have chosen Ribbed Palm because it is known by that name to more people, preferring in all such cases to favor the majority rather than the minority. Where the pattern had no name at all, I have tried to give it a short descriptive title. The essential point was to give it a name by which it could come to be known everywhere. Baltimore Pear, known also as Maryland Pear and in some places as Twin Pear, shows a fruit that looks more like a pear than a fig, but the leaf belongs to the fig tree rather than to the pear. But "Fig" is not liked, and since most collectors and dealers have called it Baltimore Pear for years it remains Baltimore Pear in this book. Its original name was "Fig," later changed to "Gypsy" by its makers, Adams and Co., of Pittsburgh, Pa.

There are various reasons why a strictly scientific or entirely logical classification of pattern glass is impossible to achieve. Pressed patterns cannot be divided chronologically into groups because the exact age of a particular design cannot be determined in the absence of reliable historical data. Moreover, many patterns enjoyed popularity during long periods so that it would be difficult to assign them to a definite decade. While undoubtedly the titles given, for the sake of convenience, to some of the chapters in this book may sound inadequate it is equally true that the concern of collectors is with specimens of their own specialty rather than with the naming of aggregations of possibly unrelated patterns.

It was the author's intention to establish the name of each pattern first and then give it a specific number as well as classify, also by number, the various "forms" or pieces found in each pattern, such as compotes, creamers, goblets, etc. If it is desired to order by mail, for example, the large covered compote on high standard, Tulip pattern, the collector can avoid errors by writing for: *Pattern No. 57, Form No. 4 a (1)*. By looking at the Classification of the Tulip pattern you will see that your compote is differentiated from the small covered compote on high standard, which is *Form No. 4 a (2)* and also from the very large open compote on standard, which is *Form No. 4 b.* It was necessary to change the form numbers in the third edition. It would be well when ordering by mail to remember this. Collectors and dealers should bear in mind the fact that the same forms vary in size, following the fashions prevailing at the time they were produced and sold. Cordial, wine and champagne glasses differ in height,* according to the patterns. Incidentally, no pressed patterns of champagne glasses appear with hollow stems except in the Three Face pattern. It is advisable when seeking to "match" pieces or forms of patterns which were popular enough to have been made by more than one glass house, to be content to approximate as closely as possible, the piece to be matched. If you wish an exact match, you must give correct dimensions. The only way for buyers and sellers to avoid mistakes is to know precisely what is wanted. Hence the need of a standardized classification. This book attempts to supply that need.

* See "Glass Terminology" on page xvii.

PREFACE TO THE THIRD EDITION

The kind reception accorded to the first and second editions of this book indicates the extent of the demand for a work devoted exclusively to patterns of our pressed glass and primarily intended to aid collectors in their quest of an essentially American product. It is a source of gratification to find that the sins of omission were much fewer than any pioneer might be pardoned for committing, when one considers the absence of precedents to guide and the dearth of documents calculated to throw light on the many phases of glass history. In publishing this revised and greatly enlarged edition of "Early American Pressed Glass," I have sought to fill as many of the gaps as I can with material and information gathered in two years of diligent search in various glass districts. I have to thank scores of correspondents the country over for their generous response to my requests for data bearing on the subject. This has enabled me to add to the classifications and to the origin of many varieties and to establish the date, place of manufacture and names of makers of divers patterns which, for years, were ascribed by dealers and collectors to Sandwich.

Fault has been found with the first and second editions, because a place was not found in my lists and Plates for this or that odd piece which had been inherited by indignant correspondents. Anyone familiar with the almost insuperable difficulties that beset American glass historians knows the utter absurdity of attempting to compile a volume that would include descriptions and illustrations of the thousands of odd goblets and other occasional items of tableware made in this country during the past hundred years. Moreover, the cost of printing such a book, even if it were ever completed, would be prohibitive. "Early American Pressed Glass," as I have been careful to state whenever the opportunity presented itself, treats exclusively of such patterns as may be collected in entire sets.

It gives me particular pleasure to record here my grateful appreciation of the help I have received in preparing this edition of my first book. I am especially indebted to Mr. Arthur Bennett, Mrs. Emma Fitts Bradford, Mrs. Edgar H. Bristol, Miss Susan Hawks, Mr. Samuel Frazier, Mr. James Gillinder, Mr. Edwin Lefèvre, Mr. Guy van Doren, Mr. C. E. Voitle, Mr. Charles H. West and officers of the U. S. Glass Company.

REVISED EDITION

Fourteen years have elapsed since the first volume of *Early American Pressed Glass* appeared and twelve years have gone by since it was revised. The nomenclature established by me in the first edition has come into such common use today that most collectors and dealers have forgotten that there was a time when most of the patterns were unknown and unnamed! During the intervening years, American pressed glass tableware has been collected so intensively that thousands of pieces which were comparatively common and easy to find in 1933, are now rare and difficult to locate except when collections come on the market. It is necessary, therefore, to bring this volume up to date once more. Additions have been made to the classifications and a few new Plates added, which will benefit all collectors. In many instances it has been possible to add valuable historical data, as to when and where patterns were made.

Collectors and dealers alike have been most kind in sending me notes regarding unlisted items and to them I feel a deep sense of gratitude, even though it is not possible to name them all here. By their good deeds they have added to the joy of all future collectors, as well as to the value of this book.

A special word should be said for Dr. Charles Ferris, who is a particularly busy man. He responded heroically by obtaining photos of the curious and interesting Monkey pattern, which has been added to this book, as well as by sending me detailed lists of items in patterns he collects. Mr. E. B. Merrill came to the rescue in a like manner, when he learned that a photograph of his beautiful Sandwich Star compote was a necessity, as well as a pleasure for all who behold it, in the completion of this nineteenth revised edition. Mrs. Harry Hussey kindly lent me her Lion lamp, a rarity which will be of interest to collectors of that well-known pattern.

Throughout the pages of this book will be found notations as to the rarity of many items enumerated, as well as asterisks to mark the pieces which have been reproduced up to this time. Considering the number of old patterns, relatively few have been copied. The fakes can be detected by those who will spend the time and effort required to learn the differences between the old and the new. There are a great many worthwhile patterns having both age and merit of design, which for some unknown reason have not come into popular demand. These patterns have not been reproduced, have not soared in price and are relatively easy to find. Collectors would do well to investigate before accumulating glass thirty-five to fifty years old, which has no more real value than reproductions.

RUTH WEBB LEE.

GLASS COLLECTORS' TERMINOLOGY

1. *Milk pitcher.* These occur in a few patterns but are rare. They are a size between a creamer and a water pitcher. Height is *approximately* 7 inches. Among the rare milk pitchers may be mentioned the Lion and the Bellflower. Bellflower in this size is found only in single vine, and ribbed to the end of the lip.

2. *Cordial.* Old trade catalogues of glass manufacturers mention cordials, wines and champagnes. A cordial and a wine, according to these catalogues, could be the same size. Cordials, in the modern meaning of the word, exist in patterns which were carried on for twenty, thirty or more years, and therefore they occur in the declining years. Usually the early patterns carried what they termed a cordial or a wine, which measure anywhere from 3⅞ inches to 4¼ inches, and a champagne which measures from 5 inches to 5¼ inches. In the later years, the Honeycomb pattern produced a cordial which measures approximately 3 to 3⅛ inches. In this book, let it be understood that the old-time terms are used and a cordial will measure 3⅞ to 4¼ inches, unless the bowl is larger than usual, when it will be noted as a wine glass. A champagne will measure approximately 5 to 5¼ inches. In the Dahlia, all three sizes were made, but this is an exception. None is the 3 inch size.

3. *Proof.* Many readers have asked for an explanation of this term. Among glass collectors, it means in perfect condition.

4. *"Three-mold."* This is a misnomer which has applied in the past only to certain patterns of *early blown glass,* known by glassmakers originally as Blown Molded glass. Mold marks on the bases of pressed glass pieces mean nothing of interest to collectors and should be disregarded. It is a fact that some

very late pressed goblets show two mold marks, whereas the preponderance of the early glass tableware has three.

5. *Claret.* Clarets are known in very few pressed glass patterns. They may be found in Ashburton, Horn of Plenty, and in a limited number of the earlier patterns but they are rare, particularly in Horn of Plenty. A claret has a long, narrow bowl, which often flares at the top. The stem is very short.

6. *Ale glass.* Ale glasses were produced in many odd patterns but are difficult to find in well-known designs, such as Excelsior, in which they exist. They are footed, with a short stem and a long bowl, quite large in diameter. Rare.

7. *Cup plate.* Most collectors are familiar with cup plates. They preceded pattern glass, for the most part. There are about 1000 designs made in clear glass and in color, by glass houses ranging from New England to Ohio and Pennsylvania. If one includes the color range in all cup plates there would be nearly 5000. It is dangerous to note the size of these plates because they vary greatly, but generally range from 3 to 3½ inches. In pattern glass this size is known in Loop and Dart with round ornament, Barberry, Maple Leaf, etc. but they are an exception. Moreover, it is debatable as to whether they were meant to be used as cup plates or as individual butter dishes. Handleless cups were a thing of the past during the era when the known 3½ inch plates occur in patterns collectible in sets of tableware, so there was no actual *need* for a plate on which to place the cup after the hot tea had been poured into the saucer!

8. *Compote.* A bowl, which can be deep or shallow, fused to a standard or stem, which can be high or low. These were used in the olden days for fruit.

9. *Toddy glass.* A tall jar-like glass, in which hot drinks were mixed during the early days. Similar to a "flip glass."

10. *Toddy plate.* There are a few lacy glass toddy plates, such as the "Grape Vine and Harp" and several in pattern glass, in a 4¼ inch size, which have come to be referred to as toddy

plates. Their original use is not known. We may surmise that some were utilized to hold the hot toddy glass so that a table would not be marred, or that they were used as cup plates for those who wished to add their spoon, when a cup plate would prove to be too small.

INTRODUCTION TO THE NEW EDITION

The Ruth Webb Lee books are so well-known and so universally acknowledged to be the best in their field they need no introduction. However, I should like to mention what I consider to be my mother's most remarkable time-proven accomplishment. The Ruth Webb Lee books cover a specific time prior to 1900. The material covered in her books is so complete that the period covered remains up-to-date without need for revision.

I have been asked, "How did your mother ever assemble the glass for the photographs, research the material and find time to write her books?" My answer is brief and to the point. It took many years of unceasing devotion and hard work.

A prominent collector once commented, "Having this book is the next best thing to owning the glass itself." This book was written for collectors, museums, dealers and all who love and appreciate early American glass.

I sincerely hope this book will bring you pleasure and the information you seek.

Robert Webb Lee

CONTENTS

Contents

ILLUSTRATIONS

EARLY AMERICAN PRESSED GLASS

Chapter I

INTRODUCTION

It is not so many years ago that collectors of American blown glass and writers on the subject did not deem worthy of mention the later commercial glassware which flooded our markets during the decades immediately preceding and following the Civil War. Snobbish lovers of antiques openly scoffed at it as "Early Woolworth." To be sure, there was no sound reason for the collector of rarities to find pleasure in acquiring anything so plentiful as glass made in America from 1840 to 1880. But the urge to buy essentially American antiques grew stronger year by year in the United States and with it a keener desire on the part of collectors to own interesting and decorative tableware which was old enough to be in harmony with the furnishings and at the same time give an American atmosphere to the dining room. To-day discriminating collectors are as keenly interested in matching sets of this popular glass, both crystal and colored, as they used to be in acquiring the rarer forms of blown glass. Pressed glass may not rival Stiegel but the urge to apologize for it is no longer felt.

It is amazing how much of it has survived the natural enemies of all fragile things during the past eighty years when one considers the average life of a modern china dinner service! On the other hand, some of the colored glass listed in this book may date as late as 1888 but you will find that even these pieces prove decidedly elusive when you are matching up sets.

Save for an occasional magazine article, very little of value has been written about our early pressed glass. There has been needed not only information but even a nomenclature. I knew that to cover all the odd specimens that come to light here and there would be an impossibility; but this book was planned with the intention of bringing some order out of the confusion. That it may prove a practical guide to the many enthusiastic collectors of American pressed glass is the extent of the author's hope.

From the very first it was my belief that the majority of readers would be less concerned with the technical details of glass and glassmaking than with the need of standardized names for the available pressed glass patterns and with the means of identifying them. As this work reached the final stages of preparation, my talks with collectors convinced me that there also existed a desire for simple answers to a few questions about old glass without going into elaborate technical explanations. For instance, fully ninety-five per cent of my correspondents ask: "How can one tell when and where these patterns were made?" After interviewing many of the recognized authorities on American glassmaking I can safely reply that no one can tell positively. This does not mean that we do not know where many of the patterns were made or that it is absolutely impossible to tell most of the earlier pressed glass from most of the late. Of course, it requires study and experience. Ask a glassmaker a question about a certain piece which you describe in great detail and he will invariably tell you: "I'll have to see the piece!" The description does not always help the expert.

The art of pressing glass into molds was known to the ancient Egyptians, but it was not until the late 1820's that Yankee ingenuity began to experiment successfully with machinery for the purpose. Machine pressed glass was known in England but English authorities as well as our own experts, award the credit for perfecting this method of glassmaking to Americans. I mention this because of the controversy over when and where pressed glass was first made by machinery.

Many amateurs have been puzzled by the earlier output of our best flint glass factories in the etched and cut glass which antedated the cruder, less artistic and much later pressed glass. The average person to-day is apt to associate "cut glass" with that relatively late American product which was nothing but special pressed glass patterns that necessitated less cutting than "blanks"; in short, an American labor saving method that was copied in Europe for the American trade. It cheapened cut glass to the point of making it unfashionable. The fine early English and American cut and etched glass was always blown and not partly pressed. It is a curious commentary on the vagaries of fashion that the once despised pressed glass is in demand to-day, while the expensive cut glass so popular for wedding gifts a generation ago, is not wanted by experienced collectors today.

The use of pressing machinery spread from 1827 on as improvements were made in apparatus as well as in processes. By 1840, factories to make pressed glass were springing up like mushrooms in various states.

It should be borne in mind by collectors who do not care to read bulky volumes on glassmaking in America that what happened with blown glass happened also with machine pressed glass, which is that at first only the more necessary articles of tableware were manufactured. As the country grew in population and wealth there was a corresponding rise in refinement in the home and a demand developed for articles that hitherto had almost been considered luxuries. What would have been called quantity production, if the term had been in use then, began, in the pressed glass industry, some time in the Forties. I have seen advertisements that show the greater variety of pieces offered for sale year by year; for example, many kinds of drinking glasses were manufactured and sold by factories in various parts of the country before 1850, such as goblets, tumblers of divers sizes, wine, rum, ale, cordial and other glasses, their great number being explained by the fact that the demand came not only from private homes but from taverns, ships, barrooms, etc.

Not only did the number and variety of articles increase, but practically all the glass houses in the Fifties were compelled to cater more and more to changing fads and modes in pattern glass. Catching the popular fancy meant sales and sales meant solvency in a highly competitive business. The tendency of the various makers to copy or plagiarize from competitors any design that proved profitably popular began then and accounts, as I have elsewhere stated, for the number of variants we find in many of the popular patterns. Incidentally, the habit persists to this day.

A question which has not yet been answered and may never be, is: "Which was the first pressed glass pattern made in America for general table use?" I mean by this, made in enough articles, such as compotes, goblets, tumblers, plates, sauce and honey dishes, to form what to-day collectors call a "set." It is reasonable to suppose that the first patterns of pressed glass tableware were the plain heavy designs, just as the earliest American pewter was simple in character. The more ornate patterns followed with the growing sophistication of the country. While I have seen several of these early heavy goblets and dishes with pontil marks, I have never found as many pontil-marked pieces of any design in which a complete service exists, as I have in the Bellflower. That is one of my reasons for believing that the Bellflower was one of the first, if, indeed, not the first, pattern made in enough articles for general table use or in what we now call a complete set. I have had goblets in this pattern crudely formed, with the base apparently blown and bearing a rough pontil mark. I have a castor set with pontil-marked bottles and a footed salt. To me it seems reasonable to assume that experiments were made with this design in at least one factory before the final perfection of the mechanical presser, and therefore the cruder specimens may well date prior to 1840, when Bellflower "sets" did not contain as many "forms" as they did later. I have a spoonholder in Bellflower in that beautiful shade of cobalt blue that is never seen in late glass.

Some molds were made of iron and others of brass. You can distinguish the ware made in brass molds by the softer contours. Later the rough scars on the bases left by the pontil rod of the glassworker were ground off. In one early catalogue, goblets were listed with "polished feet." By "crimped handles," in my descriptions of articles, I mean handles that were applied by hand to the piece instead of being pressed into place by machinery. The workmen usually flipped over the end of the handle in a series of little crimps at the bottom where it joined the bowl. This method was used until after the Civil War. It is by the study of these differences that the approximate age of certain articles may be judged.

We know that pressed lead flint glass was made before 1830, the lead and flint giving to the glass a clear bell-like tone when tapped, as well as greater brilliancy and weight. Impurities in the sand that would color the glass were overcome by the proper addition of manganese dioxide, which the workmen in England called "glass-maker's soap." Bottle glass, for example, was merely glass in which the impurities had not been rendered colorless by the proper addition of manganese. A greenish or bluish cast was imparted by impurities that had not been fully eliminated just as a purple tinge came from an excess of manganese. With the exception of a few factories, practically the last of the lead flint glassware for table use ceased to be made shortly after the Civil War, when it became commercially imperative to find cheaper products. Lime glass came in and with it disappeared the bell-like ring of the old glass.

With the advent of this cheaper lime glass came also the production in quantity of the colored pattern glass so largely collected to-day. There is a grape pattern, manufactured about twenty years ago, which to-day is found in almost a violet shade. Many people insist it therefore must be very old. A purple cast is not necessarily evidence of age. While it is true that sunlight and time impart the amethystine hue we see on old window panes, too much manganese will do the same thing. Moreover, we know that clear glass left exposed to the sunlight in the desert will acquire the same color within a few months.

I wish I might make clear, once for all, the unfortunately too common error of indiscriminately referring to some pressed glass as "three-mold" because it shows three mold-marks or lines. What old-time collectors always meant by the misnomer "three-mold," was one certain type of early blown glass, known by the makers as "Blown Molded." The latter original designation is a more sensible name, since this particular style of blown glass was produced from two, three, four or five-part molds. So why was it ever called "three-mold"? An endless amount of confusion has resulted from the erroneous term, since amateurs have persisted in commenting on the number of mold-marks noted on pressed glass goblets and dishes, which mean nothing of value to the collector and should be disregarded.

The designs of the true Blown Molded glass consist usually of combinations of vertical, horizontal or diagonal ribbing, diamond quilting, sunbursts, daisy-in-the-square, as well as the arched and baroque patterns, many of which may be found illustrated in my volume "Sandwich Glass." Originally aiming to produce decorative effects similar to the English or Irish cut glass, at a much cheaper cost, the Blown Molded patterns were obtained by blowing glass into hinged molds on whose interior surfaces the desired pattern had been cut. In examining pieces of this type, one will find the inside of the article to be the reverse of the outside. This happened because, since the glass was in the plastic state when blown into the mold, what was concave on the outside, was convex on the inside. Pressed glass, on the other hand, is smooth on the inside. The three lines which are seen so clearly on the bases of many pressed glass goblets, gave way to two lines when the later and cheaper pressed glass was made. One occasionally sees pressed glass bearing four or five mold-marks. But the point to establish clearly is that the term "three-mold glass" does not refer to any pattern of pressed glass of which this book treats. The stubborn insistence of a few collectors of blown glass in continuing this incorrect term, will forever cause confusion to new collectors.

Chapter II

COLONIAL GROUP

ASHBURTON

The series of patterns treated in this chapter, in the absence of specific names, is generically called "Colonial." The glass is distinguished by its heaviness and brilliancy. Of course, it is much later than the Colonial period, since that came to an end in 1776. Perhaps the thickness of the ware and the simplicity of design suggesting primitive times are responsible for the designation. They date, in some cases, during the 1840's, while others were listed in old catalogues as late as the 1880's. There is a marked similarity between many of them, and close observation is necessary to distinguish the differences. These patterns did not lose their popularity, commercially speaking, until about 1875, which accounts for the variations and differences in the quality of glass.

The first of the group is the "Ashburton." This was the name given to it in old catalogues of the Fifties and Sixties. It has not been known by any other name than "Colonial" of late years and as it is not an easy task to give it a descriptive title that would differentiate it instantly from the other designs it so closely resembles, it seems fitting to retain the original name of "Ashburton." It consists of a loop below with large oval above. The goblet is large and very heavy, with hexagonal stem that spreads out, forming a knob close to the base, which is clear. It is simple and dignified and is found in a satisfying number of forms, including one most unusual large covered mug or toddy glass, with plate. It has been definitely established that this pattern was made in three factories, though doubtless it was produced at others as well. The general design is the same, but it varies in minor details and in the quality of the glass, the product of later years being

9

less brilliant and lighter in weight. There is one point I wish to emphasize about the Ashburton pattern, because it may help to avert trouble from those seeking to match pieces. The top row of ovals or circles may vary and they were shown this way in at least one original catalogue. On the page of line drawings, Plate 3, are shown three types of goblets, all of the same period, one with ovals which do not connect and two with ovals joined. Sometimes the top row has circles, though this is generally on the smaller pieces, such as wines or cordials. These varying types were all shown and listed under the name of Ashburton. In her interesting book on Cambridge Glass, Mrs. Watkins speaks of this as one of the earliest of the New England Glass Company's patterns and since she found an inventory listing the design in 1849, it may be accepted as one of the earliest pressed glass patterns made for general table use. In the inventory referred to, a list of pressed glassware was given that was shipped to California during the '49 gold rush, under date of October 29, 1849. Included were "large size Ashburton goblets" to sell for $4.50 a dozen. Also decanters, tumblers, champagnes, jelly glasses, wines and cordials. This proves conclusively that pressed pattern glass was being turned out during the Forties, for it must have been produced in large quantities prior to the date of that shipment.

It is amazing that the popularity of the Ashburton was so long lived. Thirty-five to forty years is a long time for one pattern to be marketed and sold. It was one of the earliest pressed patterns at the old firm of Bakewell, Pears & Co., whose catalogue of about 1875-80 still shows samples of it. An Ovington Brothers' catalogue of the period 1854-59, during which time they were located at 218 and 220 Fulton Street, Brooklyn, Long Island, advertises in this manner: "Double Flute, or Ashburton pattern, of all the various sizes: Lemonade, Bar, Beer, Table, Soda and Sarsaparilla Tumblers. The largest size Tumbler of this style is one of the most desirable patterns, being very perfectly and beautifully moulded." The catalogue further states on another page, under "Pressed or Moulded Glassware. Tumblers": "The subscribers assortment of this article includes every known de-

PLATE 1—GOBLETS

Ashburton   Loop
Flute   Excelsior

PLATE 2—GOBLETS

Colonial
Argus

Crystal
Mirror

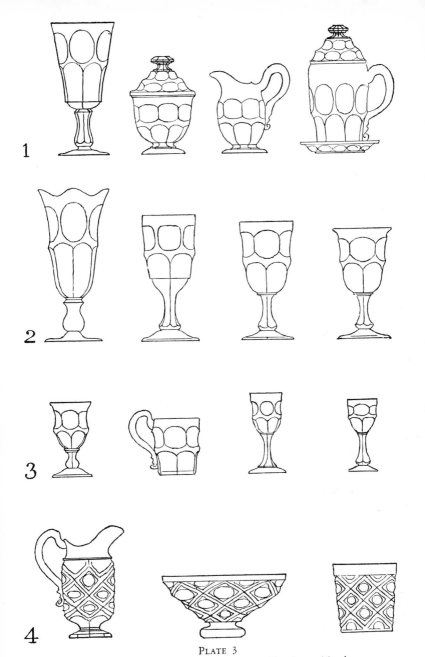

PLATE 3

1. ASHBURTON celery vase, sugar bowl, creamer, toddy glass with plate.
2. ASHBURTON celery vase, goblet with disconnected ovals, goblet in usual form,
   goblet with flaring bowl.
3. ASHBURTON egg cup, handled mug, wine, cordial.
4. DIAMOND THUMBPRINT creamer, bowl with low foot, tumbler.

PLATE 4

1. EXCELSIOR goblet, footed tumbler, double egg cup, egg cup.
2. EXCELSIOR tumbler, wine, cordial, claret.
3. LOOP covered compote on high standard, deep plate, covered bowl.
4. PETAL and LOOP open compote, sugar bowl, sauce dish.

sirable style and pattern, and will generally comprise between seventy-five and one hundred different sizes and designs of pressing; the stock includes all the modern patterns, so much admired, some of which are so perfectly moulded as to compare favorably with cut glass." Proof enough that pressed glass made a considerable headway during the 1840's.

While the clear flint glass is all one can usually find in this pattern, an occasional colored piece comes to light. I have seen a few, including a footed tumbler with applied handle in a beautiful shade of golden amber, a champagne in a fine shade of green, and several yellow, opaque white and opalescent pieces, mostly sugar bowls. "Gold Colar" cordials were listed in the inventory of the items shipped to California. "Colar" is the original spelling in the inventory. The rarest and most beautiful Ashburton specimen known to date is a celery vase in amethyst.

We learn that in subsequent shipments other pressed patterns were sent. We are unable to identify them in the absence of illustrations. Who can tell to-day what "York Shell," "General Taylor" or "Astor" patterns looked like? Doubtless specimens survive but they are not known by the original trade names, given to them by the New England Glass Company. Fragments of the Ashburton design have been excavated from the site of the Boston & Sandwich Glass Company, so this pattern must be included among that factory's products.

Classification

ASHBURTON

PATTERN 1

(See Plates 1, 3, 8)

Form Number.
  1. Bitters bottle.
  2. Celery holder (now generally referred to as celery vase).
  3. Champagne.
  4. Claret. 5¾ inches.

Form Number.

5. Cordial. Shape and size vary.

6. Creamer. Two styles.

7. Decanters.
    a. With heavy collar.
        (1) Pint.
        (2) Quart.
        (3) Three pint.
    b. With Stopper.
        (1) Half-pint.
        (2) Pint.
        (3) Quart.
        (4) Three pint.

8. Egg cup. Some do not ring when tapped.
    a. Double egg cup.

9. Flip glass.

10. Goblets.
    a. Flaring sides.
    b. Straight sides.
    c. Rarity may be found in goblet having engraved designs in the panels.

11. Honey dish. 3⅝ inches.

12. Jelly glass.

13. Jugs.
    a. Pint.
    b. Quart.
    c. Three pint.

14. Lemonade glass.

15. Long Tom ale glass.

16. Mugs.
    a. Beer.
    b. Pony (quoted from old catalogue price list).

17. Sauce dish. Two sizes.

18. Sugar bowl. Two sizes.

19. Toddy jars, covered.
    a. With plate, quart size.
    b. Same with handle.
    c. Extra large flip glass.

Form Number.
20. Tumblers.
    a. Handled, large half-pint.
    b. Quart size.
    c. Sarsaparilla.
    d. Ship tumblers.
        (1) Half-pint.
        (2) Large half-pint.
        (3) One-third pint.
    e. Soda.
    f. Taper tumblers.
        (1) One-third pint.
        (2) Pint.
    g. Water.
    h. Whiskey tumblers.
21. Water bottle with "tumble-up," or matching tumbler.
22. Wine glass. Large and small sizes, which vary in shape of bowl and stem.

Colors: Clear glass; a few occasional pieces in opaque white, yellow, amber, green, etc., are rare. The finest piece to date is a particularly beautiful amethyst celery vase.

ARGUS

This design would be exactly like the Ashburton except for a row of elongated thumbprints running between the upper and lower band of connected loops. The quality of the glass is much the same and shows careful workmanship. Not any pattern of the group miscalled "Colonial" can be called plentiful. It does not seem possible that they could have been made in the large quantities that others were because so little remains to-day. Not many of these early patterns were copied by other factories as extensively as some of the later designs, except Ashburton.

Much pleasure may be derived from the use of this lovely early flint glass, and as collectors become more familiar with the less known designs, it seems certain that the demand will grow far beyond the small supply that survives. I have in my possession several pieces of this glass, which I have compared carefully with some of the wood-cut illustrations of the Argus pattern shown in M'Kee Brothers, Pittsburgh, Pa., catalogues printed before and after the Civil War. They are exactly alike in every detail. Yet in the same catalogues are shown other pieces under the name of "Argus" which look like a plain thumbprint. One is a lamp and another an ale glass. These are shown on Plate 11, of line drawings, copied carefully from the catalogue illustrations.

Characterized as "the first successful flint glass factory in the United States" in various histories and reports on the progress of glass manufactories in America, is that of Bakewell, Pears & Co. of Pittsburgh, Pa., established in 1808. A complete history of this interesting firm and its wares would make a valuable book in itself. Originally Bakewell, Page & Bakewell, their factory was known as the Pittsburgh Flint Glass Manufactory. Their specialty was flint glass, and they were the first to manufacture cut glass and to do all kinds of ornamenting and engraving in glass work. Lafayette visited the famous works on his tour of the United States in 1825 and took to France specimens of their work which he considered equal to Baccarat glass. They sold their product in almost all parts of the world but particularly in the West and in Mexico. From the Pittsburgh *Mercury* (1832) we learn that "President Jackson has ordered from Bakewell, Page & Bakewell, of the city of Pittsburgh, a set of glass for his own use. It consists of large and splendid bowls, with and without stands, celery glasses, pitchers, quart and pint decanters, tumblers, wines and champagne glasses, salts, etc., all executed in the very best style of workmanship. The glass is as pellucid as crystal and the beautiful cuttings give a brilliancy of effect not easily described." "We understand the order is valued at $1,500." They had previously made a full set for President Monroe.

In an illustrated trade catalogue of Bakewell, Pears & Co. which is undated but appears to be of their later period (1875-80) is shown an ale glass in the Argus pattern, under the name of "Concave Ashburton." The Argus pattern of Bakewell, Pears & Co. is fully illustrated in a pattern given in this book under the title of Thumbprint. The old trade names of the various early patterns have been lost for many years. It may be just as well, since confusion would have been inevitable due to the fact that every factory used a different name for the same design. The Ashburton is one of the very few that remained Ashburton throughout the thirty-five or forty years that its popularity endured.

It has been definitely established that Argus was produced at Sandwich, though probably in limited quantities.

Classification

ARGUS

PATTERN 2

(See Plates 2, 11)

Form Number.

1. Ale glass, two types.
2. Beer glass, two sizes.
3. Bitters bottle.
4. Celery. Two types, one pressed and the other cut.
5. Champagne.
6. Decanters.
   - *a.* Pint.
   - *b.* Quart.
7. Egg cup.
8. Goblets.
9. Jelly glass.
10. Lamps.
    - *a.* Footed.
    - *b.* 4 inch colored base.
11. Mug, handled (same as whiskey tumbler).
12. Spoonholder.
13. Sugar bowl.
14. Tumblers.
    - *a.* Footed.
    - *b.* Ship.
    - *c.* Whiskey.
15. Wine glass.

Color: Clear glass. Any colored pieces are rare. A spoonholder has been noted in yellow.

EXCELSIOR

The design of this pattern is more elaborate than the others. It shows a row of loops with large indented centers around the base, an inverted row directly overhead and a large diamond point with blunt end at each intersection through the center. That this was one of the very early patterns made by the M'Kee Brothers, is borne out by the character of the pieces and the bell-like ring to the glass. The goblet is large and very heavy, with pointed knob stem. The egg cup comes in two types, one having an inverted bowl-shaped base, much like those made to-day. One page taken from the M'Kee Brothers catalogue of 1868 is shown on Plate 7. This pattern also appeared in a much earlier list, *circa* 1859. The line drawings on Plate 4 are taken from pieces in my possession. It is to be noted that in many of the early as well as in some of the later patterns, goblets were made in two sizes. This is also one of the earliest of the pressed patterns in which candlesticks were made to match, aside from the well-known Sandwich Petal and Loop. The Excelsior candlesticks were made in two sizes, the larger being shown on Plate 34.

Classification

EXCELSIOR

Pattern 3

(See Plates 1, 4, 7, 34)

Form Number.

1. Ale glass, tall and fairly large in diameter.
2. Bitters bottle.
3. Bowls.
    a. Round, flat, covered.
    b. 10 inch.

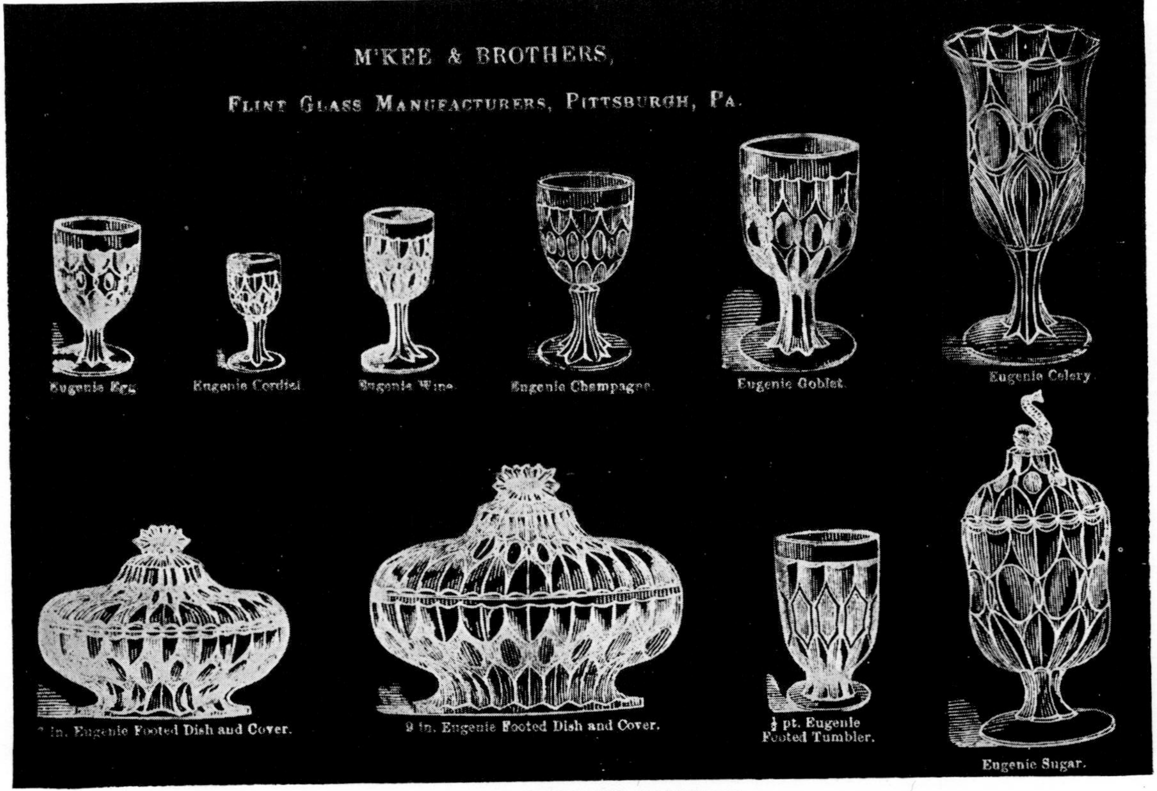

M'KEE & BROTHERS,
FLINT GLASS MANUFACTURERS, PITTSBURGH, PA.

Eugenie Celery.

Eugenie Sugar.

Eugenie Goblet.

½ pt. Eugenie Footed Tumbler.

Eugenie Champagne.

Eugenie Wine.

Eugenie Cordial

Eugenie Egg.

8 in. Eugenie Footed Dish and Cover.

9 in. Eugenie Footed Dish and Cover.

PLATE 5—EUGENIE PATTERN

Reproduced directly from page of old trade catalogue, M'Kee & Brothers, Pittsburgh, Pa.

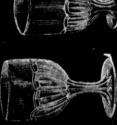

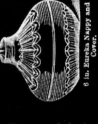

M'KEE & BROTHERS.

FLINT GLASS MANUFACTURERS, PITTSBURGH, PA.

4 in. Eureka Nappy.

6 in. Eureka Nappy.

7 in. Eureka Dish.

8 in. Eureka Dish.

9 in. Eureka Dish.

Eureka Cordial.

Eureka Egg.

Eureka Wine.

Eureka Champagne.

Eureka Ft. Tumbler.

Eureka Goblet.

6 in. Eureka Nappy and Cover.

6 in. Eureka Footed Nappy and Cover.

6 in. Eureka Sweetmeat and Cover.

PLATE 6—EUREKA PATTERN

M'KEE & BROTHERS,

FLINT GLASS MANUFACTURERS, PITTSBURGH, PA.

Pt. Ex. Decanter.

Pt. Ex. Pitcher.

Ex. Bitter.

Ex. Ale.

3 qt. Ex. foot Tumb.

½ qt. Ex. Ship Tumb.

10 in. Ex. Bowl.

Qt. Ex. Pitcher.

Qt. Ex. Decanter.

PLATE 7—EXCELSIOR PATTERN

Reproduced directly from page of old trade catalogue, M'Kee & Brothers, Pittsburgh, Pa.

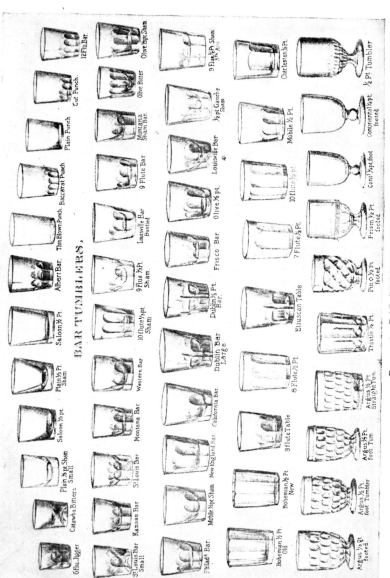

BAR TUMBLERS.

PLATE 8—BAR TUMBLERS

Reproduced directly from page of old trade catalogue, Bakewell, Pears & Co., Pittsburgh, Pa.

Form Number.

4. Candlesticks, 9½ inch. One smaller size.

5. Celery vase, with knob stem.

6. Champagne.

7. Compote, 10 inch, open on high standard.

8. Creamer. Two styles: Usual type and a rarity produced from a tumbler mold.

9. Decanters.
    - *a*. Pint.
    - *b*. Quart.
    - *c*. Small footed, like sauce bottles.

10. Dish, oval. Two sizes.

11. Egg cups.
    - *a*. Double.
    - *b*. Usual style.
    - *c*. Covered.

12. Goblets, two sizes. Variations in bowl and stem.

13. Jelly glass.

14. Pitchers.
    - *a*. Pint.
    - *b*. Syrup.
        - (1) Metal top.
        - (2) Tin top.
    - *c*. Water.
        - (1) Pint.
        - (2) Quart.

15. Salts, footed.

16. Spoonholder.

17. Sugar bowl. Two styles, one with double knob finial.

18. Tumblers.
    - *a*. Footed. Sizes and height vary.
    - *b*. Water, four sizes.

19. Water bottle, with tumble-up.

20. Wine glass. Sizes vary.

Color: Clear glass. Variants in this pattern, closely similar in design, have been found in a brilliant opalescent.

PETAL AND LOOP

An early Sandwich pattern is the Petal and Loop. A similar design with a heavy, brilliant loop was produced by the O'Hara Glass Company of Pittsburgh, Pa., where it was well known as the "O'Hara" pattern. At least one other Pittsburgh factory produced a similar glass under the name of "Leaf." The only reason for changing the name must have been the desire to avoid calling it by the designation given it by another factory. The Pittsburgh copyist might have found a more fitting title. There certainly is no resemblance to a leaf in the large clear loop which is the feature of the design. The glass has the heavy lead-flint quality of all the early pressed glass and has the usual bell-tone. Mention is made so frequently to the ring of the glass because in the product of later years it is entirely lacking. I have seen three different types of goblets in this pattern, two of which are shown on Plate 154 and one on Plate 1. The glass is so brilliant that it reflects its own varied surfaces.

The Sandwich ware, which could have been earlier than the Pittsburgh glass, I believe may be distinguished by the smaller petals and the fact that the standards of the Sandwich pieces have a loop design on the base, while the Pittsburgh have hexagonal stems and a plain circular base. The line drawings on Plate 4 will plainly show the difference between the products of the two factories. These drawings were copied directly from the Pittsburgh catalogue and from photographs of the old wooden molds of the "petaled and looped" Sandwich pieces which were found after the closing of the Cape Cod factory.

The Loop pattern must have been one of the very earliest designs made in enough pieces for general table use, as it is mentioned in a Pittsburgh catalogue issued about 1859. I also find it illustrated in an old but undated trade catalogue of the Central Glass Co. of Wheeling, W. Va. Many of the pieces are found with the rough pontil mark. The well-known "Petal and Loop" candlesticks, which are certainly of the early pressed glass period, match the tableware. These are found in various colors besides crystal, including yellow, opalescent, opaque, combinations of colors such as blue tops and opaque white base; jade green, peacock blue, amethystine, blue, purple, amber. The candlesticks could date as early as 1830. The tableware would be later.

Classification

PETAL AND LOOP

PATTERN 4

(See Plates 1, 4, 154)
Made at Pittsburgh

Form Number.
1. Bowl, covered, 6 inch, no standard.
2. Compotes.
   a. Covered.
       (1) 6 inch on high standard.
       (2) 7½ inch hexagonal standard and round base.
   b. Open, 10 inch on high standard. Hexagonal standard and round base.
3. Goblets, three styles. Two shown on Plate 154. Photo on Plate 1. None has petal design on foot.
4. Salt. Plain, without foot.

Made at Sandwich

PATTERN 4-A

1. Bowls, flat, deep. Similar to finger bowls.
2. Candlesticks. Crystal and various colors, such as opaque jade green, clear yellow, opaque white, opaque white base and blue top, lavender, purple, blue, opalescent and bluish green.
3. Compotes.
   a. Large and deep, loop on base.
       (1) Same, smaller.
   b. On high standards. Various sizes with petal on bowl, loop design on base.
4. Creamer, footed.

Form Number.

5. Lamp, all glass, similar to candlesticks, with loop design on base. Whale oil period.

6. Salts, footed.

    a. Salts, covered.

7. Sauce dish.

    a. Opalescent.
    b. 4 inch size, also varying sizes to fairly large bowl. Clear glass.

8. Sugar bowl. Petal on bowl, loop design on base.

9. Vases.

Made at unidentified works

PATTERN 4-B

1. Bowl, covered. Deep, without standard. Very heavy loops, $5\frac{1}{2}$ inch.

2. Celery vases, three sizes.

    a. 9 inch, very large and heavy
    b. $8\frac{1}{4}$ inch, medium.
    c. $7\frac{1}{2}$ inch, fairly small.
    These may vary in size as this pattern was widely copied.
    One type has heavy wide scallop at top.

3. Cordial.

4. Champagne.

5. Creamer.

6. Decanter, quart size.

7. Dishes.

    a. Covered, flat. Heavy, $5\frac{1}{2}$ inch diameter.
    b. Open, large, flat. Very heavy, $7\frac{1}{4}$ inch.

8. Egg cups.

9. Pitcher, water.

10. Salt, footed.

11. Spoonholder.

12. Sugar bowl, covered, footed.

13. Tumbler, footed.

14. Wine glass.

Colors: Clear glass, with the exception of a few pieces. These may be found in opalescent or opaque white more often than in color.

DIAMOND THUMBPRINT

Another very early pressed glass pattern is the Diamond Thumbprint. The design consists of large diamond-shaped blocks with a large thumbprint in the center of each diamond. From the weight of the glass and the beautifully crimped handle of the pitchers, I conclude that it must have been made in the 1850's. The glass is fine and clear with a silvery sheen to it. In one of the early illustrated price lists I have seen the name "Diamond Thumbprint" used but as the design was not illustrated by a cut it is impossible to say whether it refers to the same pattern that we now call "Diamond Thumbprint."

A certain crudeness in some of the pieces that I have seen in this pattern makes me suspect that they were made at a much earlier date than has been generally believed. I own a large tumbler of a lovely light green, but of a far more primitive quality of workmanship than we associate with the majority of our pressed glass patterns, and I have also seen a pontil-marked creamer. On the other hand, certain other pieces, such as the whiskey tumbler, have a few oval shaped depressions in a row around the top of the glass. These particular pieces are so beautifully molded as to appear cut instead of pressed. Of course, these specimens of obviously finer workmanship may have been made either by the same factory at different periods or by different factories. The cruder pieces assuredly have every appearance of being much earlier, probably between 1840 and 1845, while the others may easily be twenty years older. Distinguishing differences in the pieces made by the various factories may be found in the footed pieces. Some have concentric circles in the bases and others have an elaborate diamond thumbprint pattern, carrying out the design on the bowl. This is especially noticeable in the compotes, creamers and spoonholders. It is known by fragment findings that the

Boston & Sandwich Glass Company was one factory who produced this pattern.

Classification
DIAMOND THUMBPRINT

PATTERN 5
(See Plates 3, 25)

Form Number.

1. Bowl. Deep, small at base, flaring at top. Scallop and point edge.
2. Butter dish.
3. Cake plate on standard. Two sizes.
4. Champagne.
5. Compotes, open, with scalloped edge. Various sizes, some deep and large on high standard, others on very low foot.
6. Cordial.
7. Creamer. Two varieties.
8. Decanter. Quart, original, stopper.
    a. Pint.
9. Goblet. Rare.
10. Honey dish. $3\frac{1}{2}$ inch.
11. Milk pitcher.
12. Pitcher, water. Quart size, applied handle.
13. Mug, applied handle.
14. Sauce dish.
15. Spoonholder.
16. Sugar bowl. Two styles. One with scalloped edge to foot, other with concentric rings in the base.
17. Sweetmeat jar, covered.
18. Tumblers.
    a. Large.
    b. Whiskey.

Colors: Clear glass. May be found delicately tinted in light green or amethystine, due to improper mixing of metal. Two pieces have been found in yellow.

M'KEE & BROTHERS,

Flint Glass Manufacturers, Pittsburgh, Pa.

10 in. Crystal Bowl.

Crystal Spoon Holder.

Crystal Cream.

Crystal Ale.

Qt. Crystal Pitcher.

8 in. Crystal Dish, footed, and Cover.

Crystal Celery.

8 in. Crystal Bowl.

Crystal Sugar.

PLATE 9—CRYSTAL PATTERN
Reproduced directly from page of old trade catalogue, M'Kee & Brothers, Pittsburgh, Pa.

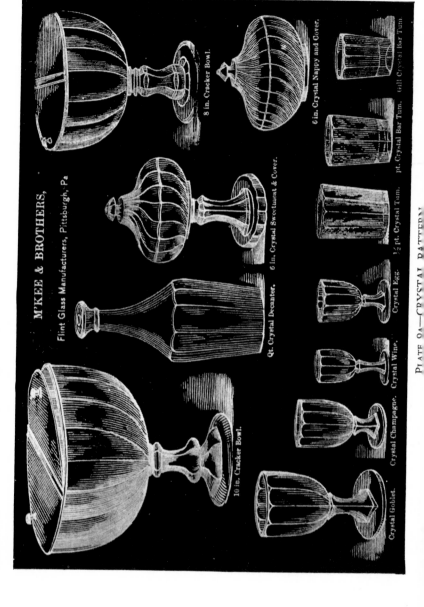

M'KEE & BROTHERS,

Flint Glass Manufacturers, Pittsburgh, Pa.

8 in. Cracker Bowl.

6 in. Crystal Nappy and Cover.

Gill Crystal Bar Tum.

pt. Crystal Bar Tum.

½ pt. Crystal Tum.

Crystal Egg.

Crystal Wine.

Crystal Champagne.

Crystal Goblet.

10 in. Cracker Bowl.

Qt. Crystal Decanter.

6 in. Crystal Sweetmeat & Cover.

Plate 9a—Crystal Pattern.

PLATE 10

1. WASHINGTON water pitcher, decanter with original stopper, decanter with bar lip.
2. COLONIAL sugar bowl, goblet, ale glass.
3. WAFFLE and THUMBPRINT decanter with patent stopper, cordial, compote, spoonholder or spill holder.
4. BIGLER goblet, tumbler, cordial

PLATE 11

1. ARGUS sugar bowl, lamp, ale glass.
2. ARGUS champagne, wine, cordial, whiskey tumbler, handled mug.
3. HUBER compote on high standard, compote on low foot, egg cup, handled egg cup.
4. HUBER sugar bowl, creamer, celery vase.

BLOCK WITH THUMBPRINT

Closely similar in many respects to the Diamond Thumbprint, is this design of large blocks in relief, each one containing a deep ovoid thumbprint. On Plate 101 is shown one of the early goblets and next to it, an early footed tumbler of heavy lead flint glass having a rayed base, the rays extending almost to the outer edge of the base. The last goblet in the row is a later copy of the earlier ware, known to have been made by Gillinder & Sons of Philadelphia, Pa., during the Seventies.

Another pattern, known to have been made at Sandwich, was in fine brilliant glass that resembles the Block with Thumbprint closely. I have seen only a few pieces and it is not illustrated in this book. It is made up of square blocks also but they are not in such high relief. The thumbprint, instead of being ovoid, is round and not as deeply indented. While it is possible this pattern may be as old as the Block with Thumbprint, I doubt it. The forms have a later appearance. The celery vase is very attractive, with its large blocks and circles, and scalloped edge. The Block with Thumbprint is a clumsily quaint old pattern, probably made in the 1850's. A few early fragments of it were discovered at Sandwich but not in a sufficient quantity for anyone to make definite assertions at this time.

Classification

BLOCK WITH THUMBPRINT

PATTERN 6

(See Plate 101)

Form Number.
  1. Celery vase (originally termed celery glass).
  2. Compote. 7 inch, on high standard, petal edge.
  3. Goblets.
       a. Early style, first period.
       b. Later copy of early style. Made by Gillinder & Sons.
  4. Tumbler, footed.
Color: Clear glass.

PILLAR

One of the very early patterns illustrated in the trade catalogue of Bakewell, Pears & Co. was called Pillar. One may occasionally find a piece or two of this heavy brilliant flint glass to-day. In an antique shop in central New York State I once found six goblets in this attractive pattern, all in perfect condition. Below the marginal band at the top of the bowl of the goblet are heavy convex panels running toward the base, each with four round thumbprints deeply impressed in it. The Pillar goblet may be seen on Plate 28 and next to it a variant in a heavy crude early glass. This variant might have been made in the Forties, or not later than the Fifties. It is found bearing a heavy, rough pontil mark.

The old Bakewell, Pears & Co. catalogue shows just two pieces of the Pillar. One is called a Pony Ale, which looks very much like a footed tumbler. The other is an Ale closely resembling our present-day parfait glass. The fact that these two pieces are found in a catalogue of the Seventies does not establish the approximate age of the glass as several of the patterns shown were made over a period of many years. In an Ovington Brothers' catalogue of the period 1854-59, a Pillar pattern is mentioned, but since the design is not illustrated I cannot be sure it is the same. Different factories often copied the same pattern but gave it a different name. It is only when the pieces are illustrated that one can be certain which one is referred to. The old models of the goblet, wine and cordial glass were among those found at Sandwich, showing that this design was made there also. I mention these few pieces because undoubtedly other forms exist.

Classification
PILLAR

PATTERN 7
(See Plates 28, 154)

Form Number

1. Ale glass (tall and footed like celery glass but stem is shorter).
    a. Pony Ale. (Shaped like parfait glass.)

Form Number.
  2. Cordial.
  3. Decanter, bar lip.
  4. Goblet.
  5. Sauce dish.
  6. Wine glass.
Color: Clear glass.

PRESSED BLOCK

On Plate 12 are shown several pieces of flint glass in the Pressed Block pattern. I can find no record of the old trade name but I am glad to be able definitely to attribute this fine quality of glass to at least one factory, that of the Bakewell, Pears & Co., of Pittsburgh, Pa. A cake plate in this design is owned by a member of the Pears family and was purchased at the old factory in 1853. While I have never seen goblets to match the other pieces, I do not doubt that they exist. The glass is heavy in weight, brilliant in quality and has a clear bell tone when struck. The few items that I have found in this design are well worth collecting. Doubtless many other examples are to be had, but so far they have avoided meeting me in my travels.

A few fragments of Pressed Block were excavated at Sandwich, so some of this pattern may have been produced there.

Classification

PRESSED BLOCK

PATTERN 8

(See Plate 12)

Form Number.
  1. Bowl, deep, covered. Varying sizes, no standard.
  2. Compotes.
      a. Covered, varying sizes on high and low standards.
      b. Open, varying sizes on high and low standards.
      c. Open, large, 8½ inch diameter.
  3. Plate.

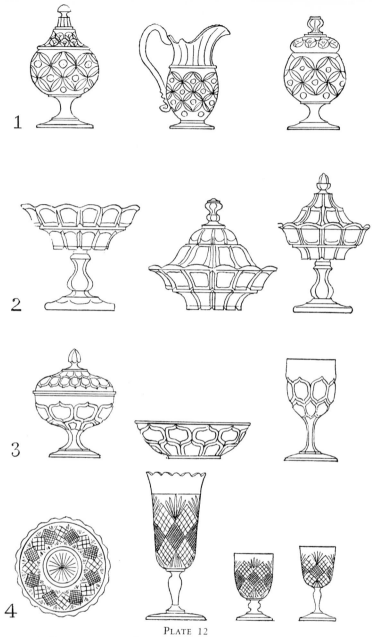

PLATE 12

1. FOUR PETAL sugar bowl, creamer, sugar bowl, with rounded lid.
2. PRESSED BLOCK compote, covered bowl, covered compote.
3. OVAL MITRE compote, oval dish, goblet.
4. SUNBURST plate, celery vase, egg cup, wine glass.

PLATE 13

1. BLAZE goblet, sugar bowl, creamer, spoonholder.
2. STEDMAN decanter with bar lip, syrup pitcher, goblet, egg cup, cordial.
3. PRISM decanter with bar lip, water pitcher, goblet, egg cup, cordial.
4. FLUTE syrup jug, goblet, champagne, wine,

PLATE 14

1. SANDWICH STAR decanter, goblet, spoonholder.
2. HARP spoonholder, handled lamp, footed salt.
3. RAY plate (six inch), sugar bowl, celery vase.
4. ENGLISH HOBNAIL and THUMBPRINT bowl, fruit dish, sauce dish.

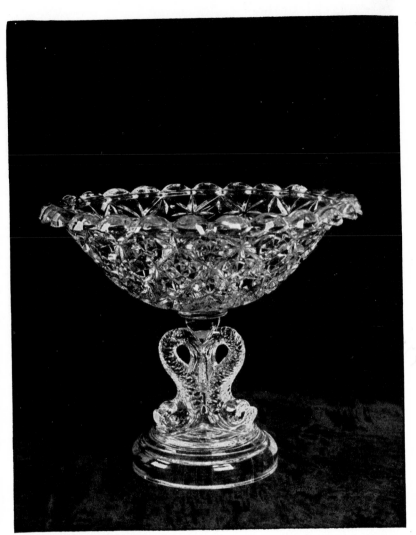

Collection of Mr. E. B. Merrill.

PLATE 14A

Extremely rare Sandwich Star compote, with triple-dolphin standard, usually found on
Sandwich glass lamps

Form Number.

4. Sauce dish, 4 inch.
5. Sweetmeat dish, covered 6 inch. High standard, hexagonal stem, round base.

Color: Clear glass.

SANDWICH STAR

It is unfortunate that so far no records are available to give us the old trade name of this early Sandwich pressed glass design. The ornament of this pattern is somewhat star-like in appearance. For lack of a better title and as a means of identification, it seems proper to call it "Sandwich Star." Not many pieces of this ware survive for us to collect to-day. A tour of New England shops failed to bring to light other pieces than a spoonholder and a quart decanter. It must be that it was not as widely copied as were most of the early designs. Of the old models found from the Sandwich factory, I find a goblet, wine, cordial and small oblong dish in this Star. Those pieces which I have seen have been very heavy in weight and sometimes lacking in brilliance or luster. I believe this to be one of the early patterns, probably of the Fifties.

Two rarities have appeared in Sandwich Star since this book was revised in 1933. The first is a compote having a bowl with petal edge, in the largest size known in this pattern, supported by three dolphins which rest on a round base. The three dolphins may be found supporting lamp bowls, in opaque-blue, opaque jade-green, opaque-lavender and probably other colors. That it is positively Sandwich may be proved by fragments of the dolphin base, in my collection, which concur exactly with the base of the Sandwich Star compote. Lamps are scarce. The most beautiful one brought to my attention was in jade-green, with a pear-shaped bowl and marble base. The compote with the three-dolphin base is the only one known, so it may have been a presentation piece, made on special order.

The second rarity is a compote in the same size as the one described above, though with the usual standard, instead of the dolphin base. It is given special mention here because it is the only one known in a brilliant shade of amethyst.

Classification

SANDWICH STAR

Pattern 9

(See Plates 14, 14a)

Form Number.
1. Compote, open on high standard. Scalloped edge similar to petal tops on candlesticks. Various sizes.
    a. Large open compote, the bowl supported by three dolphins which rest on a round base.
2. Cordial.
3. Decanter, quart size.
4. Dish, oblong, flat.
5. Goblet. Rare.
6. Lamps.
7. Spoonholder. Very heavy glass.
8. Wine glass.
Color: Clear glass. Any colored piece is a rarity.

FOUR PETAL

An early but not very well-known design is the Four Petal. It is a heavy, brilliant glass, probably made in the 1850's. Having found first a covered sugar bowl, I was delighted when I saw the creamer to match. Later I found another sugar bowl, with a different shaped cover. I find no record of where this pattern was made, but certainly it was executed by careful workmen. The pieces are of an excellent quality of flint glass with a clear bell-like tone. The pitcher is footed, has a large applied handle crimped at the base and the mouth has vertical panels a third of the way down, which terminates in a heavy band of glass. This is a delightful pattern, evidently produced in a limited quantity. Little of it is seen to-day and no one can give me any information about it.

Classification

FOUR PETAL

PATTERN 10

(See Plate 12)

Form Number.
1. Bowl, round and deep.
2. Creamer.
3. Sugar bowl.
    a. Footed, two styles.
    b. No foot, round base.

Color: Clear glass. Brilliant blue, or any other colors, are extremely rare.

COLONIAL

Whatever the original trade name of this pattern may have been, I have never met anyone who could tell it to me. It is not mentioned in any of the early catalogues I have studied. Dealers and collectors usually refer to it by the generic name of "Colonial." Under the circumstances it has seemed proper so to designate it in this book for, after all, it deserves a name of its own. It is really an interesting design which probably was not copied extensively, as I have seen but very few pieces of it. The sugar bowl pictured on Plate 10 was found in Ohio; an ale glass in New Jersey; goblets and champagne glasses in Pennsylvania. The more elusive the pieces are the more interesting the chase, and this pattern must be hunted over a wide area. All collectors have stories to tell of how they ran across unlisted pieces in places where they least expected to find anything of interest. The Colonial footed tumbler was found in a New York City shop. According to fragment findings, some of this design was produced at Sandwich.

Classification

COLONIAL

PATTERN 11

(See Plates 2, 10)

Form Number.
1. Ale glass, tall, footed.
2. Celery glass.
3. Champagne.
4. Goblet.
5. Sugar bowl.
6. Tumbler, footed.

Color: Clear glass. Opal, or any other color, very rare. Fragments in amethyst and peacock-blue were excavated at Sandwich.

FLUTE

Lacking a better name, I am using the title given to this pattern in an old Pittsburgh catalogue. The goblet, illustrated elsewhere, is before me as I write. It has a luster similar to that observed in the Bull's Eye, which is not as brilliantly clear as the others of this series. The design consists of six flattened panels arched at the top. The knob of the stem is hexagonal and close to the base of the bowl. The stem is balloon-shaped at the base, and an odd hexagonal-shaped step connects the stem with the round clear base of the goblet. It was an early glass, produced at the Sandwich factory as well as elsewhere. One goblet made at Sandwich did not have a knob stem, though the champagne glass did. Another goblet shows only two mold-marks, made long before this became a common practice. An interesting point in this pattern is to be noted in the tumblers. These were made and listed by the number of "flutes." There is a one-third pint nine-flute tumbler, one-third quart ten-flute ale, an eight-flute beer mug, six-flute soda, pint six-flute tumbler, etc. They counted their "flutes" in this catalogue, dated 1868, but this only seems to hold true of the tumblers which were chiefly manufactured for ships, hotels and bar-rooms. The tableware is both heavy and attractive and seems to come under the heading of "Six Flute." It is interesting to note that all bases in every pattern of this series are clear, while in the ribbed patterns, which are more elaborate, the bases are almost always rayed. It is also a point of interest to note some of the titles given to these early Bar tumblers. Suggesting that they were shipped to many points are these pattern names taken from the Bakewell, Pears & Company catalogue, such as: Richmond Soda, Mobile, Charleston, Continental, St. Louis Bar, Montana Bar, Western Bar, Kansas Bar, Louisville Bar, California Bar, Philadelphia Bar, Frisco Bar, etc. No thoughts of the day when prohibition would somewhat agitate our country entered the minds of these glass factory owners during that period when one of their chief sources of revenue was derived from all sorts of glasses made for ships, hotels and bar-rooms.

The designs described so far in this series are all typically American, none of them showing European influences.

Classification

FLUTE

PATTERN 12

(See Plates 1, 13)

Form Number.
1. Ale glass.
2. Bitters bottle (six- and eight-flute)
3. Candlesticks. Six-flute, no sockets.
4. Champagne.
5. Decanter, quart size.
6. Egg cup.
7. Goblet.
8. Jelly cups, footed.
9. Jug, syrup.

Form Number.

  10. Tumblers.
      a. Gill.
      b. Half-pint.
      c. Jelly, ten-flute.
      d. Toy, one-half gill size.
  11. Wine glass.

Colors: Clear glass. An occasional piece may be found in color. This holds true of most of the glass in this group.

BIGLER

Before the first edition of *Early American Pressed Glass* appeared in 1931, when there was no established nomenclature to guide collectors, Bigler was the least known of the early designs. It is a scarce pattern, the articles encountered most frequently being goblets and cordials. The goblets are usually of the early lead-flint glass type, heavy and brilliant. One style has a short stem almost low enough to be termed a footed tumbler. In others, the panel which divides the ovals is not so long on one variety, as on another. Not many pieces of Bigler have come to light but reports on other items than those listed may come to us in the future.

Undoubtedly Bigler was produced by more than one factory. That it was made by the Boston & Sandwich Glass Company has been established by fragments unearthed at the site of the old glasshouse.

Classification

BIGLER

PATTERN 13
(See Plate 10)

Form Number.

  1. Ales.
  2. Bowls.
  3. Celery vase.
  4. Champagne.

Form Number.
   5. Cordial.
   6. Goblet. Three styles.
   7. Mug, applied handle.
   8. Plate, 6 inch.
   9. Tumbler, water.
Color: Clear glass.

OVAL MITRE

While the Oval Mitre was undoubtedly produced by a number of factories, both early and late, I am using the old trade name given to it by the M'Kee Brothers in their 1859 catalogue. Only a few pieces are given in this price list but it must be remembered that in those early days glass was not on the same wholesale merchandizing basis it later came to be, and "sets" were not produced in the sense we now use the term. Only those articles for which the greatest demand existed were manufactured. With the increasing prosperity of the country came the call for additional luxuries and other pieces of tableware were made. It was a gradual development.

Oval Mitre is one of those patterns which evidently did not enjoy as widespread a popularity as others. It probably was not made in as great a variety of articles since relatively few pieces seem to be available to-day. I gave up hope of ever finding a goblet in this design, but one finally turned up, though of a later variety, the quality of glass not being what it might have been had it been produced in the late Forties or Fifties. I find that the majority of the early patterns of pressed glass were copied in later years and as a rule underwent slight changes although scarcely enough to justify their being called variants. While I do not doubt that many other forms exist in Oval Mitre, the list given below contains all I have actually seen.

The old trade catalogues indicated the difference in the height of certain footed pieces by specifying that they were either on a high or low foot. "Footed" meant a base of one sort or another

To-day the word "standard" has replaced "foot" almost exclusively. In this book both words are used. While most collectors and dealers refer to high or low standards they should keep in mind that footed means the same thing.

Classification

OVAL MITRE

PATTERN 14

(See Plate 12)

Form Number.

1. Butter dish.
2. Compotes.
   a. Covered.
      (1) High standard, $5\frac{3}{4}$ inch diameter.
      (2) Footed, 6 inch diameter.
   b. Open.
      (1) Eight inch.
      (2) High standard, $6\frac{3}{4}$ inch.
      (3) High standard, 10 inch.
      (4) Six inch.
3. Creamer.
4. Dish, oval, no foot.
5. Goblet.
6. Sauce dish, flat, 4 inch.
7. Spoonholder.
8. Sugar bowl.

Color: Clear glass.

HUBER

Quite the opposite of the Flute, which has flattened panels, is the Huber, which is made up of narrow, slightly convex panels. It was listed as the Huber pattern in an old catalogue issued in 1869, but it may well have been produced earlier. It is a good pattern though one can scarcely call it a particularly handsome design. Its effectiveness lies in its simplicity. It was a practical ware for hotels being heavy enough to withstand hard usage. It was suitable also for home use, the glasses being well adapted for jelly and custards. It must have sold well for it comes in a wide variety of pieces. The forms are shown on Plate 11. I first found it mentioned in a New England Glass Company price list, but the name "Huber" also appears in a Pittsburgh catalogue. Not being illustrated there, I cannot tell if the pattern is the same. A Huber decanter with stopper to match was priced at $13.25 per dozen in the 1868 Pittsburgh price list. A Huber pattern was an early one produced by Bakewell, Pears & Co., of Pittsburgh, though their design is not the same as the Huber listed here. The Boston & Sandwich Glass Company also made some of it.

Classification

HUBER

PATTERN 15

(See Plate 11)

Form Number.

1. Ale glass.
2. Bitters bottle.
3. Celery vase.
4. Champagne.
5. Compotes.
    a. Covered.
        (1) High standards. Five sizes, 6 to 10 inches.
        (2) On low foot, 6, 7, and 8 inches.
    b. Open.
        (1) High standards. Five sizes, 6 to 10 inches.
        (2) On low foot. Five sizes, 6 to 10 inches.
6. Cordial.
7. Creamer
8. Decanter.
    a. With stopper.
        (1) Pint.
        (2) Quart.
    b. Without stopper and with heavy collar.
        (1) Pint.
        (2) Quart.

Form Number.

9. Dishes.
    a. Covered, 6, 7 and 8 inch.
    b. Oval, 7, 8, 9 and 10 inch.
    c. Shallow without foot, 3½ to 8 inches.

10. Egg cups.
    a. Egg cups, applied handle.

11. Goblets.
    a. Hotel.
    b. Large.
    c. Small.

12. Honey dish, 3½ inch.

13. Jelly glass.

14. Jugs.
    a. Quart.
    b. Three Pint.

15. Lemonade glass.

16. Mugs.
    a. Beer.
        (1) Half-pint.
        (2) Tall.
    b. Pony beer.
        (1) Large.
        (2) Small.

17. Nappies. (Dishes.)
    a. Covered, low foot, 6, 7 and 8 inch.
    b. Open, low foot, 6, 7 and 8 inch.

18. Pitcher, water. Two styles.

19. Plates, 6 and 7 inch.

20. Preserve dishes.
    a. Covered, 6 and 7 inch.
    b. Open, without foot, 6 and 7 inch.

21. Salts.
    a. Footed.
    b. Individual.
    c. Small.

22. Sauce dish, 4 inch.

23. Spoonholder.
    a. Large.
    b. Small.

Form Number.

24. Sugar bowl.
25. Tumblers.
      a. Gill.
      b. Large half-pint.
      c. Small half-pint.
      d. Taper.
      e. Taper bar tumbler.
26. Wine glass.
Color: Clear glass.

WASHINGTON

In the New England Glass Company price list, printed, it is believed, in 1869, are listed numerous pieces of this heavy flint glass pattern under the title of "Washington." Since I have found that examples of it are exceedingly scarce, it is reasonable to believe that this is another design that was not copied to the extent that many others were. It has fine, dignified lines, and it is to be regretted that it is not more plentiful.

On Plate 10 is shown a Washington decanter, complete with the original glass stopper to match and another decanter made with what was termed the "bar lip." I have found that those bottles and decanters with the heavy collar or "bar lip" were obviously designed to use corks as stoppers, either plain solid cork, or the so-called patent stoppers, which were a combination of cork and pewter, one style having a tiny glass ball that acted as a cover for the liquor when the decanter was not in use. When the bottle was tipped, the glass ball fell forward, being attached to a pewter stem. These were cheaper to manufacture than the glass stoppers to match, which necessitated hand work to grind to size. That is the reason why it is not usual to find, in the earlier wares, stoppers made in the same design as the container. In the Tulip decanter on Plate 53 is shown another cork and pewter stopper such as I have described though glass stoppers to match were made for decanters and cruets in Tulip. It is interesting to note that in the M'Kee Brothers price list, of Pittsburgh, dated April 1, 1868, thirteen decanters out of fourteen are priced per dozen with "patent corks." The only pattern in that catalogue listed with "glass stopper" is the "Huber." A group of varied types of patent corks is shown on Plate 189. These were copied directly from an Ovington Bros.' trade catalogue of 1854-59. The items found in the Washington are quoted from the list given in the old catalogue of the New England Glass Company.

Classification

WASHINGTON

Pattern 16

(See Plate 10)

Form Number.
1. Ale glass.
2. Bitters bottle.
3. Bowls.
   a. Highfoot, 6, 7, 8, 9 and 10 inch.
   b. Low foot, 6, 7, 8, 9 and 10 inch.
4. Celery vase.
5. Champagne.
6. Compotes.
   a. Covered.
      (1) On high foot, 6, 7, 8, 9 and 10 inch.
      (2) On foot, 6, 7 and 8 inch.
   b. Open, on foot, 6, 7 and 8 inch.
7. Cordial.
8. Creamer.
9. Decanters.
   a. Bar lip.
      (1) Pint.
      (2) Quart.
   b. With stopper.
      (1) Pint.
      (2) Quart.
10. Dishes.
    a. Covered, 10 inch.
    b. Oval, 7, 8, 9 and 10 inch.
    c. Shallow, 6, 7 and 8 inch.

Form Number.

11. Egg cup.
12. Goblet, large and small.
13. Honey dish, 3½ inch.
14. Jelly glass.
15. Jug. Three pint.
16. Lemonade mug.
17. Nappies, low foot, 6, 7 and 8 inch. (Dishes.)
18. Pitcher, water. Two styles.
19. Plates, 6 and 7 inch.
20. Salts.
   a. Footed.
   b. Individual.
   c. Large, round.
21. Sauce dish, 4 and 5 inch.
22. Spoonholder.
23. Sugar bowl.
24. Tumblers.
   a. Half-pint.
   b. One-third pint.
25. Wine glass.

Color: Clear glass.

WAFFLE AND THUMBPRINT

The old trade name of the New England Glass Company for this early flint glass pattern, was the Palace. Today it is widely known as Waffle and Thumbprint, which is, of course, a home-made descriptive title of recent origin.

While I have found one crudely finished goblet in this design, for the most part the only pieces one may see will be so sharply pressed as to appear cut rather than moulded. The glass is brilliantly clear, as is typical of the New England Glass Company's product. It is not plentiful to-day and is eagerly sought by discriminating collectors. It is a fine, dignified pattern of great appeal, probably first produced not later than 1860. It was undoubtedly copied and made by more than one factory. The Boston & Sandwich Glass Company is known to have been responsible for some of it.

Classification
WAFFLE AND THUMBPRINT

PATTERN 17

(See Plates 10, 26)

Form Number.
1. Celery vase.
2. Champagne.
3. Claret.
4. Compotes, open.
    a. Large, on high standard.
    b. Small.
    c. Small, on low standard.
5. Decanters
    a. Pint.
    b. Quart.
    These are found in several types, both blown and pressed, with matching stoppers. Also in a rare decanter jug, with matching stopper. The jug has an applied handle.
6. Egg cup
7. Goblet.
8. Lamps. Hand lamps, small, with applied handle.
9. Pitcher, water.
10. Sugar bowl.
11. Spoonholder.
12. Tumblers, water.
    a. Whiskey tumbler.
13. Wine.
Color: Clear glass. Rarities appear in milk-white and also in yellow.

Chapter III

OTHER PITTSBURGH PATTERNS

RAY

A pattern which bears the closest resemblance to the so-called "lace glass" of the Sandwich factory, is the "Ray." It was listed at Pittsburgh late in the 1850's and again in 1868, so it must have enjoyed some popularity. It is an effective design, undoubtedly copied from the earlier Sandwich "peacock eye" or "peacock feather," said to have been suggested by the appearance of Halley's Comet. A few forms are shown on Plate 14, copied directly from the old catalogue. The six-inch plate is shown on Plate 163.

I have never seen goblets in this attractive pattern, and they were not listed in either catalogue. There are many charming designs in odd goblets, however, which could be combined attractively with the lovely Ray dishes, so that a collection of the latter need not suffer from the absence of tumblers or goblets.

Some fragments in this design were unearthed at Sandwich, so it may possibly have been one of their products, as well.

Classification

RAY

PATTERN 18

(See Plates 14, 163)

Form Number.
1. Bowls, round, 6 and 7 inch.
2. Celery vase.
3. Dish, oblong, fairly deep. 7 and 9 inch.
4. Plate, 6 inch.
5. Sauce dish, round. 4 and 5 inch.
6. Sugar bowl.

Color: Clear glass.

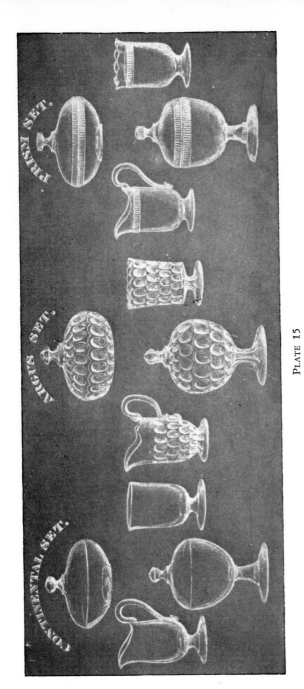

PLATE 15

Page from Bakewell, Pears & Co. catalogue, showing "sets" of Continental, Argus (now known as Thumbprint) and Prism (now known as Prism and Flute).

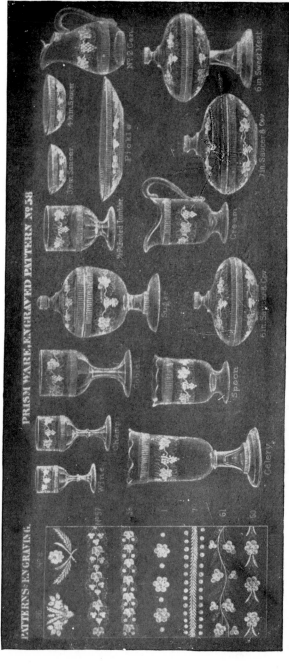

PLATE 16

Page from Bakewell, Pears & Co. catalogue, showing "Prism" pattern (Prism and Flute), engraved, together with patterns used for engraving.

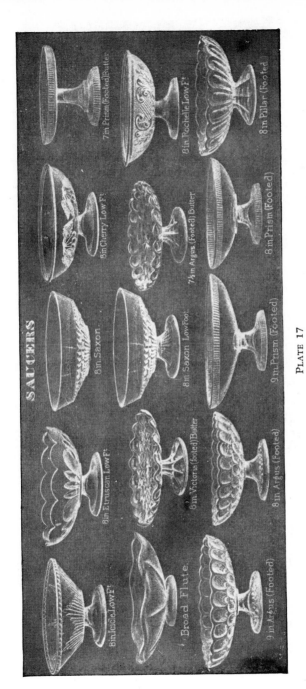

SAUCERS

8 in. Icicle Low F†.   8 in. Etruscan Low F†.   8 in. Saxon.   8 in. Cherry Low F†.   7 in. Prism (Footed) Butter.

Broad Flute.   8 in. Victoria (footed) Butter.   8 in. Saxon Low Foot.   7½ in. Argus (Footed) Butter.   8 in. Rochelle Low F†.

9 in. Argus (Footed)   8 in. Argus (Footed)   9 in. Prism (Footed)   8 in. Prism (Footed)   8 in. Pillar (Footed)

PLATE 17

Page from Bakewell, Pears & Co. catalogue, showing their "saucers" and footed butter dishes.

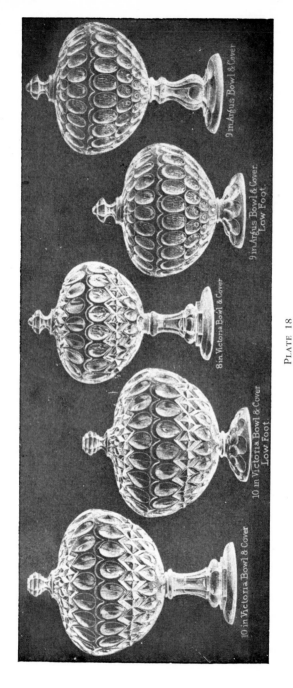

9 in Argus Bowl & Cover

9 in Argus Bowl & Cover.
Low Foot.

8 in Victoria Bowl & Cover

10 in Victoria Bowl & Cover
Low Foot

10 in Victoria Bowl & Cover

PLATE 18

Group of covered compotes in the Victoria and Argus patterns, of the Bakewell, Pears & Co.
(Argus is now known as Thumbprint).

EUGENIE

A popular pattern of the late Fifties and the only one which showed pronounced foreign influence, is the Eugenie. This was evidently produced during the reign of the last Empress of France. It appears in both the early and the late Pittsburgh catalogues, so it must have been favorably received from the first. The brilliant court of Napoleon III set the fashion for the world and in the American pressed glass named after his Empress, the design reflects the splendor of the times. It is much more ornate than the more distinctive American patterns. The knob of the sugar bowl cover is in the form of a dolphin flipping its tail with quite Gallic insouciance. A page from the old catalogue is displayed on Plate 5. It is interesting to see how this glass was shown in advertisements of that time. The old wood-cut illustrations do not adequately convey the beauty of the glass as a modern photograph would do.

Classification

EUGENIE

PATTERN 19

(See Plate 5)

Form Number.
1. Castor bottles.
2. Celery vase.
3. Champagne.
4. Dishes.
   a. Covered on foot, 7 and 8 inch.
   b. Covered on low foot, 7 and 9 inch.
5. Egg cups.
6. Goblet.
7. Sugar bowl.
8. Tumbler, footed.
9. Wine glass.
Color: Clear glass.

PRISM

An attractive pattern which is unknown to a great many collectors is the Prism. I am using the name given to it in the 1868 M'Kee price list, because no other could suit it better. That this glass was made for some years prior to that date seems clear from its excellent quality and the bell tone of earlier glass. The goblet has brilliant, coarse ribs which terminate in points at the top, leaving a plain half-inch marginal band about the edge of the bowl. The stem is hexagonal and the base of the goblet rayed to the extreme edge. Prism is found in many forms, and is one of those unusual patterns which has been neglected by the collector, probably due to the fact that it is so little known. Moreover, it is another of those designs which should be seen in a group to be appreciated. A single piece seen here or there in an antique shop does not convey an adequate impression of its high decorative value.

Another design, also called Prism, produced at an early date by Bakewell, Pears & Co. of Pittsburgh, is treated separately in this book under the title of "Prism and Flute." The "Brooklyn" pattern, also by Bakewell, Pears & Co., is shown on Plate 154 of odd items. This was probably made in a number of forms not listed in their late catalogue, so it should be mentioned among the earlier patterns. I have seen large compotes, goblets and ale glasses, in the Brooklyn.

Among the rarities should be listed a pair of six-inch covered compotes on a high standard in opaque white or "Opal." These could be from Sandwich, as the pattern is known to have been made there.

Classification

PRISM

PATTERN 20

(See Plates 13, 27, 154)

Form Number.
1. Butter dish, without foot.
   a. Footed.

Form Number.

2. Celery vase.
3. Champagne.
4. Compotes. Various sizes, including 6 inch, covered on high foot.
5. Counter jars, in 6 sizes.
6. Creamer.
7. Decanter, quart.
8. Egg cups. Footed and double form. The latter is rare.
9. Goblet.
10. Lamps.
    a. All glass, colored base. One has been found bearing Atterbury's patent dates of Feb. 11th and June 3, 1862.
    b. Marble base.
11. Pickle dish.
12. Pitcher, water.
    a. Half-gallon.
    b. Quart.
13. Plates, 6 and 8 inch.
14. Spoonholder.
15. Sugar bowl.
16. Wine glass.

Color: Clear glass; Opal.

BLAZE

This design seems to have been a product of both New England and Pennsylvania. It appears in a catalogue of the New England Glass Company of 1869, as the "Blaze" pattern and in the list of M'Kee Brothers of Pittsburgh in 1868 as the "Stedman." There is a considerable difference, though the effect is the same. The "Blaze" of the New England Company is so fine that it almost appears to be cut. The ribbing is similar to the Bellflower, and the glass is of good quality, with a clear bell tone. The base of the footed pieces is clear.

The "Stedman" is a heavier glass and the design is coarser. It shows more clearly its pressed glass character. The ribbing, which is even in the "Blaze," in the "Stedman" has wide loops near the base. In both varieties the stem is a plain hexagonal, the base rayed in the Pittsburgh and not in the New England.

The line drawings on Plate 13 show clearly the marked differences. The forms of the two factories are listed separately.

Classification

BLAZE

PATTERN 21

(See Plate 13)

The "Blaze"—New England Glass Company

Form Number.
1. Bowls.
    a. Covered, on foot, 6, 7 and 8 inch.
    b. Open, on high foot, 6, 7, 8, 9 and 10 inch.
    c. Open, on low foot, 6, 7, 8, 9 and 10 inch.
2. Celery vase.
3. Champagne.
4. Compotes.
    a. Covered on foot, 6, 7 and 8 inch.
    b. Covered, on low foot, 6, 7 and 8 inch.
    c. Open, on foot, 6, 7 and 8 inch.
    d. Open, on low foot, 6, 7 and 8 inch.
5. Cordial.
6. Creamer.
7. Dishes.
    a. Covered, on low foot, 5½, 6, 7 and 8 inch.
    b. Oval, 7, 8, 9 and 10 inch.
8. Egg cup.
    a. Egg cup, handled.
9. Goblet.
10. Lemonade glass.
11. Plates.
    a. Cheese plate, 6 and 7 inch, with and without covers.
        (1) Plain cover.
        (2) Blaze cover.

Form Number.

12. Salt, oblong.
13. Sauce dish, 4 and 5 inch.
14. Spoonholder.
15. Sugar bowl.
16. Tumblers, two sizes.
17. Wine glass. Two sizes.

Color: Clear glass.

STEDMAN—Pittsburgh factory—1868

PATTERN 22

(See Plate 13)

1. Champagne.
2. Decanter, quart.
3. Egg cup.
4. Goblet.
5. Lamps.
    a. All glass, bowl in pattern, round base.
    b. 5 inch colored base.
    c. Peg lamps.
6. Pitcher, syrup.
7. Plate, 6 inch.
8. Salts.
    a. Flat.
    b. Round.
9. Sugar bowl.
10. Tumbler, half-pint.
11. Wine glass.

Color: Clear glass.

MIOTON

One of those patterns listed in 1868 in Pittsburgh by the M'Kee Brothers was called Mioton. It is mentioned here only to make my list complete, as this was a pattern produced largely for hotels and bar-room use. Under the heading of "Goblets" in the old catalogue this is called "Pressed Mioton Hotel." The classification contains only the pieces mentioned in the catalogue. The goblet may be see on Plate 154. The panels are narrow and arched at the top, leaving a wider plain band at the top than on any others of this type. It is possible other forms exist.

Classification

MIOTON

PATTERN 23

(See Plate 154)

Form Number.
1. Champagne.
2. Cordial.
3. Goblet.
4. Tumbler, half-pint.
5. Wine glass.
Color: Clear glass.

CRYSTAL

On Plates 9 and 9A may be seen a most comprehensive illustration of the Crystal pattern. It should be of interest to all collectors to see just how these pressed glass patterns were pictured originally. The crude wood-cuts do not enhance the beauty of the old glass. On Plate 2 may be seen a goblet in this same design, which is a brilliant, clear, heavy piece of flint glass. It is simple but pleasing in its simplicity. The old cracker jars, with metal tops, were useful articles. They were made largely for hotels, but it is difficult to imagine what they might be utilized for in our day. One old catalogue lists them as "Bar Sugars."

This pattern is listed in both the 1859 and 1868 catalogues of the M'Kee Brothers of Pittsburgh, so it must have had a wide range of sale. It is fairly plentiful, particularly the goblets.

Classification

CRYSTAL

PATTERN 24

(See Plates 2, 9, 9A)

Form Number.

1. Ale glass.
2. Bowl, cracker, 8 and 10 inch.
3. Butter dish.
4. Celery vase.
5. Champagne.
6. Compotes.
   a. Covered, on high standard, 6 inch.
   b. Open, on standard, 8 and 10 inch.
7. Creamer.
8. Decanter, quart.
9. Dishes.
   a. Covered, on foot, 8 inch.
   b. Shallow, 6 inch.
10. Egg cup.
    a. Egg cup with applied handle. Rare.
11. Goblet.
12. Pitcher, water.
13. Spoonholder.
14. Sugar bowl.
15. Tumblers.
    a. Bar, two sizes.
    b. Half-pint.
16. Wine glass.

Color: Clear glass.

PRESSED LEAF

On Plates 29 and 29A are shown two full pages from the M'Kee Brothers', Pittsburgh, Pa., trade catalogue under date of 1868. The pattern illustrated is their "N. P. L." design. Having found in an older catalogue a "Pressed Leaf" I believe that to differentiate one from the other, the initials stand for "New Pressed Leaf." It took a little time and much searching for me to decide that this glass has a later appearance in actuality than would appear from the old wood-cut pictures. The heavy lines in the photographs might seem to indicate ribs, but in reality it is a plain, fairly heavy glass. After studying and comparing sample pieces, such as those shown in line drawings on Plate 125, no doubt was left that the two are one and the same.

The two pages give a comprehensive idea of what one may collect in the Pressed Leaf.

It is claimed that the Boston & Sandwich Glass Company produced some of this pattern.

Classification

PRESSED LEAF

PATTERN 25

(See Plates 29, 29A, 125)

Form Number.

1. Bowls, open.
    a. On high foot, 7 and 8 inch.
    b. On low foot, 7 and 8 inch.
2. Butter dish.
3. Cake plate, on standard.
4. Champagne.
5. Compotes, covered.
    a. On high foot, 6, 7 and 8 inch.
    b. On low foot, 7 and 8 inch.
6. Creamer.
7. Dishes, open, 5, 6, 7, 8 and 9 inch.
8. Egg cup.
9. Goblet.
10. Lamp, applied handle. Known as "hand lamp."
11. Pitcher, water.
12. Salt, footed.
13. Sauce dish, 4 inch.

Form Number.
14. Spoonholder.
15. Sugar bowl.
16. Wine glass.
Color: Clear glass.

EUREKA

A favorite pattern after the Civil War seems to have been the Eureka, if the large number of pieces featured by the M'Kee Brothers is any indication of popularity. It is a design seldom seen to-day but that may be due to the fact that it is little known. An active demand always brings to light glassware that has long lain hidden away on pantry shelves. There is a wide range of pieces to choose from in the Eureka, which is shown in two full pages in the old price list of 1868. These illustrations do not do justice to the glass, which is heavy and brilliant, with panels that are most effective. There is an unusually large number of compotes shown, both open and covered. The knobs of the covers are most attractive. Every needed form for general table use seems to be there, with the exception of plates and celery holders. Not any plates are listed in the catalogue. This fact need not deter the collector of this design, as there are any number of odd plates and vases that combine nicely with it.

Classification

EUREKA

PATTERN 26

(See Plate 6)

Form Number.
1. Butter dish.
2. Champagne.
3. Compotes.
    a. Covered, on high foot, 6, 7 and 8 inch.
    b. Covered, on low foot, 6, 7 and 8 inch.
    c. Open, on high foot, 7 and 8 inch.
    d. Open, on low foot, 7 and 8 inch.

Form Number.

    4. Cordial.

    5. Creamer.

    6. Dishes.

        a. Oval, shallow, 9 inch.
        b. Shallow, 6, 7 and 8 inch.

    7. Egg cup.

    8. Goblet.

    9. Salt, footed.

  10. Sauce dish, 4 inch.

  11. Spoonholder.

  12. Sugar bowl.

  13. Tumbler, footed.

  14. Wine glass.

Color: Clear glass.

BAND

One of the early patterns made at Pittsburgh was the Band. This is the original trade name for it. I find few pieces listed, so its popularity must have been short-lived. The items on Plate 61 were copied directly from the old catalogue price list. This design must have been made in the late Fifties and since only the sugar bowl and footed tumbler are mentioned in the 1868 list, it would seem that not much of it was produced at any time. It is pictured here to identify it for collectors who may have found an occasional piece.

Classification

BAND

PATTERN 27

(See Plate 61)

Form Number.

    1. Celery vase

    2. Goblet.

Form Number.

   3. Sugar bowl.

   4. Tumblers, footed, one-third quart.

Color: Clear glass.

PRISM AND FLUTE

The "Prism" pattern produced by Bakewell, Pears & Co. in the Seventies is among those listed as the earliest of their pressed glass designs. While some of the pieces were simply decorated with a narrow band of dainty fine ribbing, as in their set shown on Plate 15, many of them were also fluted below the band of ribbing, with wide arched panels. Another pattern that I believe may antedate this one is so well known by the name of Prism, that I am adding "Flute" to the old trade name used by Bakewell, Pears & Co., since few collectors know this pattern by any name at all.

Such pieces as the butter dish, creamer, sugar bowl and spoon-holder are plain, while the water pitcher, egg cup, wine glass, footed tumbler and goblet have the wide panels around the base of the bowl, below the band. It seems obvious that the Prism was designed for use in engraving to satisfy those who desired something more elaborate. On Plate 16 is shown "Prism Ware, Engraved," together with a small sample of their designs for engraving. A separate classification is given for the benefit of those collectors who might find use for it.

That the Prism and Flute was very popular in its day seems unquestionable, judging by the large number of articles made. One dish which is unusual is the seven-inch footed butter, as shown on Plate 17. The butter dishes in the earliest forms were flat and covered. Later they sometimes appeared on a low foot but always covered. In the "gay Nineties" the butter dish was something in the nature of a saucer with a high domed lid. The flat open butter on a high foot is a style which I imagine to have been short-lived.

The glass in this design is heavy, clear and brilliant. The articles listed are taken from the old catalogue.

Classification

PRISM AND FLUTE

Pattern 28

(See Plates 15, 16, 17)

Form Number.

1. Ale glass.
2. Bowl, covered 9 inch, with low foot.
3. Butter dish, footed. Shallow, open on high standard, 7 inch.
4. Cake plate, 7½, 9, 10½ and 12½ inch.
5. Cake salver on standard.
6. Celery vase.
7. Compotes.
    - a. Covered.
        - (1) High foot, 6, 7 and 8 inch.
        - (2) Low foot, 7, 8 and 9 inch.
        - (3) Solid foot, 9 inch.
    - b. Open, on low foot, 8 and 9 inch.
8. Cordial.
9. Dish, round, flat, covered, 7 and 9 inch.
10. Egg cup.
11. Goblet.
12. Jelly glass.
13. Pickle dish, oval, 7, 8 and 9 inch.
14. Pitcher, water, half-gallon.
15. Plate, 6 and 8 inch.
16. Salts, individual and large.
17. Sauce dish, 3½ and 4½ inch.
18. Sweetmeat jar.
    - a. On high foot, 6 inch.
    - b. On low foot, 7 inch.
19. Tumbler, footed, half-pint.
20. Urn, covered, half-gallon.
21. Wine glass.

Color: Clear glass.

PRISM WARE, ENGRAVED

The Prism and Flute has already been described on previous pages, but for the benefit of those who may be collecting it in one of the engraved patterns, another classification is given.

Classification

PRISM WARE, ENGRAVED

PATTERN 29

(See Plate 16)

Form Number.
1. Butter dish, covered, 6 inch, no foot.
2. Celery vase.
3. Champagne glass.
4. Compote, covered, on high foot, 6 inch.
5. Creamer.
6. Dish, covered, 7 inch, no foot.
7. Goblet.
8. Pickle Dish.
9. Pitcher, syrup, metal top.
10. Sauce dish, 3½ and 4½ inch.
11. Spoonholder.
12. Sugar bowl.
13. Tumbler, footed.
14. Wine glass.

Color: Clear glass.

CONTINENTAL

The name of this exceedingly simple ware suggests that it may have been inspired by some European model. "Continental" is the old trade name given to it by Bakewell, Pears & Co. It is quite possible that this was made for use in engraving, as was the case with the Prism and Flute. A large number of articles was made which is given in the classification taken directly from the catalogue. The group on Plate 15 is taken from the same source.

Classification

CONTINENTAL

PATTERN 30
(See Plate 15)

Form Number.

1. Ale glass.
   - *a.* Flared ale.
   - *b.* Sham ale.

2. Butter dish, flat, covered.
3. Celery vase.
4. Creamer.
5. Compote, covered, low foot, 6, 7 and 8 inch.
6. Compote, covered, high foot, 6, 7 and 8 inch.
7. Goblet.
   - *a.* Heavy.
   - *b.* Continental sham.
   - *c.* Hotel.

8. Sauce dish, 4 inch.
9. Spoon holder.
10. Sugar bowl.
11. Tumbler, footed.
    - *a.* One-third pint.
    - *b.* One-half pint.

Color: Clear glass.

VICTORIA

The title of this handsome glass must have been inspired by the popularity of England's Queen. Many times in my travels have I found an open or covered compote and lived in hope that a goblet might come to light. It was a pleasure to find the photographs identifying the ware, in the Bakewell, Pears & Co. catalogue. A few more pieces than I had encountered were shown but not many.

The glass is heavy and brilliant, in many ways similar to the Thumbprint. While it is shown in a catalogue of the Seventies, I believe that it was first made about 1860, or even earlier. It is disappointing that more forms do not appear to exist, though they may possibly have been made at an earlier date and not pictured in the later trade catalogue. The footed open butter dish, mentioned under Prism and Flute, is again shown in the Victoria, only with a much lower foot. The salvers in this particular pattern are quite beautiful. The group on Plate 18 is taken from the original catalogue.

Classification

VICTORIA

PATTERN 31
(See Plates 17, 18)

Form Number.

1. Butter dish on low foot, 8 inch.
2. Compotes, covered.
    a. On high foot, sweetmeat compote, 6 inch.
    b. On high foot, 8 and 10 inch.
    c. On low foot, 8 and 10 inch.
3. Salvers, on foot, 9, 13 and 16 inch. (Cake plate on standard.)

Color: Clear glass.

ETRUSCAN

An interesting heavy ware that was made by Bakewell, Pears & Co. of Pittsburgh, was named by them Etruscan. The pleasing simplicity of the lines suggests that it might have been produced much earlier than 1875, though it is shown in one of their catalogues of about that period. The glass is heavy and brilliantly clear. The design consists of a fairly broad, arched panel alternating with three finger-like flutes. The goblet is attractive with its rounded bowl and square-cut knob stem. The salver or cake dish on standard is unusual, the rim being upturned in wide scallops. Oval dishes and compotes are found in several sizes.

The so-called "set" of Etruscan of that period is shown on Plate 20. Other articles were made because I have seen plates. The classification is taken from the old catalogue.

Classification

ETRUSCAN

PATTERN 32

(See Plates 17, 20)

Form Number.
1. Butter dish.
2. Compotes.
    a. Covered, on high foot, 8 inch.
    b. Open, on high foot, 8 inch.
    c. Open, on low foot, 8 inch.
3. Creamer.
4. Dish, oval, 7, 8 and 9 inch.
5. Egg cup.
6. Goblet.
7. Plate, 6 inch.
8. Salt, footed.
9. Salver, cake plate on high standard, 9 inch.
10. Sauce dish, flat with wide scalloped edge, 4½ inch.
11. Spoonholder.
12. Sugar bowl.
13. Tumbler, water.
Color: clear glass.

SAXON

Not having seen any variants of the Saxon design, I believe it may have been an exclusive pattern of Bakewell, Pears & Co. It is shown in their catalogue dating about 1875, though it may well have been produced some years earlier since most patterns were carried over a period of years.

Lightning changes in style were not so common in those days of the horse and buggy as they are now, in this 16-cylinder age!

The six-inch plate in the Saxon is particularly appealing, having an unusual star-shaped ornament in the center. It is interesting to note in the illustration taken from this old catalogue, Plate 21, that the oval platter is marked "12 inch bread plate." These oval

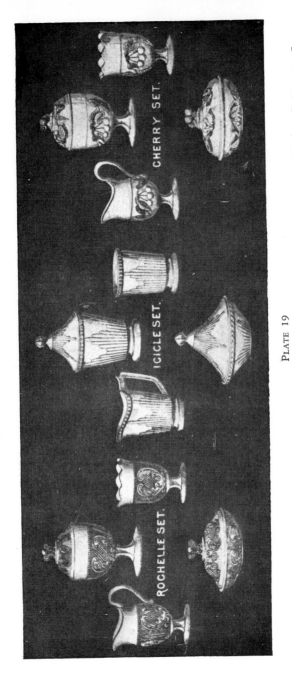

PLATE 19

"Sets" showing Rochelle, Icicle and Cherry patterns, taken directly from an old trade catalogue of Bakewell, Pears & Co., Pittsburgh, Pa. (Rochelle is now known as Princess Feather).

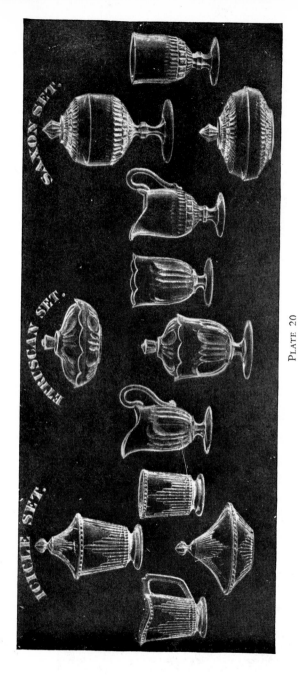

PLATE 20

"Sets" showing Icicle, Etruscan and Saxon patterns, taken directly from an old trade catalogue of Bakewell, Pears & Co., Pittsburgh, Pa.

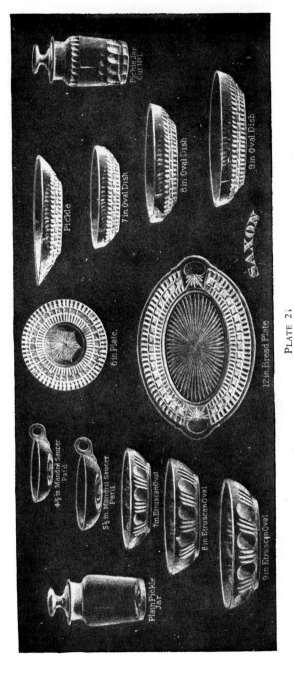

Pickle Jar Cut Lid

9 in Oval Dish

8 in Oval Dish

7 in Oval Dish

Pickle

SAXON

6 in Plate.

12 in Bread Plate

4½ in Mandril Saucer Pat'd

5½ in Mandril Saucer Pat'd

7 in Etruscan Oval

8 in Etruscan Oval

9 in Etruscan Oval

Plain Pickle Jar

PLATE 21

Page taken from Bakewell, Pears & Co., trade catalogue, illustrating Saxon pattern.

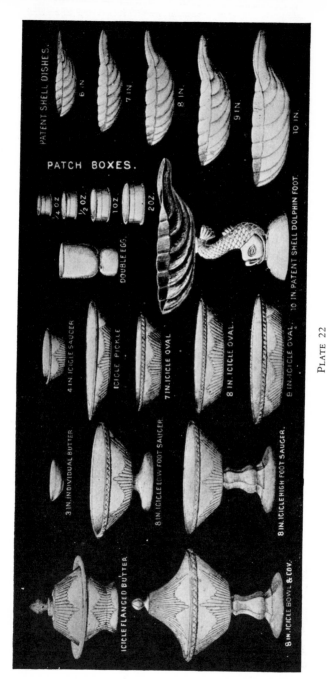

PATENT SHELL DISHES.

6 IN.
7 IN.
8 IN.
9 IN.
10 IN.

PATCH BOXES.

¼ OZ.
½ OZ.
1 OZ.
2 OZ.

DOUBLE EGG.

4 IN. ICICLE SAUCER

ICICLE PICKLE

7 IN. ICICLE OVAL

8 IN. ICICLE OVAL

8 IN. ICICLE OVAL

10 IN. PATENT SHELL DOLPHIN FOOT.

3 IN. INDIVIDUAL BUTTER

8 IN. ICICLE LOW FOOT SAUCER

8 IN. ICICLE HIGH FOOT SAUCER.

ICICLE FLANGED BUTTER

8 IN. ICICLE BOWL & COV.

PLATE 22

Group of Icicle pattern and Dolphin dish, as taken from an old trade catalogue of Bakewell, Pears & Co., of Pittsburgh, Pa.

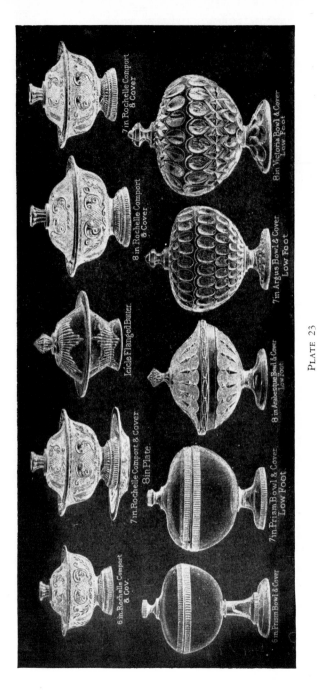

PLATE 23

Group of covered dishes, taken from old trade catalogue of Bakewell, Pears & Co, Pittsburgh, Pa.

PLATE 24

Group of goblets, in patterns made by Bakewell, Pears & Co., carried on both early and fairly late.

bread plates were first in evidence when the change for the more sophisticated forms came about, or, approximately, in 1870. One of the first series having the footed sauce dish, round bread plate bearing the customary inscription "Give us this day our daily bread," oval platters, etc., is the group which includes Lion and Westward-Ho.

The Saxon appears principally in clear glass and the forms are numerous, so that a pleasing set may be accumulated. The pieces which comprised a "set" in those days are shown on Plate 20. The forms listed are taken directly from the old trade catalogue. The only colored pieces I have seen are a celery vase in a dense amber and an oval platter in deep blue.

Classification

SAXON

PATTERN 33

(See Plates 20, 21)

Form Number.

1. Bread platter, oval, 12 inch. Handle at each end.

2. Butter dish.

3. Celery vase.

4. Compotes.

    a. Covered, on high foot, 7 and 8 inch.
    b. Covered, on high foot (sweetmeat dish), 6 inch.
    c. Open, on high foot, 8 inch.
    d. Open, on low foot, 8 inch.

5. Creamer.

6. Dish.

    a. Oval, 7, 8 and 9 inch.
    b. Round, no foot, 8 inch.

7. Egg cup.

8. Goblet.

9. Pickle dish.

Form Number.

10. Pitcher, water.

  a. Half-gallon.
  b. Quart.

11. Plate, six inch.

12. Salts.

  a. Individual.
  b. Large.

13. Sauce dish, 3 and 4 inch.

14. Spoonholder.

15. Sugar bowl.

16. Tumbler, water, half-pint.

17. Wine glass.

Color: Clear glass. Amber. Blue. Pieces in color are rare.

ICICLE

A pattern now seldom encountered, was made in Pittsburgh by Bakewell, Pears & Co. during the Seventies and was called by them Icicle. It was made in milk-white glass as well as in clear glass. One may call to mind icicles at the sight of these narrow panels in uneven lines, but the same thought was carried out by the New England Glass Co. in an earlier ware they called "Blaze" and again by the M'Kee Brothers of Pittsburgh in their "Stedman" pattern. To be sure, each factory varied the lines slightly, but the effect in each case is very much the same. The milk-white in "sets" was an innovation. There is something about the Icicle which suggests a slightly later period. The handle of the creamer, for instance, is obviously pressed, lacking the crimps at the base, and for the first time the dawn of the machine age is most apparent. However, this attractive pattern has its usefulness for certain purposes. The complete classification as taken from the old catalogue is given below. The group shown on Plate 19 was also taken from this same catalogue, clearly indicating how the milk-white glass was presented for the inspection of prospective purchasers.

PLATE 25
Diamond Thumbprint
Popcorn Pattern

PLATE 26—GOBLETS

Waffle and Thumbprint	Cube
Lincoln Drape	Lincoln Drape with Tassel

PLATE 27—GOBLETS

Bull's Eye with Diamond Points
Prism

Ribbed Grape
Fine Rib

PLATE 28—GOBLETS

Stipped Medallion   Arched Leaf
Pillar   Variation of the "Pillar"

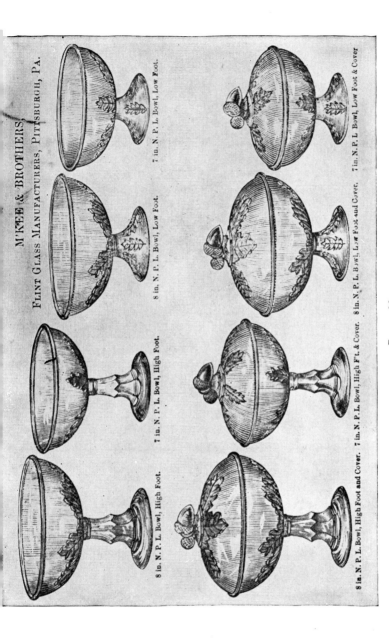

M'KEE & BROTHERS,
FLINT GLASS MANUFACTURERS, PITTSBURGH, PA.

7 in. N. P. L. Bowl, Low Foot.

8 in. N. P. L. Bowl, Low Foot.

7 in. N. P. L. Bowl, High Foot.

8 in. N. P. L. Bowl, High Foot.

7 in. N. P. L. Bowl, Low Foot & Cover.

8 in. N. P. L. Bowl, Low Foot and Cover.

7 in. N. P. L. Bowl, High F't. & Cover.

8 in. N. P. L. Bowl, High Foot and Cover.

PLATE 29

Group showing the "N. P. L." pattern of M'Kee & Brothers, as shown in their trade catalogue.
This pattern is now known as Pressed Leaf.

M'KEE & BROTHERS, FLINT GLASS MANUFACTURERS, PITTSBURGH, PA.

½ gill. N. P. L. Pitcher.

4 in. N. P. L. Nappie.

7 in. N. P. L. Dish.

N. P. L. Salt.

6 in. N. P. L. Nappie & Cover.

8 in. N. P. L. Dish.

N. P. L. Spoon.

N. P. L. Egg.

N. P. L. Wine.

N. P. L. Champagne.

9 in. N. P. L. Dish.

N. P. L. Cream.

N. P. L. Goblet.

6 in. N. P. L. Sweetmeat & Cover.

N. P. L. Sugar.

PLATE 29A

Group showing the "N. P. L." pattern of M'Kee & Brothers, as shown in their trade catalogue.
This pattern is now known as *Pressed Leaf.*

Classification

ICICLE

PATTERN 34

(See Plates 19, 22)

Form Number.
1. Butter dish, covered, flat.
2. Butter dish, covered, flanged, on foot.
3. Compotes.
    a. Covered.
        (1) High foot, 8 inch.
        (2) Sweetmeat, 6 inch.
    b. Open on low foot, 8 inch.
4. Creamer.
5. Dish, oval, 7, 8 and 9 inch.
6. Goblet.
7. Pickle dish, tapered at one end.
8. Pitcher, water.
9. Salt, large.
10. Saucer.
    a. Flat, 3 and 4 inch.
11. Spoonholder.
12. Sugar bowl.
Colors: Clear glass; milk-white.

Chapter IV

RIBBED GROUP

BELLFLOWER

From my earliest days of glass collecting, it has been apparent that the first of all patterns of American pressed glass for which a really popular demand developed, was the Bellflower. Moreover, I am led to believe this to be one of the earliest designs of pressed glass made for general table use, one of my reasons being the fact that I have found a greater variety of crude pieces of this pattern bearing pontil marks than in any other pressed patterns that also come pontil-marked. To be sure, this is merely a personal opinion, since no record exists of when the first Bellflower piece was made. But it seems clear that experiments must have been made with this design before the end of the so-called blown glass period. The pontil-marked Bellflower goblets have every appearance of having been blown into a mold before mechanical pressure processes were fully perfected. If so, they should date prior to 1840. One collector tells me that she has a Bellflower cruet bearing the patent date of 1857 on the brass top and the glass obviously antedates it; but I have seen still earlier, though unmarked, pewter standards for Bellflower cruets. An illustrated price list issued by the M'Kee Brothers' factory of Pittsburgh in 1868, contains many cuts advertising numerous pieces of tableware in this design. Other factories in various parts of the country had been copying and producing Bellflower over a period of many years and during all that time it enjoyed great popularity. Therefore no one should be surprised at the quantities of this glass that have survived for us to collect to-day.

In studying this pattern, it is interesting to note the many variants to be found, more than in any of the patterns that follow it chronologically. This is doubtless due to its having been produced by many factories, each of which made slight changes in minor details of the design. The quality of the glass also varies. Some pieces are silvery and fine, like the early "lace glass" of the Boston & Sandwich Glass Company, while others are rather dull, though any of them will generally resound like a bell with a tap of the finger. I have observed a few pieces in which the design can barely be distinguished in the rays, probably due to a worn mold. Occasionally a piece will show a distinctly amethystine hue, due to the causes mentioned in Chapter One. A few have been found in opaque and opalescent glass, and I own a spoonholder in a beautiful cobalt blue. A friend tells me that she has a creamer and a syrup pitcher in the same sapphire blue, an egg cup in amber and another unusual piece is an opaque cologne bottle with a small smooth space for the label. The cologne bottles are not true Bellflower design. By some they are thought to be French but in coloring they bear characteristics of a Sandwich origin. Possibly Deming Jarves produced these at his Cape Cod glass works, which he began in 1858. These colored pieces are extremely scarce, clear glass being almost exclusively what a collector can find.

Though a vast quantity of Bellflower glass has survived, it must be noted that certain articles of tableware are much scarcer than others, possibly because, being more fragile, they were less able to withstand hard usage; or it may well be because they were made in lesser quantities. Compotes, goblets and sauce dishes may be plentiful, but the collector will discover that it takes time and effort to find the six-inch plates or the decanters, champagnes and cordials. He will be lucky to obtain these one at a time. But it is precisely this finding of the one plate needed to complete a set which makes the hunt so fascinating; and the elusiveness of that one missing piece may persist for a long time. And do not always expect to find the plates in perfect condition. While I do not advocate buying badly nicked or chipped specimens, it has been my experience that the edges of the plates are nearly always imperfect. It must be remembered, too, that this early glass is susceptible enough to variations of heat and cold to check or crack easily.

Another rare item of unusual interest is the covered salt. I happen to know of only one specimen in Bellflower, but having found them in other ribbed patterns, such as the Ribbed Ivy and Fine Rib, I am convinced that they were made in practically all the early pressed patterns as well as in some of the later ones. The use of the covers was abandoned for various reasons at such an early date that the complete covered salt is almost impossible to find to-day. The cover fits the salt base, having a beaded edge. Of equal rarity is the hat, produced from a whiskey tumbler mold. I have never owned a cake plate on a standard but I have heard of three perfect specimens, and one cracked.

At the M'Kee Brothers' factory, Bellflower was listed in their price list as "R. L.," which meant "Ribbed Leaf." That it was produced in variations by several factories, there is no doubt. For instance, the rare octagonal sugar bowl, of which few whole or perfect specimens have been found, has always come to light in the Midwest. Eastern factories contributed their share of this pattern, which date approximately from 1840 to 1860. It is known to have been made by the Boston & Sandwich Glass Company and possibly by the New England Glass Company, too, though I have no authentic record about the latter.

In collecting Bellflower I must mention again the variants to be found, for it is well to decide, for instance, on one form of sauce dish, and concentrate on completing the set with exact mates. The collector must study the differences. The following classification containing a list of the various forms in which it comes, should be of assistance:

Classification

BELLFLOWER

PATTERN 35

(See Plates 30, 31, 31A, 32, 33, 34, 35)

Form Number.

1. Bowls.

> *a.* Berry bowl. Flat, with wide, scalloped edge. 8 inch.

Form Number.

> *b.* Deep, no standard. Oval, scalloped edge, rayed center. $9\frac{3}{8} \times 6\frac{1}{4}$; $2\frac{1}{2}$ inches deep.
>
> *c.* Round and flat, 6 and 8 inch. Fine rib, single vine. Plain rim, rayed base. Scallop and point edge. Rare.

2. Butter dish, covered. Flat, without standard. Fine rib, single or double vine. Rims with edges like 4, 5, 6. Design in base varies as in sauce dishes. Rim No. 6 goes with base No. 7. Size, 6-inch diameter. Knob of covers usually like No. 11. Three distinct styles. (See details, Plate 31.)

> *a.* Beaded edge where cover joins rim.
>
> *b.* Rayed edge and plain rim.
>
> *c.* Scalloped edge where cover joins. Scallop curls over and is plain, without ribbing.

3. Cake plate on standard. Extremely rare. See *Plates*.

4. Castor sets. A few of these castor sets have been found, in pewter or Britannia standards. There are usually five bottles in a set—salt, pepper, mustard, oil and vinegar. Some have Bellflower design on lower part of bottles, as well as above. Fine rib, single vine. Scarce.

5. Celery vase. Fine rib, single vine, scalloped edge, rayed to edge of scallop. Straight sides. Very scarce.

6. Champagnes. These follow style of goblets closely. Those most readily found are:

> *a.* Barrel shape, fine rib, single vine, knob stem.
>
> *b.* Straight sides, plain stem, rayed base.
>
> *c.* Straight sides, fine rib, single vine, plain one-fourth inch marginal band around top.
>
> *d.* Barrel shape, plain stem, coarse rib. Bases vary, as in goblets. $5\frac{3}{8}$ to $5\frac{1}{4}$ inches in height. Rare.

7. Cologne bottle, plain space for label. Not true Bellflower but closely similar. Usually found in opaque green or translucent white. Sometimes marked "Cologne."

> *a.* Clear.
>
> *b.* Opaque white or green.

8. Compotes.

> *a.* Covered, on high or low standard, generally in 8-inch size. Ribbing fine, single vine, plain rim where cover joins. Very scarce.

Form Number.

    b. Open on high standards. Fine or coarse rib, single vine, base like small inverted bowl, ribbed and with vine. Edge of bowl with plain clear scallop or rayed to extreme edge of scallop. Usual size, 8-inch diameter.

    c. Open on low standards.

        (1) Coarse rib, single vine, deep scalloped edge, plain glass without ribbing. Solid glass base with practically no standard.

        (2) Same as above in finer rib.

        (3) Fine rib, single vine, scalloped edge like line drawing A, rayed to edge of scallop. Low standard with base like small inverted bowl, bearing vine like top.

        (4) Same as above, with scallop of plain glass without ribbing.

    d. Open, extra large on high standard. Large enough to use as a punch bowl. 9¾ inches diameter, 8½ inches high.

Compotes are usually six or eight inches in diameter, single vine, coarse or fine ribbing.

9. Cordial. Same as champagnes, except ribbing is considerably finer on some than may be seen on any other pieces. Scarce. 4 to 4¼ inches.

10. Creamer, fine rib, single or double vine. Base of handle crimped. Footed, with round base, usually rayed. Single vine is seen in two varieties and is more desirable.

11. Decanters.

    a. Pint, fine rib, single vine. Rare. Matching stoppers.

    b. Quart, fine rib, single or double vine. Original stoppers with Bellflower design were made but are generally missing. Decanters are very scarce and vary so much as to make exact classification impossible. Some have flange on neck and others have heavy glass collars of varying size. Any decanters with Bellflower stoppers are rare.

12. Egg cups. Two styles, fine or coarse rib. Straight sides or flaring. Single vine. Rayed base. Rare examples may be found in amber and in milk-white or opalescent.

13. Goblets.

    a. Barrel shape with knob stem. Ribbing fine.

    b. Barrel shape with plain stem. Coarse rib or fine rib.

    c. Straight sides with plain stem. Ribbing fine to extreme edge of bowl.

Form Number.

    d. Straight sides in coarse rib, plain stem.

    e. Variation carries 12 rounded, fluted panels about the lower part of the bowl, beneath the Bellflower design. The goblet bowl rests on a hexagonal knob stem, and plain foot. Rarest goblet form, aside from those having Bellflower pattern cut against ribbed background, instead of being pressed.

    f. Straight sides with plain stem. Fine ribbing but plain one-fourth inch marginal band around top of bowl. Stems are never round. The design in the bases vary as in line drawings, 1, 2 and 3. Single vine only. (Plate 31.)

14. Hat, made from tumbler mold. Extremely rare.

15. Honey dish, fine rib, single vine. Three sizes, 3, $3\frac{1}{4}$ and $3\frac{1}{2}$ inch diameter. No standard. Smaller has plain rim, rayed base. Three-inch size, very rare, has scallop and point rim and star base.

16. Lamps. Lamps are found with bowl of Bellflower design, with brass standards and marble base and also of all glass, usually with scalloped base. Sizes and heights vary too much for classification. Bowls of some lamps have designs inverted —i.e. design on inside, smooth on surface.

17. Mug, small with handle. Fine rib, single vine. Base of handle crimped. Same size as whiskey tumbler, with handle added. Very scarce.

18. Pickle dish, oval. Fine rib, single vine. Two sizes.

19. Pitchers.

    a. Syrup, fine rib, single vine, metal top. Two sizes. Base of handle crimped. Scarce. Tops were either of tin, Britannia or metal. Milk-white syrup. Sapphire blue syrup. Rarest form is fine ribbed ten-sided syrup jug with a flaring foot and ten-pointed rosette in base.

    b. Water, two sizes and two shapes. Usually with double vine but may be found in single. Ribbing fine. Third, or smallest size is often referred to as "milk pitcher." Ribbed to end of lip. Rare.

20. Plates.

    a. Cake plate on standard. Fine rib, single vine, scalloped edge, rayed to edge of scallop. Low standard, with design of vine around base. Bowl flat, with scalloped edge curling up slightly. Rare. $8\frac{1}{2}$ inch diameter, 3 inches high.

Form Number.

       b. Six-inch size only. Fine rib, plain scalloped edge, single vine, large sunburst in center. Only one usual type and these were apparently made quite early, as many are uneven and fairly crude. Scarce. See illustration. One rare oddity has appeared with the design against a fine diamond point background. Rare.

21. Salts, footed, fine rib, rayed base. Some flare more than others. Edge may be:

       a. Rayed to edge of scallop.
       b. Beaded edge. This type was made with covers, similar to Ivy, illustrated on Plate 39.
       c. Scalloped edge, plain without rays.
       d. Wide scallop alternating with point, on rim. Rough pontil, with faint five-pointed star pressed in center. Rayed base.

22. Sauce dishes. (See Bellflower details. Plate 31.)

       a. Earliest have flat rim like No. 6, base like No. 7.
       b. Plain scalloped rim like B.
       c. Scalloped rim like A.
       d. Plain flat rim like No. 8.

Bases of sauce dishes may have concentric circles like No. 9, small sunbursts like No. 8, large sunbursts like No. 10, or design like No. 7, common.

23. Spoonholders, fine rib, single or double vine. Usual style has scalloped edge with rays going to top. Variant has short stem with plain scalloped edge.

24. Sugar bowls.

       a. Extremely rare octagonal shape, with high, domed lid. Height with cover, 8¼ inches. 5¾ inches across without lid. 4⅛ inches across base. Scalloped edge and rayed base. Probably earliest type, usually found in the Midwest.
       b. Single vine, illustrated on Plate 30.
       c. Double vine, illustrated on Plate 30.

25. Tumblers.

       a. Footed, double vine.
       b. Water.
           (1) Usual tumbler has straight sides, single vine, fine ribbing, plain base.
           (2) Same, with plain one-fourth inch marginal band around top. See illustration.
           (3) Same as No. 1, only with coarse ribbing.
           (4) Flares slightly from base and the vine has two veined leaves, two three-petalled clovers and two bellflowers rotating together instead of alternating.

c. Whiskey—Small tumbler with fine rib, single vine, plain base. Very scarce.

Colors: Clear glass; a few occasional pieces in sapphire blue, milk-white, opalescent and amber. Amber is the rarest color in this design.

RIBBED GRAPE

During the Bellflower period, or from about the 1840's on, which is as close as we can come in the absence of definite records, other patterns were in vogue that used the same rayed background as a basis for the design. This marked similarity in both general appearance and quality of glass is found in the "Ribbed Grape." This distinctive pattern, of great charm and appeal, must have been exclusive with the Boston & Sandwich Glass Company, where fragments were found in color, because the pieces vary so slightly. It is not nearly as plentiful as the Bellflower. The rayed ground has a vine threading gracefully through it, with a finely ribbed grape leaf alternating with a large cluster of clear grapes.

Ribbed Grape is essentially a clear glass pattern, though a few odd pieces may be found in color. I have seen a spoonholder in brilliant sapphire blue. That this glass was made during the Bellflower period is proved conclusively by a pair of compotes in my possession which have the Bellflower design around the base, the bowl being in the Grape. The list below is as complete as I can give it from personal knowledge. It is usually found in clear glass. Fragments in blue were recovered from Sandwich but perfect pieces in color are extremely rare.

Classification

RIBBED GRAPE

PATTERN 36

(See Plates 27, 32, 35, 36)

Form Number.

1. Butter dish.
2. Compotes.
    a. Covered, 6 inch, on high standard. A rarity in milk-white.
    b. Open, on low standard. 7¾ inch. Sizes may vary.

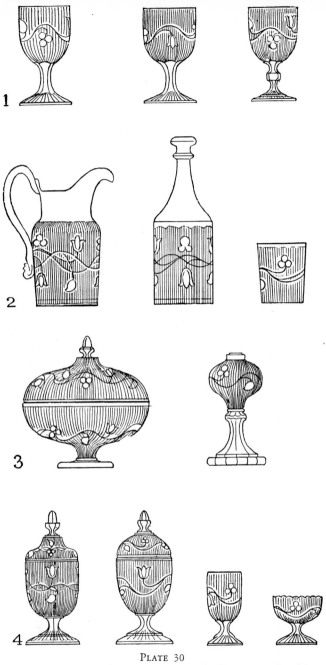

PLATE 30

1. BELLFLOWER goblet with coarse rib; barrel-shaped goblet with fine rib; barrel goblet, fine rib, knob stem.
2. BELLFLOWER water pitcher with double vine; decanter with double vine and bar lip, tumbler.
3. BELLFLOWER covered compote on low foot, lamp.
4. BELLFLOWER sugar bowl with double vine; sugar bowl with single vine, egg cup, salt.

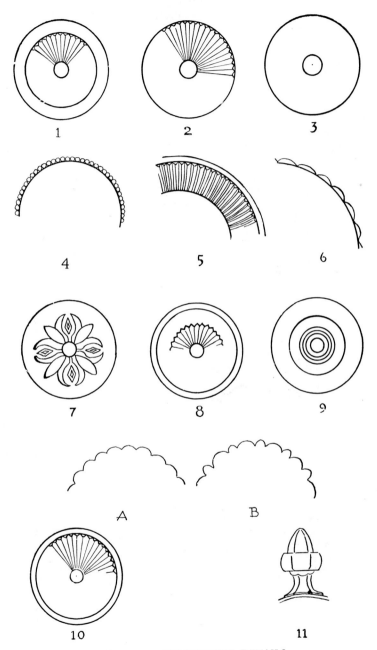

PLATE 31—BELLFLOWER DETAILS

PLATE 31A

Rare octagonal Bellflower sugar bowl. of Midwestern origin.

PLATE 32—SIX INCH PLATES

Bellflower
Ribbed Grape

Horn of Plenty
Cable

PLATE 33—GOBLETS

Ribbed Ivy   Bellflower
Ribbed Palm   Inverted Fern

PLATE 34

1. BELLFLOWER castor set in pewter standard, celery vase, footed tumbler.
2. RIBBED VARIANTS of BELLFLOWER ERA, cut against a fine rib background.
3. Candlesticks in EXCELSIOR pattern. One of the earliest pressed glass designs to match table ware. Found in two sizes.

RIBBED GRAPE COMPOTE   OPAL BELLFLOWER EGG CUPS

PLATE 35

Form Number.

3. Cordials.

4. Creamer, crimped handle. Attractive size for use, being smaller than most early creamers.

5. Goblets.

   a. One-fourth inch marginal band around top. Straight sides.
   b. Rayed to top edge, straight sides.

6. Plates, 6 inch. One style, with finely serrated edge and sunburst in center, similar to Bellflower. See illustration.

7. Sauce dish, one style only. Flat, with scalloped edge.

8. Spoonholder, usual type, similar to Bellflower.

9. Sugar bowl. Footed, same style as Bellflower.

Color: Clear glass. A few pieces may be found in milk-white and in color, but they are rare. Deep blue and peacock-green shades are extreme rarities.

RIBBED IVY

Following the Ribbed Grape very closely is the Ivy, which seems to have been made in larger quantities. It is found more readily and comes in a greater variety of forms. The background is rayed like the Bellflower or Ribbed Grape. Here again we have the vine threading its way around, with a design consisting of clear three-pointed leaves which stand out against the fine ribs. The stems are clear and round on the footed pieces, with a rayed base. The quality of the glass is usually brilliant and clear, and rings like a bell. That it was copied by many factories may be doubted for the variants are few. The wanted pieces are comparatively easy to match.

Lamps may be had with bowls in the Ribbed Ivy pattern, generally with brass stem and marble base, though they also come with all glass and opaque glass bases.

I have been assured by dealers that they have owned a water pitcher and a six-inch plate in this design which is so similar to the Bellflower. There is no reason why they should not exist but I myself have never seen any and collectors who have specialized in this pattern for years assure me they have never found either one. In some cases the confusion may have arisen from the fact that another pattern, showing a five-pointed instead of a three-pointed leaf, with coarser ribbing and obviously of a later period, has been mistaken for Ivy. This pattern, christened Southern Ivy in the North, is illustrated on Plate 166. Ribbed Ivy was produced by the Boston & Sandwich Glass Company.

Classification

RIBBED IVY

PATTERN 37

(See Plates 33, 39)

Form Number.

1. Bowl, 8½ inches diameter, 2½ inches deep. Design in base same as in sauce dish. Very scarce.
2. Butter dish. Clear scalloped edge that rolls out where cover joins. No standard.
3. Castor bottles.
4. Celery vase. Extremely rare. 7¼ inches high; bowl, 5½ inches long; top and base, 4 inches diameter. Two or three known specimens.
5. Champagnes.
6. Compotes.
   a. Open.
      (1) On high standard, with scalloped edge. Extra large, similar to same style in Bellflower. One is 8¾ inches in diameter, 7½ inches high.
      (2) On low standard, with scalloped edge. Deep bowl.
   b. Small, covered on standard. Same size as butter dish. Extremely scarce. 6 inch.
   c. Small, on low foot. Shallow bowl.
7. Cordials.
8. Creamer. Same type as Bellflower. Footed, with crimped handle.
9. Decanters.
   a. Half-pint decanter or sauce bottle. Vary in height. One style eight inches high. These are found both with pewter shaker

Form Number.

> top and ornate glass stopper. Usually found with stoppers missing.
>
> *b.* Pint, same as quart. Usual type.
>
> *c.* Quart, usual type.

10. Egg cups. Straight sides, clear round stem. Base usually rayed, but sometimes found clear.

11. Goblets. One type only, rayed to edge of bowl. Base may be rayed or plain glass. Round plain stem.

12. Hat, produced from tumbler mold. Rare.

13. Honey dish, $3\frac{1}{2}$ inch.

14. Lamps. Bowls in Ivy pattern found in lamps with clear glass or milk-white standards; also brass stem and marble base.

15. Mugs, with handles.

> *a.* Exactly like whiskey tumblers, only with handles. Very scarce.
>
> *b.* Same, smaller size.

16. Salts, footed.

> *a.* Covered. Rim beaded. Extremely scarce with covers.
>
> *b.* Open, with beaded edge.
>
> *c.* Scalloped edge.

17. Sauce dish.

18. Spoonholder. Same as Bellflower, with scalloped edge.

19. Sugar bowl. Base of sugar has scalloped edge in plain glass that rolls out slightly where cover joins.

20. Tumblers.

> *a.* Water. Straight sides, plain base.
>
> *b.* Whiskey. Same as water tumblers, only smaller.

Color: Clear glass.

FINE RIB

A pattern in this early series of ribbed glass consists exclusively of the fine rib without either vine or flower being used to decorate it. The rib is as fine as the Bellflower and the glass as clear and bright as the Ribbed Ivy. Though simple it is very pleasing. It has not been collected as extensively as many other patterns and it is not plentiful. It is recommended to those seeking something different, for it has dignity and refinement of line and the quality of the glass is all that one could desire. It has been definitely established that this glass was made at the New England Glass factory, as it was pictured in their trade catalogue of about 1869, though it was unquestionably made at a much earlier date. If records were obtainable I think we would find that this was being produced in the late Fifties. While this design must have been made by other factories, I have not found any variants. The classification is taken from the New England Glass Co.'s illustrated catalogue, augmented by some pieces I have seen. It was used as a blank for cutting, as noted in the chapter on "Rayed Variants."

Fragments of Fine Rib were excavated at Sandwich, so some of this ware must have been produced there.

Classification

FINE RIB

Pattern 38

(See Plates 27, 36)

Form Number.

1. Ale glass.
2. Bitters bottle.
3. Bowls.
   a. Covered.
      (1) High foot, 6 and 7 inch.
      (2) Low foot, 6 and 7 inch.
   b. Open, on foot, 6, 7, 8, 9 and 10 inch.
4. Butter dish.
5. Castor set.
6. Celery vase.
7. Champagne glass, 5¼ inches high.
8. Compotes.
   a. Covered.
      (1) On foot, 6 and 7 inch.
      (2) On higher foot, 6, 7 and 8 inch.
      (3) On low foot, 6, 7 and 8 inch.
      (4) On low standard, 8 inches high.
   b. Open.

Form Number.

9. Cordials.

10. Creamer.

11. Custard, handled. Small mug.

12. Decanters.
    - *a.* Bar lip.
        - (1) Pint.
        - (2) Quart.
    - *b.* With stopper.
        - (1) Pint.
        - (2) Quart.

13. Dishes.
    - *a.* Covered.
        - (1) 5½, 6 and 7 inch.
        - (2) Shallow on low foot, 6 and 7 inch.
    - *b.* Oval, 7, 8, 9 and 10 inch.
    - *c.* Shallow, 5½, 6, 7 and 8 inch.

14. Egg cups.
    - *a.* Double; also covered. May be found in translucent white and in colors.

15. Goblets.
    - *a.* Usual type, ribbed to top of bowl.
    - *b.* Plain marginal band around the top.

16. Honey dish, 3½ inch.

17. Jelly glass.

18. Jugs.
    - *a.* Pint.
    - *b.* Quart.
    - *c.* Three pint.

19. Lamps, two sizes. Applied handles.

20. Lemonade glass.

21. Mugs, small with handles. Two sizes.

22. Pitcher, water.

23. Plates, 6 and 7 inch.

24. Salts.
    - *a.* Covered on stems.
    - *b.* Individual.
    - *c.* Large open, footed.
    - *d.* Oval.

25. Sauce dish.

Form Number.

26. Spoonholder.
    - *a.* Large.
    - *b.* Small.
27. Sugar bowl.
28. Tumblers.
    - *a.* Taper.
    - *b.* Water.
    - *c.* Whiskey.
29. Water bottle with tumble-up.

Color: Clear glass. Egg cups, open or covered, may be found in several fine shades of opaque colored glass, as well as in translucent white and colors.

ACORN

An early ribbed pattern of which we know very little beyond the fact that it was made during the Bellflower period, is the Acorn. The quality of the glass and the ribbing are the same as the Bellflower, the difference being that the Acorn motif is substituted for the former. I have a compote in which the vine motif shows a clear Acorn, alternating with a very finely ribbed leaf almost identical with the Ribbed Grape leaf. The base is also rayed and has the Bellflower design. Another Acorn variation has a differently shaped acorn and a plain clear leaf like that used in the Bellflower. Of the pieces that match, one will find that the centers all have concentric circles like those shown in the line drawings on Plate 39. It is an interesting design but the pieces are exceedingly scarce. Its popularity must have been short lived as so little of it appears to survive for us to collect to-day. A dealer tells me that he has owned the goblet and the six-inch plate but a collector who owns one hundred six-inch plates has never seen one or had one offered to her. It seems reasonable to believe that the goblet, plate and other pieces must exist, though I have not seen either one over a period of twenty years.

Deming Jarves, founder of the Boston & Sandwich Glass Company, was exceedingly fond of the Acorn motif, so it is not surprising to know that fragments of this pattern were discovered at the site of the old factory.

The articles listed are the only ones I have actually seen.

Classification

ACORN

PATTERN 39

(See Plate 39)

Form Number.
1. Butter dish.
2. Compotes.
    a. Covered.
        (1) On high standard, 6 inch. This type usually termed originally "Sweetmeat dish."
        (2) On low standard, 6 inch.
    b. Open, 8 inch. Scalloped edge.
        (1) Plain base.
        (2) Bellflower design on base.
        (3) Acorn design on base.
3. Honey dish, $3\frac{1}{2}$ inch.
4. Sauce dish.
Color: Clear glass.

RAYED VARIANTS

A word should be said here about the variants of those patterns using a ribbed or rayed background as a basis of design. Possibly those patterns of which I have found only one or two of a kind should be classed with the "collectibles," but I cannot list them as such unless I find enough items to make a set. On Plate 34 is shown a ribbed water tumbler using a three-leaved clover in a most effective manner. On the same Plate is shown a goblet in the double Bellflower. I found three of these in one day, but the only other piece I have ever seen to match is a water tumbler. These goblets are all of a very beautiful clear flint glass, and the workmanship is much finer than on the average Bellflower piece. Another variant shown on the same Plate seems to be of the same

PLATE 36

1. RIBBED GRAPE creamer, sugar bowl, spoonholder.
2. FINE RIB goblet, covered compote on low foot, footed salt, cordial.
3. INVERTED FERN sugar bowl, butter dish, egg cup, sauce dish.
4. CABLE goblet, open compote, footed salt, egg cup.

PLATE 37—SIX INCH PLATES

Tulip
Ribbed Palm

Waffle
Rayed, with Loop border

M'KEE & BROTHERS.

FLINT GLASS MANUFACTURERS, PITTSBURGH, PA.

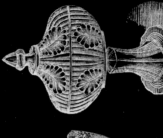

6 in. Sprig Nappy and Cover.

6 in. Sprig Sweetmeat and Cover.

6 in. Sprig Nappy.

4 in. Sprig Nappy.

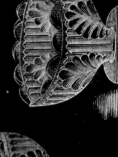

7 in. Sprig Bowl, Low Foot.

6 in. Sprig Plate.

8 in. Sprig Bowl, High Foot.

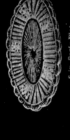

8 in. Sprig Bowl, Low Foot.

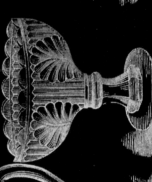

½ gall. Sprig Pitcher.

PLATE 38.

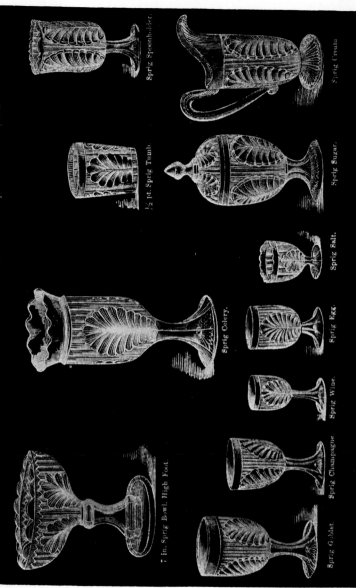

M'KEE & BROTHERS, FLINT GLASS MANUFACTURERS, PITTSBURGH, PA.

Sprig Spoonholder.

Sprig Cream.

½ pt. Sprig Tumbl.

Sprig Sugar.

Sprig Celery.

Sprig Salt.

Sprig Egg.

Sprig Wine.

7 in. Sprig Bowl, High Foot.

Sprig Goblet.

Sprig Champagne.

PLATE 38A

Group of Ribbed Palm, originally termed "Sprig," as shown by M'Kee & Brothers of Pittsburgh, Pa., in the 1860's.

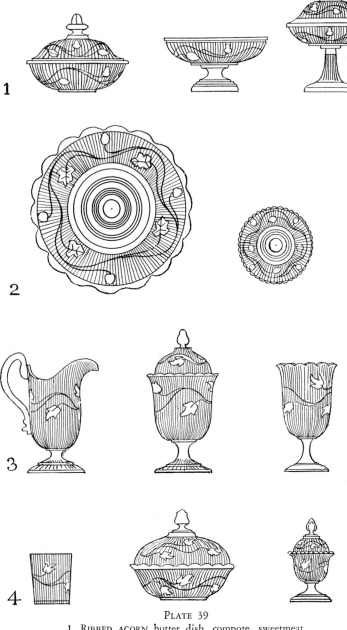

PLATE 39

1. RIBBED ACORN butter dish, compote, sweetmeat.
2. Bowl of RIBBED ACORN compote and sauce dish.
3. RIBBED IVY creamer, sugar bowl, spoonholder.
4. RIBBED IVY whiskey tumbler, butter dish, covered salt.

high quality of material and workmanship. In the pieces having the clear elongated thumbprint, I have seen two or three goblets and a cordial. The existence of the cordial causes me to suspect that there must be other forms, but so far they have not come to light. These variants are apparently "blanks" in the Fine Rib pattern, which have been used for cutting. The goblets and other articles are unquestionably of pressed glass, the design having been cut against the rayed background. Since the New England Glass Company produced the Fine Rib pattern, it is reasonable to assume that they are responsible for these unusual, attractively cut glasses.

RIBBED PALM

In a catalogue and price list issued by M'Kee Brothers, flint glass manufacturers, of 17 Wood Street, Pittsburgh, dated April 1, 1868, containing numerous illustrations of their wares, are shown many pieces of "Sprig" pattern. This pattern has of late years become so generally known by the title of "Ribbed Palm" that it is too late now to return to the old trade name. Indeed, the new is a more appropriate description. Against the rather heavy ribbing is displayed a clear palmette, or ribbed leaf. It is a bold and handsome design, in relief, and follows closely in form that of the Bellflower.

Fragments of Ribbed Palm have been unearthed at the site of the old Boston & Sandwich Glass Company, so it is impossible to state today which factory produced this design first. That there is evidence one or the other wished to avoid plagiarism is certain, because some goblets are discovered with the ribbing convex while on others, it is concave. So are there other minor variations. A tentative date of manufacture can be fixed, because the pattern is pictured in wood cut illustrations in an earlier, undated M'Kee catalogue, known to be of the 1850's. Undoubtedly the Ribbed Palm was a popular pattern, carried on by both factories for many years.

The forms are many so that this pattern lends itself to effective table decoration. The pieces are not difficult to match, with the exception of those which prove scarce in nearly all other patterns, like the plates, champagnes, wines and tumblers. An interesting collection may be assembled in a short time. The glass is fairly heavy, especially the goblets. The stems of the footed pieces are hexagonal and the bases rayed, both of these being distinguishing marks of the earlier table glass. The handles of the water pitcher and creamer are crimped at the base, as on the blown glass pieces. The bases of the known compotes are of plain solid glass but the sugar bowl, salts, egg cups, goblets and smaller footed pieces have rayed bases. The center of the plates is rayed as in the Bellflower, the only difference being a larger circle in the center of the rays. Goblets, egg cups, tumblers, champagnes and wines all have a plain clear glass band above the ribbed design.

In various states this glass has been known from time to time by different titles, such as "Oak Leaf," "Leaf" and "Acanthus." I never knew anyone to call it by its catalogue name of "Sprig." The best and most generally known is "Ribbed Palm."

Classification

RIBBED PALM

PATTERN 40

(See Plates 33, 37, 38, 38A)

Form Number.
1. Butter dish.
2. Celery vase.
3. Champagne.
4. Compotes.
    a. Open on high standard, 7, 8 and 10 inch.
    b. Open, on low, plain solid glass standard. Plain, deeply scalloped edge. 7 and 8 inch.
    c. Sweetmeat compote. 6 inch, covered, on standard.
5. Creamer.
6. Dish, deep. No cover, 6, 7, 8 and 9 inch.
7. Egg cups.
8. Goblets.

Form Number.
  9. Lamps.
     a. All glass.
     b. 5 inch colored base.
     c. Peg lamps.
  10. Pickle dish, oval. Two sizes.
  11. Pitcher, water.
  12. Plates, 6 inch.
  13. Salts, footed.
  14. Sauce dish, 4 inch.
  15. Spoonholder.
  16. Sugar bowl.
  17. Tumblers, water.
     a. Whiskey tumbler.
  18. Wine glass.
Color: Clear glass.

INVERTED FERN

This is a dainty and well-known pattern which has been popular with collectors for some years. The descriptive title of Inverted Fern no doubt came from the desire to differentiate it from the Ribbed Palm when the various designs were not as well known as they are to-day. This glass is lighter in weight though it is brilliant in quality. It is one of the first to show considerably less of the lead-flint quality. The design, of very fine ribbing, fairly covers the objects, with the exception of the clear fern leaves (as they have come to be designated) which stand out in relief. The glass rings though not so clearly as the earlier glass. This design is much more delicate than the Ribbed Palm. Probably that is the reason why it has been more widely sought.

It is to be noted that the goblets and egg cups were made with both a clear and a rayed base. Those pieces in my possession having a clear base are of a noticeably clear white glass, while those with rayed bases are less brilliant, sometimes bordering on amethystine. Fragments of Inverted Fern were found at the site of the old Boston & Sandwich Glass Company.

Classification

INVERTED FERN

Pattern 41

(See Plates 33, 36)

Form Number.

1. Butter dish.
2. Champagne.
3. Compotes, open. Various sizes.
4. Creamer.
5. Egg cups. Base either plain or rayed.
6. Goblets.
     a. Fine rayed base. Heights may vary slightly.
     b. Plain base, always plain band at top, except on plates.
7. Honey dishes.
8. Pitcher, water. Rare.
9. Plates, 6 inch. Very rare.
10. Salts, footed.
11. Sauce dishes, flat only. 4 inch.
12. Spoonholder.
13. Sugar bowl.
14. Tumblers, water.
     a. Whiskey tumbler.
15. Wine glass.

Color: Clear glass.

SOUTHERN IVY

Quite different from the earlier Ribbed Ivy is this pattern which has been christened Southern Ivy. Some confusion has existed over these designs due to the fact that both show ivy leaves against a rayed or ribbed background. When a piece of each is placed side by side the differences are quite marked. The earlier ware is of a brilliant flint glass having a bell-like tone, and the vine motif carrying the three-pointed ivy leaves stands out clearly against a finely ribbed surface. The later ware is lighter in weight and with very little ring to the glass. The ribbing is coarser and instead of the vine there are sprays of clear five-pointed ivy leaves. The forms vary also, those of the Southern Ivy having shapes that were not made during the earlier period. The title of this glass came about because of the resemblance of the leaves to the Virginia Creeper.

As nearly as can be ascertained this glass was produced during the Seventies. Where it was made is unknown though probably in a mid-Western glass house.

The pieces that match in this pattern have a large nine-pointed star in the base. I refer, of course, to such dishes as the large berry bowl, sauce dish, etc. The star is heavily rayed, giving a rather unusual effect. I have not seen many forms, but perhaps the ware is more plentiful in sections which I have not visited. At present it is not well known or in demand.

Classification

SOUTHERN IVY

PATTERN 42

(See Plate 166)

Form Number.
1. Berry bowl, scalloped edge, 8¼ inch diameter, 3¼ inches deep.
2. Egg cup.
3. Cruet, small.
4. Pitcher, water.
5. Sauce dish, 4 inch.
6. Tumbler, water.
Color: Clear glass.

PRISM WITH DIAMOND POINTS

A brilliant and beautiful glass neglected and nameless for years, is now in demand under the name of Prism with Diamond Points. This glass was evidently produced at different periods, as the earlier ware shows sharply defined lines and has a clear bell tone when struck. The goblet is almost chalice-shaped, with a knob stem close to the base of the bowl. The stem is hexagonal and the base clear. This goblet, with its fine dignified lines, may be seen on Plate 96. Some years later this same pattern was used again, but the glass lacks the fine tone, the ribs and diamond points are duller and the knob is lacking on the goblet. The earlier ware is seldom encountered, though goblets in the later ware are not rare. Other forms were made but they are not plentiful. From fragment findings, it would appear that the earlier forms were made at Sandwich.

Classification

PRISM WITH DIAMOND POINTS

PATTERN 43

(See Plate 96)

Form Number.

1. Butter dish.
2. Celery vase.
3. Compote. Sweetmeat dish. 6 inch, covered, on high foot.
4. Creamer.
5. Dish. Deep, round bowl.
6. Egg cups. Two styles, single and double.
7. Goblets.
    a. Knob stem, earlier ware.
    b. Same design, but without knob stem.
8. Pickle dish, oval.
9. Pitcher, water.
10. Plates, large. Later period.
11. Salts, footed.
12. Spoonholder.
13. Sugar bowl.
14. Tumblers, water.
15. Wine glass.

Color: Clear glass.

Chapter V

OTHER EARLY PATTERNS

SAWTOOTH

This pattern is known to have been made by the New England Glass Company of Cambridge, Mass., probably in the 1860's, and at the Sandwich factory, presumably during the same period. More than one factory in the old Pittsburgh glass district also was turning it out. In a catalogue of Bryce Bros., of the Seventies, numerous pieces of their "Diamond" Pattern are illustrated, and in one of Gillinder & Sons, of Greensburg and Philadelphia, Pa., of the Eighties, are found their "Deep Diamond Bowls," "Diamond Covered Bowls," "Cake plates" and "Celeries." Their sugar bowl is shown on Plate 41. Still other factories must have been producing it at an earlier date, as I find the "large diamond pattern" mentioned several times in an Ovington Brothers catalogue of the period 1854-59. It is a heavy glass, made up of coarse, sharp points. There is always something fascinating about the absolute precision with which the sawtooth edges of the covers fit the body of the dishes. The earlier pieces ring clearly and show, in both material and workmanship, that they are a characteristic product of their period. Later on this same design was copied and made lighter in weight, with very little ring to the glass. Ripley & Co. of Pittsburgh made one of these later copies, which they called their "Roanoke" pattern. The covered dishes had knobs that resembled the curved stem of a pumpkin. The forms, as a whole, would indicate the late period when they were produced. Bryce Bros. made during the Eighties a pattern which they called the "Amazon." This design has the Sawtooth points around the base of the bowl of each object, the remaining portion being plain. It is in no way to be compared with the earlier ware, some of which may well have been made during the Fifties and possibly earlier.

In the Cambridge factory this design was called "Mitre Diamond," but today it is so generally known as "Sawtooth" that it would be unwise to insist on calling it by any of its original trade designations. Many of the forms are also to be had in opalescent or opaque white and, at a later period, compotes were made in several colors. This pattern has also been called "Pineapple" in some states, but this title has gradually fallen into disuse. It should be abandoned altogether.

Having warned collectors that there are many Sawtooth variants due to its having been copied by so many factories over a period of forty odd years, I can only point out the best-known forms. It is also necessary to bear in mind that there is a difference in the size of the Sawtooth points. The earliest is heavy and coarse. This does not detract from its beauty, for it is very brilliant and effective. There is a later Sawtooth with only slightly smaller points and still another of the early period which is very fine. It is called "Diamond Point." The latter I shall take up in subsequent pages. The best-known and most collectible goblet is the earliest type, shown on Plate 42. It is of heavy flint glass, and has a fine knob stem. Goblets of a much later period are lighter in weight, generally without the knob stem and with a wider marginal band at the top of the bowl. I have seen a late one in which the design is carried only two-thirds of the way up the bowl. The still later "Amazon" pattern has the sawtooth edges only at the base of the goblet bowl. Generally speaking, most of the earliest pieces, with the exception of the goblets, have rayed bases. The sugar bowl, butter dish, creamer and pomade jar on Plate 40 show the earliest forms. Note the difference in the shape of the covers on the covered pieces. I have heard the style of the covers of the butter dish and of the large compote referred to as "Pagoda" type. The celery holders, or vases, as we call them now, I suspect, are slightly later. The covered sugar and creamer on Plate 41 show the first change from the earliest period. The pair of oblong dishes with knobs and handles formed of lion's heads, were made by Bryce

Bros. of Pittsburgh, during the Eighties. A "Toy Set" consisting of sugar bowl, creamer, butter dish and spoonholder, was made by Gillinder & Sons of Philadelphia.

The classification I give is based chiefly on those known to have been made at the Cambridge factory and by Bryce Bros., together with many others I have found in my travels. The candlesticks shown on Plate 40 are classified under Diamond Point instead of under Sawtooth, because of the small points. They may be used appropriately with either pattern.

Classification

SAWTOOTH

Pattern 44

(See Plates 40, 41, 42)

Form Number.

1. Bottle, water, with tumbler. Originally known as "water bottle and tumble-up." Ovington advertised "either bottle or tumble-up sold separately."
2. Bowls.
    a. Covered.
        (1) On low foot, 7, 8, 9 and 10 inch.
        (2) 6 and 7 inch, no foot.
    b. Fruit or preserve, on foot, large diamond patterns, 6, 7, 8, 9, 10, 11 and 12 inch.
    c. Fruit or preserve, on low foot, scallop edge, 8, 9 and 10 inch.
    d. Open, no foot, 6, 7, 8, 9 and 10 inch.
3. Butter dish.
4. Cake plate, on standard, 7, 8 and 9 inch, marked "flared to 9, 10 and 12 inch."
    a. Bryce Bros. 9, 11 and 13 inch.
5. Celery vase.
6. Champagne, knob stem.
7. Compotes.
    a. Covered.
        (1) On high standard, 6 and 7 inch.
        (2) On low standard, 6 and 7 inch.
        (3) On standard, 7, 8, 9 and 10 inch.

Form Number.

    b. Open.

        (1) On high foot, 6, 7, 8 and 9 inch. Bowls deep or flaring.
        (2) On low foot, 6 and 7 inch.
        (3) 7, 8, 9 and 10 inch. (Nappies.)

8. Cordials.
9. Creamer, footed, rayed or clear base.
10. Cruet, small.
11. Decanter, quart size.
12. Dishes.

    a. 5 and 7 inch.
    b. Oval.

13. Egg cups.
14. Goblets.
15. Honey dishes.
16. Lamps.
17. Pitcher, water. Quart and ½ gallon.
18. Pomade jar.
19. Salts.

    a. Covered.
    b. Footed.
    c. Open, with smooth edge.

20. Sauce dishes, flat, round, 4, 4½ and 5 inch.
21. Spoonholder.
22. Sugar bowls.

    a. Covered, with plain or rayed base. Believe rayed is the earliest.
    b. Footed, rayed base.

23. Toy sets, made for Centennial. Butter, sugar, creamer and spoonholder.
24. Trays, 10, 11, 12 and 14 inch.
25. Tumbler. Several styles.
26. Wine glass.

Colors: Milk-white; clear glass; colors, particularly in compotes, were made during later period. Creamer, sugar bowl and spoonholder sometimes found in sapphire blue. Goblets of earlier period were not made in color.

PLATE 40—SAWTOOTH

Sugar bowl   Wine glass   Butter dish   Pomade jar   Creamer
Pair of celery vases   Pair of candlesticks   Compote on high foot

PLATE 41—SAWTOOTH OF LATER PERIOD

Pair of covered dishes with lion handles and knobs   Open compote in center

Sugar bowl   Cake plate on standard   Creamer

PLATE 42—GOBLETS

New England Pineapple   Tulip
Sawtooth   Diamond Point

PLATE 43—GROUP OF DIAMOND POINT

Celery vase Egg cup Open compote Tumbler Water pitcher

PLATE 44—PLATES

Beaded Tulip   Diamond Point
Pinwheel   Daisy

PLATE 45—PLATES

Diamond Point, star and circle center
Willow Oak

Diamond Point, star center
Single Tulip

DIAMOND POINT

The Diamond Point, as it is now known, was originally called "Sharp Diamond" by the New England Glass Company. This name describes it very well, as it is made up of small diamond points that sparkle radiantly. At the Sandwich factory it was produced in the late Fifties, or in the earlier years of the subsequent decade. I should mention here that it was once fairly well known by the titles of "Grant" or "Grant Pineapple." The origin of these later names is a matter for conjecture. It has been suggested that some wide-awake manufacturer took advantage of General Grant's popularity to re-name this pattern in his honor after Appomattox.

Diamond Point is fairly plentiful, due to its having been copied extensively by so many factories early and late. This makes it more difficult for the collector to match sets for there is an amazing number of variants, impossible to classify closely enough. The best known goblet and the earliest, is shown on Plate 42. This is of a heavy flint glass, with clear bell tone. Plates were made in various sizes, which is an interesting point, as this is the first of the early designs treated in which plates were made in other than the six-inch size.

From the illustrations shown in the New England Glass Co. price list, it is plain that two forms were made by them. For instance, water pitchers are shown, one with a small stem and circular base, and another style without a foot, the base being flat and octagonal. A number of pieces in both forms are shown on Plate 43, making a more detailed verbal description unnecessary. On Plate 44 is shown a six-inch plate of very small diamond points and undoubtedly of early origin. Two other plates of a slightly later period, are illustrated on Plate 45. On Plate 153, Number 11, is shown another type of Diamond Point goblet, the panels suggesting the trend of those pieces having the octagonal shaped base. This particular shape is thought to have been made at Sandwich. A footed tumbler in my possession has a scalloped foot, diamond points on the lower part of the bowl, nine small panels above and a plain circular top, flaring slightly. This being the same style as the goblet, I believe all the stemware may have been made in this shape, as well as with the knob stem, as shown on Plate 42. (See *Victorian Glass*.)

This pattern was undoubtedly a typical New England product. In the Pittsburgh M'Kee Brothers list I find only a "Three inch diamond plate."

Classification

DIAMOND POINT

PATTERN 45

(See Plates 42, 43, 44, 45, 153)

Form Number.

1. Ale glass, 6¼ inches high, 2¼ inches diameter at top. Knob stem.
2. Bowls.
    a. Covered, 6, 7 and 8 inch.
    b. 5, 6, 7 and 8 inch. Open.
3. Butter dish.
4. Cake salvers, 9, 10, 11, 12 and 14 inch.
5. Candlesticks, 6½ inch. Clear glass, opaque white, green, sapphire blue.
6. Castor bottles.
7. Celery vase.
8. Champagne. Knob stem, clear bases on all.
    a. Large.
    b. Small.
9. Compotes.
    a. Covered.
        (1) On high standard, 6, 7, and 8 inch.
        (2) On low standard, 6, 7, and 8 inch.
    b. Open.
        (1) On low standard, 6, 7, 8, 9 and 10 inch.
        (2) On standard. 6, 7, 8, 9 and 10 inch.
10. Cordials. Knob stem, clear bases on all.
    a. Large.
    b. Small.

Form Number.

11. Creamer, footed.

12. Cruets.

13. Decanters.

    a. With stopper.
        (1) Pint.
        (2) Quart.
    b. Without stopper, heavy collar.
        (1) Pint.
        (2) Quart.

14. Dish, oval, 7, 8, 9 and 10 inch.

15. Egg cups. Rare in colors, especially when covered.

16. Goblets. Knob stem, clear bases on all.

    a. Large.
    b. Small.

17. Honey dishes, $3\frac{3}{4}$ inches, plain rim, ten-pointed star in base. Also $3\frac{1}{2}$ inch.

18. Jelly glass.

19. Jugs.

    a. Half-pint.
    b. Pint.
    c. Quart.
    d. Three-pint.

20. Lemonade glass.

21. Mugs, handled, same size as whiskey tumblers.

22. Mustard, with Britannia cover.

23. Pepper, cut neck, Britannia screw cap.

24. Pitcher, water. Four sizes from one-half pint to three pints, with and without foot. Flat ones octagonal.

25. Plates.

    a. 6, 7 and 8 inch.
    b. $5\frac{1}{2}$ inch. Star center.
    c. Large, fairly deep, 8 inch. Six large circles and star in center.
    d. Smaller, like *c*—6 inch.
    e. Three-inch diamond plate, Pittsburgh.
    f. With very fine diamond points. See plate 44.

26. Salts, covered, footed. Opaque covered types especially desirable.

27. Sauce dish, plain edge, 4 inch.

Form Number.

28. Spoonholder.
29. Sugar bowls. With and without foot. Flat ones have octagonal bases.
30. Tumblers.
    a. Water.
    b. Whiskey.
31. Vinegar, cut neck.
32. Wine glass, knob stem. Clear bases on all.
    a. Large.
    b. Small.

Colors: Clear glass; opaque-white may be found in a few articles, including the candlesticks. Covered egg cups are found in clear and in colored opaque glass. Rare. Some of the covered styles were used for pomades. One in my possession carries original paper label, marked "Floral Perfumery, New York."

FLATTENED SAWTOOTH

An interesting variation to the Sawtooth pattern is the Flattened Sawtooth. Instead of a sharp pointed apex to the diamond it is truncated, the flattened end looking as though a knife had cut off the point. It is a heavy glass, apparently of the same period as the better known pattern. The usual pieces are found though they are not plentiful. In an old catalogue, issued by George Duncan & Sons of Pittsburgh, are listed a number of pieces which were continued by the United States Glass Co. after they absorbed the Duncan firm. It is possible other factories also may have produced this pattern.

Classification

FLATTENED SAWTOOTH

PATTERN 46

(See Plate 65)

Form Number.

1. Bowl. Flat, round, 10 inch. Various other shapes.
2. Celery vase.

Form Number.

3. Celery tray. Two styles, straight and crimped.
4. Compotes, open and covered. Various sizes
5. Cordials.
6. Decanters.
7. Egg cups.
8. Finger bowls.
9. Goblets.
10. Ice tub.
11. Lamp.
12. Pitcher, water.
13. Plates, 6 and 7 inch.
14. Salts.
    a. Covered.
    b. Footed.
15. Sauce dishes.
16. Tumblers.

Color: Clear glass.

WAFFLE

If the Waffle pattern were better known it would undoubtedly be much more popular. One may see an odd piece of it in an antique shop, such as a celery holder and admire it as a flower vase and never realize that it is a design collectible in sets. Individual specimens of any pattern give but the vaguest idea of the effectiveness of that same pattern when grouped together. It has taken us a long time to realize the decorative value of our old American pressed glass.

The Waffle was one of the early patterns produced at Sandwich. This was established some years ago when a number of the old original mahogany models were found long after the factory had ceased operations. Later on, fragments were excavated at the site of the Boston & Sandwich Glass Company. It is a most attractive design, of heavy flint glass. The edges of many of the pieces, such as the celery vases, butter dishes, etc., have a thick clear scalloped edge, that greatly increases their effectiveness. The stemware all has knob stems. The Waffle may be found in the needed forms for table use. It is a pattern that I believe belongs to the late Fifties or early Sixties.

Collectors not familiar with the design must beware of the variants which are so similar that a careful scrutiny is needed to avoid mistakes. The earliest Waffle has three panels of cubes, divided by a double bar. Another and much later pattern, consists of four panels of cubes, divided by four bars, three bars in each column. Still another pattern is made up entirely of cubes, without any bars to form panels. These are shown on Plates 26 and 153.

Classification

WAFFLE

PATTERN 47

(See Plates 26, 37, 46, 153)

Form Number.
1. Butter dish.
2. Celery vase.
3. Champagne.
4. Compotes.
    a. Covered, on high standard. 6 inch. Various sizes.
    b. Open, on standard. 8 inch.
5. Cordials.
6. Creamer.
7. Decanters.
8. Egg cups.
9. Goblets.
10. Lamps.
    a. Glass base.
    b. Brass stem, marble base.
11. Plates, 6 inch.
12. Salts, footed.
    a. Covered. Very rare.
13. Sauce dish, flat, 4 inch.
14. Sugar bowl.

Form Number.
 15. Tumblers.
   a. Water.
   b. Whiskey.
Color: Clear glass. Milk-white or colors are unusual and rare.

HARP

A pattern which was made by the M'Kee Brothers of Pittsburgh during the Fifties was called the Harp. This same pattern was also made at an early date, I believe, at Sandwich. The design was apparently copied over a period of a few years, and it may be numbered among the earliest of the pressed glass patterns. Those pieces found most readily to-day are footed salts, spoonholders, small handled whale oil lamps (see Plate 14) and the larger glass whale oil lamps, the bowl showing the harp in its panels. Some of the spoonholders show evidence of being very early. It is interesting to remember that these so-called "Spoonholders" did more than double duty in the old days. They were also sold as cigar holders and as spill holders. One in my possession is hexagonal, with a round foot. It has a clear metallic ring, denoting its flint glass quality. Taper holders were made to match many of the early lamps.

Any of the Harp pattern, aside from the larger lamps, is heavy and generally rather crudely made. The rim of the cover of a butter dish is often found rough and unfinished in appearance. The goblets are exceedingly rare.

Variants of the Harp have an oval alternating with the harp, in the panels.

Classification

HARP

PATTERN 48

(See Plate 14)

Form Number.
 1. Butter dish.
 2. Honey dish.

Form Number.

3. Goblet. Rare.
4. Lamps, whale oil.
   a. Handled. Double wick with snuffers.
   b. Larger, on glass standard.
5. Salt, footed.
6. Sauce dish.
7. Spoonholder. Hexagonal, round base.
8. Sweetmeat dish. 6 inch covered dish on low foot.

Color: Clear glass.

Chapter VI

BULL'S EYE AND CONTEMPORARY PATTERNS

HORN OF PLENTY

In this chapter are included a series of patterns generally believed to have been made during the early Sixties but in my opinion produced before the end of the previous decade. All of these are of a noticeably brilliant glass, heavier in weight and bold in design.

Collectors who have gathered Horn of Plenty glass assiduously for years may now learn that in the old catalogues of one of the makers, M'Kee Brothers, of Pittsburgh, it was listed as "Comet," probably plagiarized from the Sandwich pattern. It is much too late to restore the original name and most collectors prefer to call it "Horn of Plenty." It is one of the patterns most in demand to-day, the plates having commanded a higher price, for a time, than those of any other design. It must have been very popular from the first for it was made in immense quantities and in a great variety of forms. This makes it possible to assemble a complete service. It is one of the most desirable and effective patterns in clear glass. The goblets are heavy, brilliant and distinctive, with a knob stem. New uses have been found for certain pieces in the various pressed glass patterns, uses that were not foreseen when they were made. Egg cups are now fashionably employed for orange juice, tomato-juice cocktails and other beverages. Bases of sugar bowls are used for grapefruit and flat butter bases for soup or finger bowls. Spoonholders and celery holders make attractive flower vases in table decoration. Some of our latter-day needs are thus met by the old glass.

A few pieces of Horn of Plenty were illustrated in a Pittsburgh trade catalogue which is believed to have been printed in the late

1850's. Six-inch dishes with and without a cover were shown. Models of this pattern were also found after the closing of the Boston & Sandwich Co., proving that it was also an early product of that factory. Due to the few variants found, I do not believe that Horn of Plenty was copied as extensively as other designs. Many fragments were unearthed at the site of the Sandwich factory. Of special note are those in color.

One of the most interesting single pieces of American pressed glass that I have ever owned is a covered butter dish, the same as the usual Horn of Plenty type except that the knob of the cover consists of a head of Washington. I personally know of but few other collectors lucky enough to own one of these unusual specimens. I have seen one of these dishes in yellow which is still more rare. The spoonholders, tumblers and six-inch plates were also made in yellow, and in my possession is a clear glass spoonholder with the edge in amber. The rarest color is a brilliant blue, in which a celery and a tumbler have been found. Other rare pieces are known in translucent white. When it comes to color, anything can be expected from Sandwich. The rarest form in clear glass in this design, is the cake plate on a standard.

Classification

HORN OF PLENTY

PATTERN 49

(See Plates 32, 47, 48)

Form Number.
1. Butter dish. Flat, no standard. One type with knob of cover in form of head of Washington. Two other styles of knobs include the conventional flattened one and the acorn-shaped.
2. Cake plate on standard. Two sizes. Extremely rare.
3. Celery vase. Tall and graceful. Knob stem. Scarce.
4. Champagnes.
5. Claret. Flaring top, scant 5 inches high. Knob stem. Rare.

PLATE 46

1. WAFFLE celery vase, water tumbler, butter dish, egg cup.
2. LINCOLN DRAPE compote, syrup pitcher, spoonholder, butter dish.
3. LINCOLN DRAPE compote, sauce dish, footed salt, egg cup.
4. LINCOLN DRAPE with TASSEL goblet, compote, spoonholder.

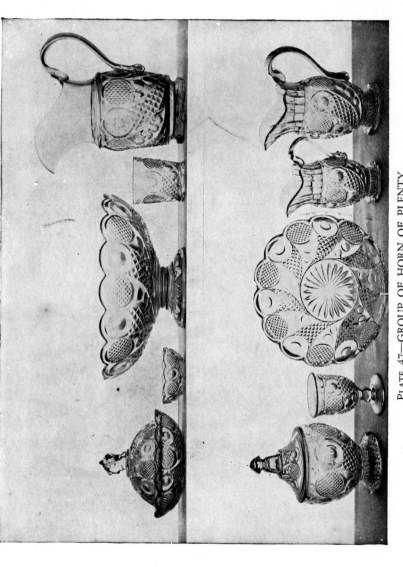

PLATE 47—GROUP OF HORN OF PLENTY

Rare butter dish with knob in form of Washington's head, oval salt, compote, tumbler, water pitcher.

PLATE 48—GOBLETS

Bull's Eye with Fleur de Lys
Comet

Bull's Eye
Horn of Plenty

PLATE 49

1. BULL'S EYE goblet with knob stem; goblet, plainer stem; cordial; egg cup; salt.
2. BULL'S EYE pickle dish, sugar bowl, tumbler.
3. COMET goblet, water pitcher, whiskey tumbler.
4. BULL'S EYE with DIAMOND POINT celery vase, cruet, egg cup, sauce dish.

PLATE 50

1. TULIP VARIANTS (later period) sugar bowl, goblet, cordial, celery variant
   without sawtooth at base of petals.
2. BULL'S EYE VARIANT goblet, footed tumbler, water tumbler, castor bottle.
3. JACOB'S LADDER creamer, jam jar, plate, cordial.
4 WHEAT and BARLEY mug, celery vase, water pitcher, footed sauce dish.

PLATE 51—BULL'S EYE WITH FLEUR DE LYS

Water pitcher   Goblet   Sugar bowl   Lamp

Form Number.

6. Compotes.
    a. Covered, on standard, 6 inch. Rare.
    b. Open.
        (1) Extra large, on high standard. Design in base also.
        (2) On low standards. These are numerous and vary in diameter by one-fourth inch. Usually found on low stem in 7¼, 8¼ or 8½ inch diameter. Bases vary accordingly. Some have plain, clear bases, others have concentric circles and still others have circle motif from Horn of Plenty design.
        (3) Open, 6-inch diameter, 6 inches high. Rare.
        (4) Oval compote on high standard. Three sizes. Very rare.

*7. Cordials. Scarce.

8. Creamer. Scalloped foot and crimped handle.
    a. Large.
    b. Small.

9. Decanters. These vary a great deal, same as in Bellflower. Sizes may vary by one-fourth inch in height. Some have neck with flange, others with heavy collar. Original stoppers having Horn of Plenty design are usually missing.
    a. Pint, more often found with original stopper.
    b. Quart.

10. Dishes.
    a. Oval. 8 x 5½ inches. 9 inches. 10 inches. Rare.
    b. Oval. Flat, large. Scarce. 11½ x 8 inches. 7 x 8 inches.
    c. Round. Flat, large. 8½-inch diameter, 2 inches deep. Rare.
    d. Extremely rare, covered oblong dish. Only three known to date. 6½ x 4. 3 inches deep, without cover. 5½ inches high, with cover.

11. Egg cups.
    a. Flaring slightly at the top.
    b. Straight sides.

12. Goblets. Fairly heavy, with knob stem.

13. Honey dish, 3¼ inch. Plain scalloped edge. Common.

14. Lamps. Sometimes found in pairs. Usually all glass with hexagonal base. May be found more rarely with brass stem and marble base. Sometimes with heavy square base, like early Sandwich types.

NOTE: Asterisk denotes item has been reproduced.

Form Number.

15. Mugs. Small, with handles. Same size as Whiskey tumblers, with applied handle. Very scarce.

16. Pickle dish, oval, 7 x 5 inches.

17. Pitcher, water. Two sizes. Crimped handle.

18. Plates, 6 inch. Scalloped plain edge. Concentric circles in center. One style only. See illustration.

19. Salts, oval, flat. Extremely scarce. A footed salt similar in design to Horn of Plenty is often used in place of the oval ones, which are so very difficult to find.

20. Sauce bottles. Evidently made especially for one manufacturer, for sauce similar to Worcestershire. All various sizes, sometimes found with plain glass stoppers.

21. Sauce dishes. One has been seen in amber.
    a. 4½ inch. Plain scalloped edge. Common.
    b. 5 and 6 inch. Plain scalloped edge. Rayed center. Scarce.

22. Spoonholder. Heavy, with plain solid glass base.

23. Sugar bowls.
    a. Scalloped base with fine diamond pattern underneath. Cover is rounded to knob on top.
    b. Base same as above. Cover is higher, sloping in and then up to the pointed knob on top.

*24. Tumblers. Scarce. Amber tumblers are recent reproductions.
    a. Water.
    b. Whiskey.

Colors: Clear glass; colored pieces, probably Sandwich, are rare. Yellow, milk-white, brilliant blue, amber, clear edged in color.

COMET

The Comet is still another pattern of this group of which the glass is both heavy and brilliant. It suggests the New England Pineapple or the Tulip, in that the design is striking and bold. The pattern consists chiefly of three ornaments suggestive of the tail of a comet, with three small bull's eyes or thumbprints in the center of each ornament. These three comets alternate with three

NOTE: Asterisk denotes item has been reproduced.

large clear bull's eyes. The stem of the goblet, which is hexagonal and has a large knob close to the bowl, tapers down to the round base, the latter being plain. This pattern is known to have been made at the Sandwich factory in the late Fifties or early Sixties. This is probably the reason why it is better known and more plentiful in New England, though even there it is scarce. It is a most attractive design and has much to recommend it to collectors though I have not seen many forms. Possibly some of my readers may add to my list. The large water pitcher, shown on Plate 49, is one of the heaviest pieces of pressed glass I have encountered. As a matter of interest I weighed it and found it tipped the scales at six pounds!

Classification

COMET

PATTERN 50

(See Plates 48, 49)

Form Number.
 1. Goblets.
 2. Mugs, with handles. Same size as whiskey tumblers.
 3. Pitcher, water.
 4. Tumblers.
    a. Water.
    b. Whiskey.
Color: Clear glass. One goblet has been found in brilliant sapphire blue and a tumbler in yellow.

BULL'S EYE

The Bull's Eye is the first of the heavy glass patterns so far described which lacks some of the glow and sparkle of the others. The old trade name for it at the New England Glass Company was the "Lawrence." It was also made by the Boston & Sandwich Glass Company. The quality of the glass has a soft luster rather than the brilliant clearness that characterizes most early designs.

The goblet shows six large bull's eyes, each one forming a panel that tapers down to the stem. The stem is hexagonal, flaring out close to the base, where it forms a knob. The base is plain. Another goblet differs only in the stem, having a small knob in the center, instead of close to the base. This type was made at the Cambridge factory.

Bull's Eye was copied by manufacturers some years later, as I have some pieces very much lighter in weight, with no ring to the glass and bearing earmarks of a ware made in the early Eighties. The present demand for this pattern does not seem to be very great though it has much to recommend it. It is early, the lines and design are excellent, it is comparatively scarce and it is to be had in all the needed forms. A variant of the early Bull's Eye has an opening above and below the Bull's Eye. This variant was also copied later, in a lightweight glass which does not ring. The classification given here includes pieces listed from the old New England Glass Co. illustrated catalogue.

The most beautiful item I have seen is an opaque jade-green covered egg cup.

Classification

BULL'S EYE

Pattern 51

(See Plates 48, 49)

Form Number.
1. Bitters bottle.
2. Castor bottles.
3. Celery vase.
4. Champagne.
5. Cologne bottle with plain stopper. No handle.
6. Compotes. Open.
    a. Large, on high standard.
    b. On low foot.
7. Cordials. Two styles.
8. Creamer.

Form Number.

9. Decanters.
   - *a*. Bar lip.
     - (1) Pint.
     - (2) Quart.
   - *b*. Usual type.
     - (1) Pint.
     - (2) Quart.
10. Egg cups. Covered, in opaque colors. Very rare.
11. Goblets.
    - *a*. Knob stem.
    - *b*. Plain stem.
12. Jar. Small, covered, with plain stopper. 5 inches high. Originally listed as "cream jar."
13. Jelly glass.
14. Lamps.
15. Mug, handled. Large, size of water tumbler.
    - *a*. Small, with applied handle. 3⅜ inches.
16. Pickle dish, oval.
17. Salts.
    - *a*. Footed.
    - *b*. Oblong, flat.
    - *c*. Covered, in clear or opaque colors, very rare.
18. Spoonholder.
19. Sugar bowl.
20. Tumblers, water.
21. Water bottle with tumble-up.

Colors: Clear glass; an occasional piece may be found in milk-white or a color. Rare.

BULL'S EYE VARIANT

A pattern that has puzzled many is a variant of the Bull's Eye which differs so slightly from the original that dealers often have purchased pieces of it thinking it was Bull's Eye. The principal point of difference is an opening just above and below the eye. Another confusing point is that this same variant was made both early and late. The water tumbler I have seen pictured in books on blown glass as an example of early pressed glassware, along with blown glass pieces. A box full of this pattern was submitted to me by a dealer in Ohio. One tumbler was probably of the late 1850's. But a footed tumbler, a goblet and a cordial were late copies, the quality of the glass indicating they might date from 1870 or even later. The earlier ware is heavy, like the Bull's Eye, while the later product is light in weight and without any ring to the glass. Recently I came upon a castor set in an elaborate Britannia standard. One of these bottles, which is the earlier glass, is shown on Plate 50. It is altogether an attractive pattern, and the fact that it is a slight variation of the Bull's Eye makes it only the more interesting. An illustrated but undated catalogue shows that these were made by Bryce Bros. of Pittsburgh, Pa.

Classification

BULL'S EYE VARIANT

PATTERN 52

(See Plate 50)

Form Number.

1. Castor bottles in standards.
2. Celery vase.
3. Cordials.
4. Egg cup.
5. Goblets.
6. Sugar bowl.
7. Tumblers.
    a. Footed.
    b. Water.

Color: Clear glass. Dark amber. Pieces in any color are rare.

BULL'S EYE WITH FLEUR DE LYS

We find, in the "Bull's Eye with Fleur de Lys," which appears to have followed the plain Bull's Eye, a brilliant and fascinating glass. That another factory may have desired to make an improvement on the original design seems possible for it is surely more elaborate. On the goblet are found six large bull's eyes forming six fairly broad panels. At the base of each bull's eye, hanging pendant-like, is a five-petaled ornament somewhat similar to a fleur de lys. The hexagonal stem forms a small knob close to the bowl of the goblet, and tapers to the base, spreading out in relief in hexagonal form, on the round base. It was the first of this particular type of stem which was repeated numberless times on the various patterns of goblets of later manufacture.

It appears that many pieces were made at the same period, with double ornaments. That is, the Fleur de Lys appears both above and below the Bull's Eye. These I have seen only on the larger pieces, such as decanters and compotes and lamps. I have never seen a goblet with the double ornament, though it is possible they were made. I have found a few pieces of a much later copy of this fine glass, decidedly inferior in quality and design. The one piece most frequently seen in the later copy is a butter dish. The design is smaller and the glass not so brilliant.

Another name for this design in certain sections is "Bull's Eye and Prince's Feather" or just "Prince's Feather." The Prince of Wales' feathers consists of three plumes, while the ornament on this glass has five petals. Therefore, it seems more fitting to call this glass by a name that may not be confused with the well-known "Princess Feather," which is illustrated and described on another page. "Bull's Eye with Fleur de Lys" has come into general use. It was produced by the Boston & Sandwich Glass Company, and possibly by other factories.

Classification

BULL'S EYE WITH FLEUR DE LYS

PATTERN 53

(See Plates 48, 51)

Form Number.
1. Ale glass. Footed piece, probably designed for this purpose. Extremely rare.

Form Number.

2. Butter dish.
3. Celery vase.
4. Compotes, open, on high or low standards.
5. Creamer.
6. Decanters.
    a. Pint.
    b. Quart.
7. Fruit bowl, round, flat.
8. Goblets.
9. Lamps. These are usually found in all glass, but may be had with glass bowl, brass stem and marble base.
10. Pitcher, water.
11. Salts, footed.
12. Sugar bowl.

Color: Clear glass. Fragments in amber were excavated at Sandwich but to date no perfect pieces in color are known.

BULL'S EYE WITH DIAMOND POINT

In a post-wartime trade catalogue of the New England Glass Co. this pattern was called "Union" and it was manufactured in the Sixties. The design is made up of a combination of bull's eyes and small diamond points, with tapering panels which are surmounted by arches over the bull's eye. The stem has a knob in the center, the glass is quite heavy, with a clear ring to it and of a fine and brilliant quality. It is a pattern so little known that personally I know of but two collectors of it. It must have been made in large quantities as many articles are listed in the catalogue.

With the progress of the American pressed glass industry, it is interesting to note the difference in the type of articles made. Up to the time of the Civil War the factories made six-inch plates, but practically none larger. We find egg cups and footed salts but no pressed glass platters or finger bowls. It is also noteworthy that there was practically no colored glass for general table use. The early blown pieces were too delicate and fragile to withstand lard usage, and moreover, they were not produced in sufficient quantities to meet the constantly increasing demand. Before colored pressed glass was made commercially in large quantities many years were to elapse during which numbers of interesting patterns n clear glass were produced and sold.

A study of the photograph of the goblet illustrated on Plate 27, will show how naturally some of the popular names were given to pressed glass patterns of which the original trade names have been forgotten. The bull's eye and the tapering diamond point panel bear a really striking resemblance to an owl's eye and beak, hence the name of "Owl" by which it was once known in some sections. The original trade name of "Union" was neither descriptive nor striking enough to be remembered.

Classification

BULL'S EYE WITH DIAMOND POINT

PATTERN 54

(See Plates 27, 49)

Form Number.

1. Bowls.
    a. Flat. 5, 6, 7 and 8 inch.
    b. On high foot. 6, 7, 8, 9 and 10 inch.
    c. On low foot. 6, 7, 8, 9 and 10 inch.
2. Celery vase.
3. Champagne.
4. Cologne bottle, with stopper.
5. Cordials. Two styles.
6. Creamer.
7. Decanters.
    a. With stopper.
        (1) Pint.
        (2) Quart.
    b. Without stopper, heavy collar or bar lip.
        (1) Pint.
        (2) Quart.
8. Egg cups.

Form Number.

9. Goblets.
10. Honey dish, 3½ inch.
11. Lamp. Small hand lamp, with applied handle.
12. Lemonade glass.
13. Sauce dish, 4 inch.
14. Spoonholder.
15. Sugar bowl.
16. Tumblers.
    - *a*. Water. One-half pint.
    - *b*. Whiskey. One-third pint.
17. Water bottle with tumble-up.

Color: Clear glass. A sauce dish and a honey dish have been found in opalescent and in milk-white.

PILLAR AND BULL'S EYE

One of the earliest pressed patterns made by Bakewell, Pears & Co. was called by them "Thistle." One cannot help but wonder what thought prompted many of these old trade names, as there is nothing suggestive of a Thistle about this heavy paneled glass. The design consists of a large Bull's Eye surmounted by a rather heavy, though short, pillar. As there are other patterns in this book which come under the heading of a real Thistle design, I am taking the liberty of changing this old trade name in order to save much future confusion. The pattern is not known by many collectors and I doubt if it was ever copied by other factories to any extent, as it is so little known to-day. The goblet is striking with its broad panels and bold design. Decanters were made in two styles, one being termed "Thistle Straight Decanter" and the tapering shape "Thistle Cone Decanter." Not as many forms are listed in this pattern in the catalogue of 1875, probably due to the fact that being one of the earliest designs, its popularity was on the wane at this late date. Very likely other articles not listed were produced at one time but since they are not mentioned, I can vouch only for those given in the only available catalogue of this company.

Classification

PILLAR AND BULL'S EYE

Pattern 55

(See Plate 24 marked "Thistle.")

Form Number.
1. Bitters bottle.
2. Candlesticks.
   - *a.* Opaque.
   - *b.* Clear, two sizes.
3. Decanter.
   - *a.* Cone shape.
   - *b.* Straight sides.
4. Goblet.
5. Pitcher, water. Half-gallon.
6. Tumbler. Half-pint.
7. Wine glasses.

Color: Clear glass.

NEW ENGLAND PINEAPPLE

When the vogue for collecting pressed glass in sets began in earnest, more confusion was derived over the title of this pattern than over almost any other. Names for patterns were made up at random by dealers and collectors as the need for identification became more urgent. In the effort to distinguish a certain design a snap description often grew into a title that was generally adopted and is now irrevocably associated with the pattern. There is, for example, one type of glass known throughout the North as "Sawtooth" which in other sections of the country is called "Pineapple." New England had its very own "Pineapple," which has now become generally known as "New England Pineapple." This seems a more fitting title than "Loop and Jewel," though it is probably equally well known by that name. It is heavy, with a striking design consisting of an ornament shaped not unlike a pineapple, with a small sawtooth center alternating with a long three-petalled flower similar to a tulip.

In this design one still may see the crimped handle on the pitchers and the forms follow closely the earlier patterns. It is not particularly plentiful but quite complete in the large number of pieces. Judging by the general characteristics, it must date from the early 1860's. Mahogany models of this pattern, which were originally used at the Sandwich factory, have been preserved and are now in the possession of A. H. Heisey & Co., Glass Manufacturers, of Newark, Ohio.

Classification
NEW ENGLAND PINEAPPLE
PATTERN 56
(See Plates 42, 52, 53)

Form Number.
1. Butter dish.
2. Castor bottles, often in pewter holders.
3. Compotes. Open, in four sizes, on high and low standards. Also extra large open compote on high standard. Rarest is 6-inch covered sweetmeat, on high standard. Knob stem.
*4. Cordials.
5. Champagnes.
6. Creamer.
7. Cruet, footed, with handle. Two sizes.
8. Decanter.
     a. Pint.
     b. Quart.
9. Egg cups.
10. Fruit bowl, flat. No standard. Round, two sizes.
*11. Goblets, two sizes. Large size reproduced.
12. Honey dishes. Two different patterns in base. One has star and another has the same design as shown in base of 6-inch plate. 3½ inch.
13. Jug. Tall, with stopper.
14. Mugs with applied handles.
15. Pitcher, water.

NOTE: Asterisk denotes item has been reproduced.

Form Number.

16. Plates, 6 inch.
17. Salts, footed.
18. Sauce dishes, flat.
19. Spoonholder.
20. Sugar bowl. Two styles, one being taller and more difficult to find covered.
21. Tumblers.
    - *a.* Water.
    - *b.* Whiskey.

Color: Clear glass.

TULIP

Very little is known about this lovely design beyond the fact that it was an early pattern made at the old Bryce Bros. factory of Pittsburgh, Pa., where it was also called Tulip. Certainly it must have been produced at the beginning of the Civil War, for it closely resembles the New England Pineapple of the same period. It derives its name from the large three-petalled flower which is its chief decoration. It has only a small amount of medium-sized sawtooth filling in the open spaces at the base of the flowers. Three tulips form the bowls of the celery vases which are illustrated on Plate 53. The knob stem is faceted and the base is rayed. The glass is heavy and brilliant though it does not ring as clearly as any of the preceding patterns. I have observed that there is a distinct difference in the pressing of some of the pieces. Most of the articles found have particularly soft contours, but occasionally one finds an article apparently made by another factory, as the lines are so sharp as to appear cut rather than pressed. The pair of jugs illustrated on Plate 54 are of this latter variety. Further evidence that these may have been the product of another factory is furnished by the stoppers, which are the original ones though not in the Tulip pattern. Of those cruets and decanters that I have seen in the softer contours, it is not unusual to find them with the original stoppers in the Tulip design.

It is always of interest to learn the original intent of the makers of some of the early articles of pressed glass. The six-inch plate, which was practically the only size made prior to the Civil War, was vaguely referred to as a "cheese plate," when given any designation at all, until the article by Mrs. Rose Lohr Ayer appeared in the magazine *Antiques* of July, 1931, entitled "Six-Inch Glass Tea Plates." I believe many collectors used to ponder over the original use for the egg cups, as they are now called. These, I find, were generally advertised in the old trade magazines as "Egg Glasses." The small tumblers, usually about two and three-fourths inches high that were made for whiskey, were changed by the addition of an applied handle into "handled custard," now usually referred to as a "handled mug" or "handled whiskey." The Tulip is one of the early patterns that added an applied handle to the water tumbler, and this type of glass was listed as "lemonades." In an Ovington Brothers' catalogue of the period 1854-59, are listed "Lemonade glasses with handle, Barrel form, Tumbler form. Lemonade glasses on foot, Goblet form, plain and fancy patterns." The ever-popular celery holders which make such attractive flower vases were listed as "Celery Glasses." To-day we speak of them as celery vases, an amusing blend of the old and the new.

The Tulip pattern has become increasingly better known during the past decade, probably because of its highly decorative possibilities. It is always the popular demand which brings to light much glassware that has been neglected on pantry shelves for years. Now that its charm has been recognized I hope many more pieces than are given in this classification may be discovered. The variants of this pattern are treated in subsequent pages.

Classification

TULIP

PATTERN 57

(See Plates 37, 42, 53, 54)

Form Number.
1. Butter dish.
2. Celery vase.

PLATE 52—SIX INCH PLATES

Diamond Quilted with Bull's Eye border   New England Pineapple
Tree of Life   Garfield

PLATE 53

1. TULIP butter dish, creamer, pomade jar.
2. TULIP celery vase, quart decanter with original patent stopper (Tulip stopper in insert), cordial, footed salt.
3. NEW ENGLAND PINEAPPLE open compote on high foot, creamer, sugar bowl.
4. NEW ENGLAND PINEAPPLE tumbler, sauce dish, egg cup.

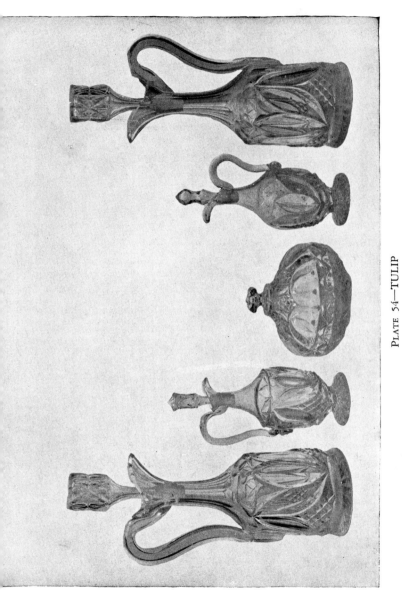

PLATE 54—TULIP
Pair of large jugs, pair of small cruets and butter dish.

Celery vase

PLATE 55—GOTHIC
Bowl

Goblet

Form Number.

3. Champagne.
4. Compotes.
    a. Covered.
        (1) Large, on high standard.
        (2) Small, on low standard.
    b. Open. Very large, on standard.
*5. Cordials.
6. Creamer.
7. Cruet.
8. Decanters.
    a. Half-pint.
    b. Pint.
    c. Quart, original Tulip pattern stopper.
9. Egg cups. Sometimes found covered, in milk-white or in opalescent.
10. Goblets.
    a. Heavy, with faceted knob stem.
    b. Later type not so heavy and knob consists of single band.
11. Honey dish.
12. Jugs, with handles.
    a. Pint size. Original Tulip stopper.
    b. Quart size. 15 inches high. Elaborate stopper.
13. Mugs, with applied handle. Large, same size as water tumblers.
14. Pitcher, water.
15. Plate, 6 inch.
16. Pomade jar.
17. Salts, footed.
    a. Smooth top edge.
    b. Pointed edge.
18. Spoonholder.
19. Sugar bowl.
20. Tumblers.
    a. Footed.
    b. Water.

Color: Clear glass. Milk-white or opalescent pieces have been found. Any piece in color is a rarity.

NOTE: Asterisk denotes item has been reproduced.

TULIP VARIANT WITHOUT SAWTOOTH

An early variant of the Tulip pattern has lately come to my notice. I have seen only celery holders, though probably other pieces were made. It is closely similar in the quality and weight of the glass but has none of the diamond sawtooth points which enhance so greatly the charm of the better known Tulip design. The space ordinarily filled with diamond points, in the original, is perfectly plain in the variant, which may be seen on Plate 50. I find this was also made by Bryce Bros. of Pittsburgh and only listed as a "Tulip celery, small."

Classification

TULIP VARIANT WITHOUT SAWTOOTH

Pattern 58

(See Plate 50)

Form Number.
  1. Celery vase.
Color: Clear glass.

TULIP VARIANT WITH SMALLER FLOWER

Recently I found what appears to be a much later copy of the early Tulip pattern. It is attractive enough, in many respects, for everyday use, but cannot compare in quality with the older product. This variant has all the earmarks of the glass produced about 1875. The design, while similar, differs in that the tulips are very much smaller, and there is a relatively larger amount of the diamond sawtooth. The glass is considerably lighter in weight, and lacks the glow and sparkle of the earlier ware. The line drawings on Plate 50 compared with those of the original Tulip on Plate 53 will show clearly the marked difference of this later design. There is no reason to doubt, when such pieces as the cordial, goblet and sugar bowl have been found, that all the usual forms of that period were produced. Diligent search will probably be rewarded by many specimens not listed in the classification below.

Classification

TULIP VARIANT WITH SMALLER FLOWER

PATTERN 59

(See Plate 50)

Form Number.
1. Cordials.
2. Goblets.
3. Sugar bowl.
Color: Clear glass.

Chapter VII

PATTERNS OF THE SIXTIES

GOTHIC

A pattern which appears to have been made about 1860, is the Gothic. A few collectors have called this "Cathedral," but a late ware is so well known by that title that to avoid confusion I am calling this Gothic. The glass is particularly brilliant and clear, and has a fine bell tone. For some little time it was not known where to attribute it, but fragments excavated from the site of the Boston & Sandwich Glass Company prove that they produced it. There are not enough variations to feel reasonably certain that the Gothic was carried on by any other factory. Articles other than the goblets and egg cups are scarce. The celery vase is a rare and brilliant piece of flint glass. I was fortunate in having the group shown on Plate 55 lent to me by a collector, as it would have taken some time to find enough pieces to illustrate the pattern adequately. I know of the following forms, listed below:

Classification

GOTHIC

PATTERN 60

(See Plate 55)

Form Number.

1. Berry bowls. 7 and 8 inch.
2. Butter dish.
3. Castor bottles. Sizes of sets and holders vary.
4. Celery vase.
5. Champagnes.
6. Compotes, footed. 8 inch, covered or open, on high or low foot.

Form Number.
   7. Cordials.
   8. Creamer.
   9. Egg cups.
   10. Goblets. Two styles, plain or rayed base.
   11. Pickle dish, oval. 4¾ x 7 inches.
   12. Salts, footed.
   13. Sauce dish, flat, 4 inch.
   14. Spoonholder.
   15. Sugar bowl.
   16. Tumblers.
Color: Clear glass.

HAMILTON

On Plate 56 is shown a most interesting and comprehensive group of the well-known and popular Hamilton pattern. Vague stories have been told to the effect that this was a favorite of Alexander Hamilton's and was named "Hamilton" for that reason. Another suggests that it was named in honor of Lady Hamilton, though there is no basis in fact for either explanation of its name. The dates to justify it would be too early. There is nothing to indicate that this ware was produced earlier than the late Sixties. There is a bell tone to the glass, though it is not as heavy as the earlier wares. That it is an American imitation of the beautifully cut Waterford, seems undeniable. The pattern is typical of many of the fine English and Irish designs. It is now well known that a number of our popular patterns were plagiarized from earlier European designs. This does not affect their value as interesting as well as distinguished patterns of pressed glass with our collectors to-day. The Hamilton is a large group and the forms are numerous enough to satisfy the most ardent seeker of a complete set. The forms follow closely those of the earliest ones, the creamer being footed and having a handle crimped at the base. The bases of the footed pieces are rayed. The knob of the covered pieces is similar to the best known one in the Bellflower. Fragments of this design were excavated at Sandwich, so it is known that it was produced there. Some pieces of dishes were uncovered in deep blue, though no whole specimens in color are known at this time.

A variant of the Hamilton is not very well known, but to those who do know it, it is generally referred to as "Hamilton with Leaf." This variant will be described under that title.

Classification

HAMILTON

PATTERN 61

(See Plate 56)

Form Number.

1. Butter dish.
2. Castor set, in standard.
3. Compotes, open, various sizes. Covered, on high foot. 6 inch.
   a. Open, bowl in Hamilton design, base in Bellflower pattern.
4. Cordials.
5. Creamer. Two styles, applied handle and pressed handle.
6. Decanter.
7. Egg cups.
8. Goblets.
9. Hat, rarity made from tumbler mold.
10. Honey dish.
11. Pitcher.
    a. Syrup, metal top.
    b. Water.
12. Salt, footed.
13. Sauce dish, with scalloped rim. 4 and 5 inch.
    a. Plain rim. 4 and 4⅞ inches.
14. Spoonholder. Two styles. Usual type and another with plain rim.
15. Sugar bowl.
16. Tumblers.
    a. Water.
    b. Whiskey.

Color: Clear glass. Pieces in color are rare.

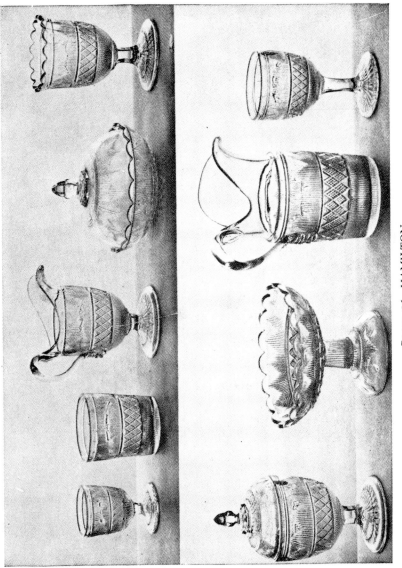

Egg cup   Tumbler   Creamer   Butter dish   Spoonholder

PLATE 56—HAMILTON

PLATE 57—GOBLETS

Dew with Raindrop　　　　Beaded dewdrop
Hamilton with Leaf　　　　Jacob's Ladder

HAMILTON WITH LEAF

Evidently produced at the same period as the Hamilton is a variation known as the "Hamilton with Leaf." The same type of mold was used for both, as they are alike in every detail, except that the leaf motif is inserted in the central band of the design instead of the conventional pressed diamond-shaped blocks as shown in the Hamilton. The leaf is clear in the better known variation, but it may also be found with the frosted leaf. The latter are exceedingly scarce. I do not believe this variation with the leaf was made in such large quantities as the Hamilton as it is not found so readily to-day. This ware dates from the same period as the Hamilton, or the late Sixties. It also appears, from fragment findings, to have been a Sandwich product.

Classification

HAMILTON WITH LEAF

PATTERN 62

(See Plate 57)

Form Number.
1. Butter dish.
2. Celery vase.
3. Cordial.
4. Compotes, open.
    a. On high standard.
    b. On low foot, 6 inch.
5. Creamer.
6. Egg cups.
7. Goblets.
8. Lamp. All glass, same style as Bellflower, with scalloped foot.
9. Honey dish.
10. Mug, applied handle.
11. Salt, footed.
12. Sauce dish.

Form Number.
  13. Spoonholder.
  14. Sugar bowl.
  15. Tumbler, water.
Colors: Clear glass; clear, partly frosted.

LINCOLN DRAPE

In the earlier days it was often the custom to commemorate deeds or events on glassware. This was particularly true of whiskey flasks, which generally carried, during a presidential campaign, the bust of the candidate. The practice is noted also in cup-plates, which portray famous Americans, like Washington, Clay, Ringgold, Harrison and others, or show famous ships or monuments and commemorate historical events. After the death of President Lincoln a pattern was introduced in tableware which ever since has been known as the Lincoln Drape. Two such designs came out at this period. They differ in that one has large tassels added to the simple drapery. The glass is clear and of good quality. They were probably placed on the market within a short time of Lincoln's death or about 1866. Lincoln Drape was made at Sandwich and possibly elsewhere. Below is listed the forms in the plain drape, without tassel.

Classification

LINCOLN DRAPE

Pattern 63

(See Plates 26, 46)

Form Number.
  1. Butter dish.
  2. Celery vase.
  3. Compotes, open, on low standard.
        a. Covered, on high foot. 6 inch.
  4. Cordials.
  5. Creamer.
  6. Decanter.
  7. Egg cups.

Form Number.
  8. Goblets.
  9. Pitchers.
    a. Syrup.
        (1) Metal top.
        (2) Sapphire blue.
    b. Water.
10. Plates, 6 inch.
11. Salts, footed.
12. Sauce dish, flat, 4½ inch.
13. Spoonholder.
14. Sugar bowl.

Colors: Clear glass; an occasional piece may be found in milk-white or sapphire blue, but these are rare.

LINCOLN DRAPE WITH TASSEL

This is a variant of the plain Lincoln Drape, described on the preceding pages. It is merely an elaboration of the simpler pattern, the quality of the glass being the same. I am of the opinion that it was produced during the same period, probably in smaller quantities, for it is extremely scarce to-day and I have been able to find only a few forms. The fact that the goblets and sugar bowl may be had indicates that the usual pieces of this period were probably produced. My search for other pieces has been in vain. Letters asking for this pattern were sent to nearly every state, without result. An egg cup has been reported but I have never seen one.

Classification

LINCOLN DRAPE WITH TASSEL

PATTERN 64

(See Plates 26, 46)

Form Number.
  1. Compotes, open, on low standard.
  2. Goblets.

Form Number.
   3. Sugar bowl.
   4. Spoonholder.
Color: Clear glass.

CABLE

This pattern was made in the 1860's to commemorate the laying of the Atlantic Cable. The design consists chiefly of a narrow panel of diagonal ribbing meant to represent a cable, alternating with wider, clear panels. The goblet has a knob next to the base of the bowl, plain hexagonal stem and clear base. It has been rather widely collected though it is a plain, simple pattern and not as artistic as many others. The glass is heavy and has a clear ring. It was made in most of the usual forms, which are listed below. Pieces in color are rare. I have owned an opaque green covered egg cup and an opaque blue spoonholder. A few pieces may also be found in opaque white.

Forms do not vary, except in the variant treated in subsequent pages. Collectors should note that the Cable with Ring variant of the plain pattern is more elaborate. This design was produced by the Boston & Sandwich Glass Company.

Classification

CABLE

PATTERN 65

(See Plates 32, 36)

Form Number.
   1. Butter dish.
   2. Celery vase.
   3. Champagne.
   4. Compotes, open. Usually found on a low foot.
      a. Extra large. 9¾ inches high, 10 inches diameter.
      b. Various sizes on low standards.
      c. Various sizes on high standards. The bowls of some are shallow, and others deep, with less flare to the edge.

Form Number.
5. Cordials.
6. Creamer.
7. Decanters.
    a. Pint.
    b. Quart.
8. Egg cups. Covered, opaque colored ones are rare.
9. Goblets.
10. Honey dishes.
11. Lamps. Usually all glass, though a few are found with brass stem and marble base.
12. Mugs, with handles.
13. Pitcher, water.
14. Plate, 6 inch.
15. Salts, footed.
16. Sauce dishes.
17. Spoonholder.
18. Sugar bowl.
19. Tumblers, footed.
    a. Whiskey tumbler.

Colors: Clear glass. Opaque green, blue and other colors very rare. Some forms have gilded decoration in the panels.

CABLE WITH RING

This design is an elaboration of the plain Cable pattern. It is heavily ornamented with rows of diagonal ribs, a clear loop through the center of each band of ribbing and a four-pointed ornament at the top of each piece between the panels of cable. This is sometimes spoken of by dealers as "Cable with ring and star." The creamer has a crimped handle and the edge of the round base has a row of cable. Underneath the base is a star pattern. I have not seen many forms in this though they must exist. I personally know of a creamer, covered sugar bowl, lamp and sauce dishes. I have also seen honey dishes but no goblets. The glass is very heavy and of the same period as the plainer design. It can be credited to Sandwich, according to fragment findings.

Classification

CABLE WITH RING

PATTERN 66

(See Plate 58)

Form Number.
  1. Creamer.
  2. Honey dish.
  3. Lamp.
  4. Sauce dish.
  5. Sugar bowl.
Color: Clear glass.

THUMBPRINT

While visiting Pittsburgh, Pa., in 1933, it was my good fortune to meet and spend part of a day with Mr. Thomas Pears, Jr., a direct descendant of a member of the firm of Bakewell, Pears & Company. Mr. Pears had long been interested in the history of the factory and he made it possible for me to publish the first authoritative history and anecdotes of what Deming Jarves, founder of the Boston & Sandwich Glass Company, termed "the finest flint glass factory in America." In fact, Deming Jarves, according to his statements, visited the Bakewell factory before he started his own company. In his "Reminiscences of Glass Making" he was most enthusiastic about their work and progress, so he undoubtedly learned much of value which he could incorporate into his own company.

The one pattern which collectors who started buying pressed glass years ago have always known by the name of Thumbprint, is of an excellent quality of flint glass. It is a highly effective pattern having large, elongated, indented thumbprints. The graceful lines and exceptional brilliancy of the glass make it particularly effective for table decoration and use. The other varieties of this group have received specific names in this book to put an end to the confusion resulting from the use of the term Thumbprint in connection with divers varieties. Undoubtedly the earliest and best forms were produced by Bakewell, Pears & Company. Sandwich made one of the later varieties.

It is easy to understand why Thumbprint always has been highly esteemed by discriminating buyers. The large covered compotes and the punch bowls are among the most interesting specimens of American pressed glass, and are so gorgeous in appearance as to justify their being classed as veritable museum pieces. The open compotes and punch bowls on standards flare outward at the rim most gracefully while the covered pieces are globular and remarkably striking. The edges of the bowl of a compote may be a half-inch in thickness and yet ring with a deep bell tone when struck.

We surmise that Thumbprint was produced early in the Sixties and possibly even earlier. It was made by Bakewell, Pears & Co. of Pittsburgh, Pa., under the title of "Argus." The reproduction of the "Argus" on Plate 15 is from a Bakewell catalogue lent to me through the kindness of Mr. Thomas Pears, Jr. It will be noted that the Thumbprint or "Argus" ware produced by Bakewell, Pears & Co. has a certain style of knob stem (see Plate 24) which appears on all such pieces as the goblets, champagnes, wines and cordials made by them. Compotes, open or covered, on low standards, usually have a double row of flattened hobnails on the inside of the base which shine through the glass in a pleasing manner. The larger compotes and punch bowls generally have a scalloped rim on the base and large thumbprints on the inside of this base. Other open and covered compotes are found with hexagonal standard and round base, or in the more elaborate form as seen on Plate 59. It distinctly differs from the round thumbprint pattern known as "Mirror" (Plate 2), which was a product of the M'Kee Brothers of Pittsburgh and of the "Punty" bowls of the New England Glass Company. Of the varying types of thumbprint designs we find that the early is heavy in weight, with a particularly fine bell-like ring. In the later pieces the thumbprints are fewer and smaller and the glass cannot be compared in brilliancy with the earlier ware. The Almond Thumbprint is described in subsequent pages under that title.

Classification

THUMBPRINT

PATTERN 67

(See Plates 15, 18, 24, 59)

Form Number.

1. Ale glass. *See Pony ale.*
2. Beer mug, half-pint, handled.
3. Bowls, flat. Several sizes.
4. Bitters bottle. Two sizes.
5. Butter dish. Globular, without foot.
   - *a.* Flat, straight flaring sides. Petalled rim where cover joins. 4 varieties.
6. Cake plate on standard. 3 sizes.
7. Castor bottles. Rare.
8. Celery vase. Two styles.
9. Champagne.
10. Claret. 5¼ inch. Bowl more slender than champagne.
11. Compotes.
    - *a.* Covered.
      - (1) On high hexagonal standard, clear round base. Varying sizes to 10 inches. 4, 7, 8, and 10 inch.
      - (2) Medium, high fluted standard. 6 inch.
      - (3) Medium high, hexagonal standard. Bowl flat where it joins standard, instead of globular. Straight flaring sides and petaled rim where cover joins. 6 inch.
      - (4) Extra large covered compote. Globular shape, 13½ inches high without cover, 10 inches diameter.
    - *b.* Open.
      - (1) On high standard in varying sizes from 4 inches.
      - (2) On low standards, various sizes. 4, 6, 8 and 9 inches. Very heavy globular shape on very short, low foot. Base has double row of flattened hobnails on under side, which reflect through the glass.
      - (3) Extra large Punch bowl. 13½ inches diameter, 12½ inches high. Thumbprints underneath heavy, scalloped base.
12. Cordials. Several styles. Old trade catalogues refer to a "cordial," which varied in size from 4 to 4¼ inches. In patterns which were carried on for thirty to forty years, cordials

Form Number.

in the modern sense of the word and size, were sometimes produced during later years. This holds true of the Thumbprint, in which a "Cordial" exists, measuring 3⅛ inches.

13. Creamer. Three variations.
14. Decanters.
   a. Quart, with bar lip and also with flange. Latter style has matching stopper.
   b. Pint. Two styles.
15. Egg cups. Rare.
16. Flip glass. Rare.
17. Goblets.
   a. Barrel-shape, plain stem.
   b. Straight sides, knob stem. 4 rows of Thumbprints. Best type. *See Plate 24.*
   c. There are ten forms in goblets, comprising an almost endless variety in shape of bowls, stem and height. Different forms occur because this pattern was produced by a number of factories, over a long term of years. The Bakewell, Pears & Co. design is at once the earliest and best.
18. Honey dishes, 3¼ and 3½ inches. Straight rim and scalloped edge.
19. Jelly glass, on stem, similar to our modern parfait glass.
20. Pitcher, water. Four varieties.
21. Pickle dish.
22. Pony ale. Same as beer mug, only smaller.
   a. Small pony ale. Like above, smaller.
23. Plate. 8 inch. Rare.
24. Salts, on standards. Rare.
   a. Individual size.
25. Sauce dishes, 4, 4½ and 5 inch. Edges vary.
26. Spoonholder.
27. Syrup jug.
28. Sugar bowl. Five variations.
29. Tumblers.
   a. Footed, ⅓ quart, ½ pint and ⅓ pint are listed in early catalogues. 10 varieties from various glass houses have been noted
   b. Water tumbler. Ten varieties.
   c. Whiskey tumblers. Small size.

Form Number.

30. Water bottle and tumble-up.
31. Wine glass. 4 inch.

Color: Clear glass, the earliest being flint glass. Milk-white items, such as tumblers and dishes, have been found.

ALMOND THUMBPRINT

During the period of the popularity of the old "Argus" pattern of Bakewell, Pears & Co., or that which is better known to-day as "Thumbprint," another similiar pattern was produced which has been known by various titles. Among these appellations may be mentioned "Almond," "Pointed Thumbprint" and "Finger Print." Almond Thumbprint seems to be the best known and it is well suited to the design, which consists of depressions pointed at each end instead of being rounded ovals. This design was copied both early and late. One will find pieces appearing to be a product of the Seventies or Eighties, lighter in weight and having no ring to the glass like the earlier ware. A wide range of shapes may be found, as I believe many factories used this same pattern with slight variations. One can distinguish the earliest forms chiefly by the weight of the glass and the clear bell tone. There is a cable edge on the rim of many of the dishes.

It is to be regretted that it was not possible to illustrate a group. The small covered pieces, such as salts, sweetmeat jar and the various sizes of compotes are particularly graceful. The drawing of the goblet, Number 14 on Plate 154, does not convey an adequate impression of the effectiveness of this striking pattern.

Classification

ALMOND THUMBPRINT

PATTERN 68

(See Plate 154, No. 14)

Form Number.

1. Butter dish.
2. Celery vase.

PLATE 58

1. CATHEDRAL sugar bowl, spoonholder, footed sauce dish, cordial.
2. LIBERTY BELL creamer, spoonholder, goblet, butter dish.
3. ANTHEMION plate with rolled edges, tumbler, sauce dish.
4. CABLE with RING sugar bowl, creamer, bowl of sauce dish.

PLATE 59—THUMBPRINT

Pair of covered compotes   Large open compote   Covered compote
Small open compote   Cordial   Decanter   Tumbler   Goblet

PLATE 60

1. HONEYCOMB handled egg cup, finger bowl, salt.
   Known as "New York" pattern by M'Kee Bros., of Pittsburgh and
   by the New England Glass Co.

2. HONEYCOMB compote on high foot, compote on low foot, celery vase.

3. HONEYCOMB sugar bowl, creamer, two styles of egg cups.
   Known as "Cincinnati" by M'Kee Bros., and as "Vernon" at the
   New England Glass Co.

4. HONEYCOMB decanter, covered salt, open salt, shakers.

PLATE 61

1. FINE CUT and PANEL sugar bowl, compote, footed sauce dish.
2. BAND sugar bowl, footed tumbler, goblet.
3. PHILADELPHIA compote on low foot, footed sauce, smaller compote.
4. BEADED BAND goblet, cordial, water pitcher.

3. Champagnes.
4. Cordials.
5. Creamer.
6. Cruet.
7. Compotes, covered.

   a. High standard, various sizes. Included are 4¾, 7 and 10 inch.
   b. Low standard.

8. Cruet, footed. Two sizes.
9. Decanter.
10. Egg cup.
11. Goblet. Several variations.
12. Punch bowl.
13. Salts.

    a. Individual.
    b. Large, flat.
    c. Footed, covered.

14. Sugar bowl.
15. Sweetmeat jar, covered, on standard, 6 inch.
16. Tumbler.

Color: Clear glass. Colors such as blue are rare. Some pieces are found in milk-white.

HONEYCOMB

There are more varieties of this pattern than of any other in the book. This indicates, of course, that it not only was made in many factories but that it was copied in later years so many times that only by the ring of the glass can one distinguish the late from the early. There were two distinct patterns made in the East, in the first place. One was originally called in New England "New York" and the other "Vernon." The principal difference is that one carries the design nearly to the top of the glass and the other extends scarcely half-way up. In one variant which was produced during the later years, the design is straight across the top instead of being arched. This is one of the first early patterns which includes finger bowls and candlesticks to match. It is unquestionably true that the earlier heavy types are not easy to find today. It will prove a rather difficult pattern to match, as much more of the later period glass will be encountered. The earlier variety may be distinguished by its weight, clarity and ring. They weigh more than the later and are more brilliant. Among the factories where this glass is known to have been produced may be mentioned the Boston & Sandwich Glass Co., Bryce Bros., and M'Kee Brothers of Pittsburgh; Richards and Hartley of Tarentum, Pa., and, in fact, nearly every factory that made tableware over a period of years.

In the beginning this was essentially a clear glass pattern, but after the Civil War it was made in quantities in the popular colored ware. To-day it is found most readily in amber. Some original catalogue terms are used in the classification.

Classification

HONEYCOMB

(Originally known as "New York." Design
on lower portion of object)

PATTERN 69

(See Plate 60)

Form Number.

1. Ale glass (old mold).
   a. Same (new mold).
   b. Number 2 size.
2. Beer mug, half-pint.
   a. Fony beer mug.
3. Bitters bottle.
   a. Ketchup bottle.
4. Bowls, on foot, 6, 7, 8, 9 and 10 inch.
5. Butter dish, individual.
6. Cake plate on standard. 11¼ inch.
7. Candlestick.
   a. Number 2 pattern.
   b. Number 3 pattern.

Form Number.

   8. Celery vase.

   9. Champagne.

  10. Claret.

  11. Cordial. Two types, one in the later 3 inch size.

  12. Creamer.

  13. Custard, handled.

  14. Dishes.

     a. Nappie, on high foot, covered. 6, 7 and 8 inch.
     b. On foot, open. 6, 7 and 8 inch.
     c. On low foot, covered. 6, 7 and 8 inch.
     d. On low foot, open. 6, 7 and 8 inch.
     e. No foot, covered. 6, 7 and 8 inch.
     f. No foot, open. 6, 7 and 8 inch.
     g. Open, no foot. $3\frac{1}{2}$, 4, 5, 6, 7 and 8 inch.
     h. Oval. 7, 8, 9 and 10 inch.

  15. Decanter.

     a. Pint, bar lip.
     b. Pint, stoppered.
     c. Quart, bar lip.
     d. Quart, stoppered.

  16. Egg cup.

     a. Flaring bowl and straight mowl.
     b. Handled. Rare.

  17. Finger bowl.

  18. Goblet.

  19. Jug, molasses, Britannia cover.

     a. Pint.
     b. Half-pint.
     c. Three pint.
     d. Quart.

  20. Lamp. Several styles.

  21. Lemonade glass. Tumbler, with applied handle.

  22. Pickle jar, stoppered.

  23. Pepper.

  24. Plate, 6 and 7 inch.

  25. Salt and pepper shakers. Pewter tops.

     a. Footed salt, rope edge.

  26. Spoonholder.

Form Number.
27. Tumbler.
    a. Half-pint.
    b. One-third pint.
28. Twine holder. Two sizes.
29. Water bottle and tumble-up.
30. Wine glass.

Classification

HONEYCOMB

(Originally known as "Vernon" and "Cincinnati."
Design covers bowl of article)

PATTERN 69A

(See Plate 60)

Form Number.
1. Bowls. Original catalogue listing.
    a. On high foot. 6, 7, 8, 9 and 10 inch.
    b. On low foot. 6, 7, 8, 9 and 10 inch.
    c. With tin hinge cover. 6, 7, 8 and 9 inch
    d. With Britannia cover. 6, 7, 8 and 9 inch.
    e. With cast foot. 6, 7, 8 and 9 inch.
    f. With cast foot, shallow, 7, 8, 9 and 10 inch.
2. Butter dish.
3. Castor bottles.
4. Celery vase.
5. Champagne.
6. Compotes.
    a. On high foot, covered. 6, 7 and 8 inch.
    b. On high foot, open, 6, 7 and 8 inch.
    c. On low foot, covered. 6, 7 and 8 inch.
    d. On low foot, open. 6, 7 and 8 inch.
7. Cordials. Knob stem. 3½ inch.
    a. Rare size, not found in most patterns. 3 inch.
8. Creamer.
9. Decanters, with matching stoppers.
    a. Quart.
    b. Pint.

Form Number.

10. Dish, oval, 7, 8, 9 and 10 inch.

    a. Round covered. 5½, 6, 7 and 8 inch.
    b. Open round. 5½, 6, 7 and 8 inch.

11. Egg cups.

12. Goblet. Many variations. One heavy flint glass type has design almost to the edge of the bowl.

13. Honey dish. 3 and 3½ inch.

14. Mug. Two sizes. 2¾ and 3¼ inch.

15. Pitcher, water. Several sizes. Engraved under handle. "Pat. 1865."

16. Pomade jar.

17. Salt, footed, open.

    a. Individual.
    b. Salt and pepper shakers.
    c. Covered, on foot.

18. Sauce dish, 4 inch.

19. Spoonholder.

20. Sugar bowl.

21. Tumbler, water.

    a. Footed tumbler.

22. Wines. Various sizes and shapes.

Colors: Earlier ware is in clear glass; later ware may be found in yellow, blue, amber, apple green and opaque-white.

PHILADELPHIA

More than one collector has remarked to me that the manufacturer who selected the name for this design must have had a grudge against Philadelphia. It is a simple and unattractive design of plain and reeded loops. The pattern was listed by this title by the New England Glass Co. and produced there during the late Sixties. For the benefit of those readers who may have a special reason for collecting this ware, I am showing it on Plate 61. The classification given is as it was listed by the Cambridge factory.

Classification
PHILADELPHIA

PATTERN 70
(See Plate 61)

Form Number.
1. Bowls.
   - *a.* Covered, low foot. 6, 7 and 8 inch.
   - *b.* Low foot. 6, 7, 8, 9 and 10 inch.
   - *c.* Open on foot. 6, 7, 8, 9 and 10 inch.
   - *d.* Shallow, on foot. 7, 8, 9, 10 and 11 inch.
   - *e.* Shallow, on low foot. 7, 8, 9, 10 and 11 inch.
2. Celery vase.
3. Compote, covered on foot, 6, 7 and 8 inch.
4. Creamer.
5. Dishes.
   - *a.* Covered. 6, 7 and 8 inch.
   - *b.* Covered, on foot. 6, 7 and 8 inch.
   - *c.* Covered, on low foot. 6, 7 and 8 inch.
   - *d.* Low foot, 6, 7 and 8 inch.
   - *e.* Oval, 7, 8, 9 and 10 inch.
6. Egg cups.
7. Goblets.
8. Jugs.
   - *a.* Quart.
   - *b.* Three pint.
9. Salt. Oval on foot.
10. Sauce dishes, 4 inch.
11. Spoonholder.
12. Sugar bowl.
13. Wine glass.

Color: Clear glass.

Chapter VIII

GRAPE GROUP

MAGNET AND GRAPE
(Frosted Leaf)

To straighten out the tangle of Grape designs is a difficult task. New variants turn up day after day until one wonders if there is any limit to their numbers. They seem to begin early and end late.

The Magnet and Grape is found in two styles, the earlier being a very heavy glass with clear ring to it and the grape leaf frosted. It was produced at Sandwich. The latter is not as heavy or old and the grape leaf is veined and lightly stippled.

The one I shall describe first is probably the earliest of all the pressed Grape patterns. One of the most interesting photographs in the book is the wine jug in this design (see frontispiece), a most unusual example of pressed glass. The stopper is the petal shape, so often used in the early ware, especially in the Ribbed Ivy design. The inscription on the top reads, "Try Me."

The goblets are found in three styles, one being unusually heavy with a large knob stem and pressed design in the base, one with plain stem and base and a variant having the addition of the American shield on the side. The tumblers are attractive also and are not as scarce as in many other designs. I have seen the following pieces:

Classification

MAGNET AND GRAPE
(Frosted Leaf)

Pattern 71
See Plate 63. Frontispiece)

Form Number.
  1. Butter dish.

Form Number.

2. Celery vase.
3. Compote, open. Various types. Scarce.
4. Cordials.
5. Champagnes.
6. Creamer.
7. Decanters, with matching stoppers.

   a. Pint.
   b. Quart.

8. Egg cups.
9. Goblets.

   a. Knob stem, pressed design in base.
   b. Plain stem, clear base.
   c. Variant, with large American shield on the bowl.
   d. Very short stem, more like a footed tumbler.

10. Salt, footed.
11. Sauce dish, 4 inch.
12. Spoonholder.
13. Sugar bowl.
14. Tumblers.

    a. Water tumbler.
    b. Whiskey tumbler.

15. Wine jug. Two styles, one without the inscription. Rare.

Colors: Clear glass, with leaf frosted.

MAGNET AND GRAPE

(Stippled Leaf)

This design closely resembles the earlier one, though the glass is not as heavy and does not appear to be nearly so old. The goblet has a plain octagonal stem and clear base. The chief point of difference is in the grape leaf, which is stippled instead of being frosted. The goblet is shown on Plate 62. This pattern is easily found in the usual pieces. It was produced by the Boston & Sandwich Glass Company.

PLATE 62—GOBLETS

Magnet and Grape
Banded Buckle

Oval Panel
Buckle

PLATE 63

1. BEADED GRAPE celery vase, tumbler, butter dish, creamer.
2. MAGNET and GRAPE (frosted leaf) goblet, tumbler, creamer, salt.
3. GRAPE and FESTOON goblet (stippled leaf), butter dish, creamer, goblet (clear leaf).
4. STIPPLED GRAPE and FESTOON celery vase, creamer, goblets (clear and stippled leaf).

PLATE 64

1. PANELLED GRAPE celery vase, spoonholder, water pitcher.
2. PANELLED GRAPE sugar bowl, creamer, goblet.
3. ARCHED GRAPE goblet, spoonholder, creamer, butter dish.
4. GRAPE BAND goblet, creamer, spoonholder, cordial.

PLATE 65

1. LATE PANELLED GRAPE goblet, covered bowl, butter dish.
2. FLATTENED SAWTOOTH compote, footed salt, water pitcher.
3. BEADED ACORN goblet, spoonholder, footed salt, egg cup.
4. CABBAGE LEAF bowl of sauce dish, celery vase, butter dish.

PLATE 66

1. BALTIMORE PEAR sugar bowl, water pitcher, spoonholder.
2. CHERRY goblet, sugar bowl, sauce dish.
3. BEADED GRAPE MEDALLION (banded) covered compote, pickle dish, creamer.
4. BEADED GRAPE MEDALLION goblets and their different bases.

Classification

MAGNET AND GRAPE
(Stippled Leaf)

PATTERN 72

(See Plates 62, 63)

Form Number.
1. Butter dish. Acorn knob.
2. Compote, open.
3. Cordials.
4. Creamer.
5. Egg cup.
6. Goblets.
7. Salt, footed.
8. Sauce dish, 4 inch.
9. Spoonholder.
10. Sugar bowl.
11. Tumbler.

Color: Clear glass with stippled leaf.

PANELED GRAPE

The most fascinating of the later Grape designs has become known as Paneled Grape. It has attracted considerable attention since it was "discovered." The design consists of lovely stippled grape leaves and clusters of grapes in high relief. The glass is heavy and brilliant, though it does not contain lead or flint and therefore has no ring to it, when tapped. All the pieces are made with narrow panels which vary in number. The water pitcher, for instance, has twelve and the spoonholder nine. The handle of the pitcher resembles a heavy stippled vine and around the base of the bowl are petal-like ornaments. The squat spoonholder makes one doubt whether it was originally designed for that purpose. It makes a most attractive glass for various beverages. The goblet is paneled also, with the bunches of grapes in high relief.

Collectors are glad to know that this design may be had in all the needed forms for general table use. It is often referred to by dealers to-day as "Heavy Grape." I have never found any record of where this glass was produced, but several Indiana dealers have asserted that it was made in their state.

Since the great popularity of pattern glass has made fraud profitable, many reproductions have been on the market, in Paneled Grape. Those copied are marked with an asterisk. Please note that plates are a new adaptation. There are no old ones as they were not among the original pieces in this set.

Classification

PANELED GRAPE

PATTERN 73

(See Plate 64)

Form Number.

*1. Ale glass. Now used as parfait glass, 6¼ inches high. Short knob stem.

2. Bowl, round, deep. Several sizes.

3. Butter dish.

4. Compotes.
   a. Large, covered, on standard. 8 inch. (Several sizes from 4 inch.)
   b. Open, on low standard. 6½ inch.

*5. Cordials.

*6. Celery vase.

*7. Creamer, vine handle. Two sizes.

*8. Cups, handled. Sherbet.

9. Dish, oval.

*10. Goblets.

*11. Lemonade glass.

*12. Pitcher, water. Two sizes.

*13. Salts.

14. Sauce dishes, oval. Several sizes.
   a. Sauce dish, round. 4¼ inch.

Form Number.

15. Spoonholder.
*16. Sugar bowl.
17. Syrup jug.
18. Toothpick holders, tiny.
*19. Tumblers.
      a. Jelly, thin top rim.
      b. Water.

Color: Clear glass.

LATE PANELED GRAPE

A grape pattern that often is combined with many others, is named Late Paneled Grape. It dates not earlier than 1890 and was sold in the country stores less than thirty-five years ago, much as some collectors may regret the youth of this design. Of course, each year adds twelve months to its age.

The goblet is often used to complete sets of the earlier heavy Paneled Grape, a pattern in which old goblets are so difficult to find. The present demand is greatly in excess of the supply. The two patterns combine nicely and are quite effective. It is paneled and the grapevine winds around in a somewhat conventional manner. The three clusters of grapes stand out in fairly high relief while the leaves are rather thin and lightly veined. The stem is clear, with a knob at the top. The base is clear also.

It is an interesting fact that while this glass is not really *old,* specimens are often obtained which show the distinctly amethystine hue that we associate with very old glass. Many different pieces are found, among them a large round covered dish not unlike a casserole. This is very heavy and the rim, where the cover joins, has a narrow ribbing which is also carried out on the edge of the sauce dishes. They, too, have a star in the base, like the covered dish. I may add that these grape sauce dishes are the deepest I have found in any pattern. The covered butter dish is in the very late style but attractive, with its high domed cover and clusters of grapes in the base.

Another grape pattern, not illustrated in this book, was produced at about this same period. It is similar in both design and forms to the Late Paneled Grape, except that the vines are heavier, with a stippled effect.

Classification

LATE PANELED GRAPE

PATTERN 74

(See Plate 65)

Form Number.
1. Butter dish.
2. Creamer.
3. Dish, covered, 8 inch.
4. Goblets.
5. Pitchers.
    a. Large, with cover.
    b. Syrup, two sizes.
    c. Water.
6. Sauce dishes, 1⅝ inches deep.
Colors: Clear glass. Often found in amethystine shades. This color is caused by careless mixing of the batch.

BEADED GRAPE

A grape pattern that is found only in emerald green or clear glass, is the Beaded Grape. The numbers of oblong trays, platters and deep dishes to be had in this design seem to be endless! It is strange that goblets should be exceedingly scarce while tumblers may be found without so much difficulty. It is a delight to have a plentiful number of items in a pattern of a color like this lovely deep emerald. Few other patterns are collectible in sets in this shade of green. The emerald Beaded Grape is charming combined with colored linen. It is a late pattern, being on the market not more than forty-five years ago.

It was made over a period of years by the United States Glass

Company of Pittsburgh, Pa., and I have no evidence that it was ever copied by any other firm. It was originally called "No. 15059" or "California Pattern."

Many of the Beaded Grape pieces are either oblong or square. The forms are decorative and a most interesting table scheme may be achieved with this "California" glass. The following classification is taken from the original trade catalogue of the United States Glass Company.

Classification

BEADED GRAPE

PATTERN 75

(See Plate 63)

Form Number.

1. Butter dish.
2. Cake plate, on standard. Two sizes.
3. Celery tray, oblong.
4. Celery vase, square.
5. Compotes.
   a. On high foot, 7, 8 and 9 inch. Open or covered.
   b. Shallow, on standard. No cover.
   c. Small, open. 4 inches high, 4¾ inches diameter. Very scarce with covers. Originally made for jelly.
6. Cordials.
7. Creamer.
8. Cruets.
9. Dishes.
   a. Oblong, deep.
   b. Square, 5¼, 6¼, 7¼ and 8¼ inch.
10. Goblets.
11. Pickle dish.
12. Plates, square, 8½ inch.
13. Olive dish, with handle.
14. Pitcher, water.
    a. Square, several sizes.
    b. Round, several sizes to extra large. One style termed "Tankard."

Form Number.

15. Platter, oblong. Scarce. Originally termed Bread Tray.
16. Salt and pepper shakers, metal tops.
17. Sauce dishes, square, flat, 3½, 4 and 4½ inch.
18. Spoonholder.
19. Sugar bowl.

> *a.* Square, flat base.
> *b.* Square, footed.

20. Toothpick holder, square.
21. Tumblers, water.
22. Vase, 6 inch.

Colors: Emerald green; clear glass.

BEADED GRAPE MEDALLION

It will surprise many to learn that this grape pattern, which has the appearance of being a fairly late glass, was made as early as 1869. It gave me pleasure to find an oval dish which is plainly marked in the base—"Mould pat'd—May 11, 1869." Evidently it had a cover at one time. It is shown on Plate 66. As there are several variants of this design it has been a problem to show them all clearly. The goblet, which has a wide clear marginal band at the top, has a snowy stippled background divided into three panels, each of which contains a clear beaded oval, enclosing a cluster of grapes. These are found in three styles, clearly illustrated on Plate 66. Goblet 1 has a stippled base showing three beaded ovals having a cluster of grapes. Goblet 2, has a stippled base containing three small clear ovals. Goblet 3, in which design all pieces of tableware are found, has same base as Number 2, but has an added stippled band over the regular design. To avoid confusion, I am listing everything in this latter design separately.

The Beaded Grape Medallion is unusual. Collectors are becoming interested in it and it is safe to predict greater popularity for it. Sandwich produced one of the variations, according to the fragment findings at the site of the old factory.

Classification

BEADED GRAPE MEDALLION

PATTERN 76

(See Plate 66)

Form Number.

1. Butter dish. Acorn knob.
2. Castor set.
3. Celery vase.
4. Champagnes.
5. Compotes.
   - *a.* Covered, on high foot.
   - *b.* Covered, on low foot.
6. Cordials.
7. Creamer. Applied handle.
8. Dish, oval, large, covered, 9½ x 6¼ inches.
9. Dish, oval, large, covered, 10 x 7 (not including cover). Four clusters of grapes in oval on cover. Knob has long oak leaf with cluster of three acorns. Dish on oval collared base.
10. Egg cups.
11. Goblets.
    - *a.* Stippled base, 3 clear beaded ovals containing cluster of grapes.
    - *b.* Stippled base, 3 small clear beaded ovals.
    - *c.* Stippled band above usual design on bowl. Base same as design *b.*
12. Honey dishes, 3½ inch.
13. Pitcher, water.
14. Salts.
    - *a.* Footed.
    - *b.* Oval, flat.
    - *c.* Round, flat.
15. Sauce dish, flat, 4 inch. Base of both types, like goblets.
16. Spoonholder.
17. Sugar bowl. Acorn knob.

Color: Clear glass.

BEADED GRAPE MEDALLION
(Banded)

This design is exactly the same as the one described, except for the addition of the narrow, stippled band above the regular design. This is plainly shown on Plate 66 of line drawings.

Classification
BEADED GRAPE MEDALLION
(Banded)
PATTERN 77
(See Plate 66)

Form Number.
1. Butter dish.
2. Celery vase.
3. Compotes, covered, on low standard.
    a. Covered, on high standard.
4. Cordials.
5. Creamer.
6. Egg cups.
7. Goblets.
8. Pitcher, water.
9. Spoonholder.
10. Sauce dish, flat, 4 inch.
11. Sugar bowl.

Color: Clear glass.

GRAPE BAND

A Grape design, dainty and attractive, has a band consisting of stippled leaves and bunches of grapes twined about the lower part of the pieces. The goblet has a wide marginal band that is clear at the top, with the band of the grape pattern just below the middle part of the bowl. The creamer has an applied handle, indicating that this ware may date from the late Sixties. A few pieces are shown on Plate 64.

Classification

GRAPE BAND

PATTERN 78

(See Plate 64)

Form Number.
1. Compotes, on high standard.
     a. Covered.
     b. Open.
     c. Covered compote, on low foot.
2. Cordials.
3. Creamer.
4. Goblet.
5. Pitcher, water.
6. Plate, 6 inch.
7. Salt, footed.
8. Spoonholder.
9. Tumbler, water. Ovals above base.
Color: Clear glass.

STIPPLED GRAPE AND FESTOON

This design, with stippled background similar to the Rose in Snow, is to be found in two styles. One has the grape leaf veined and lightly stippled and the other has the grape leaf perfectly clear. As the design is the same in other details, I am listing the two variants together. It is a matter of choice which design one prefers and the same pieces are to be had in both. It is most attractive, with the snowy background and the festoon of clear leaves standing out in bright relief. It is a pattern not yet widely collected. The large number of variants in the grape designs has made collectors hesitate to collect them, but now that the different types are classified it will be an easy matter to choose.

This glass is fairly heavy and well made. The pattern with stippled background appears to be somewhat older than the clear Grape and Festoon. It will be noted that the stippled glass has clear festoons of leaves, while the clear Grape and Festoon has lightly stippled leaves that are not in relief. The forms on Plate 63 show distinctly the plain and stippled leaves, being compared and shown on one line. Acorn knobs are generally used on all covered dishes of both varieties, so one classification will cover both. The design with the stippled leaf was made by Doyle & Co. of Pittsburgh. Evidently more than one factory produced it, since the pattern appears to have a wider marginal band in the old catalogue illustrations by Doyle, than on some specimens I have seen. Fragments in this design were found at the site of the old Sandwich factory after this book was revised in 1933. Probably they produced the type having the clear leaf.

Classification
STIPPLED GRAPE AND FESTOON
PATTERN 79 (Clear Leaf)
PATTERN 79A (Veined Leaf)
(See Plate 63)

Form Number.
1. Butter dish.
2. Celery vase.
3. Compotes, covered on low foot, 8 inch. Acorn knob.
4. Cordials.
5. Creamer.
6. Egg cups.
7. Goblets.
8. Pitcher, water.
9. Sauce dish, flat, 4 inch.
10. Spoonholder.
11. Sugar bowl.
Color: Clear glass.

GRAPE AND FESTOON
(Clear)

This design, like the Stippled Grape and Festoon, is found in two styles, with either a clear leaf or veined leaf. The design in either case is thinner and the glass is not quite so heavy. It was probably produced during the 1870's, and continued into the 1880's. It is known that the Boston & Sandwich Glass Company made it and Doyle & Co. also produced the clear pattern as well as that with the stippled background.

The forms follow closely those of the earlier ware, the covered dishes having an acorn knob. The leaves over the cluster of grapes may vary on some of the goblets, but otherwise the pieces will match. The point of difference is shown carefully on Plate 63 of Stippled Grape and Festoon. Mention should be made here of the goblet variant having an American shield added to the design. This is undoubtedly plagiarized from the early Magnet and Grape design, which also had a variant bearing the shield. On the Grape and Festoon goblet, the shield is much smaller.

Classification

GRAPE AND FESTOON

(Clear)

PATTERN 80 (Clear Leaf)
PATTERN 80A (Veined Leaf)

(See Plate 63)

Form Number.
1. Butter dish.
2. Celery vase.
3. Compote, covered.
    a. On high standard.
    b. On low standard.
4. Cordials.
5. Creamer, two styles.
6. Egg cups. Two sizes.
7. Goblets. Two styles, one having small American shield.
8. Mug, small, with shield.
9. Pickle dish, oval.
10. Pitcher, water.

Form Number.
    11. Plate, 6 inch.
    12. Salt, footed.
    13. Sauce dish, flat 4 inch.
    14. Spoonholder.
    15. Sugar bowl. Acorn knob.
Color: Clear glass.

ARCHED GRAPE

Of the many grape patterns, probably the least known is one now called Arched Grape. It is cool-looking and dainty in appearance and the glass is quite light in weight. The goblet has eight arched panels, each of which contains a cluster of leaves and a bunch of grapes in low relief. The flat covered butter dish has a knob in the form of a small cluster of grapes, with a leaf overlaying it. This has twelve panels, one containing two grape leaves alternating with another having a cluster of grapes and some leaves. The creamer is footed and has the later type of pressed handle. Patterns of this type are picked up in antique shops at exceedingly low prices, as the demand for many of these little known designs has scarcely started. Apparently this was a Sandwich pattern, probably of the 1870's.

Classification
ARCHED GRAPE

PATTERN 81
(See Plate 64)

Form Number.
    1. Butter dish.
    2. Celery vase.
    3. Creamer.
    4. Goblet.
    5. Pitcher, water.

Form Number.

    6. Sauce dish, 4 inch.

    7. Spoonholder.

    8. Sugar bowl.

Color: Clear glass.

GRAPE WITH THUMBPRINT

Another dainty grape pattern that will probably become more popular as it is better known is the Grape with Thumbprint. The goblet has eight panels slightly arched at the top, each containing two lightly stippled grape leaves and a cluster of grapes. Above the panels is a row of small thumbprints. The stem is plain and round and the base is the same. A dealer tells me that he has a water pitcher and twelve goblets which were purchased from an old lady who bought them sixty-five years ago for nine dollars for the set. This may be true, though the glass itself and the forms are very similar to those of the Late Paneled Grape, which was sold in the stores thirty-five years ago. I do not find any records of this grape, and as it has not been collected to any extent, it is difficult to classify it.

Classification

GRAPE WITH THUMBPRINT

Pattern 82

(See Plate 164, No. 4)

Form Number.

    1. Butter dish.

    2. Creamer.

    3. Goblet.

    4. Pitcher, water.

    5. Spoonholder.

    6. Sugar bowl.

    7. Syrup jugs. Several sizes.

Color: Clear glass.

Chapter IX

RIBBON GROUP

RIBBON

An early piece that must have been popular, produced by Bakewell, Pears & Co., was a dolphin-footed dish of pressed glass. The round base and dolphin are frosted and the edge of the bowl consists of a striped effect produced by alternating one frosted panel and one clear indented panel. Two of these dishes were shown in an article by Thomas C. Pears, Jr., which appeared in *Antiques,* issue of March, 1927. Mr. Pears, who collected considerable data about this early Pittsburgh establishment, figured that these were made about 1850, or slightly later. On Plate 68 is shown one of these dolphin compotes, together with one of the Ribbon goblets. The dolphin dishes had bowls of various designs and sizes. Some were round, some oblong and some were in clear glass in the form of shells, similar to the "patent" shell dishes which, in many sizes, were a product of this factory. It seems reasonable to believe that the beautiful Ribbon glass being collected to-day must have been produced at this same factory, following the dolphin dishes. The glass is heavy, having one frosted panel, alternating with one clear indented one. A comprehensive group showing the forms to be had, is shown on Plate 67. It is to be noted that the earlier frosted (not stippled) effects appear to have been ground or sandblasted and are slightly rough to the touch, on the surface. Later on, in patterns such as Westward-Ho, Lion, Three-face, etc., the frosted surface is smooth, which was accomplished by the use of acid. This latter type used to be referred to by some collectors and dealers as "camphor glass," doubtless because of the coat of crystallized camphor often left on the inside surface of glass containers of spirits of camphor after the alcohol has evaporated. This term was never used by the glass workers. Of the earlier patterns that show a ground effect on the frosted surface, is the Magnet and Grape pattern (described in the Grape series) which has a large grape leaf with the rough surface, and a goblet that is a variant of this design and has an American shield with the same rough surface. The Frosted Leaf pattern, as shown on Plate 94, is another example.

Compotes are found more readily in the Ribbon pattern than almost anything else. They must have been made in large quantities as they are not difficult to find to-day. Goblets are elusive, but that is true of almost any pattern, particularly when one is attempting to complete a set in a hurry. There is a very large tray made originally for a water set that is most unusual in shape and has a handle at each end. The goblets are found in two forms, one having slightly straighter sides than the one pictured on Plate 68. The panels on the base of the footed pieces are all clear glass. Various other Ribbon effects were produced at a later period, which are treated in subsequent pages.

Classification

RIBBON

Pattern 83

(See Plates 67, 68)

Form Number.

1. Bowl for water set. Size of finger bowl.
2. Celery vase.
3. Compotes.
    a. Covered, on high foot, 6, 7 and 8 inch.
    b. Open, on low foot, 8¼ inch.
4. Champagnes.
5. Cordials.
6. Creamer.
7. Dolphin compotes, with dolphin and base frosted. Bowl in Ribbon glass. The bowl of the compote may be oblong in Ribbon pattern, various sizes, and is also found with round

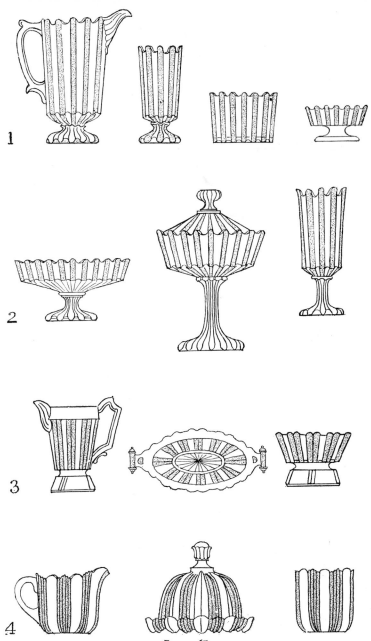

PLATE 67

1. RIBBON water pitcher, spoonholder, bowl, footed sauce dish.
2. RIBBON compote on low foot, compote on high standard, celery vase.
3. DOUBLE RIBBON creamer, pickle dish, footed sauce dish.
4. FLUTED RIBBON creamer, butter dish, spoonholder.

PLATE 68

Pair of relish dishes with frosted centers, showing mountains and a St. Bernard dog.
Plate in Frosted Stork, Dolphin dish with bowl in Ribbon pattern. Ribbon goblet.

PLATE 69
1. FROSTED RIBBON celery vase, goblet, footed sauce dish.
2. DEW and RAINDROP berry bowl, tumbler, sauce dish.
3. SWIRL celery vase, butter dish, tumbler.
4. MOON and STAR berry bowl, sugar bowl, butter dish.

PLATE 70

1. CLEAR RIBBON goblet, spoonholder, sauce dish, bread tray.
2. CLEAR RIBBON compote, butter dish, cake plate on standard.
3. CUPID and VENUS celery vase, creamer, footed sauce dish, cordial.
4. CUPID and VENUS water pitcher, sugar bowl butter dish.

Form Number.

bowl, various sizes. Same style of dolphin dish was made both frosted and clear, the bowl being in form of large shell.

*8. Goblets.
    a. Sides bulging slightly.
    b. Straight sides.

9. Pickle jar.

10. Pitcher, water, two sizes.

11. Plates. Extremely rare.

12. Sauce dish.
    a. Footed.
    b. Round, flat.
    c. With handle.

13. Spoonholder.

14. Sugar bowl.

15. Tray, large. Originally designed to hold water pitcher, bowl and goblets. Very heavy. Size $16\frac{1}{4}$ x 15 inches.

Color: Frosted and clear combined.

FROSTED RIBBON

It would seem as if nearly every pattern which enjoyed enough popularity to sell well, was copied by competing glass houses a little later on, usually in a less attractive form. This is not strictly true of the later Ribbon glass. The first Ribbon, so far as I can learn, was made by Bakewell, Pears & Company. In the very earliest form it was used in a dolphin dish, like the one pictured in Plate 68. The glass was of splendid quality and the design carefully carried out. I believe the next Ribbon to follow this type was produced by George Duncan & Sons of Pittsburgh, and simply designated by them as "No. 150 Pattern, Frosted." Therefore I am calling it the Frosted Ribbon. An old catalogue in my possession is undated, but appears to be of the Seventies. It also carries the Three Face and other patterns known to have been made before the Centennial in 1876.

There is no question about this being a particularly attractive glass. The goblet is especially pretty. The knob stem has tiny

thumbprints running through it, and the clear base is in twelve
little panels. The footed sauce dish has a dainty, scalloped top,
like the celery holder. It is a little-known pattern that lends itself
to attractive decorative schemes. It was also made in several
variations, such as with a frosted and clear panel, the clear one
being etched; with a double, clear panel alternating with a frosted,
the clear being etched; and in all clear crystal, plain or etched
The classification given below is taken directly from the old trade
catalogues.

Classification

FROSTED RIBBON

PATTERN 84

(See Plate 69)

Form Number.

1. Bitters bottle.
2. Celery vase.
3. Compotes.
   a. Covered, on high foot. 6, 7, 8 and 9 inch.
   b. Open, on high foot. 5, 6, 7, 8, 9 and 10 inch.
   c. Covered, on low foot. 6, 7, 8, 9 and 10 inch.
   d. Open, on low foot. 5, 6, 7, 8, 9 and 10 inch.
   e. Open, shallow bowl on high foot. 5, 6, 7, 9 and 10 inch.
4. Cordials.
5. Champagnes.
6. Creamer.
7. Dish, octagon (relish), 8 and 9 inch.
8. Egg cup.
9. Clarets.
10. Goblet.
11. Pickle jar (marmalade).
12. Pitcher, water. Quart and $\frac{1}{2}$ gallon.
13. Sauce dish, footed.
    a. 4 and $4\frac{1}{2}$ inch.
    b. 4 inch, two styles. Flaring bowl and plain bowl.
    c. $4\frac{1}{2}$ inch, with flaring bowl.

Form Number.
14. Salt, footed.
15. Spoonholder.
16. Sherry.
17. Sugar bowl.
18. Tumbler.
Color: Frosted and clear, combined; all crystal.

DOUBLE RIBBON

A variation of the well-known Ribbon glass occurs in the Double Ribbon. It is undoubtedly a somewhat later adaptation, to judge by the quality of the glass. Instead of having one frosted panel alternating with one indented clear panel, this design has a double frosted panel alternating with a clear one which is not as deeply indented as in the earlier ware. The footed sauce dish has a clear collared base, as has also the creamer. These are shown on Plate 67, contrasted with the single Ribbon. This is a very attractive glass, even though it is not as heavy as the one that preceded it. A few pieces of a variation of the Double Ribbon have come to my attention, which is the opposite of the one just described. The variation has two clear panels alternating with one frosted one. Sometimes this glass is found with the clear panel etched.

One variation of a ribbon effect is shown by the group on Plate 69 of line drawings. This has a wide frosted panel alternating with a clear one which is not indented. It is treated elsewhere under Frosted Ribbon.

The known pieces of Double Ribbon are as follows:

Classification
DOUBLE RIBBON
PATTERN 85
(See Plate 67)

Form Number.
1. Butter dish.
2. Compote on high foot, open.

Form Number.
   3. Creamer.
   4. Egg cup.
   5. Goblet.
   6. Sauce dish, footed, 4½ inch.
   7. Spoonholder.
   8. Sugar bowl.
Color: Frosted and clear, combined.

FLUTED RIBBON

The Fluted Ribbon was known simply as Pattern No. 15022, when it was produced during the Nineties by the United States Glass Company of Pittsburgh, Pa. The design places it with the Ribbon group in this book and as the old trade name would tax the memory of the most inveterate hunter of patterns, the new title is deemed more helpful. The weight of the glass, which is particularly heavy, would suggest that it is fairly early, while the type of butter dish, which shows a design not used before the Nineties, disproves it. In other words, the weight of the glass hints at the early Sixties, while the domed-cover fitting over the plate is a "family" butter dish, belying its age. In any event, it is an unusual glass, with its heavy frosted panel alternating with the clear, which is fluted in between each panel. The classification is taken from the original illustrated catalogue.

Classification

FLUTED RIBBON

Pattern 86

(See Plate 67)

Form Number.
   1. Bowls.
         a. Berry. 5, 6, 7, 8 and 9 inch.
         b. Berry, with plates. 9 and 10 inch.
         c. Berry, with plate. 7 inch.
   2. Butter dish.

Form Number.

3. Celery tray with or without handles. 10 and 12 inch.

4. Compotes.
   a. Open, on high standard. 7 and 8 inch.
   b. Covered on high standard. 7 and 8 inch.

5. Creamer.

6. Custard cup and saucer.

7. Dish, oblong. 6, 7, 8, 9 and 10 inch.

8. Finger bowl.

9. Molasses jug. (Syrup pitcher.)

10. Oil bottle.

11. Olive dish.

12. Pickle dish, with or without handles. 8 inch.

13. Pitcher. ½ gallon.

14. Plates. 7, 9 and 10 inch.

15. Salt and pepper shaker.

16. Sauce dishes.
    a. **Flat.** 4 and 4½ inch.

17. Spoonholder.

18. Sugar bowl.

19. Tumbler.

20. Water bottle.

Color: Frosted and clear, combined.

CLEAR RIBBON

A variant which has been called "Ribbon" by the few who know it, is really a much later ware, probably of the Eighties. This is shown fully on Plate 70. It is a clear glass, fairly heavy, and with a wide threaded band which would naturally make one think of a ribbon. The goblets have an unusual type of base which is rather attractive. Some of the pieces are all of clear glass and others are etched in the panels. This design may be found in a large number of forms, which include the following:

Classification
CLEAR RIBBON

PATTERN 87

(See Plate 70)

Form Number.
1. Bread tray.
2. Cake plate on standard.
3. Compote, covered, large.
4. Creamer, footed.
5. Dish, oblong, covered, 6, 7 and 8 inch.
6. Goblets.
7. Pitcher, water.
8. Sauce dish, on four feet, 4 inch.
9. Spoonholder.
10. Sugar bowl.
Color: Clear glass.

Chapter X

DEWDROP GROUP

DEWDROP WITH STAR

Of the middle and late period of pressed glass, no style of decoration has ever surpassed in duration of popularity that of the various Dewdrop patterns. They began during the Sixties and were still being produced during the Eighties. I refer not to the plain dewdrop design, but to all of those which used or com- bined dewdrops as the important decorative motif to enhance the artistic value of the glass. Probably the earliest of this group, and certainly one of the outstanding patterns to-day, is the Dew- drop with Star. The title is self-explanatory. The dishes are covered with very small pointed hobnails, known as dewdrops. In the center of many of the pieces are stars, formed entirely of these dewdrops. In the covered dishes the dewdrops form points on the inside of the cover that sparkle brilliantly. Additional evidence of the great popularity of this pattern is found in the large number of plates in varying sizes that are to be had. Collectors have always found the goblets disappointing when matching this design, be- cause the dewdrops in them not only are too fine but extend upward only a small distance on the bowl. This leaves a very wide plain marginal band so that the goblets are the least attractive pieces of the set. Indeed, many have doubted if the generally accepted gob- lets are, after all, a true match. Fortunately there are other dew- drop patterns, with more character, that combine nicely. (See the Popcorn design, plate 71.) All these goblets are illustrated, as well as the eleven-inch plate. The sauce dishes are on a small standard, almost a collared base, and may be had in more than one size. Another style is not footed.

The Dewdrop bread plates (found in ten- and eleven-inch sizes) appear to have been made at this period. They are similar to the star plates, as may be seen by comparing them in the illustration on Plate 73. They have the same inscription found on nearly all those which were made at this time: "Give Us This Day Our Daily Bread," and show a sheaf of wheat in the center. These plates are usually found in clear glass, but I have also seen them in blue, yellow and amber. They are lovely in color but rare. The fine Dewdrop goblets also may be found in the same colors. I have never seen or heard of them in green or amethyst.

This is an unique and satisfying pattern—one that can never grow tiresome.

Worthy of particular note is the eleven-inch plate with large cover, presumably a honey or cheese dish. It seems almost unbelievable that so many plates and sauce dishes were made in this design. They all vary by one-fourth inch. It is altogether likely that Dewdrop with Star enjoyed a wide popularity over a period of years and was copied extensively. This would account for the large number of varying sizes in the dishes.

Classification

DEWDROP WITH STAR

PATTERN 88

(See Plates 71, 73)

Form Number.
1. Butter dish, covered, star base.
2. Cake plate on standard.
    a. Extra large size.
3. Celery vase. Star in base.
4. Cordial.
5. Creamer, star base.
6. Dishes, covered. Two types of dome cover, one rounding out and one curving in.
    a. Footed, star base, 6 and 7 inch.
    b. On high standard, various sizes.
    c. On low standard, various sizes.

Form Number.

   7. Goblet.

   8. Lamp. All glass, with patent mark in base, Aug. 29, 1876.

   9. Pickle dish.

  10. Pitcher, water.

*11. Plates.

     a. $4\frac{1}{2}$, $5\frac{1}{4}$, $5\frac{1}{2}$, 6, $6\frac{1}{4}$, $6\frac{1}{2}$, 7, $7\frac{1}{4}$,* $7\frac{1}{2}$, $7\frac{3}{4}$, $8\frac{1}{4}$, 9 to $9\frac{3}{8}$, 11 inch. The $7\frac{1}{4}$ size is only one reproduced.

     b. 11 inch plate with large cover (probably honey dish).

  12. Sauce dish.

     a. Footed, round base, $3\frac{1}{2}$, 4, $4\frac{1}{2}$ inch.

     b. Without standard, 4, 5, $5\frac{1}{4}$, $5\frac{1}{2}$, 6 inch.

*13. Salt, footed. Scalloped top, $3\frac{1}{8}$ inches in diameter, $1\frac{1}{2}$ inches high.

  14. Spoonholder.

  15. Sugar bowl, covered, star base.

(Other Dewdrop goblets may be combined with this pattern as follows:)

  16. Popcorn. Plate 71.

  17. "101." Plate 72.

  18. Panelled. Plate 72.

  19. Beaded. Plate 57.

  20. Dewdrop. Plate 71, only with light thumbprint effect covering usual plain wide marginal band. Not illustrated.

*21. Dew with Raindrop. Plate 57.

  22. Flattened hobnail. Plate 71.

  23. Hobnail with fan. Plate 71.

*24. Lace dewdrop. Plate 154.

Colors: Clear glass, with the exception of the goblets and bread plates with sheaf of wheat center. These may be had in amber, blue and yellow.

DEWDROP

Of this same period, or the late Sixties, we also have the plain Dewdrop. This differs from the Dewdrop with Star only in the base of the dishes, which are completely sprinkled over with rows of dewdrops, instead of having the star pattern in the center. There is no particular goblet to match, but any of them combine nicely. The covered dishes are the same as those with the star and the footed pieces usually have a clear base. There are a number of sizes of pickle dishes, but I have not found any plates that match. It is my belief that this glass was all on the market at the same period and that buyers chose the plates or goblets or sauce dishes to combine, according to the individual taste.

Classification

DEWDROP

PATTERN 89

Form Number.

1. Butter dish, covered, 6¼ inch, dewdrop base, no standard.

2. Compote, covered, 9 inch on high standard; three rows of dewdrops around base; small knob stem; plain center; usual cover.

3. Dish, oval.

   a. Dewdrop base, 6½ x 9¼ inches.
   b. Plain base, 5½ x 8 inches.

4. Goblets, fine dewdrops. Plate 71.

5. Pickle dish.

   a. Double, with leaf separating the two parts.
   b. Ten-inch, small handle with star at each end, dewdrop base.

6. Pitcher, water, plain base.

7. Salts, round; individual, 2⅝ inch diameter, collared foot.

   a. Base rayed.
   b. Base of dewdrops with small six-pointed ornament in center.

8. Sauce dish, flat, dewdrop base, 4 and 5¼ inch.

9. Sugar bowl.

Color: Clear glass.

PLATE 71—GOBLETS

Hobnail with Fan top   Flattened Hobnail
Dewdrop   Popcorn

PLATE 72—GOBLETS

"101" Panelled Dewdrop
Printed Hobnail Late Buckle

PLATE 73—LARGE PLATES

Rose in Snow
Dewdrop with Sheaf of Wheat

Dewdrop with Star
Arched Leaf

PLATE 74—SEVEN INCH PLATES

Stippled Forget-me-not   Snakeskin with Dot, three sizes
Hobnail   "101"

POPCORN

Apparently the widespread popularity of the Dewdrop patterns inspired the producers to try varying the design. One, which has become better known as Popcorn, is greatly admired to-day. There is every reason why it should, as it is brilliant in effect and most attractive. A group is shown on Plate 25 and the goblet on Plate 71. The goblet is one of the most satisfying to collect in this group. The bowl tapers from the top, and the dewdrops are divided by three ovoid ribbed panels. The base of the bowl and the stems are fluted, and a row of these, extending outward for half an inch, may be seen from underneath the base. The pieces, such as creamer, sugar bowl and spoonholder, are divided by an outstanding stippled ornament which may slightly resemble, from a distance, an ear of corn.

That this pattern was undoubtedly made by a factory which produced large quantities of Dewdrop seems certain because the same type of cover is found on the covered dishes and the details of the knob are identical. The quality of the glass also appears to be the same. I judge it all dates from the late Sixties.

The base of the butter dish is of solid dewdrops, that sparkle brilliantly from every angle. I do not know of any plates that match, other than the star pattern. The bases of butter dishes may be used for plates, as they are flat with practically no rim.

Classification

POPCORN

PATTERN 90

(See Plates 25, 71)

Form Number.
1. Butter dish.
2. Cordial.
3. Creamer.
4. Goblet. Two types. On one style, the ear does not stand out.
5. Pitcher, water (oval panels like goblet).

Form Number.

6. Spoonholder.
7. Sugar bowl.

Color: Clear glass.

"101"

Very popular at the present moment is this lovely dewdrop pattern, known as "One hundred and one." The title came about because the design shows an O pattern, with an ornament that looks like a figure 1. These follow alternatively in a border. A glimpse of the goblet on Plate 72 will show this very plainly. The oval is in relief and bordered with dewdrops. The glass is brilliant and sparkling. Plates are found in four sizes including an eleven-inch plate which is inscribed, "Give Us This Day Our Daily Bread." This has a sheaf of wheat in the center, with the "101" border.

Collectors have become particularly interested in this pattern during recent years. It is presumably a ware of the Seventies, judging by the forms and the quality of the glass. It was evidently popular and produced over a long period. The handled lamp appears to be of a later date than many of the other forms. At least some of this ware was made by the Bellaire Goblet Company of Findlay, Ohio, which was absorbed by the U. S. Glass Company of Pittsburgh, Pa., in 1891.

Classification

"101"

Pattern 91

(See Plates 72, 74, 141)

Form Number.

1. Butter dish.
2. Celery vase.
3. Compote, covered, on high foot. 8 inch.
4. Creamer.

Form Number.

    5. Goblet.

    6. Lamp, kerosene type; flat, handled.

    7. Pickle dishes.

        a. Oval, on collared base.
        b. Tapered at one end.

    8. Pitcher, water.

    9. Plates, 7, 8 and 9 inch.

        a. Bread plate, round. 11 inch. Sheaf of wheat, farm implements, etc., in center.

  10. Sauce dish, flat, 4 inch.

  11. Spoonholder.

  12. Sugar bowl.

  13. Relish dish, oval, deep.

Color: Clear glass.

PANELLED DEWDROP

A brilliant and popular pattern to-day is one generally known as Panelled Dewdrop. There is reason enough for collectors to become enthusiastic over this brilliant glass. During the past few years, when the vogue grew for assembling sets of the old pressed glass, many designs came to light which had been neglected for a long time. The Panelled Dewdrop, called by some "Striped Dewdrop," is bound to be much sought after as it becomes better known. The goblets, showing the rows of brilliant rounded panels alternating with a stripe of the same width with three close-set rows of dewdrops, is found in two forms. One has the round stem with plain clear base, and the more elaborate one has eight loops of the dewdrops underneath the base, alternating with panels as shown on the bowl. Either one is equally desirable and it is only a case of which one the collector finds first, as a rule. The quality of the glass indicates this to be a pattern of the late Sixties. The water tumblers may be found with applied handles, crimped at the base. These were listed in old catalogues as "lemonades."

Classification
PANELLED DEWDROP

Pattern 92
(See Plates 72, 75)

Form Number.
1. Butter dish, covered, with dome lid.
2. Celery vase.
3. Champagne.
4. Compotes.
   a. Covered, on foot, 8 inch.
   b. On high standard, open.
5. Cordials.
6. Creamer. Two sizes.
7. Dish, oval, collared base.
8. Goblets.
   a. Eight loops of dewdrops on base.
   b. Plain base.
9. Pickle dish, oval.
10. Pickle jar.
11. Plates.
    a. Seven inch.
    b. With unusually large cover. May have been honey dish. 11 inch.
12. Platters.
    a. Oblong, inscribed with "Give Us This Day Our Daily Bread." Handle at each end.
    b. Oval.
13. Sauce dish, flat, 4 inch.
    a. Footed, 4 inch.
14. Spoonholder.
15. Sugar bowl.
16. Tumblers.
    a. Water.
    b. With applied handle, for lemonade.

Color: Clear glass.

DEW AND RAINDROP

A late dewdrop pattern which should not be overlooked merely because it is not as ancient as others, is called Dew and Raindrop. The goblet is one of the most attractive of this series, either early or late, and may be seen on Plate 57. The delicate row of dew-drops around the center of the stem adds a final touch of dainti-ness. Goblets are scarce and the tumblers in this pattern are found far more readily. I have never seen many forms, though this glass combines nicely with any of the other dewdrop designs. The sauce dishes are so large and deep that they may readily serve as finger bowls. I have found no record of where it was made, but I believe it may have been in Indiana, probably during the Eighties.

Classification

DEW AND RAINDROP

PATTERN 93

(See Plates 57, 69)

Form Number.

1. Butter dish.
2. Berry bowl, round, large, deep.
*3. Cordials.
*4. Goblets.
5. Mug.
6. Salt shakers.
7. Pitcher, water.
8. Sauce dish, round and flat; 4 and $4\frac{1}{2}$ inches.
*9. Sherbet cups.
10. Sugar bowl.
11. Tumblers.
12. Wines.

Color: Clear glass.

BEADED DEWDROP

The dewdrop designs must have been popular over a period of many years, as so many varied patterns with them as the decorative motif are found. An unusual one came to light which was known to very few before this book was written. The goblet, so dainty and appealing that it will speak for itself, is shown on Plate 57. The attractive sherbet cup is an additional find in this pattern. That this glass dates from the Eighties there is little doubt, but it has much to recommend it. The design consists of stippled arched panels alternating with a clear one. Dewdrops in various sizes stand out against the stippled background of these panels. It was made by the United States Glass Co. of Pittsburgh, Pa., and by them called "Wisconsin Pattern." The following classification is taken from their trade catalogue.

Classification

BEADED DEWDROP

Pattern 94

(See Plate 57)

Form Number.

1. Butter dishes. Two sizes, covered. Third is open, with handles.
2. Bon Bon dish. 4 inch, handled.
3. Cake plate on standard. 6½, 8½, 9½ and 11 inch.
4. Creamer. Two sizes, one individual.
5. Condiment set. Tall salt and pepper, round mustard and horse radish. Also made with salt and pepper and individual sugar and creamer.
6. Compotes.
   a. Covered, on high standard. 6 , 7 and 8 inch.
   b. Open, on high standard. 8½, 9½ and 10½ inch.
   c. Open, on high foot, deep bowl. 6, 7 and 8 inch.
   d. Shallow, with collared base. 7 inch.
   e. Shallow, footed. 5 inch.

Form Number.

  7. Celery tray.
  - *a.* Tall celery.

  8. Dishes.
  - *a.* Deep preserve dish. 6 and 8 inch.
  - *b.* Oval, with handles. 6 inch.
  - *c.* Handled olive dish. 5½ inch.
  - *d.* Sweetmeat, footed. 5 inch.
  - *e.* Oval, covered dish. 6 inch.
  - *f.* Covered nappy. 6, 7 and 8 inch.
  - *g.* Mustard dish.

  9. Goblet.

10. Individual sugar and creamer.

11. Jelly dish, footed, with and without cover. 5 inch.

12. Molasses can. (Syrup pitcher.)

13. Mug, large.

14. Nappies (bowls). 6, 7 and 8 inch.

15. Oil bottle, with or without handle.

16. Pickle jar.

17. Pitcher, water. ½ gallon and 3 pints.

18. Plates.
  - *a.* Square, deep in center. 7 inch.
  - *b.* Candy plate. 5 inch.

19. Relish dish.

20. Sauce, flat. 4 inch.

21. Sherbet cup and saucer.

22. Sugar shaker.

23. Sugar bowl. Three styles, one large for hotels, one medium and one individual.

24. Salt and pepper shakers. Two styles.

25. Syrup jug.

26. Spoonholder.

27. Toothpick holder.

28. Tumbler.

29. Vase. 6 inch.

30. Wines.

Color: Clear glass.

BEADED LOOP

A ware, late but nevertheless effective, is called Beaded Loop. Apparently produced during the Eighties, if not later, it evidently was not made in large quantities, as little of it is found to-day. On Plate 76 is shown a group consisting of the covered sugar bowl, goblet and a bowl of which the cover is missing. The glass in those pieces I have seen has not been as brilliant as one often finds in other patterns of an equally late or an even later period. The goblet is pleasing, the beaded loops enclosing a small pressed diamond pattern. The sugar bowl is the type which follows the earlier footed style. I have been assured that this pattern was made by the U. S. Glass Co. of Pittsburgh, Pa., in the late Nineties and continued into the 1900's.

Classification

BEADED LOOP

Pattern 95

(See Plate 76)

Form Number.
1. Bowls, deep. 6, 7 and 8 inch.
2. Bread plate, oval.
3. Butter dishes.
    a. With flange.
    b. Usual style.
4. Cake plates on standard. 8, 9 and 10 inch.
5. Celery vase.
6. Compotes.
    a. Shallow bowl on high foot. 7¼, 8½ and 10 inch.
    b. On high foot. 6, 7 and 8 inch.
7. Creamer.
    a. Flat.
    b. Footed.
8. Cruet, vinegar.
9. Dish, oval. Deep. 7½, 9½ and 10½ inch.

Form Number.

10. Goblet.
11. Jelly dish, with or without cover. Footed. 5 inch.
12. Molasses jar. (Syrup pitcher.)
13. Mug, handled.
14. Olive dish, boat shape.
15. Pickle dish, boat shape.
16. Pitcher, water. ½ gallon.
17. Salt and pepper.
18. Sauce dishes.
     a. Flat. 3½ and 4 inch.
     b. Footed. 3½ inch.
19. Spoonholders.
     a. Flat.
     b. Footed.
20. Sugar bowls.
     a. Flat.
     b. Footed.
21. Toothpick holder.
22. Tumbler.
23. Wine.

Color: Clear glass.

BEADED OVAL AND SCROLL

Touring through Pennsylvania one encounters more frequently than anywhere else, a pattern composed of dewdrops forming an oval alternating with a scroll shaped very much like an hour-glass. Some of the pieces are bright and sparkling, while others may be rather dull. Following the vogue of the dewdrops, this glass should be popular. The goblet is pleasing, and the deep sauce dishes with scalloped rim come in a useful size and are moreover dainty to look upon. The creamer has a round foot and a late style of pressed handle. This glass probably is of the Eighties, judging by the quality and the forms.

Classification

BEADED OVAL AND SCROLL

PATTERN 96

(See Plate 77)

Form Number.

1. Butter dish.
2. Compote on high standard.
3. Cordial.
4. Creamer.
5. Dish, 6¼ inch.
6. Goblet.
7. Pickle dish.
8. Pitcher, water.
9. Sauce dish, flat, 4 inch.
10. Spoonholder.
11. Sugar bowl.

Color: Clear glass.

BEADED BAND

Dewdrop patterns, of one sort or another, endured longer in popular favor than any other design. To-day they are still in demand. The Beaded Band, I suspect, was made in the late Seventies, if, indeed, not later. The glass is of medium weight, brilliant and clear. The design is simple in character but pleasing. The goblet has a tapering bowl, plain round stem with simple turnings at the top and bottom and a clear base. The design shows three rows of tiny dewdrops, the center one being slightly larger. Below is a pointed ornament, stippled in the center, which alternates with a rounded one having a clear center but embellished with an oval outlined with beads or tiny dewdrops. I believe a large group of this glass was made, though I have actually seen only the pieces listed. It is said to be found more readily in Ohio, than elsewhere.

Classification
BEADED BAND

Pattern 97
(See Plate 61)

Form Number.
1. Compote, covered, on high foot, 10 inch.
2. Cordial.
3. Goblet.
4. Pickle jar.
5. Pitcher, water.
6. Sauce dish, flat.
7. Spoonholder.
8. Sugar bowl.
9. Syrup pitcher. Metal top, marked with patent date, June 29, '84.

Color: Clear glass.

TEARDROP AND TASSEL

The Teardrop and Tassel belongs to that series of designs which employed dewdrops as the chief embellishment. Variations of the dewdrop pattern seem almost numberless. This one appeals to many because of its brilliant large teardrop surrounded by leaves alternating with a tassel that forms the border of the cover and decorates the lower part of the bowl of the covered pieces. It is suggestive of Victorian times when tassels ornamented chairs, footstools and sofa cushions. It is a dainty design, a group of which may be seen on Plate 78. Some of this glass may be found in a shade of blue not quite as dark as sapphire. The water pitcher and tumblers in this color have the design in not quite as high relief, and the metal appears later than in most of the pieces one finds in clear glass. The blue looks like a ware of the Eighties, while many of the clear dishes might well date from the Seventies. I have not found many forms in this pattern but they must exist.

Classification

TEARDROP AND TASSEL

PATTERN 98

(See Plate 78)

Form Number.
1. Butter dish.
2. Compote, covered, on high foot; 6 inch diameter, 9¼ inches high.
3. Creamer.
4. Pickle dish.
5. Pitcher, water.
    a. Blue.
    b. Clear.
6. Salt and pepper shakers.
7. Sauce dish, 4 inch.
8. Tumblers, blue.

Colors: Blue; clear; opaque jade green; light clear green.

JEWEL WITH DEWDROP

While the earlier Dewdrop patterns show more careful execution, some of the later pieces are highly decorative when gathered in sets. Of the later period belongs the Jewel with Dewdrop. The design consists of one clear, rounding panel, alternating with a stippled one containing one oval and two rounded bright ornaments. These stand out in relief against the stippled background, surrounded by a single row of dewdrops. The panel is also outlined with dewdrops. The general effect is dainty, and though this glass may well date from the late Nineties, it is worthy of consideration. It was made by the United States Glass Co. of Pittsburgh, Pa., and designated by them as "Kansas" pattern. A wide range of pieces was produced, and the classification given is taken from their old trade catalogue.

PLATE 75

1. PSYCHE and CUPID sugar bowl, goblet, celery vase.
2. CLEMATIS goblet, spoonholder, sauce dish.
3. JEWEL with DEWDROP pitcher, sauce dish, cordial.
4. PANELLED DEWDROP celery vase, lemonade, goblet.

PLATE 76

1. FROSTED CIRCLE spoonholder, compote on high standard, butter dish.
2. BEADED LOOP sugar bowl, bowl (cover missing), goblet.
3. FAN with DIAMOND sugar bowl, creamer, spoonholder.
4. PLAID sugar bowl (cover missing), pickle dish, celery vase.

PLATE 77

1. BEADED OVAL and SCROLL goblet, creamer, sauce dish.
2. PANELLED FLOWER STIPPLED spoonholder, oval dish, sugar bowl.
3. SWAN creamer, oval covered dish, goblet.
4. FORGET-ME-NOT and SCROLL creamer, sugar bowl, spoonholder.

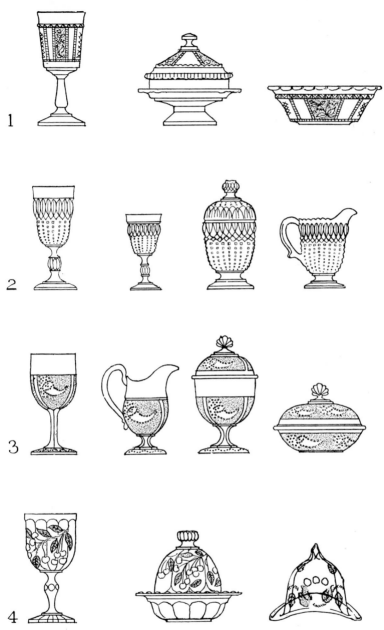

PLATE 79

1. **PANELLED FORGET-ME-NOT** goblet, butter dish, bowl (cover missing).
2. **LOOP with DEWDROPS** goblet, cordial, sugar bowl, creamer.
3. **POWDER and SHOT** goblet, creamer, sugar bowl, butter dish.
4. **PANELLED CHERRY** goblet, butter dish, rare hat made from goblet mold.

Classification

JEWEL WITH DEWDROP

PATTERN 99

(See Plate 75)

Form Number.

1. Bowls, deep. 6, 7 and 8 inch.
2. Bread plate, oval. Lettered as "Cake plate" or with "Our Daily Bread."
3. Butter dishes.
   - *a.* Flanged.
4. Cake plates on standards. 8, 9 and 10 inch.
5. Celery vase.
6. Compotes.
   - *a.* Covered, on high foot. 6, 7 and 8 inch.
   - *b.* Open, with deep bowl, on high foot. 6, 7 and 8 inch.
   - *c.* Open, shallow, on high foot. 7½, 8½ and 9½ inch.
   - *d.* Open, with deep bowl, on high foot. 6, 7 and 8 inch.
7. Cordial.
8. Creamer.
9. Cup, handled. Tall and slender.
10. Dish, oval. 8½ x 6¼. 2½ inches deep.
11. Goblet.
12. Jelly dish, with cover. Footed. 5 inch.
13. Molasses jar. (Syrup pitcher.)
14. Mug, handled.
15. Pitchers. ¼ and ½ gallon.
16. Preserve dish. 8 inch.
17. Salt and pepper.
18. Sauce dish, flat. 4 inch.
19. Spoonholder.
20. Sugar bowl.
21. Sweetmeats. Covered, footed. 5, 6 and 7 inch.
22. Toothpick holder.
23. Tumbler.

Color: Clear glass.

LOOPS WITH DEWDROPS

Belonging to the popular Dewdrop group, is this slightly later pattern called Loop with Dewdrops. Many collectors will be interested in this attractive glass, which has received the attention it deserves. It is an interesting design of interlaced loops forming a wide band at the top of each dish, the rest of the bowl showing vertical rows of small square pointed dewdrops. These seem almost to form chains hanging straight down from the loops above. The entire object is covered with the design, which is both sparkling and pretty. The glass is obviously of the later pressed glass period, or at least 1880. A group is shown on Plate 79. The goblet is particularly attractive and will combine nicely with any of the other numerous dewdrop patterns in so many of which, as collectors know, goblets that match exactly are exceedingly difficult to find. This glass was produced by the United States Glass Company of Pittsburgh during the Nineties, but it is likely that it was made still earlier and proved popular enough to justify the company in producing it for a long time. The classification is taken directly from the old trade list.

Classification

LOOPS WITH DEWDROPS

PATTERN 100

(See Plate 79)

Form Number.
1. Bowls. 5, 6, 7 and 8 inch.
2. Butter dish.
3. Cake plate on standard. 9 and 10 inch.
4. Celery vase.
5. Compotes
   a. Covered, on high foot. 5, 6, 7 and 8 inch.
   b. Open, on high foot. 5, 6, 7 and 8 inch.
6. Condiment set. Salt and pepper with plain oil bottle in glass tray, or with cruet instead of bottle.

Form Number.

7. Creamer.
8. Cup and saucer.
9. Dish, oval. 7, 8 and 9 inch.
10. Goblet.
11. Jelly dish. Footed, 4½ inch.
12. Molasses jar, tin or nickel top. (Syrup pitcher.)
13. Mug with cap.
14. Pickle jar.
15. Pickle dish.
16. Pitcher, water, ½ gallon.
17. Plate, bread.
18. Salt and pepper shakers.
19. Sauce dishes. Flat, 4 inch.
    a. Footed. 4 inch.
20. Sugar bowl.
21. Spoonholder.
22. Tumbler.
23. Wines.

Color: Clear glass.

Chapter XI

HOBNAIL GROUP

HOBNAIL (Pointed)

The Hobnail is a large and interesting group. That it was a popular pattern, widely copied, there is no doubt. So large was the number of articles produced that one could never feel sure that every known piece of this glass had been properly listed and classified. All that I shall hope to do is to name the various types and give as complete a list of forms in each as possible.

In the Pointed Hobnail, which has every indication of being the earliest in this group, there is only one well-known goblet form. It is illustrated among the pieces in this pattern on Plate 81. The photograph cannot do justice to the beauty of this glass. The goblet pictured is barrel-shaped, with plain round stem and base. On Plate 153, goblet number 8 is a true early form but unfortunately, difficult to find. It is slightly more elaborate with a knob stem. Collectors should bear in mind that the pieces just described are in a *Pointed Hobnail,* and not the later variety with blunted ends. These earlier goblets may be found in a brilliant, clear, deep amber, as well as a fine shade of blue slightly darker than the average blue found in the pressed glass of the late Seventies and Eighties. They represent the best types obtainable in this design. Nearly all forms found in clear glass may also be found in the two last-named colors.

It should be noted that to match sets in this glass one must compare either the top edge or the base. One style has heavy glass ball feet; another has a collared base imprinted with deep thumbprints; still another has deeply pointed edges to the bowls and sauce dishes. The "fan top" pieces are fairly well known, though not many collectors realize that a goblet may be had to match. This is shown on Plate 71. Still another form has little pressed ornaments in the marginal band, as may be noted on the cup in Plate 82. A complete set comprising such pieces as a butter dish, sugar bowl, creamer, celery vase, cups and saucers, etc., may be had in this last named type, which was made during the Seventies by the Columbia Glass Company of Findlay, Ohio. They also are responsible for the barrel-shaped goblet shown on Plate 81 and for the cake plate on standard shown on Plate 83. All of their other Hobnail pieces (designated "Dewdrop" by them), such as the sugar bowl, creamer, etc., have a collared base covered with the pointed knobs. The dishes with Fan Top were made by Adams & Company, while the later frosted and colored ware can practically all be attributed to Hobbs, Brocunier & Company of Wheeling, W. Va. Their output included a full line of heavy hobnails ornamenting all sorts of gas globes and light shades, barbers' bottles, "Acorn" night-lamps and numerous pieces of tableware in frosted and colored effects, many of which had the "fluted" or "ribbon" tops. A favorite color was called "Rubena Verde," which was rose-red shading to opalescent. A full line called "Frances Ware" was a frosted white with a light amber fluted band around the top edge of each dish.

Along about 1933 a leading department store in Philadelphia carried a full table setting in an opalescent hobnail, which included goblets, wines and plates. This glass was not harmful because the pieces were not reproductions of any old forms. Collectors should remember that *old* hobnail goblets, wines or plates were not made in *opalescent*. There is a variety of old opalescent hobnail described later on in this chapter, which is authentic and may be easily identified by students.

The classifications given are taken wherever possible from the old original trade catalogues.

Classification
HOBNAIL (Pointed)
Pattern 101
(See Plates 74, 80, 81, 82, 83, 88, 153)

Form Number.

1. Berry bowl.
2. Bone dish, crescent shaped. Scarce.
3. Butter dish.
4. Cake plate on standard.
5. Celery vase.
6. Compote, 8 inches high, 8 inches diameter. Hobnails on bowl and standard, with a single row around the base.
7. Cordials.
   a. Barrel shape, plain stem.
   b. Knob stem.
8. Creamer. Plain round collared base.
9. Cruets. Several sizes, from small to pint.
10. Cups and saucers.
11. Dish, oblong. 12 x 8 inches.
12. Goblet.
    a. Barrel shape, plain stem.
    b. Knob stem.
13. Inkwell, covered.
14. Mugs, handled.
15. Mustard jar.
    a. Handled. Clear round base.
    b. Metal top and handle.
16. Pen tray, oblong.
17. Pickle dish, oval.
18. Pitcher, water. Pint and quart.
19. Plates, 7 inch.
20. Platter, oblong, deep. Plain edge. 7 x 4½ inches.
21. Salt and pepper shakers. Metal tops.
22. Salt dips, individual.
23. Sauce dish. Round, flat, plain edge.
24. Spoonholder.

Form Number.

25. Sugar bowl. Plain round, collared base.
26. Tray for water pitcher and goblets. Round with low rim, 11½ inch.
27. Tumblers.
    a. Wide marginal band. (Illustrated.)
    b. Design carried nearly to top.
28. Vinegar cruets. Several sizes.

Colors: Clear glass; amber; blue. Yellow, apple green, dark green are rare.

HOBNAIL (BALL FEET)

It is safe to assume that the Pointed Hobnail pieces having the heavy clear ball feet, may be listed among the earliest articles made in this pattern. Such dishes as are found with this type of base have a scalloped or pointed top edge. A verbal description would prove to be inadequate. The reader may see this particular group illustrated on Plate 81. The forms are extremely interesting and well worth collecting. Handsome, large, sparkling bowls with a deep, sharply defined, pointed edge and plain round, clear base, combine well with the footed pieces which also have a pronounced though not as deeply pointed, edge. A bowl may be seen on Plate 83, and the sauce dish to match on Plate 80. These two dishes were mentioned previously under Hobnail (Pointed). All the plain pieces which combine with any of the variants, such as water tumblers, cordials and goblets are listed under Hobnail (Pointed).

This glass will be found to be fairly heavy in weight, brilliant and sparkling.

Classification

HOBNAIL (BALL FEET, POINTED EDGE)

PATTERN 102
(See Plate 81)

Form Number.

1. Berry bowl. Round, collared base, deep pointed edge.
2. Butter dish.

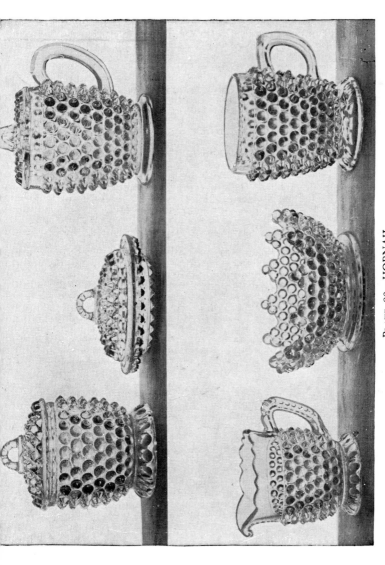

PLATE 80—HOBNAIL

Mustard jar (Thumbprint base), butter dish of child's set, mustard jar with handle
Creamer (Thumbprint base), sauce dish, mug (Thumbprint base)

PLATE 81—HOBNAIL

Creamer	Butter dish	Spoonholder (Ball feet)
Finger bowl (Thumbprint base)	Goblet	Open sugar (Ball feet)

PLATE 82—HOBNAIL

Salt and pepper shakers   Butter dish of child's set   Sherbet Cup
Sugar bowl of child's set   Tumbler   Cordial   Cup showing ornamented band

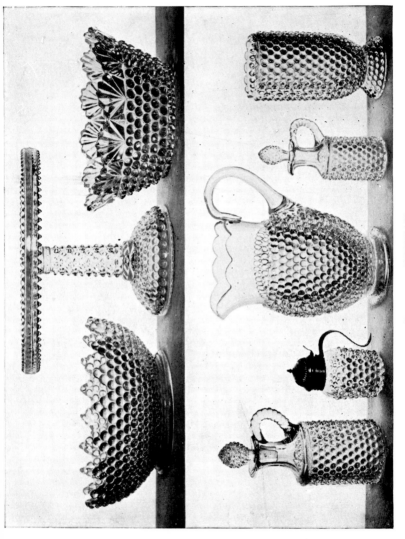

PLATE 83—HOBNAIL

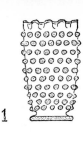

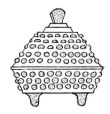

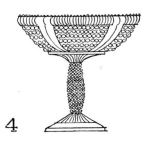
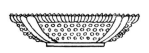

PLATE 84

1. OPAL HOBNAIL (frilled top) celery vase, creamer, tumbler.
2. OPAL HOBNAIL (three feet) celery vase, creamer, tumbler.
3. OPAL HOBNAIL (four feet) sugar bowl, creamer, butter dish.
4. PANELED HOBNAIL compote, berry bowl.

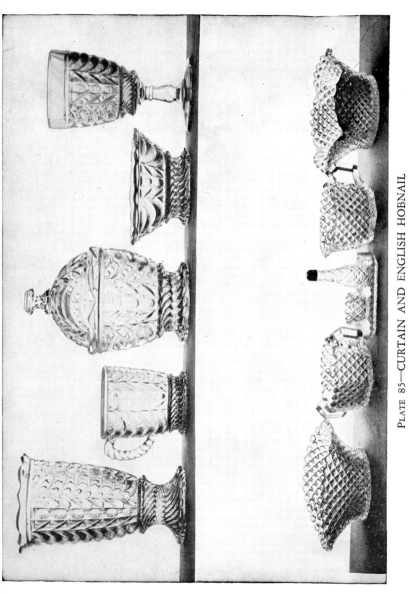

PLATE 85—CURTAIN AND ENGLISH HOBNAIL

| Curtain celery vase | Mug | Sugar bowl | Sauce dish | Goblet |

Form Number.

    3. Celery vase.

    4. Creamer.

    5. Sauce dish. Round collared base, deep pointed edge.

    6. Spoonholder.

    7. Sugar bowl.

Color: Clear glass.

HOBNAIL (Thumbprint Base)

There is little to be said about this pattern beyond the fact that it is a variant of the well-known Hobnail. Any of the pieces of Pointed Hobnail combine well with it, though it is wise to match such articles as the sugar bowl, creamer and butter dish. This particular type also comes in color, though it is most often seen in clear glass. Its chief point of difference is in the base, which is collared, with thumbprints deeply impressed in a single row. It was produced by Bryce Bros. of Pittsburgh, during the Seventies.

Classification

HOBNAIL (Thumbprint Base)

Pattern 103

(See Plates 80, 81, 82)

Form Number.

    1. Bowls. 5, 6, 7, 8, 9 and 10 inch.

    2. Butter dish. Flanged, with hobnails underneath base.

    3. Child's set on tray, consisting of butter dish, creamer, spoonholder and sugar bowl. Referred to as Toy Set.

    4. Celery vase.

    5. Creamer.

    6. Finger bowl.

    7. Individual sugar and creamer.

    8. Mustard jar.

    9. Pitcher, water.

  10. Puff box.

Form Number.
11. Salts, individual.
12. Spoonholder.
13. Sugar bowl.
14. Tray. Large, round, for water set.
Colors: Clear glass; amber; blue.

HOBNAIL (Fan Top)

Most collectors who have been at all interested in this group of glass are familiar with those pieces having the so-called "fan top." The large berry bowls and round deep sauce dishes in colors have been eagerly sought. The bowl in this style is shown in the group on Plate 83. The goblet (Plate 71) to match has slightly flatter hobnails, but is nevertheless an attractive one. Few collectors have realized it could be obtained at all, as they are comparatively scarce.

The berry bowls and sauce dishes are found in both a light amber and a deep rich shade. The blue is slightly deeper than the usual shade found belonging to this period. This pattern is most often seen in clear glass, though the colored pieces are not particularly scarce at this time. While this particular group is small, any other hobnail pieces combine nicely with it. The following classification is taken from an Adams & Company catalogue, which is undated but appears to be of the Seventies. A few additional pieces which I have seen in my travels, are added.

Classification
HOBNAIL (Fan Top)
Pattern 104
(See Plates 71, 83)

Form Number.
1. Bowls, berry.
   a. Large and deep.
   b. Sweetmeat, not footed. 6 inch.
   c. Bowls, shallow. 5, 6, 7, 8, 9 and 10 inch.

Form Number.

2. Butter dish. Flange, with hobnails under the rim.
3. Creamer.
4. Celery vase.
5. Dish, oblong. Three sizes.
6. Goblet.
7. Platter, oblong. 12 inch.
8. Salts, individual, plain edge.
9. Sauce dishes. 4½ and 5 inch.

Colors: Clear glass; light amber; dark amber; blue.

HOBNAIL (ORNAMENTED BAND)

This group is in every way similar to the Hobnail previously described, except that the marginal band at the top carries a simple pressed conventional design and all collared bases are decorated with hobnails. In nearly all of these groups it will be noted that goblets do not come to match, except in the earliest Pointed Hobnail and the variant with fan top. This particular group was made by the Columbia Glass Co. of Findlay, Ohio, which was eventually absorbed by the United States Glass Co. of Pittsburgh. The following classification is taken from an original catalogue of the Columbia Glass Co.

Classification

HOBNAIL (ORNAMENTED BAND ON SOME PIECES. THIS LISTING PRODUCED BY COLUMBIA GLASS CO., OF FINDLAY, OHIO)

PATTERN 105

(See Plate 82)

Form Number.

1. Berry bowls.
    a. Deep, with ornamented band at top. 8 inch.
    b. Deep, with plain top edge. 8 inch.
    c. Same as above, covered.
2. Butter dish.

Form Number.

3. Cake plate on standard. 10 inch. Plate 83.
4. Celery vase.
5. Compotes.
     a. Open, on high foot. Flared bowl. 9 inch.
     b. Open, on high foot. Deep bowl. 8 inch.
     c. Covered, on high foot. 8 inch.
6. Creamer.
7. Cups and Saucers.
8. Goblet. Plain marginal band. Plate 81.
9. Inkwell and cover. Square.
10. Mustard with metal top.
11. Pickle dish.
12. Pitcher, water. Round, ½ gallon. See *Water Set.*
13. Salts.
     a. Square.
     b. Salt and pepper in metal holder.
     c. Shaker salt (large, for hotel use).
14. Sauce dish. 4½ and 5 inch.
15. Spoonholder.
16. Sugar bowl.
17. Syrup jug, metal top. Originally termed molasses jug.
18. Tankard. ½ gallon, pint and cream size.
19. Toothpick holder, round.
20. Toy set. Sugar bowl, creamer, spoonholder and butter dish.
21. Water set. Large round tray, pitcher (tumblers or goblets), and ice bowl. Goblet, plate 81.
22. Wines. Plain edge.

Color: Amber; blue; clear glass.

FLATTENED HOBNAIL

Following the earlier sharp-pointed Hobnail patterns are many others with a smaller round knob. To differentiate the earlier from the later ware, or the sharp-pointed from the blunt rounded hobnails, this is called Flattened Hobnail. The goblet may be found in many forms, as this pattern was copied over a period of years, but the best known one is shown on Plate 71. This has a large rounded bowl with plain marginal band at the top and a rounded stem with clear base. Another goblet, very similar but not illustrated, has a wider marginal band at the top and a pretty knob stem. These are the two best known types in the later ware.

No doubt all the usual pieces were made in this pattern, as it was produced during the height of the highly commercialized pressed glass era or in the Eighties, but the classification includes only those articles I have found.

Classification

FLATTENED HOBNAIL

PATTERN 106

(See Plate 71)

Form Number.
1. Ale glass.
2. Berry bowl.
3. Butter dish.
4. Cake plate on standard.
5. Celery vase.
6. Creamer.
7. Cruets.
8. Goblets.
    a. Barrel shape, round stem.
    b. Knob stem, 1¼ inch marginal band.
9. Salt and pepper shakers, metal top.
10. Pitcher, water. Two styles, globular and with straight sides.
10A. Plates. 4½ inch. Squares in center, clear scalloped edge.
11. Sauce dish, round. Plain top.
12. Spoonholder.
13. Sugar bowl.
*14. Tumbler, water. Reproductions in color.
15. Wine glass.
Color: Clear glass.

PANELED HOBNAIL

To differentiate this hobnail pattern from the many others it is called Paneled Hobnail. Plates are often found in this design in two sizes, both clear and colored, so the pattern is familiar to most collectors. Other pieces than the plates are scarce and seldom seen in shops. On Plate 84 is shown a compote on high foot and a large fruit bowl, both being unusual pieces. I have never seen a goblet or tumbler that match exactly though they may exist. The goblet with plain rounded or flattened hobnails, shown on Plate 71, is the nearest match. It may be doubted if they were ever made with the four short panels, like the plates. Incidentally, the toddy plate, in the clear as well as the colored, has been a favorite of collectors for years. I refer to the 4½ inch size. It is difficult to determine when this glass was produced, but it was probably in the Seventies.

Classification

PANELED HOBNAIL

PATTERN 107

(See Plates 84, 88)

Form Number.
1. Celery vase.
2. Compote, on high foot.
3. Fruit bowl, round, flat. 8 inches diameter, 2¼ deep.
4. Plates, 4½, 7 inch.
5. Sauce dish, 4 inch.
6. Sugar bowl.

Colors: Amber; blue; clear; opaque white; yellow.

OPAL HOBNAIL

The four types of opalescent hobnail, which are also found in a yellowish tinge and a blue, will be treated together, to avoid confusion. The four kinds most often encountered, may be, first, those that are round with a "frilled" or ribbon-top edge and plain base; second, those that are round and always stand on three little feet; third, those that are square and stand on square feet; fourth, those that are octagonal in shape. Any of these will most often be seen in opalescent with considerable opal color; next in blue-opalescent and less often in yellow-opalescent. Three of these types may be seen on Plate 84, together with the two styles of tumblers most often found to match the above. The hobnails on all these pieces are fairly large and coarse, but they are most effective. They are charming combined with those dainty colored dolphin compotes and so-called "petticoat dolphin" candlesticks. These occur in opalescent, bluish green, yellow, amber and very rarely in a greenish-peacock shade. Unfortunately, good copies of the dolphin compotes have flooded department stores and gift shops. It is not difficult for an expert to differentiate the old from the new but a novice should be wary of them. The tiny dishes of hobnail on three feet are used largely for cigarettes or matches to-day, though originally designed as toothpick holders. The celery holders are readily adaptable for flowers. Of the four styles of colored hobnail, those standing on three feet seem to be the favorite at this moment. The four kinds are classified separately. All four styles were made in the 1880's.

The Hobnail pattern, being popular over a period of years and widely copied by different factories, is naturally found in a large number of variations. Immediately following the opal hobnail, a larger and still coarser hobnail was made, in plain colors as well as in combinations of colors. The one form most often employed, even though in the larger hobnail, is that type with the frilled or ribbon top. A lovely set of this in a vivid clear blue was called to my attention lately. A favorite seems to have been a frosted hobnail which is quite effective. A more startling effect was achieved in those pieces having a bright yellowish-orange band at the top, and frosted hobnail base. These pieces are highly decorative, and were produced during the Eighties by Hobbs, Brocunier & Co. of Wheeling, W. Va. They called it their "Frances Ware."

A favorite in the smaller hobnail, which is not often seen, is a rose color, with soft opalescent tinge over all. These are found most readily in tumblers and large dessert dishes, of a size often used now for finger bowls. The cranberry red hobnail was made, but apparently not in the quantity of the other colors, as it is exceedingly scarce to-day.

A great many reproductions have been produced in colored hobnail, which are treated in my book, *Antique Fakes and Reproductions*.

Classification

OPAL HOBNAIL (Round, with Frilled Top)

Pattern 108

(See Plate 84)

Form Number.
1. Bowls.
   a. Berry bowl, large and deep. Two sizes. Made round and square. 8 and 9 inch.
   b. Finger bowl.
   c. Bowl with plate. Large, with frilled edges.
2. Butter dish. Frilled flange and frilled ornament on cover.
   a. Plainer style, with ribbon edge.
3. Celery vase.
*4. Creamer.
5. Cups, sherbet. Plain marginal band.
6. Decanter.
7. Dish. Oblong, deep.
8. Finger bowl and plate. Frilled edge.
9. Pickle dishes. Long, oblong tray.
10. Pickle jar with cover.
*11. Pitcher, water. Several variants. Square-mouthed top and round top best known. See *Water tray*.
12. Sauce dishes. Two styles, round and square. 4½ inch.
13. Spoonholder.

Form Number.
  14. Sugar bowl.
  15. Syrup pitcher.
  16. Toothpick holder.
*17. Tumblers.
  18. Vase.
  19. Water bottle.
  20. Water tray. Clover shape.
Colors: Opalescent; yellow-opalescent; blue-opalescent; cranberry
  red. Same style, of later period, with coarser hobnails: Blue;
  frosted; frosted with yellow-orange banded top; blue frosted;
  plain frosted.

OPAL HOBNAIL (THREE FEET)

PATTERN 108-A

(See Plate 84)

Form Number.
  1. Bowl, large.
  2. Celery vase.
  3. Creamer.
  4. Cups, sherbet.
  5. Pitcher, water.
  6. Sugar bowl.
  7. Toothpick holder.
  8. Tumbler (not footed).
Colors: Opalescent; yellow-opalescent; blue-opalescent; blue; amber. Ruby red and ruby-opalescent very scarce.

OPAL HOBNAIL (SQUARE)

PATTERN 108-B

(See Plate 84)

Form Number.
  1. Butter dish.
  2. Celery vase.

Form Number.

3. Creamer.
4. Dessert dishes, large.
5. Spoon holder.
6. Sugar bowl.

Colors: Opalescent; blue-opalescent; yellow-opalescent.

OPAL HOBNAIL (Octagon)

Pattern 108-C

Form Number.

1. Butter dish.
2. Celery vase.
3. Creamer.
4. Cups, sherbet.
5. Spoonholder.
6. Sugar bowl.

Colors: Opalescent; blue-opalescent; yellow-opalescent.

PRINTED HOBNAIL

The various Hobnail patterns enjoyed a wide popularity for many years. During that time an interesting pattern was produced which I have never heard called by any name except Strawberry. It is not difficult to look at this glass and imagine how it came to be called by this name, as the surface of the flat hobnails is suggestive of the pitted surface of a strawberry. Since an older pattern has been known for some years as Strawberry, it will prevent future confusion to christen this glass by another name now, while it is still neither well known nor widely collected.

A large number of forms were made in this interesting pattern and it may be found in several colors. It might be your good fortune to find a set of it in amethyst for it was made in that lovely color. It appears to be a product of the Eighties.

Classification

PRINTED HOBNAIL

PATTERN 109

(See Plate 72)

Form Number.

1. Bowls.
2. Butter dish.
3. Celery vase.
4. Creamer.
5. Goblets.
6. Mugs, handled.
7. Pitcher, water.
8. Sauce dish, 4 inch.
9. Spoonholder.
10. Sugar bowl.
11. Tray, for water set.
12. Tumblers.
13. Wines.

Colors: Amethyst; blue; yellow; amber; clear glass.

ENGLISH HOBNAIL

Following the pointed Hobnail glass is another pattern of the same series which has come to be known as English Hobnail. It is an all-over pressed design similar to that seen on some of the early Sandwich glass salts, which in late years is referred to as "Waffle." This is not the same Waffle pattern described in this book, but a design of truncated pyramids with a cross impressed on the apex. It was made during the Seventies and it is still being made to-day, though in many modern forms not used originally. It has been a favorite selling pattern for many years of the Westmoreland Glass Co. of Grapeville, Pa. They call it their "Diamond" pattern. A student of glass may distinguish the early from the later ware, but the novice has need to be wary. The earliest plate was flat, while the later copy is deeper in the center. The plates of either period are sparkling and effective. I have never

seen a tumbler or goblet that matches exactly. There is an unusually attractive goblet shown on Plate 86, which is a combination of broad panels of English Hobnail with a clear, narrow
convex panel that collectors of English Hobnail use in forming
sets.

It will be noted in the group shown on Plate 85 that most of
the forms appear to conform to a more modern vogue than the
old designers would have been influenced by at the time the plate,
for example, was first made. I have never seen English Hobnail
in any but clear glass with the exception of a few plates in amber.

Classification

ENGLISH HOBNAIL

Pattern 110

(See Plates 85, 86)

Form Number.

1. Bowl, 6½ inch. Bowls of this average size are found in
   various shapes.
     a. Hexagonal.
     b. Round.
     c. Round with two sides bent up.
2. Creamer.
3. Dish, round, with handles, 5¼ inches.
4. Pickle dish, oblong.
5. Plate, 8 inch.
     a. Same, deeper in center.
6. Salt and pepper shakers, with metal tops.
6a. Sugar bowl, open.
7. Tray. Small oblong, to hold salt and pepper.
Colors: Clear glass; amber.

ENGLISH HOBNAIL AND THUMBPRINT

There is one late pattern which is not well known to-day, though
quite recently a demand has sprung up for it. As no one has known
by what name to call it, it has caused no end of confusion for both
dealers and collectors. It has been decided to christen it English

PLATE 86—GOBLETS

Paneled Diamond Point
Forget-Me-Not in Scroll

English Hobnail, Paneled
Rose Sprig

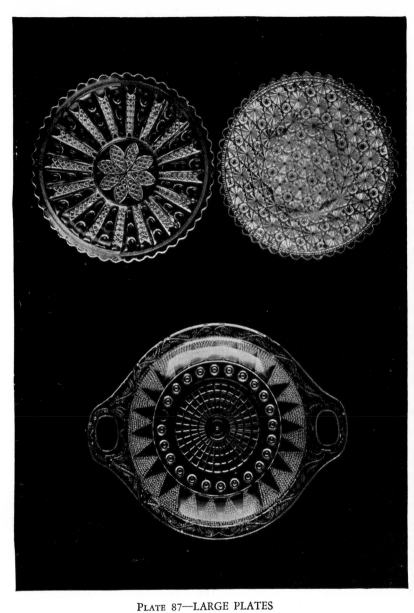

PLATE 87—LARGE PLATES

English Hobnail and Thumbprint   Daisy and Button
          Dewdrop in Points, vine border

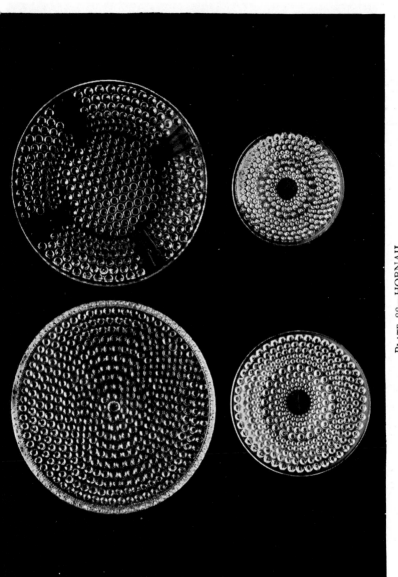

PLATE 88—HOBNAIL

Tray for water set   Plate in Paneled Hobnail

Saucers for cups, illustrated on Plate 82

Hobnail and Thumbprint. English Hobnail is described on another page and one will find that the panel in English Hobnail and Thumbprint corresponds with the design covered in the English Hobnail pages.

The plates in English Hobnail and Thumbprint are particularly admired. They are found in two sizes. The design consists of panels which taper toward the center, one having a band of the fine English Hobnail and the other three thumbprints, graduating in size. In the center is a large rosette, filled with the English Hobnail. There is a band of cable cord near the edge and the rim is scalloped. Though a late ware, this glass is exceedingly brilliant, and it sparkles under artificial light. Not many forms have come to my attention but I am listing it here as a means of identification. One of the plates may be seen on Plate 87 and the group is shown on Plate 14. Now that it is possible to identify it, doubtless other forms will be found, such as goblets, sugar bowl, etc. The classification only lists the few pieces I have actually seen.

Classification

ENGLISH HOBNAIL AND THUMBPRINT

PATTERN 111

(See Plates 14, 87)

Form Number.
1. Bowls.
   a. Large, with two sides bent upward.
   b. Size of deep finger bowl.
2. Celery vase.
3. Plates, 8 and 10½ inches.
4. Sauce dish, 4½ inch.
Color: Clear glass.

ENGLISH HOBNAIL, PANELED

One of the most attractive patterns in this series is that known to-day as the English Hobnail, Paneled. It was made during the

Eighties by the old firm of Bryce Bros. of Pittsburgh, Pa. Evidently a great amount of it was not produced, as it is quite scarce to-day. One seldom finds any of the pieces aside from the goblets, one of which is shown on Plate 86. The original trade name used by Bryce Bros. for this glass was simply "No. 100 Pattern." The following classification is taken from their illustrated catalogue.

Classification

ENGLISH HOBNAIL, PANELED

PATTERN 111A

(See Plate 86)

Form Number.

1. Bowls.
   a. Large, oval. 9 inch.
   b. Smaller. 5 inch.
2. Butter dish.
3. Creamer.
4. Goblet.
5. Pitcher, water.
6. Sauce dish. 4 inch.
7. Spoonholder.
8. Sugar bowl.

Color: Clear glass.

Chapter XII

FROSTED AND CLEAR GROUP

WESTWARD-HO

The title given to this extraordinarily popular pattern is aptly chosen. "Westward the course of empire takes its way" and our grandfathers well knew it. In this frosted design in relief, depicting the log cabin of the pioneer, the bison charging wildly across the plain, the deer fleeing from an unseen hunter, surmounted on all the covered pieces by a knob in the shape of a crouching Indian (see Plates 89, 90), we find a patriotic reminder of the state of our country west of the Mississippi before the transcontinental railroads were built. It is the distinctly American appeal of this glass that has made it so widely and eagerly sought by our most discriminating collectors. The goblets, wines and cordials are particularly scarce, as collectors have discovered when they endeavored to complete sets. Compotes on standards are found both oval in shape, and round. Westward-Ho has also been called "Tippecanoe" and "Pioneer," the latter, as a matter of fact, being the manufacturer's designation, but the vast majority of collectors know it by its more picturesque name. Stories abound regarding the popular ware, but have no basis in fact. That it is one hundred years old is a myth, pure and simple. Any student of glass would recognize it by quality and forms as a product of the late Seventies, even if we did not have the testimony of a son of the manufacturer.

It is of the greatest interest to collectors to know at last, definitely and authoritatively, when and where this glass was made. It was designed by a German mold maker named Jacobus for Gillinder & Sons, of Philadelphia, who produced it exclusively at their factory in Philadelphia shortly after the Centennial in 1876. It was originally named "Pioneer" by them, and the story is that the design was suggested by Western scenes in Currier & Ives prints. The room in which the frosted or satin finish was applied by the use of acid, was called in the factory their Pioneer Room. Mr. James Gillinder, a member of the original firm bearing that name, now engaged in the manufacture of glass in Port Jervis, N. Y., is authority for settling once for all the question as to where, when and by whom Westward-Ho was produced. In my possession is a sworn statement, duly notarized, as to the origin, name and producer of Westward-Ho.

This is the first series in which we find a noticeably different change of forms. It is more sophisticated. The footed sauce dish appears for the first time, the platter also being an innovation. The marmalade jar is another addition, though it was intended for India relish or small pickles originally.

Classification

WESTWARD-HO

Pattern 112

(See Plates 89, 91, 92)

Form Number.

1. Butter dish, covered, on standard.
2. Celery vase.
3. Compotes, round, covered, 5 inch and large sizes.
   - *a.* On high standard. Several sizes, including 5 inch. Rare.
   - *b.* On low standard. Several sizes, including 5 inch. Rare.
   - *c.* Oval, in various sizes.
4. Cordials.
5. Creamer.
*6. Goblets.
7. Marmalade jar.
8. Mug. Odd piece, not of the early period of this ware.
9. Pickle dish.
10. Pitcher, water; two sizes.
11. Platters, oval.
12. Sauce dishes, footed, 3 sizes, 3½, 4, 4½ inches.

Form Number.
13. Spoonholder.
14. Sugar bowl.
15. Wines.
Color: Clear with frosted scene. Blue goblets were never made
originally. These are recent reproductions.

LION

The Lion is another of the partly clear and partly frosted patterns, the principal difference being a wide frosted collared base
on many of the footed pieces. It was so plentiful when this book
was first written that it has been well known and collected for some
years. The covered compotes were so common that they could be
purchased for less than was asked for the same sort of piece in
other patterns. This does not hold true today. The goblets have
now become scarce, and sell for considerably more than the average. Unfortunately, a number of items in this pattern have been
reproduced, though it is easy to detect the frauds if one will take
time to study. Fakes have been made in all lines of antiques, and
the popular pattern glass is no exception. The copies are thor-
oughly treated in my book devoted to reproductions.

The Lion forms follow closely those of Westward-Ho. The
sauce dish on a standard or collared base came into general use
at this period, as well as the oval platter. The large round bread
plates, another innovation at this time, have found their place on
modern tables as service plates. The platter and bread plate are
illustrated on Plate 92. The tumbler seems to have disappeared.
It has been replaced by goblets exclusively for the time being,
though a Lion tumbler, partly frosted, was made apparently at a
later period. It does not seem to belong properly to the original,
earlier pattern. Of all the Lion forms the cologne bottles and
powder jar are the rarest.

There are several variants to be found in the Lion pattern,
mostly in the covered pieces. The goblets, sauce dishes and bread
plates will match, but the difference is generally in the knob of

the covers. These are shown in the line drawings on Plate 93. One knob is a large frosted crouched lion; another is the same lion but smaller; the third is a very large rampant lion with front paws on a log; the fourth consists of only the frosted head of the lion while the fifth appears in a much later adaptation of this design, and is a small unfrosted lion. Usually the bowls of the goblets, sauce dishes and compotes are clear, but I have seen a few sets in which the bowls were etched. The covered dishes are usually round but they also come in an oblong shape, the round being the more abundant.

This is a distinctive pattern and a complete set may be formed, though the old goblets, egg cups and wines are quite rare now. The platters and pickle dishes are also uncommon. The only plates are the ten-inch round bread plates.

The one record I have of the Lion pattern is an illustration of the bread plate in an 1888 catalogue of the Richards & Hartley Glass Company of Tarentum, Pa. The fact that the plate is shown at this late date would indicate that it continued to be in demand years after the manufacture of the other pieces of tableware was discontinued. No record has been found that will tell where the different variants of this pattern were made. According to Mr. James Gillinder, a grandson of William Gillinder, who founded Gillinder & Sons, their firm produced a full line of the earliest forms. Mr. Gillinder owns pieces which came from the old factory. In fact, the Gillinders were responsible for three of our most popular patterns of the 1870's—Westward-Ho, Lion and Classic, all of which were designed by a man in their employ named Jacobus.

A very late Lion pattern, probably forty-five years old, consists of clear lion heads on the glass, in low relief. At this period a covered salt was made, which was all of clear glass.

The covered sugar bowl at the end of line 2, on Plate 93, may be found with either a clear base or a frosted finish. The preponderance of them were frosted, so the clear base is unusual.

Classification

LION

PATTERN 113
(See Plates 90, 91, 92, 93)

Form Number.

*1. Butter dish, round, covered.

*2. Celery vase.

3. Champagne.

4. Cheese dish. Round plate with cable edge, center frosted and decorated with large figure of lion standing on limb of tree. 8¾ inch diameter. Cover is clear with round frosted circle on top, and knob in form of large frosted rampant lion. Rare.

5. Cologne bottles. Rare.

6. Compotes, round.
   a. Covered, on high standard.
   b. Covered, on low standard.
   c. Covered, on standard, 5 inch.

7. Cordials. 4¼ inch.

8. Creamer.

9. Dish, oblong, covered, on collared base. Various sizes, including one extra small, 7 x 4 inches. Medium-sized oval covered dish reproduced.

*10. Egg cups.

*11. Goblets. Bowl usually clear, but sometimes etched.

12. Lamp. Burner dated 1888.

13. Marmalade jar.

14. Miniature set consisting of creamer, spoonholder, butter dish, sugar bowl and cup and saucers. These found in all frosted; in all clear glass and a few pieces in amber. Undoubtedly a Philadelphia Centennial novelty, 1876.

15. Pickle dish.

16. Pitchers.
   a. Syrup, with metal top.
   b. Water. Two sizes. Smaller is rare. Sometimes termed "milk pitcher."

PLATE 89

1. WESTWARD-HO compote. sugar bowl, creamer, marmalade jar.
2. WESTWARD-HO butter dish, celery vase, footed sauce dish.
3. THREE-FACE compote, salt shaker, sugar bowl, butter dish.
4. BABY-FACE sugar bowl, spoonholder, goblet.

PLATE 90

Lion lamp, clear glass with frosted heads. It is 7¾ inches high to the top of the collar and 5 inches across the widest part of the bowl.

PLATE 91—GOBLETS

Lion
Polar Bear

Three-Face
Westward-Ho

PLATE 92—PLATES AND PLATTERS

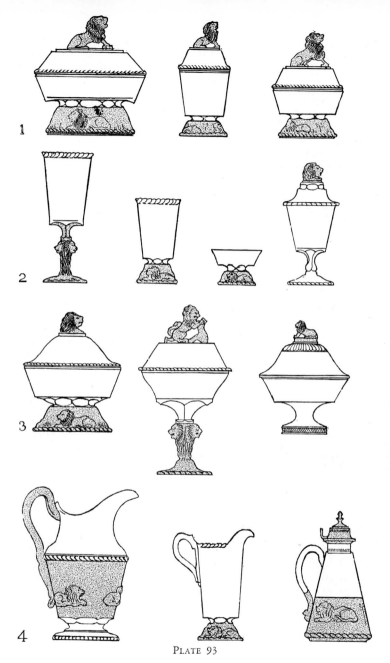

PLATE 93

1. LION oblong covered dish, sugar bowl, butter dish.
2. LION celery vase, spoonholder, footed sauce, sugar bowl.
3. LION covered dish, compote on high standard, compote on low foot.
4. LION water pitcher, creamer, syrup pitcher.

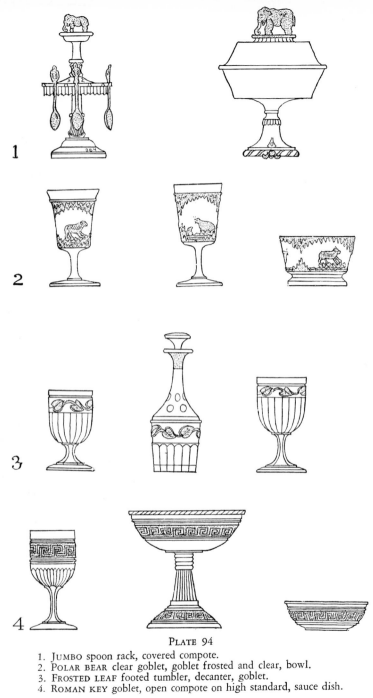

PLATE 94

1. JUMBO spoon rack, covered compote.
2. POLAR BEAR clear goblet, goblet frosted and clear, bowl.
3. FROSTED LEAF footed tumbler, decanter, goblet.
4. ROMAN KEY goblet, open compote on high standard, sauce dish.

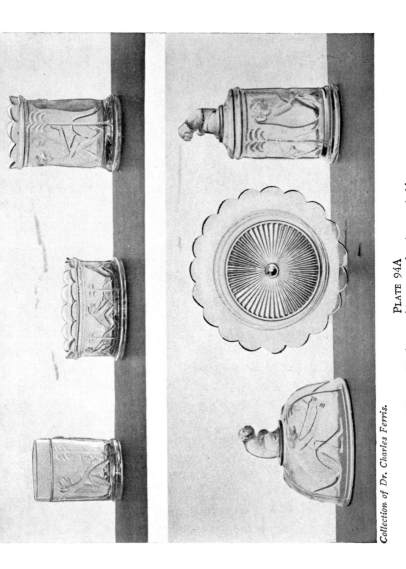

Collection of Dr. Charles Ferris.

PLATE 94A

Upper: Monkey tumbler, waste bowl, spoonholder.
Lower: Butter dish, showing rayed base; pickle jar.

Form Number.

*17. Plates, bread; often referred to as cake plates. Inscribed, "Give us this day our daily bread." Rare in blue, amber or yellow.

18. Platter, oval.

19. Powder jar. Rare.

*20. Salt, oval on collared base; extremely scarce.

21. Sauce dish, footed, two sizes. 4 inch.

*22. Spoonholder.

*23. Sugar bowl, covered, round.

24. Tumbler. Frosted band 1¼ inches high, with round base, containing four lion heads in relief and two raised circles between the heads. Top clear glass, flaring. 3¾ inch.

25. Wine glass.

Color: Clear and partly frosted. Colored round bread plates are rare. Rarest pieces in this design are the cologne bottles and powder jar.

THREE-FACE

From the beginning of the interest in American pressed glass there has been much speculation as to the date, origin and meaning of the trio of countenances in the pattern known as Three Face. Many legends, all apocryphal, circulated for years. For example, there was the tale of a beautiful member of a well-known Philadelphia family who ordered a portrait from a distinguished artist but was told that her extraordinary beauty could be captured only by three likenesses—full face, profile, and fifty-fifty. Getting three commissions instead of one was not only high art but high finance.

Classical students called the ware the Three Graces. However, Aglaia has exactly the same face as Euphrosyne, and Thalia is an exact counterpart of her sisters. None of the three looks like either father or mother. Other stories circulated. Many well meaning souls contended that Three Face was a Sandwich product, though without any corroborative evidence other than the desire to call everything in pressed glass Sandwich. No collector knew even approximately the date when this pattern was made, or where it was made.

It is, therefore, gratifying to have found, in an old trunk, a catalogue issued by George Duncan & Sons of Pittsburgh, Pa., in which several pages are devoted to Three Face, known simply to the trade in those days as Pattern No. 400. It is to be doubted that Three Face was made at any other factory, for no variants of any of its forms have been found. When a factory copied a pattern that had been originated by a rival concern and had proved popular enough to be plagiarized profitably, slight differences or variations were introduced, probably because they were considered a safeguard against accusations of infringement. In the case of Three Face, no variations have been found to indicate that more than one master model was used for any of the different items, all of which are known to have been made by George Duncan & Sons. It is reasonable to assume that no other glass house produced Three Face.

Collectors always wish to know when and by whom a particular pattern was made, as well as to have a full list of its various items, in order to know when the series is complete. It is also desirable to know the original trade name, though we are all agreed that only confusion would ensue were collectors to substitute long-forgotten pattern names for familiar descriptive titles now in use.

For most pattern glass it is obviously impossible to establish the date of manufacture, the reason being that, as a rule, the old catalogues are not only scarce but undated. Nobody deemed trade lists worthy of preservation for the benefit of collectors yet unborn. Moreover, the memory of glassworkers and salesmen is untrustworthy. It is too much to ask the average man to recall exactly the first making of an article, which may have been one of dozens that he sold year after year four or five decades ago. The only way to judge the age of glass is by ascertaining its period, which, in turn, is determined by the character of the pattern and the number and variety of articles made in the particular design. The changes in fashion between 1870 and 1885 afford the most reliable guide to the age of certain forms. It was between these years that many of the combined frosted and clear effects were produced, as, for example, Three Face, Lion, Westward-Ho, Polar Bear, and so on. For years Eastern collectors have credited many of these to Sandwich; but we now know that they were made in the Pittsburgh district. Incidentally, "camphor glass," used to designate a frosted finish, was a term unknown to the old glass makers, who always referred to it as "satin finish," or "frosted."

The trade name of Three Face in the Duncan catalogue is Pattern No. 400; but among the Duncan workmen it was known as the Three Sisters. One old glass blower assured me that he recalled making it at the Duncan factory in 1872. Though he was well along in years, his memory was apparently as reliable as human memory ever is. It should be borne in mind that much pressed glass was made in 1874 and 1875 in expectation of an active demand from the souvenir-loving public that was planning to attend the Philadelphia Centennial Exposition in 1876. Many novelties were manufactured then, some at Sandwich, some at the old Pittsburgh glass houses.

After *Early American Pressed Glass* was revised in 1933, a woman wrote to me from Washington, Pa., whose mother, still living at the time, was the model used for the Three Face pattern by her father, John E. Miller, who was designer for the Duncans. She sent me a profile view of her mother, then ninety-two years of age, so that I could see the likeness, which was still apparent. Her father was associated with the glass business for seventy-six years and died in 1931 at the age of ninety-one. She sent me numerous newspaper clippings to bear out her stories, so I presented this information at a lecture in Boston, Mass., in 1935.

The following classification covers the pieces of Three Face listed in the Duncan catalogue. I have seen all of them. Nearly all the forms come both etched or frosted and clear, being etched more frequently than happens with the Lion pattern. There are two types of salts, the small individual which is frosted and open and the other the shaker type with metal top. It is the first metal top shaker in the pressed glass patterns and as such came in pairs, pepper as well as salt. These I have also seen in clear glass, which is in no way so attractive as the frosted.

Classification
THREE-FACE

PATTERN 114

(See Plates 89, 91)

Form Number.

1. Biscuit jar, covered. 9 inches high, 5 inches diameter. Rare.
2. Butter dish, covered, on standard. 6 inch.
3. Cake plates, on standard. 8, 9, 10 and 11 inch.
4. Celery vase.
    a. Plain edge at the top.
    b. Scalloped edge at the top.
*5. Champagnes.
    *a. Saucer bowl.
    *b. Deep bowl.
    *c. Hollow stem.
6. Clarets.
7. Compotes.
    a. Open compotes, on high standard (foot and base all frosted). Rounded bowls with beaded edge. 7, 8, 9 and 10 inch.
    b. Open compotes, on high standard (foot and base all frosted). Bowls not rounded and rim plain. 7, 8 9 and 10 inch.
    c. Covered compotes, on high standard (foot and base all frosted). Rounded bowl with beaded edge where cover joins. 7, 8, 9 and 10 inch.
    d. Covered compotes, on high standard (foot and base all frosted). Bowls not rounded. 7, 8, 9 and 10 inch.
8. Creamer. Two styles, one having medallion face underneath the lip.
*9. Goblets.
10. Lamps.
    a. Clear, round bowls. Three sizes.
    b. Ornamented bowl. Three sizes.
    c. Rare lamp in amethyst, with plain bowl.
11. Pickle jar. Sold with set but does not match. Frosted, bird knob to cover.
12. Pitcher, water, ½ gallon. Rare.
13. Salts.
    a. Salt dips, or celery dips, all frosted.
    b. Salt and pepper shakers with metal top.

Form Number.

*14. Sauce dish, footed. 4, 4½ inch.

15. Spoonholder.

16. Sugar bowl.

17. Wines.

Color: Clear, partly frosted. A lamp exists in deep amethyst. **Very** rare.

BABY-FACE

This pattern is so little known that not many pieces have come to light, though doubtless it was made in all the usual forms. The stem of the standard pieces is formed of three chubby baby faces which are frosted, as is also the base. The knob of the covers is also frosted and also shows the three baby faces. The rest of the glass is perfectly clear. The rim of the lower part of the covered pieces is scalloped and flares out.

This pattern was probably not made in the quantities of the more popular ones of this series. It is seldom seen and at this time collectors rarely ever ask for it. To date no record has been found to tell us where it was made.

Classification

BABY-FACE

Pattern 115

(See Plate 89)

Form Number.

1. Butter dish.

2. Celery dips.

3. Compotes.
   a. Covered, small.
   b. Open, large.
   c. Covered, on high foot.

4. Cordials.

5. Creamer.

6. Goblets.

7. Pitcher, water.

Form Number.
   8. Spoonholder.
   9. Sugar bowl.
Color: Clear, partly frosted.

POLAR BEAR

One of the most fascinating patterns of all is the one popularly called "Polar Bear." In certain sections of the country it has been known by other names, such as "Iceberg," "Arctic" and "North Pole." Any one of these descriptive titles might serve as well, though the bear is an outstanding feature. The glass is mostly clear, though frosted enough to give the desired effect. The lower part of the bowl of the goblet is frosted, and the upper part too, leaving three clear panels. In one panel is a seal (frosted), resting on a large block of ice in the water; in another panel is a seal in a similar position, while a small one has its head just out of the water; the third panel has the large polar bear standing on the ice. The top part of the goblet is made to simulate icicles hanging down, the upper part being frosted and the tips very cleverly left clear, giving a most realistic appearance. The stem of the goblet is plain, clear and round, as is also the base. This glass is scarce, though not very much in demand at present. Prices are almost equal that of the ever popular "Westward-Ho." It is certainly interesting and unusual.

The large round water tray belonging to this set has a ship in the center bearing a flag, with "C. G. Co." on it. An old glass blower, whose whole life was spent working with glass companies in and about Pittsburgh, told me that this pattern was made by the Crystal Glass Company of Bridgeport, Ohio. The lettering would bear out his statement. This company was out of business by 1892, according to an old directory in my possession. I have no records of their patterns, so I can neither tell the original trade name nor give a complete classification beyond such items as I have seen.

The glass is also found perfectly clear, without any frosted effect. The clear goblets flare more at the top.

Classification
POLAR BEAR

PATTERN 116

(See Plates 91, 94)

Form Number.

1. Bowl, round; ice bowl, formerly used with water sets.
2. Creamer.
3. Goblets.
4. Pickle dish.
5. Pitcher, water.
6. Tray, large, round. Used for water sets.
    a. Oval water tray.
7. Sauce dish.
8. Spoonholder.
9. Sugar bowl.

Color: Clear glass; clear, partly frosted.

ROMAN KEY

The Roman Key belongs to that early series described under the Ribbon glass, which carries a design having a frosted surface resembling ground glass. The goblet is of clear glass, adorned by a fairly wide band, or fret, displaying the Roman Key in relief, between two rather heavy horizontal ribs. The lower part of the bowl is decorated with a plain vertical ribbing, similar to that seen in the coarse Bellflower but not so heavy as in the Prism. The stem is hexagonal and the base clear. The glass has a clear bell tone and was probably produced soon after the Civil War. A variant, of which I have seen a few pieces, has a clear key, instead of frosted. The forms follow those of that period, all the pieces being footed. Fragments of both the frosted and the clear Roman Key have been unearthed at Sandwich, in sufficient quantity to feel certain the pattern was made there. It may have been produced elsewhere, though there is no known proof to sustain such a claim at present.

It is interesting to know that this same pattern was made in England, in a slightly more elaborate form. The English style is shown by the celery vase on Plate 95, where it may be noted that the background is frosted, the key in clear relief and the base more ornate. The one pictured was not marked but I found the exact duplicate in one double the size of the usual celery holder, stamped on the inside near the base of the bowl, with the diamond-shaped English registry mark with crown, in heavy relief. The same mark was found on the inside of goblet number 18 on Plate 164. It is so unusual to find these marked pieces that I show them in order that collectors and dealers may see how easily we can mistake for American certain English pressed glass made at the same period as our own.

The Roman Key is not particularly plentiful, though many more pieces may come to light when the demand becomes more urgent.

Classification

ROMAN KEY

PATTERN 117

(See Plates 94, 95)

Form Number.

1. Berry bowl. Cable edge. 9½ inches diameter.
2. Butter dish, flat.
3. Castor set. Bottle, shaker and mustard jar.
4. Celery vase.
5. Compotes, open:
   Low with short 6-sided concave stem. Rayed foot.

   a. 7 inches diameter, 5¾ high.
   b. 7½ inches diameter, 5¼ high.
   c. 8 inches diameter, 4¾ high.

   Medium with 9-sided stem. Clear. Roman key on foot. Cable rim.

   d. 8 inches diameter, 6⅛ inches high. 10 pointed star center.

   Tall with reeded stem. Clear. Roman key on foot. Cable rim.

   e. 10⅛ inches diameter, 9⅛ high. Flared at top.
   f. 9¼ inches diameter, 8 high.
   g. 8⅛ inches diameter, 6¼ to 6½ high. 24 rays at center.
6. Creamer, footed, applied handle.

Form Number.

    7. Decanter, pint. Matching stopper. Some with 30 rays, others with 36.

        a. Quart size. Matching stopper. 36 rays.

    8. Egg cup.

    9. Goblet. Heights vary.

  10. Pitcher, water. Flat base.

        a. Milk pitcher, 7 inches at lip.

  11. Plates. Rare.

  12. Relish dish, oval. 6¼ x 9¼ inches. Cable edge.

  13. Salt, footed. Barrel-shaped, straight sided and slightly flaring bowl.

  14. Sauce dish. Styles and sizes vary slightly.

  15. Spoonholder.

  16. Sugar bowl. Two styles. Hexagonal or octagonal stems.

  17. Tumbler, footed.

        a. Tumbler, water.

  18. Wines. Two styles, one with 36 rays; other with 42 rays.

Colors: Clear glass, partly frosted; all clear glass. A later Roman key appears in lime glass with clear key. It is still quite early and may be found in a number of forms.

FROSTED CIRCLE

This attractive design of clear glass and frosted circles seems to be little known. The quality and weight of the pieces vary greatly, some appearing to be fairly early while others are obviously of a later period. This pattern also may be found all clear, the circles being entirely clear instead of frosted. It is attractive in either style though rather more effective with the frosted medallions. The glass in such pieces as the butter dish, sugar bowl or cake plate is very heavy, while other pieces are noticeably lighter in weight, probably because they were made either at different factories or at different periods. The pieces that are all clear have a plainly later appearance.

The Frosted Circle is a striking pattern consisting of large round circles with a star-shaped ornament impressed in the center of each, alternating with a large conventionalized fan-shaped ornament. The goblet is attractive, with a plain round stem and base. This glass was produced originally by the Nickel Plate Glass Co. of Fostoria, Ohio, which was later absorbed by the United States Glass Co. of Pittsburgh, Pa. Having been made by two different factories explains the variations. It probably dates from the late Seventies. The classification is taken from an original catalogue of the United States Glass Co.

Classification

FROSTED CIRCLE

PATTERN 118

(See Plates 76, 96, 131)

Form Number.

1. Bowl, berry.
   - *a.* Flat, covered. 6, 7 and 8 inch.
   - *b.* Open. 8 and 9 inch.
   - *c.* Open. 5, 6 and 8 inch.
2. Butter dish.
   - *a.* Open.
   - *b.* Covered. 5 inch.
3. Cake plate, on standard. 9 and 10 inch.
4. Celery vase.
5. Champagne.
6. Claret.
7. Compotes.
   - *a.* Covered, on high foot. 5, 6, 7 and 8 inch.
   - *b.* Open, on high foot. 5, 6, 7 and 8 inch.
8. Creamer.
9. Cruet.
10. Cup and saucer.
*11. Goblet.
12. Honey dish. 3½ inch.
13. Pickle jar.
14. Pitcher, water. See *Tankard*.
15. Plates. Round. 7 and 9 inch.
16. Salt and pepper.
17. Sauce dishes. Flat, 4 inch.
18. Spoonholder.
19. Sugar bowl.

Form Number.

20. Syrup pitcher.
21. Tankard. ½ gallon.
22. Tumbler.
    a. Champagne.
    b. Water.
23. Wine.

Color: All clear; clear with circles frosted.

CLASSIC

Another partly frosted and partly clear glass pattern that is now widely known, is the Classic. It is ornate and suggestive of mid-Victorian taste. Every other panel is frosted and contains a classical figure in relief. The alternating panels have an all-over pressed design that is quite attractive. Acorns and oak leaves also figure in the decorative scheme in an effective way. The large sauce dish may be found either on stippled feet like many of the larger standard dishes, or on a collared base which is covered with dense clusters of the acorns and leaves. An unusual feature is the stippled feet of such pieces as the covered sugar, creamer, etc. These are meant to simulate small logs, or limbs of trees.

Mr. James Gillinder, a direct descendant of the founder of Gillinder & Sons, of Philadelphia and Greensburg, Pa., told me that Classic was designed by their Mr. Jacobus, who was also responsible for Westward-Ho and Lion. Mr. Jacobus was a capable man, well-known in the trade during his day. The statement by Mr. Gillinder is borne out by the fact that the name "Jacobus" appears on one piece of Classic glass. There are two large round plates, one of which may be found containing the bust of Cleveland and the other showing a warrior on a horse. In the latter there is a stone at one edge of the scene and close inspection will reveal the name "Jacobus" in rather small lettering under it. This would seem to prove beyond all doubt that Mr. Jacobus designed this interesting glass, for Gillinder & Sons of Philadelphia. It is a ware of the 1870's.

Mr. Gillinder also informed me that the pieces with the stippled feet were so susceptible to breakage that they were soon abandoned

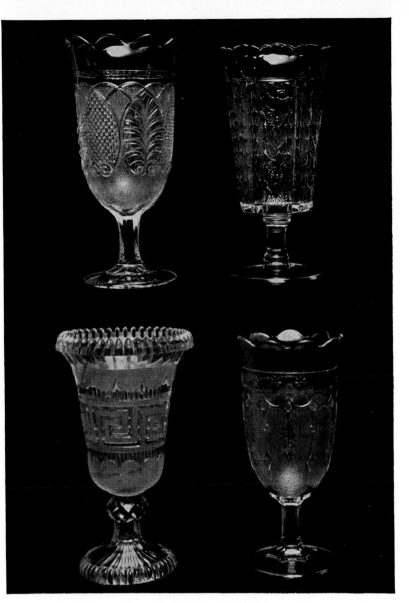

PLATE 95—CELERY VASES

Palmette
Roman Key (English type)

Paneled Daisy
Leaf and Dart

PLATE 96—GOBLETS

Three Panel
Teasel

Frosted Circle
Prism with Diamond Points

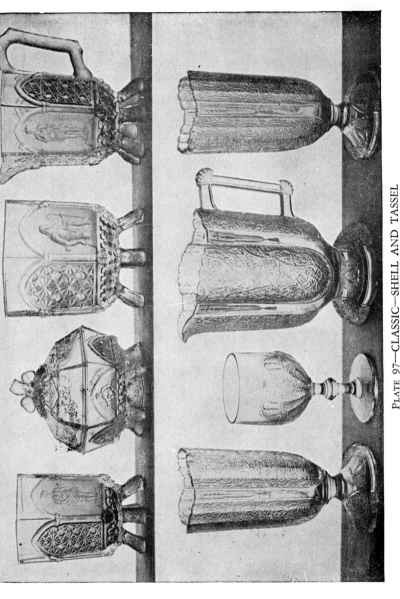

PLATE 97—CLASSIC—SHELL AND TASSEL

Classic spoonholder   Butter dish   Sugar bowl (cover missing)   Creamer
Shell and Tassel pair of celery vases   Goblet   Water pitcher

PLATE 98—GOBLETS

Garfield Drape
Star Rosetted

Cardinal Bird
Classic

PLATE 99—COVERED DISHES

Pair of compotes with frosted eagle knobs
Compote with knob in form of large dog, frosted

Pair of oval dishes with knobs in form of pheasants, frosted
Frosted Stork sugar bowl

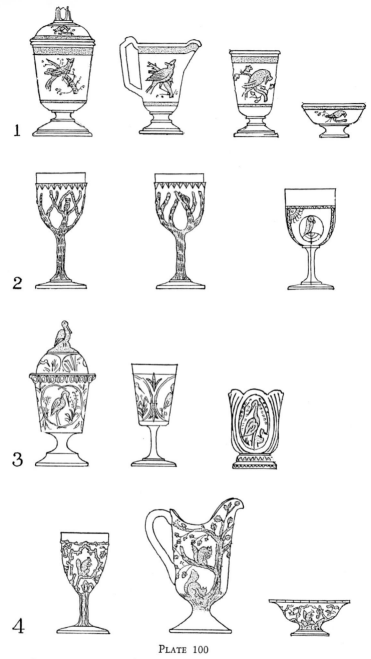

PLATE 100

1. CARDINAL BIRD sugar bowl, creamer, spoonholder, footed sauce dish.
2. OWL and POSSUM goblet, showing both sides of bowl, PARROT goblet.
3. FROSTED STORK sugar bowl, goblet, spoonholder.
4. SQUIRREL goblet, water pitcher, footed sauce dish.

in favor of a collared base. Those who own pieces with the little log feet should feel fortunate in having glassware of this type which has survived after seventy-five years.

Classification

CLASSIC

PATTERN 119

(See Plates 97, 98)

Form Number.
1. Butter dish, on stippled feet, 5¾ inches.
2. Celery vase.
3. Compote, covered, on stippled feet. Various sizes.
   a. Compote on foot, 6 inch.
4. Creamer.
5. Goblet.
6. Pitcher, water. Two sizes.
7. Plate, 10½ inch. Two styles of frosted center, one containing Cleveland's bust and the other showing a warrior on a horse. Latter is marked "Jacobus" under large stone.
8. Sauce dish, collared base, 4¼ inch.
   a. On stippled feet.
9. Spoonholder.
10. Sugar bowl.

Color: Clear glass; clear with frosted panels. Most of the pieces may be found either on feet or on a collared base.

FROSTED STORK

There seems to be considerable difference of opinion as to whether the bird displayed on this glass is a stork or a crane. But because it has been referred to rather more often as Frosted Stork, I have given it that name. It is found in all-clear glass as well as in frosted-and-clear, though more of the plates and platters are seen in the frosted glass. The same bird adorns them all, a curious looking old fellow perched atop the sugar bowl to form the knob.

On the big plate he is seen with his long bill opened, ready to swallow a large butterfly. In each panel of every piece, the position of the bird and the landscape is altered. Altogether it makes an interesting glass to collect. The border of the plates and platters (Plate 68), is the same as shown on the sugar bowl in the group on Plate 100. The same border is found on many odd plates and platters showing all manner of different frosted scenes in the center. These were made in the early Seventies by the Crystal Glass Company of Bridgeport, Ohio, so an aged glass-blower told me. I believe his assertion to be correct, since this company is responsible for the Polar Bear, another frosted and clear combination, as well as the Oval Bee Hive (Industry) platter, not illustrated. In such pieces as the sugar bowl there are three panels on the bowl, each different, with a spray of flowers separating each panel. It is a quaint pattern collected quite extensively in the West. I am listing only those pieces I have seen, and as this glass was made both frosted and clear, one classification is being used for both. The collector should specify which variety he has in mind.

Classification

FROSTED STORK

Pattern 120

(See Plates 68, 99, 100)

Form Number.
1. Bowl. Originally ice bowl for water set.
2. Butter dish.
3. Creamer.
4. Dish, oval, deep. 9 x 6. 2 inches deep.
5. Goblet.
6. Pickle jar. Frosted stork as knob for the lid.
7. Pitcher, water.
8. Plate, round with closed handles. 9 inch.
9. Platter, oval.
10. Spoonholder.

Form Number.
  11. Sugar bowl.
  12. Tray, large, for water set.
Colors: Clear glass; frosted and clear, combined.

DEER AND DOG

While the series of combined frosted and clear patterns such as the Three Face and Westward-Ho were in vogue, several animals were used as decorative motifs to attract the popular fancy. One of these is called the Deer and Dog. The knob of all the covered pieces shows a dog standing on four feet, done in an all-frosted effect. The bowls of all the pieces are in clear glass and have a scene frosted on the surface, depicting a deer hunt. The covered butter dish has, on the rim of the cover, two dogs pursuing deer. The narrow band on the lower part has the same scene, while on the bowl of the sugar bowl is the same picture as on the butter dish. The goblet of this pattern is not illustrated, but it is of clear glass with the same picture frosted, on the surface. While I have not found this pattern to be particularly abundant, it may be more frequently encountered in sections I have not visited. As a rule the old glass was widely distributed. The forms follow those in Three Face. Probably because it is scarce is the reason why this pattern has not seemed to be properly appreciated. It is most attractive. Only the pieces I have actually seen are listed. It was produced in the Seventies.

Classification

DEER AND DOG

PATTERN 121
(See Plate 101)

Form Number.
  1. Butter dish.
  2. Celery vase.
  3. Compote, open or covered.
  4. Creamer.

Form Number.
  5. Goblet.
  6. Pitcher, water.
  7. Sauce dish, footed.
  8. Spoonholder.
  9. Sugar bowl.
Color: Clear glass, with frosted design. Also clear glass, minus scene but with frosted dog knob to covers.

JUMBO

During the Seventies and Eighties many interesting patterns in pressed glass were developed that combined clear glass with frosted effects. In this series is included the Elephant. Jumbo, the wonderful elephant of circus fame, was the inspiration for this design. It will be remembered that Jumbo was the widely advertised elephant of the generation before our own. Purchased by P. T. Barnum in London in 1882 for $10,000, he was eleven and one-half feet high and weighed seven tons. Special accommodations had to be provided for him on his voyage to America, as there was not room enough between the decks for his ponderous body. Jumbo was very fond of children and became an immense favorite with circus audiences in the United States. In England he had learned to like whiskey but on his arrival in this country he became a beer drinker, though a very moderate one. He took only a quart of beer a day and five gallons of water. He was twenty-five years old when he was killed in a railway accident in St. Thomas, Ontario, Canada, on September 16, 1885.

This glass commemorating the elephant must have been produced at the height of Jumbo's popularity. A large oblong-shaped butter dish came to my attention lately, which carries the frosted elephant as a knob for the cover, and on the blanket adorning him is the word "Jumbo." Forming the knob of a cover atop a large covered compote he stands in frosted glass, his long trunk apparently busy with a small mound of hay. One of the most amusing pieces is the spoon rack illustrated with a few spoons in place, on Plate 94. This unique piece is dated on the base "Patented Sept.

23, 1884." In nearly all of the elephant glass the animal is frosted and the balance of the glass is all clear. Curiously, the Jumbo goblet is quite a rarity. When this book was first written there was no report on one. It was not until after 1933 that a goblet came into my possession. Lately a collector wrote that she is the proud owner of another. These goblets are not found by the half-dozen! For the benefit of those who have never seen a Jumbo goblet, the design shows three elephants, two with their trunks down and one holding up his trunk. By commemorating in glassware this famous, friendly elephant who met such an untimely death, his memory will thereby outlive him.

One might think that it would be a comparatively simple matter to trace the history of dated glass but as a matter of fact, it is not. Starting with the date on the Jumbo spoonholder, the first step was to study the Patent Office records. To whom and for what was the patent granted? It took some time to find it because it was listed under "spoonholder." The application was filed February 14, 1884, by David Barker, of Canton, Ohio, assignor to the Canton Glass Co. The patent was granted on February 23, 1884. Barker's claim was that it was "a novel article for table use for the purpose of holding spoons, forks, etc., made of glass instead of the usual metal or part metal articles." His drawings showed not only the holder but the molds used and he specified the method of manufacturing it. There was no elephant on the knob of the holder shown in the drawings filed, but the third paragraph of the application read: "The object of this invention is to provide a holder of compressed glass which can be cheaply constructed but at the same time adapted to allow much latitude in the matter of ornamentation."

This information was not particularly interesting to collectors of the Jumbo pattern. The next step therefore was to learn from the Canton Glass Co. if they could shed any light on Jumbo glass. When was the ware produced? Was it true that Jumbo was the inspiration for the elephant knob? When did the manufacture of this pattern cease and what other forms were made? A letter asking for this information was sent to the Canton Glass Co.,

Canton, Ohio, but the postoffice there returned it unclaimed. Evidently the company went out of business so long ago that information about it was not obtainable from the present generation. The name of the company does not appear among the Ohio glass houses named in any printed reference I could find of the early glass factories. It will be seen how difficult it is to trace the makers of pressed glass even when it is late and dated.

The goblet is probably the rarest form and most sought after item in this pattern.

Classification

JUMBO

PATTERN 122

(See Plate 94)

Form Number.
    1. Butter dish, round.
        a. Oblong butter dish on four feet, with rack for butter knife attached to the side. "Jumbo" written on his blanket. Rare.
    2. Compote on high standard. Various sizes.
    3. Creamer.
    4. Goblet. Rare.
    5. Sauce dish.
    6. Spoon rack. Rare.
    7. Sugar bowl. Cover knob in form of elephant.
Color: Clear; clear, partly frosted.

MONKEY

Following the "Jumbo" elephant pattern, is one which properly belongs in the same series—or else in a zoo! It is the Monkey design. Many collectors will not be familiar with it because it apparently was not produced in large quantities or widely distributed. Those who do know it are enthusiastic, either because it represents something novel or else because the well-executed figures of the monkeys evoke admiration.

In the illustration on Plate 94A, there may be seen the pickle jar and the base to the butter dish, which is encountered more frequently than the dome-shaped lid, which reposes beside it. The same rayed center found in the bottom of the butter dish also appears on the spoonholder, tumbler and waste bowl, but not on the pickle jar, which has a plain base. The waste bowls, incidentally, originally went with nearly all the old-time water sets. Today they have divers uses.

The Monkey glass is seen most frequently in opal, or in clear glass. The design consists of monkeys, each holding the tail of the one in front and usually clinging to a palm tree as well. One odd feature is that three distinct types of handles may be discovered. That on the water pitcher is ribbed, while the two different types of mugs, one of which has an ornamented collared base, have handles dissimilar in shape. Cover knobs are in the form of a monkey.

It is not known where this glass was produced but it has been seen in Illinois more frequently than elsewhere, so that State may be its birthplace. Other forms than those listed will undoubtedly come to light, since this pattern is still an unfamiliar one today. So far, I have not heard of a compote.

Classification

MONKEY

PATTERN 122A

(See Plate 94A)

Form Number.
1. Butter dish.
2. Celery vase.
3. Creamer
4. Mugs. Two styles.
5. Pickle jar.
6. Pitcher, water.
7. Spoonholder.
8. Sugar bowl.

Form Number.

9. Tumbler, water.
10. Waste bowl.

Color: Opal; clear glass.

FROSTED LEAF

A highly decorative pattern which is attributed to the Portland Glass Company, of Portland, Maine, is known as Frosted Leaf. This factory was in operation a brief ten years—from the fall of 1863 until 1873.

The Frosted Leaf may well be considered one of the finest designs they produced. From the quality of the metal it appears to be of the early 1860's, as it has a certain amount of lead-flint, even though it is not so heavy as some of the earlier patterns. The design consists of a band of leaves, which are as heavily frosted as the grape leaf in the well-known Magnet and Grape. These leaves may have been sand blasted, rather than treated to a bath of acid, for the frosted finish. Below the band of leaves are narrow panels, which run to the stem, in the footed pieces.

The Frosted Leaf has a charm and grace which excels many of the patterns collectible in sets. It is seen more often in Maine than other places. While it is possible to accumulate a set within a reasonable length of time, a diligent search is necessary in the New England territory, where it is found more readily than elsewhere. It is one of my favorites and graces my table more frequently than any other glass. Plates have been reported but I have not seen them.

Classification

FROSTED LEAF

PATTERN 122B

(See Plate 94)

Form Number.

1. Butter dish.
2. Compotes, covered. Several sizes.
   a. Compotes, open.

Form Number.

3. Celery vase. Two styles, one having a scalloped edge and plain base; the other, plain edge and star cut base, with a leaf design pressed about the lower part of the bowl below the band of frosted leaves.

4. Champagne.

5. Cordial.

6. Creamer.

7. Decanter. Quart, with matching stoppers.
   a. Pint, cut on shoulders.

8. Egg cup.

9. Goblets, two sizes.

10. Lamp, brass stem and marble base. Matching shade. One lamp has been found in amethyst.

10A. Pitcher, water.

11. Salts, footed. Almost as large as egg cups.

12. Sauce dish, round, flat. Two sizes, both with star base. One is much deeper than the other. 4 and $4\frac{1}{4}$ inch.

13. Spoonholder.

14. Sugar bowl.

15. Tumbler, water.
   a. Footed tumbler.

Color: Clear, partly frosted. Amethyst or any colored piece is rare.

Chapter XIII

CLEAR CONVENTIONAL GROUP OF THE SEVENTIES

BUCKLE

The Buckle pattern has been collected for some years and it is more generally known by this title than by any other. The old trade name was undoubtedly quite different. The only record I have found is in a Gillinder & Sons (Philadelphia) catalogue of the early Seventies. A goblet is shown as "No. 15." Whether it had any other name than this we may never learn, unless an earlier catalogue is found illustrating the pattern more fully. The fact that only the goblet is shown indicates that this design was being carried over from an earlier date of manufacture. Apparently it was fairly popular, since several variants exist. The one described here is the best known. It is found either rayed or plain at the base of the bowl. This applies to all the dishes as well as the goblets and to the covers of the dishes which were either rayed or plain just below the knob. Another style is banded above the buckles, but this will be treated on another page. I believe at least two factories produced this glass, probably during the Sixties, since many of the pieces have a clear bell tone. It should be noted that the diamond points in the buckle vary considerably. On some pieces the points will be quite fine and on others, fairly coarse. The knobs of the covered dishes are attractive, being in the shape of an acorn with fine diamond points on the lower part and the top plain, bright and clear. The handle of the creamer is crimped and the forms follow closely those of all the earlier patterns.

On Plate 62 are shown the two goblets and the differences will be clearly noted. The bases of either style are plain. On Plate 102 is pictured a group of the dishes. One large deep fruit or berry bowl is sometimes found in the original wire basket which acted as a support or frame. These bowls have a small plain base without any foot and usually show a ground pontil mark. This same style of bowl may also be found in deep sapphire blue, though they are scarce in this color. I have never seen this type of bowl in the Banded Buckle though it may exist.

Since there are these variations in design, it is not surprising that fragments of both the Buckle and the Banded Buckle were discovered at Sandwich, since this book was revised in 1933.

Classification

BUCKLE

PATTERN 123

(See Plates 62, 102)

Style 1, plain; rayed.

Style 2, without rays; same forms as style 1.

Form Number.

1. Bowl, fruit or berry; found with wire basket container.
2. Butter dish, covered, flat, acorn knob.
3. Champagne.
4. Compote, open, on low standard.
5. Cordials.
6. Creamer.
7. Egg cup.
8. Goblet.
9. Pickle dish, large, oval, deep.
10. Pitcher, water.
11. Salt, footed. Two styles, one with plain edge and one scalloped. An oval, flat one is very scarce.
12. Sauce dish, 4 inch, flat; center has nine-pointed star, stippled in center. Two styles. Plain rim and cable edge on rim.
13. Spoonholder.
14. Sugar bowl, covered, acorn knob.
15. Tumbler.

Colors: Clear glass; sapphire blue (rare).

BANDED BUCKLE

There is quite a noticeable difference in the quality of the glass in the plain Buckle and the Banded Buckle. I believe the former pattern to have been produced earlier, for the glass is bright, with a clear bell tone to it, while the Banded Buckle is lighter in weight, less brilliant and lacks the ring. Moreover, the design varies. The plain Buckle has a large oval shaped motif arched fairly close to the top of the glass, while the Banded has buckles not much less than half the size. Of course, the narrow band of fine diamond points takes up some of this space at the top of the glass. I should judge that this ware was not made before 1870, though the forms follow closely those of the Buckle. It was produced at Sandwich and possibly elsewhere.

Classification

BANDED BUCKLE

PATTERN 124

(See Plates 62, 102)

Form Number.
1. Butter dish.
2. Compote, open, on low standard.
3. Cordials.
4. Creamer.
5. Egg cup.
6. Goblet.
7. Pickle dish, oval, deep.
8. Pitcher, water.
9. Salt, footed.
10. Spoonholder.
11. Sugar bowl.
12. Tumbler.
Color: Clear glass.

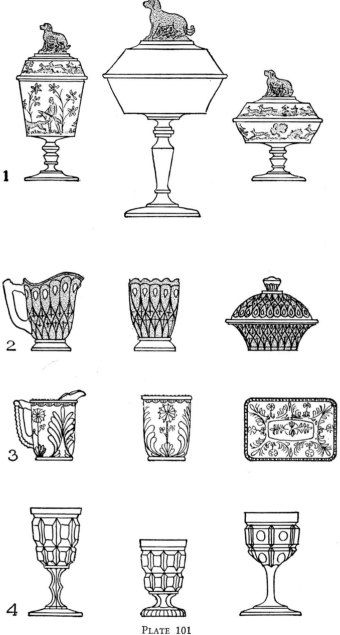

1. DEER and DOG sugar bowl, Dog compote on high standard, Deer and Dog butter dish.
2. DOUBLE LOOP creamer, spoonholder, butter dish.
3. STIPPLED DAISY creamer, spoonholder, oblong dish.
4. BLOCK with THUMBPRINT goblet, footed tumbler, goblet variant.

PLATE 102

1. HONEYCOMB with STAR butter dish, sugar bowl, creamer, spoonholder.
2. MEDALLION water pitcher, butter dish, goblet.
3. BANDED BUCKLE sugar bowl, egg cup, spoonholder.
4. BUCKLE sugar bowl, creamer, egg cup, sauce dish.

PLATE 103—GOBLETS

Moon and Star   Gooseberry
Ivy in Snow   Diamond Band

PLATE 104
1. DIAMOND QUILTED sugar bowl, celery vase, butter dish, tumbler.
2. GARFIELD DRAPE water pitcher, pickle dish, footed sauce dish.
3. BASKET WEAVE water pitcher, goblet, cup and saucer.
4. PANELLED DIAMOND POINT celery vase, sauce dish, spoonholder.

PLATE 105—PLATTERS

Chain and Shield
Shell and Tassel

Dahlia
Pleat and Panel

PLATE 106

1. ROSETTE compote, spoonholder, sugar bowl.
2. LOG CABIN creamer, spoonholder, compote.
3. PEACOCK FEATHER (late) creamer, sauce dish, handled lamp.
4. SHIELD and CHAIN goblet, cordial, sauce dish.

DIAMOND BAND

A heavy glass, handsome in effect and rather widely collected to-day particularly in and near New York City, is hereby christened Diamond Band. No dealer seems to call it by any particular name and it should have a means of identification. It was made during the Seventies by the Central Glass Co. of Wheeling, W. Va., whose designation was simply "No. 439 Pattern." It has none of the lead-flint quality of the earlier metal. Though the Diamond Band was made at a period in our glass history when commercialism held sway and a decline in artistic lines had been noted, still there are many patterns which are dignified and graceful. The Diamond Band is one of them. All the pieces in this design seem to carry a distinct appeal. The goblet (shown on Plate 103) speaks for itself. All the articles of tableware have marginal bands with the wider band of diamond points below, covering the bowl of the object to a pleasing extent. Around the top edge of such pieces as the sugar bowl, compotes, etc., is a scalloped or draped effect in light relief, on the surface. The forms are many and interesting in this highly collectible glass. The following classification is given from an original catalogue.

Classification

DIAMOND BAND

PATTERN 125

(See Plate 103)

Form Number.
1. Bowls. Round, flat. 5, 7, 8 and 9 inch.
2. Butter dish.
3. Cake plate on standard. 8, 9, 10, 11 and 12 inch.
4. Champagne.
5. Compote, scalloped foot.
6. Cordials.
7. Creamer.
8. Dish, oval. 6, 7, 8 and 9 inch.
9. Goblet.

Form Number.
  10. Jam jar.
  11. Pickle dish.
  12. Pitcher, water. Two sizes, $\frac{1}{2}$ gallon and quart.
  13. Plates. Scalloped edge. 5, 6, 7, 8 and 9 inch.
  14. Salts, round, large and individual.
  15. Sauce dish.
        a. Footed. 4 inch.
        b. Round, flat. 4 inch.
  16. Spoonholder.
  17. Sugar bowl.
Color: Clear glass; yellow or any colors are scarce.

PANELED DIAMOND POINT

Not infrequently we find a pattern which suggests the influence of some of the early "lace glass" designs. The Paneled Diamond Point is almost a replica of some odd little flint glass honey dishes I have seen. It is of an excellent quality of glass, apparently of the Sixties. The pattern is composed of a panel about three-quarters of an inch wide, of diamond points, alternating with a clear panel having a narrow band of fluting on each side of it. At the top of the panel of diamond point is a fan-shaped ornament. The top edge of the celery holder has a flat scalloped rim. The stem is rather plain, with a round knob and the base is clear. So far this design has not been widely collected and therefore is not well known. It may have been made in a large variety of forms but they are so scarce that I have seen very few of them.

Classification
PANELED DIAMOND POINT

PATTERN 126
(See Plate 104)

Form Number.
  1. Celery vase.
  2. Goblet.

Form Number.

    3. Sauce, 4 inch.

    4. Spoonholder.

    5. Sugar bowl.

Color: Clear glass.

CURTAIN

A brilliant, scintillating clear glass will be found in a pattern which is not well known or widely collected to-day. Because of its draped effects, which may be seen in a group illustrated on Plate 85, it is called Curtain. Not a single piece of this ware was encountered during my many years of collecting until a number of pieces came to my attention in Hershey, Pa. It was originally called "Sultan" by Bryce Bros. of Pittsburgh, who produced it, but the old name must be discarded and the later one used because too much confusion would result if one insisted on keeping the old trade names, after having been abandoned so many years.

Collectors will undoubtedly be interested in this glass when it is better known, for it has character. The following classification is taken from an old illustrated catalogue of Bryce Bros.

Classification

CURTAIN

Pattern 127

(See Plate 85)

Form Number.

    1. Bowls, collared base.

        a. Covered. 5, 6, 7 and 8 inch.

        b. Open. 5, 6, 7 and 8 inch.

    2. Butter dish.

    3. Celery vase.

        a. Plain top edge.

        b. Scalloped top.

    4. Cake plate on standard. 8, 9 and 10 inch.

Form Number.

    5. Celery boat.

    6. Compotes.

        a. Covered, on high standard. 6, 7 and 8 inch.

        b. Open, on high standard. 7, 8 and 10 inch.

    7. Creamer.

    8. Finger bowl.

    9. Goblet.

  10. Mug, large.

  11. Pickle dish.

  12. Plates.

        a. Square. 7 inch.

        b. Bread. Square, large.

  13. Pitcher, water. $\frac{1}{2}$ gallon and quart.

  14. Salt and pepper shakers.

  15. Sauce dish.

        a. Collared base. $4\frac{1}{2}$ inch.

        b. Flat. $4\frac{1}{2}$ inch.

  16. Spoonholder.

  17. Sugar bowl.

  18. Tray, for water set. Large, round.

  19. Tumbler.

  20. Water set.

Color: Clear glass.

CHAIN AND SHIELD

A most attractive pattern that has been overlooked by collectors because it is so little known, is called Chain and Shield. It is a rather spectacular design. The oval platter, shown on Plate 105, shows plainly what suggested this title. In the center of the base is a large sunburst with small dewdrops scattered in the background like stars. There is a large row of heavy hobnails underneath, which compose the feet that the platter stands on. In the border is a chain effect, with shield-shaped ornaments to finish the outer edge. The handles are petal-shaped and stippled. The glass is fairly heavy, especially the little four-inch sauce dish. The design follows that of the platter, the dish resting on the large hobnails. The edge of the sauce dish is beaded with a single row of tiny dewdrops. The goblet has a lacy appearance with a prettily reeded stem. A group of the Chain and Shield is shown on Plate 106.

Unfortunately I can find no record of where this interesting glass was made. It appears to be a pattern of the Seventies. Not many pieces have come to light but they doubtless will when the demand makes the search for it profitable.

Classification
CHAIN AND SHIELD

PATTERN 128

(See Plates 105, 106)

Form Number.
1. Cordial.
2. Creamer.
3. Goblet.
4. Platter, oval.
5. Spoonholder.
6. Sugar bowl.
7. Sauce dish, flat, 4 inch.
Color: Clear glass.

HAND

For some years this glass has been known as the Hand pattern and it is too late to attempt to change the name now. The title was derived from the knob of the covered pieces, which is in the shape of a tightly clenched fist grasping a short round bar. A more fitting name might have been used at the beginning but dealers and collectors usually cling to that with which they are familiar.

The Hand pattern was made during the Eighties by the O'Hara Glass Co. of Pittsburgh, and it was called by them the Pennsylvania pattern. It is a brilliant, clear glass. The goblet is sparkling and lovely, with the short panels of fine diamond points alternating with the plain, clear panels. Through the center of each piece is a narrow horizontal band dividing the panels. The bowl of the goblet has especially delicate lines, being long and tapering. The rim of the sugar bowl and other covered pieces has a clear, flat, scalloped rim where the cover joins.

This has been a popular pattern over a period of years and the pieces are by no means plentiful. It may be assumed that a wide range of articles was made but I give only those I have seen, together with those taken from an old but incomplete O'Hara catalogue.

Classification

HAND

PATTERN 129

(See Plate 107)

Form Number.
1. Cake plate on standard.
2. Celery vase.
3. Compotes.
    a. Covered, on high foot.
    b. Open, tall slender dish with scalloped edge, on foot.
4. Creamer.
5. Dishes, oval. 7, 8, 9 and 10 inch.
6. Goblet.
7. Jam jar. Originally termed pickle jar.
8. Pickle dish.
9. Pitcher, water.
10. Platter.
11. Sauce dish. Flat, 4 inch.
12. Spoonholder.
13. Sugar bowl.
Color: Clear glass.

DIAMOND CUT WITH LEAF

The tendency to copy successes was as strong among glass makers as among other manufacturers. When a firm produced a pattern that won profitable popularity imitations and variants followed as a matter of course. During the vogue of the Fine Cut appeared the Diamond Cut with Leaf. Radiating from the center of the plate is a border of single stippled leaves, pointing toward the edge of the rim. In the creamer, the leaves are comparatively larger, extending upward well above the middle. The goblet is particularly attractive, with an unusual knob stem, as may be noted on Plate 109. The plates may be found in two sizes, and there are many items in this charming, lacy design.

The quality of the glass of the plates appears to be different from that of the other pieces, so that one wonders whether the plates were not earlier. They have a clear ring which the creamer, for instance, entirely lacks. With no records to guide us, we can only note these points and hazard a guess. It is a delightful pattern, well worthy of the collector's notice. I have seen the plates in amber and in blue.

Classification

DIAMOND CUT WITH LEAF

PATTERN 130

(See Plates 108, 109, 138, 144)

Form Number.
1. Butter dish.
2. Cordial.
3. Creamer.
4. Cup, small, handled. 2½ inch.
5. Goblet.
6. Plates. 7¼ and 9½ inch.

Colors: Clear; amber; blue. Colors are scarce.

SUNBURST

During the early blown glass period our now sought-after Blown Molded glass was produced to give a cheap imitation of the fine English and Irish glass. Later on the same idea was carried out in several patterns of pressed glass. The Sunburst is one of them. It is an effective pattern, not so widely known as others though a few collectors have been buying it for years. The attractive plates are found in three sizes. One unusual piece is the large, double pickle dish. The egg cups are slightly larger than the usual size and most attractive, with the star base which is really like a sunburst. The design of the Sunburst pattern is too complicated for adequate description and it can best be understood by examining the group on Plate 12. It is a later glass than the Hamilton, which it resembles, probably dating about 1870.

Classification

SUNBURST

PATTERN 131

(See Plate 12)

Form Number.

1. Bread plate, round, with inscription: "Give us this day our daily bread."
2. Cake plate, on standard.
3. Compote. $7\frac{1}{2}$ high x $10\frac{1}{2}$ inches diameter.
4. Celery vase.
5. Creamer.
6. Dish, deep, oblong, and large.
7. Egg cup.
8. Goblet.
9. Pickle dish, large; double, 8 x 10 inches.
10. Plates.
    a. 6 inch.
    b. 7 inch.
    c. 11 inch.

Form Number.
  11. Sauce dish. Flat, with handle on one side.
  12. Sugar bowl.
Color: Clear glass.

CANADIAN

One cannot help wondering what could have inspired the names attached to some of the old pressed glass patterns. Since this design seems to be so well known by the name of "Canadian," it may well be that there is some basis for the rumor that it was made in Mallorytown, Ontario, Canada. I tried to verify the report but I did not succeed. I am assured that there was a glass factory there and residents like to imply that they know a good deal about it, but no one could speak positively about this one pattern of glass. It seems certain that wherever the Canadian was produced, the Cape Cod must also have been made, as the two are so similar.

The scenes depicted in the Canadian might be any rural spots anywhere. The goblet has three panels, arched at the top, each one including a scene showing a house and trees, some flying birds and a fence. Between the panels the glass is lightly stippled and has sprays of ivy with berries. The stem of the goblet is clear and round with fine ribbing around the base of it. It was a difficult glass to photograph, the design being so thin. Judging only by the quality of the glass, this pattern must date in the 1870's. Another design closely similar to the Canadian, shows a water scene, and is called "Cape Cod." It is treated in this book under that name.

The Canadian seems to be in great demand in certain states at this time. Prices are fairly high considering that it is not generally well known. I have limited the classification to those pieces I have actually seen. I am told of a seven-inch plate, but I have not come across one.

Collectors will probably be able to add to my list. It would not surprise me if we learn, by way of future research work, that this was made in America.

Classification

CANADIAN

PATTERN 132

(See Plates 111, 112, 113)

Form Number.
1. Butter dish.
2. Celery vase.
3. Cordials.
4. Compotes, open, on high and low standard.
5. Compote, covered, 6 inch.
   a. Compote, covered, 7 inch.
   b. Compote, covered, 8 inch.
6. Creamer.
7. Dish, round. Handles on each side. 6 inches diameter, $1\frac{1}{2}$ inches deep.
8. Goblets.
9. Jam jar.
10. Pitcher, water. Two sizes.
11. Plates, 6, 8, 10 inch, with small closed handles.
12. Sauce, footed, 4 inch.
   a. Sauce, flat, 4 inch.
13. Spoonholder.
14. Sugar bowl.
Color: Clear glass.

CAPE COD

Of the series that includes the Canadian is another pattern of exactly the same style and period, which has come to be known as Cape Cod. It is very similar to the Canadian, having the sprays of ivy on a stippled background between the scenes. The Cape Cod goblet has an oval medallion enclosing the views, instead of the oblong panel arched at the top. The title of Cape Cod probably was inspired by the water scene in one of the medallions, which shows small sailboats off the Cape! This glass dates from the

Seventies. Forms are the same as Canadian, with the exception of the goblet.

Classification

CAPE COD

PATTERN 133

(See Plates 114, 115)

Form Number.
1. Bowl, with small handles; 6-inch diameter, 2 inches deep.
2. Butter dish.
3. Celery vase.
4. Compotes.
    a. Covered, 6, 7 and 8 inch.
    b. On high foot.
    c. On low foot.
5. Cordials.
6. Creamer.
7. Goblets.
8. Jar, marmalade.
9. Pitcher, water.
    a. Pint.
    b. Quart.
10. Plates.
    a. Six inch, small, closed handles.
    b. Eight inch, small closed handles.
    c. Ten inch, small closed handles.
11. Sauce dish, footed, 4 inch.
    a. Flat, 4 inch.
12. Spoonholder.
13. Sugar bowl.
14. Water tumblers.
Color: Clear glass.

BARLEY

A very delicate and dainty effect is produced by the misnamed Barley pattern. It is simple and its tracery of long fern-like leaves is charming. This rather conventional design was never really meant to be called Barley, but since the glass has long been known by this title in many sections, I shall not attempt to change it. The six-inch plates have a large star in the center and a scalloped rim which is edged with dewdrops, thereby adding a sparkle that relieves the plainness. The footed sauce dish has a double vine and the same scalloped rim edged with dewdrops. The goblet has a plain marginal band at the top and the design has the double vine. The stem is plain and round and the base is the same. It should not be confused with the Wheat and Barley pattern.

Little is known about this pattern. The set I found was in Ohio, and most of the pieces I have had came from that state. It would appear, by the quality of the glass, to have been made in the late Sixties or early Seventies. Many more pieces may be had than in my classification, but I have listed only those I actually have seen.

Classification
BARLEY

PATTERN 134
(See Plates 113, 116)

Form Number.
1. Butter dish, scalloped rim with row of thumbprints.
2. Cake plate on standard.
3. Celery vase.
4. Compotes. Open and covered, on high or low foot.
5. Cordials.
6. Creamer.
7. Dish, oval, $9\frac{1}{2}$ x $6\frac{1}{2}$ inches. $7\frac{1}{2}$ x $5\frac{1}{4}$.
8. Goblets.
9. Honey dish. $3\frac{1}{2}$ inch.
10. Marmalade jar.
11. Pickle dish.
12. Pitcher, water.
13. Plate, 6 inch.
14. Platter, oval.

Form Number.
  15. Sauce dish, footed, 4 and 5 inch.
        a. Flat, sunburst center, 4½ inch.
  16. Spoonholder.
  17. Sugar bowl.
Color: Clear glass. A plate has been found in light amber. Colored pieces are rare.

LIBERTY BELL

Of the patriotic designs the Liberty Bell stands out as the one most generally collected. It is not a beautiful glass though it has a certain historical interest. It is our Centennial ware and for years it was known by that name. The goblet is all clear glass, with a large Liberty Bell on one side and the inscription "Declaration of Independence" over it. On the reverse, "100 years ago" in large stippled lettering. Small pennants, one on each side, bear the dates 1776-1876. The stem is hexagonal, forming a knob close to the clear base. It is needless to record that this pattern was made in 1876. The oval platters bear the names of all the signers of the Declaration on the lower border. In the center is a large Liberty Bell. The little six-inch plate is very plain, with scalloped edge and clear border bearing the words "100 years ago." There are two small closed handles. In the center is the Liberty Bell with "Declaration of Independence," 1776-1876. Below, in very small lettering, is "Pat. Sept. 28, 1875." If only it had been a trade custom to date all pressed glass, what an easy task it would be to group the various periods together in chronological order. I have never seen wines or egg cups in this pattern.

Of interest is the fact that this glass was made by Gillinder & Sons of Philadelphia, for the Centennial. The mugs with snake handles were actually made on the grounds for the benefit of the spectators. I have found them inscribed "Manufactured at the Centennial by Gillinder & Sons." These little cups are unusually interesting and, strange as it may seem, are exceedingly scarce to-day. Interesting also are the little bells which have a metal arrangement on the top, so that they may be hung up. These were made for souvenirs or possibly as containers for candy. One I found was inscribed—"Proclaim Liberty Throughout all the Land" and on the reverse, "1776-1876 Centennial Exposition."

The Gillinders made a full line of what the trade came to know as "Centennial Ware" and so did many other factories. Between them they produced a large number of Liberty Bell novelties as souvenirs for visitors to the Centennial Exhibition at Philadelphia. A correspondent wrote me that some of the Liberty Bell platters were made by Bakewell, Pears & Co. of Pittsburgh, but I have not been able to verify this. A glass worker in Pittsburgh assured me that the Penn Glass Co., which was incorporated in 1875 and went out of business in 1877, made a Liberty Bell plate and other Centennial specialties. According to him the Penn Glass Co. took over some old works under their own name and failed the following year. It is my conviction that the greatest volume of Centennial ware was turned out by Gillinder & Sons. They were on the ground and fully utilized their strategic position. A plain oval platter, showing a Liberty Bell in the center, was patented by J. C. Gill, of Pittsburgh, on September 28, 1875.

Classification
LIBERTY BELL

PATTERN 135
(See Plates 58, 113, 117)

Form Number.
1. Bells. Metal tops, for candy.
    a. Ornaments. Metal tops, open, to hang up by.
2. Butter dish.
3. Celery vase, tall.
4. Compotes, all open, with collared base. 6, 6¾ and 8 inches.
5. Creamer.
6. Goblets.
7. Mugs, shaped like Liberty Bell. Handle in form of snake. Inscribed on the base, "Manufactured at the Centennial Ex-

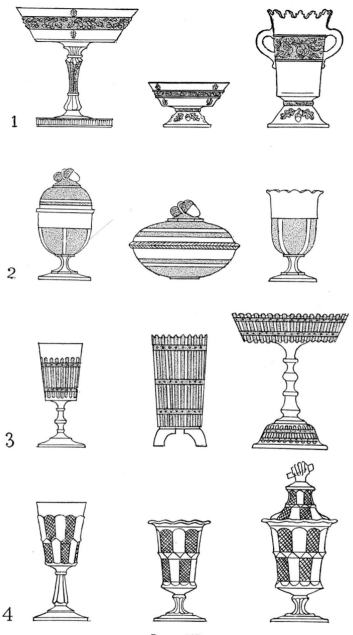

PLATE 107

1. FLOWER BAND compote, footed sauce dish, celery vase.
2. STIPPLED BAND sugar bowl, butter dish, spoonholder.
3. PICKET goblet, celery vase, open compote on high standard.
4. HAND goblet, spoonholder, sugar bowl.

PLATE 108

1. DIAMOND CUT WITH LEAF creamer, plate, handled cup.
2. SUNFLOWER creamer, spoonholder, butter dish.
3. DRAPERY creamer, spoonholder, sugar bowl.
4. NAILHEAD goblet, butter dish, bowl of sauce dish.

PLATE 109—GOBLETS

Roman Rosette   Diamond Cut with Leaf
Princess Feather   Flower Band

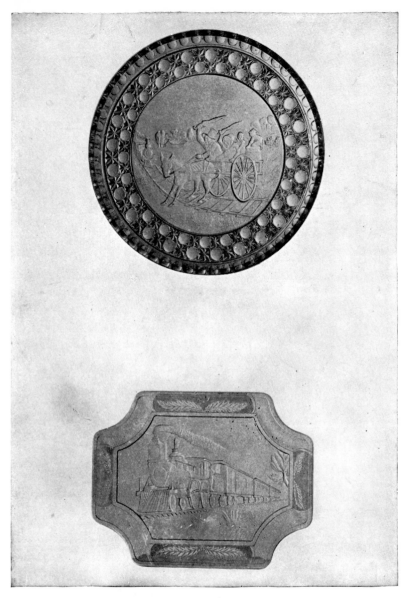

PLATE 110

Tray in "Currier and Ives" pattern
Railroad Train platter

PLATE 111—GOBLETS

Pleat and Panel
Cupid and Venus

Canadian
Egyptian

PLATE 112

1. PRINCESS FEATHER sugar bowl, egg cup, water pitcher, covered bowl.
2. PALMETTE creamer, spoonholder, pickle dish, footed salt.
3. CANADIAN jam jar, goblet, cordial, footed sauce dish.
4. HORSESHOE or GOOD LUCK goblet, jam jar, covered bowl, butter dish.

PLATE 113—SIX INCH PLATES

Grape   Barley
Liberty Bell   Canadian

PLATE 114—LARGE PLATES

Wheat and Barley
Paneled Thistle

Primrose
Cape Cod

hibition by Gillinder & Sons." These are usually in clear glass, but may be found in milk-white. Rare.

8 Pickle dish.

9. Pitcher, water.

10. Plates, round, small closed handles; 6, 8 and 10 inch.

11. Platters.
> *a.* Oval. 9¼ x 13 inches. Border contains the signers of the Declaration of Independence.
> *b.* Oval. 7 x 11¼ inches. No signers on border.
> *c.* Opaque white. Rare. May be found in 11½-inch size with name John Hancock, and in 13-inch size with John Hancock's name in place of signers of Declaration of Independence.

12. Salts.
> *a.* Small, open.
> *b.* Shaped like Liberty Bell, with pewter shaker tops.

13. Sauce dishes.
> *a.* Flat, round.
> *b.* Footed, round.
> *c.* Flat, with two closed handles. 4½ inches.

14. Spoonholder.

15. Sugar bowl.

16. Toy, or miniature set. Comprised of sugar, creamer, spoonholder and butter dish.

Colors: Clear glass; milk-white, rare.

EGYPTIAN

Quite different in style and feeling from other designs of American pressed glass, is one known as Egyptian. A few dealers call this "Parthenon," which may be a more appropriate name, but it is widely known at this time as Egyptian. The goblet has three panels, one containing the ruins of a temple underneath which is printed "Ruins of Parthenon." Another shows a palm tree and a sphinx and the third a camel, tent and palm trees. These panels are divided by a stippled band containing a row of daisy-like flowers in dewdrops and the band also runs around the top of the bowl below the clear marginal band. This flower motif lends considerably more character to the glass. It serves as a border on ali the pieces, including the oblong bread plate. This plate is inscribed, as most of them were during the Seventies and Eighties, "Give us this day our daily bread." In the oval center is the figure of an Egyptian woman holding some heads of wheat on her lap, and gazing off across the landscape. The compotes have a stippled figure of the sphinx in the base. Not many pieces of this glass have come to my attention, though all the usual forms employed during the late Seventies were probably made.

Classification

EGYPTIAN

PATTERN 136

(See Plates 111, 118)

Form Number.
1. Bread plate.
    a. Shaped like oblong platter. Figure of woman in center. Inscribed, "Give Us This Day Our Daily Bread."
    b. Same shaped plate, with building, Salt Lake Temple, in center.
2. Butter dish.
3. Celery vase.
4. Compote, covered, on low foot.
5. Creamer.
6. Goblets.
7. Pickle dish, oblong.
8. Pitcher, water.
9. Plate. Small closed handles. 8 inch.
10. Sauce dish, round, flat. 4 inch.
    a. Footed. 4 inch.
11. Spoonholder.
12. Sugar bowl.
Color: Clear glass.

DEER AND PINE TREE

Almost everyone knows the Deer and Pine Tree, or as it has sometimes been called, the Deer and Doe. It is a familiar pattern.

found in colors as well as in clear glass. It is most often seen in the latter, though the oblong platters are not rare in colors. Recently I found a pretty little handled mug in apple green. The amber in this glass is really charming, being lighter than the usual shade and clear and vivid. A covered butter dish in this bright amber was a late find, also. The goblet is of an unusual shape, four oblong panels giving it flattened sides, though the top is round. The stem is fairly heavy and round. The two panels on the sides contain the deer and doe, with an attempt at a pine tree on one side. While I have seen a number of pieces in color, I have not found any colored goblets. The oblong platters are very popular as service plates. They have flattened diamond points that cover the center, with a band of diamond points around the ends and sides and the two deer and pine trees at each end.

This glass is not plentiful today, because it has been so widely collected. It dates in the 1870's.

Classification
DEER AND PINE TREE

PATTERN 137

(See Plate 119)

Form Number.

1. Butter dish.
2. Bowl, small. Slightly larger than usual finger bowl.
3. Cake plate on standard.
4. Celery vase.
5. Creamer.
6. Compote, covered, various sizes.
7. Compote, large oblong, covered.
8. Dishes, oblong, $5\frac{1}{2}$ x $7\frac{1}{4}$ inches; $5\frac{1}{2}$ x 8; $5\frac{3}{4}$ x 9.
9. Goblets.
10. Jam jar.
11. Mug, small.
12. Pickle dish, oblong, deep.
13. Pitcher, water. Two sizes.

Form Number.
   14. Platters, oblong, 13¼ x 8 inches.
   15. Sauce dish, flat.
      a. Sauce, footed. 2 sizes.
   16. Sugar bowl.
   17. Spoonholder.
   18. Tray, large, 11 x 15 inches.
Colors: Clear; amber; blue; apple green; yellow.

PALMETTE

Years ago I heard this design called either "Spades," or "Hearts and Spades." They were not suitable titles and I never felt satisfied until I was informed one day that it was originally called "Palmette." This is a descriptive name that fits admirably. It is a dainty and effective pattern, combining leaves shaped like the old palm-leaf fans. One leaf is ribbed and the alternating one is filled with fine diamond points. The background is entirely stippled. On some of the pieces, such as the spoonholder, there is a very narrow band above the design, having tiny four-petalled ornaments. These are so small that one would scarcely notice them at the first glance.

Palmette is, generally speaking, a clear glass pattern belonging to the Seventies. I have seen handled cake plates in both amber and blue, which have a variation of the Palmette design, but I believe were meant to be used with this pattern.

Classification

PALMETTE

PATTERN 138

(See Plates 95, 112, 120)

Form Number.
   1. Butter dish, small handles on each side. No standard.
      a. Butter dish. No handles, no standard.
   2. Cake plate, handles, 9 inch. Not true Palmette, but closely similar.

Form Number.
3. Castor bottles.
4. Celery vase.
5. Compote, on low **foot.**
6. Cordials.
7. Creamer.
8. Egg cups.
9. Goblets.
10. Pickle dish.
11. Pitcher, water.
12. Sauce, flat, 4 inch.
13. Salt, footed.
14. Spoonholder.
15. Sugar bowl.
16. Tumblers.
   a. Footed tumbler.

Colors: Clear glass. Cake plates in amber, blue and possibly other colors.

JACOB'S LADDER

Just where the title for this pattern originated nobody has been able to tell me. It is true that the clear prism-like panels which alternate with a panel having a lattice effect may have a suggestion of the steps of a ladder, and thus inspired this biblical name. While it is a fairly late pattern, at least of the Seventies, the glass has considerable brilliancy. The bowl of the goblet tapers toward the base. Almost directly below it is a knob-stem faceted so that it catches the light on all sides. The base is plain and clear.

A very interesting set may be accumulated in this attractive design, as there is a wide range of pieces. The creamer is footed and the marmalade or pickle jar, as well as the other covered pieces, have a knob in the shape of a maltese cross. In fact, the original trade name was "Maltese," as designated by the makers, Bryce Bros. of Pittsburgh, in their catalogue. Compotes are found in a large open size with a scalloped rim, but the rarest one in

Jacob's Ladder has a dolphin standard. Lucky, indeed, is the collector who finds one these days! The six-inch plates are particularly pretty, with their deeply scalloped edges. These pieces may be seen on Plate 50. While the usual articles in this pattern are of clear glass, I have seen a few colored ones, including a six-inch plate in amber.

Classification

JACOB'S LADDER

PATTERN 139

(See Plates 50, 57)

Form Number.

1. Bowl. Round, flat. 6 inch.
2. Butter dish.
3. Cake plate on standard. 8, 9, 11 and 12 inch.
4. Castor bottles.
5. Celery vase.
6. Compotes.
    a. Covered, large, on high standard; knob in form of Maltese Cross. 6, 7, 8 and 9 inch.
    b. Open, large, on standard, with scalloped edge. 7, 8, 10 and 12 inch.
    c. Compote with dolphin standard. Rare.
7. Cordials.
8. Creamer.
9. Dishes, oval. 7, 8, 9 and 10 inch.
10. Goblet, knob stem.
11. Marmalade jar.
12. Mug.
13. Pickle dish.
14. Pitcher, water.
15. Plate. 6 inch.
16. Relish dish, oval.
17. Salt, footed, with scalloped edge.
18. Sauce dish, flat, scalloped edge.
    a. Round, flat. 3½, 4 and 5 inch.
    b. Footed. 4½ inch.

Form Number.

19. Spoonholder.
20. Syrup pitcher. Metal top, plain or with knight's head as a knob.
21. Sugar bowl.
22. Tumbler.
    a. Tumbler, handled.

Colors: Clear glass; amber; yellow. Colors are scarce.

CUPID AND VENUS

One of the effective later patterns is generally called "Cupid and Venus." In some states it was called "Minerva" but this title leaves Cupid unaccounted for! Since he has wings I feel he deserves to be in the picture. Another name I have heard is "Guardian Angel." My informant claims that her grandmother purchased this ware when it was known by that name, and she believes it to be the original one. We find few patterns known to-day by their original appellations, the old records containing trade names with few exceptions having been lost. I was fortunate enough to find an old illustrated catalogue of Richards & Hartley of Tarentum, Pa., who made this pattern, and it surprised me to find that their only term for this glass was "No. 500 Pattern." It is, therefore, better to have a recognizable alias than a meaningless birth certificate.

It is a comparatively simple design, the main feature being a beaded oval bearing the figures of Cupid and Venus. The goblet has two of these medallions, a narrow conventional band connecting the two. The stem of the goblet has a double ring in the center and the outer edge of the base has a very narrow band of fine ribbing underneath.

The Cupid and Venus is found in a satisfying number of forms. It is effective when grouped together, especially the ten-inch plates, which are most attractive combined with any pattern as service plates. It was probably made between 1875 and 1880.

When *Early American Pressed Glass* was first written, this was a comparatively common pattern and a set could be accumulated within a reasonable length of time. Pattern glass has been collected so intensively since my nomenclature was established in 1931, that today the designs which came into the most active demand are now scarce and much higher in price. It requires time and patience to find bargains today.

Classification

CUPID AND VENUS

PATTERN 140

(See Plates 70, 92, 111)

Form Number.

1. Butter dish.
2. Celery vase.
3. Champagnes.
4. Compotes.
    a. Covered, on high and low standards.
    b. Open, on high standards.
5. Cordials.
6. Creamer.
7. Goblets.
8. Jam jar.
9. Mugs, in three sizes.
10. Pitcher, water, two sizes.
11. Plates, round, 10 inch, for bread or cake.
12. Relish dish, oval, deep, three sizes.
13. Sauce dish.
    a. Round, flat.
    b. Footed, 3½, 4 and 5 inch.
14. Spoonholder.
15. Sugar bowl.

Colors: Clear glass. A few of the plates may be found in color, chiefly in yellow or amber.

PSYCHE AND CUPID

A fanciful design that appears to date from the Seventies is one that I find most generally known as Psyche and Cupid. Some may

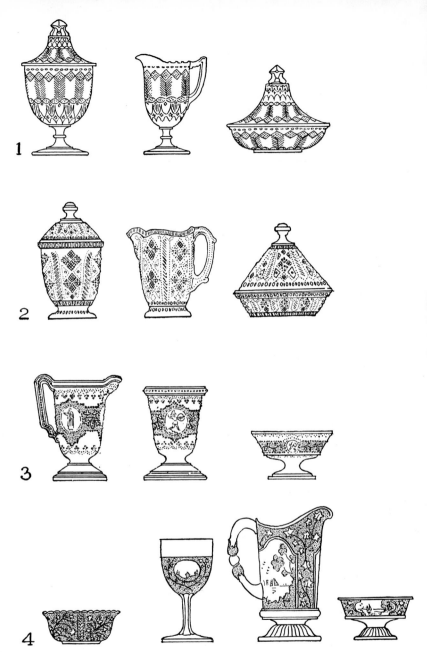

PLATE 115

1. HERRINGBONE sugar bowl, creamer, butter dish.
2. JACOB'S COAT sugar bowl, creamer, butter dish.
3. MINERVA creamer, spoonholder, footed sauce.
4. CAPE COD sauce dish, goblet, water pitcher, footed sauce.

PLATE 116

1. HOLLY covered compote, goblet, egg cup.
2. CORD and TASSEL wine, celery vase, water pitcher.
3. BARLEY celery vase, jam jar, footed sauce, goblet.
4. BEADED TULIP butter dish, sugar bowl, footed sauce, goblet.

PLATE 117—PLATTERS AND GOBLETS

Liberty Bell   Prescott and Stark "The Heroes of Bunker Hill"
                                      Centennial goblet

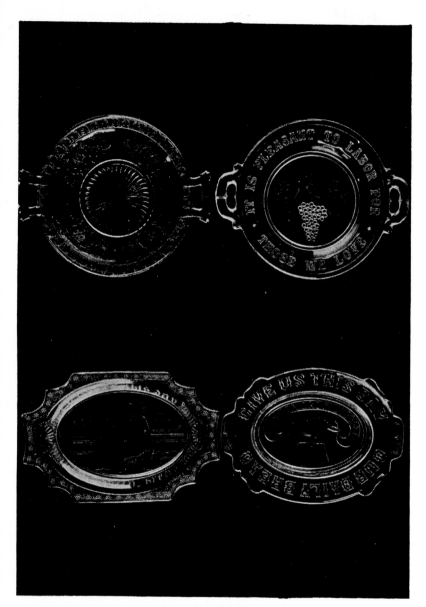

PLATE 118—BREAD PLATES

Scroll with Flowers
Egyptian

Grape
Centennial, with eagle

PLATE 119

1. DEER and PINE TREE celery vase, butter dish, goblet, footed sauce dish.
2. BUDDED IVY goblet, creamer, spoonholder, butter dish.
3. STIPPLED IVY goblet, sugar bowl, spoonholder, footed salt.
4. IVY in SNOW covered compote, celery vase, cordial, cup and saucer.

PLATE 120—GOBLETS

Rose in snow
Palmette

Fishscale
Windflower

PLATE 121—GOBLETS

Arabesque
Herringbone

Minerva
Drapery

reverse the order and call it Cupid and Psyche, but since there is another, known as the Cupid and Venus pattern, future confusion may be avoided by using the order named. The design is in such low relief as to appear etched on the surface. Possibly this may have been a special process tried out by one factory as few other patterns are found that resemble it. The goblet has three medallions, showing Cupid holding the mirror in front of Psyche who appears to be combing her hair. The three medallions are divided by a thin conventional scroll. The bowl of the goblet is long and tapering with a short round stem. The base is clear on all the footed pieces. The design shows much more clearly on the larger pieces, such as the celery vase and sugar bowl. The knob of the covered pieces is a rather curious conventionalized ornament. Very little of this glass seems to be found in New York State and I have never seen much of it in antique shops elsewhere, so it may be assumed that it was not made in as large quantities as most other patterns.

Classification

PSYCHE AND CUPID

PATTERN 141

(See Plate 75)

Form Number.
1. Celery vase.
2. Compote, on high standard.
3. Creamer.
4. Goblet.
5. Pitcher, water.
6. Spoonholder.
7. Sugar bowl.
Color: Clear glass.

MINERVA

The Minerva is a pattern that appears to be a product of the late Seventies. It is most attractive when grouped together. Small dewdrops contribute in large measure to the effectiveness. There is a double scallop of them around the top of the creamer and they form the edges of the three round medallions depicting a Greek warrior in varied postures. Many useful pieces are to be found and so far the Minerva is one design not yet known widely enough to cause prices to soar. Fortunately there are enough old glass patterns to suit individual tastes and purses. A collector who has a home on Squirrel Island has a unique pattern in the quaint old pressed glass Squirrel and those who like the races have a penchant for the Good Luck or Horseshoe. The originators of these patterns, which after all were chiefly made not as examples of fine workmanship but as a commercial product to meet growing competition, would be amazed at the eagerness with which they are sought to-day.

One of the most amusing pieces of pressed glass is the Minerva pickle dish, which bears the inscription "Love's Request is for Pickles." In the center of this dish is a large figure marked "Minerva." It was this dish which gave the pattern its name.

A complete set of this glass may be assembled and it is plentiful enough so that the search need not be a long one.

Classification

MINERVA

Pattern 142

(See Plates 115, 121)

Form Number.
1. Butter dish.
2. Cake plate, on standard.
3. Compotes.
      a. Covered, on low foot.
      b. Covered, on high foot.
4. Creamer.
5. Dishes. Oblong, 2½ inches deep. 5 x 8. 6 x 9.
6. Goblet.
7. Jam jar.

Form Number.

8. Pitcher, water.
9. Plate. 9 inch, with closed handles.
   a. Smaller size.
10. Platter. Oval, inscribed "Give us this day our daily bread."
11. Relish dish. Oblong, inscribed "Love's Request is for Pickles."
12. Sauce dish.
    a. Round, flat.
    b. Round, footed. 4 and 4½ inch.
13. Sugar bowl.
14. Spoonholder.

Color: Clear glass.

Chapter XIV

FLOWER GROUP

ROSE IN SNOW

Probably one of the most popular and best known patterns collectible to-day in a great variety of pieces is the Rose in Snow. It is found most readily in clear glass though it was also made in yellow, blue and amber. The forms are both round and square. This does not apply to the goblets or plates. The creamer, sugar bowl, covered butter dish and compotes may be had in the square style and all the needed pieces may be had in the round. The square butter dish is not footed and has a pretty conventional design in the base. The round butter dish is most attractive, with its wide scalloped rim. The round sugar is on a low round foot. One of the most unusual pieces in this pattern is a double pickle dish. This has four roses on each of the oval sides, and a rose at each end, which forms a handle. All the pieces have a stippled background with the clear roses and leaves in relief. The goblet is shown on Plate 120, and the forms, both round and square, on Plate 122. The 9-inch plate is shown on Plate 73. In this size the plates are found with small handles, as pictured. The 5-inch, 6-inch and 7¼-inch plates are round, without handles. There is no need to dwell on the beauty of the Rose in Snow, which is always in demand. Egg cups, celery vases and wines were never made originally. The only record I have found of this pattern is that it was made by Bryce Bros. of Pittsburgh in the Seventies. It did not have any name beyond "No. 125." I presume it may also have been produced by other factories, which would account for the two different forms.

Unfortunately, there are some fakes now on the market, but they are adequately treated in my book on reproductions. The pieces copied are marked in this classification, and are made in clear, amber, blue and yellow.

Classification

ROSE IN SNOW

PATTERN 143

(See Plates 73, 120, 122)

Form Number.

1. Butter dish.
   - *a.* Round, wide scalloped rim. Rare.
   - *b.* Square, no foot.
   - *c.* Round, no rim, flat.
   - *d.* Round, collared base.
2. Cake plate on standard.
3. Compotes.
   - *a.* Covered, on high standard. Several sizes.
   - *b.* Covered, on low standard. Several sizes.
   - *c.* Open, various sizes.
   - *d.* Square, on low base.
4. Creamer.
   - *a.* Round.
   - *b.* Square.
5. Dish, oval, deep, 8½ x 11¼, 1½ inches deep.
   - *a.* Smaller.
*6. Goblets.
7. Mugs.
   - *a.* Large, with applied handles; same size as tumblers.
   - *b.* With handles, inscribed "In Fond Remembrance."
8. Pickle dish. Plain and scalloped edge.
   - *a.* Double, 8¼ x 7 inches.
   - *b.* Oval, small handle at each end. Two sizes.
   - *c.* Oval, without handles.
9. Pitcher, water.
10. Plates, 5, 6, 7¼ and 9 inch (9 inch is 10 inches to edge of handles).
11. Platter.
12. Sauce dish.
    - *a.* Footed.
    - *b.* Round, flat.

Form Number.

13. Spoonholder.
    a. Round.
    b. Square.

14. Square bowl, flat, 8 and 9 inch.
    a. Square, covered.

15. Sugar bowl.
    a. Round.
    b. Square.

16. Sweetmeat jar, covered, on standard. 5¾ inch.
17. Toddy jar, covered, with plate.
18. Tumbler, water.

Colors: Amber; blue; clear glass; yellow.

CABBAGE ROSE

A dainty and attractive Rose pattern of the late Sixties is called the Cabbage Rose. It is not widely known or collected though popular among those who know it. One collector tells me she has purchased pieces of it in the South, in central New York and in Pennsylvania so it must have enjoyed a wide sale once upon a time. The design covers the object fairly well, which always tends to make any glassware more attractive. The goblets are particularly dainty and pretty. Above the design of open roses and leaves is a narrow panel containing ovals. This seems to follow on all of the stemware, as the cordials also have it. The large covered compote, shown on Plate 122, has the design on the inside of the cover and the knob is formed of a large rosebud, some leaves and a smaller bud. The base of the pickle dish is quaintly pretty, having in the center a horn of plenty filled with roses. This is probably the most popular Rose pattern to-day after the Rose in Snow. It was gratifying to find that this popular design was produced by the old Central Glass Co. of Wheeling, W. Va., which was absorbed in 1891 by the United States Glass Co. of Pittsburgh. The following classification is taken from the original catalogue and from a list furnished to me by a collector of the

"Cabbage Rose." The old name for it is rather disappointing: "No. 140."

A few fragments in Cabbage Rose were discovered at Sandwich but not enough for me to go on record as saying it was positively made there.

Classification

CABBAGE ROSE

Pattern 144

(See Plate 122)

Form Number.
1. Butter dish.
2. Cake plate, on standard.
3. Celery vase.
4. Compotes, covered, 6, 7, 8 and 9 inch, on low and high standards. Rose knobs to covers.
5. Cordials.
6. Creamer.
7. Dish. Round, no cover. 7 inch.
8. Egg cups.
9. Goblet.
10. Pickle dish.
11. Pitcher, water. Two sizes, quart and 3 pint.
12. Salts, footed.
13. Sauce dish. Round, flat. 4 and 5 inch.
14. Spoonholder.
15. Sugar bowl.
16. Tumbler, water.
Color: Clear glass.

OPEN ROSE

A quaint, old-fashioned pattern is the Open Rose. It would appear to be later than the Rose in Snow, though the principal reason for thinking so may be that the glass is all clear, without any stippling. A frosted background somehow always looks older. The goblet in this Rose pattern has a wide marginal band at the top and three sprays of open roses, each being divided by a sprig containing two leaves and a bud. The stem is in nine tiny panels, with a clear round base. The sugar bowl has the design on the inside of the cover in high enough relief so that it is most effective. Many of the usual forms are found though they are not plentiful. This pattern was probaby made during the Seventies. There are several variations to be found among the goblets, as to shape and size. Enough fragments of this pattern were found at the site of the Boston & Sandwich Glass Company, to be sure some of it was produced there.

Classification

OPEN ROSE

PATTERN 145

(See Plates 122, 123)

Form Number.
1. Butter dish.
2. Compote, on high standard.
3. Creamer.
4. Dish, oval, 9½ x 6 inches.
5. Egg cup.
6. Goblets, two sizes. Height and size of bowl varies.
7. Pickle dish, oval.
8. Pitcher, water.
9. Salt, footed, cable edge.
10. Sauce dish, flat, 4 inch.
11. Spoonholder.
12. Sugar bowl.
13. Tumbler.

Color: Clear glass.

ROSE SPRIG

A Rose pattern which is very attractive but is among those made during the Eighties, is the Rose Sprig. The existence of a number of rose designs has caused some confusion, particularly in regard to this, which is the last of the series. To give a complete classification of the pieces made in this pattern would be impossible without the old records, but the list given will be enough to assist those collecting it.

For some reason, tumblers in the Rose Sprig are found much more readily than the goblets. Dealers who have handled pattern glass for a number of years told me they had never seen one and I thought they did not exist until I found five in clear glass, in an antique shop in Atlantic City. Antique shops, it seems, are found even in this resort city! Rose Sprig is also found in yellow, blue and amber, but I have not found it in apple green or in amethyst in my travels. The forms vary, some of the pieces being square and others round. The plates are square and have slightly upturned scalloped edges, with a large star in the center. They are divided into four panels, each containing a rose and bud with a cluster of leaves, all of which are stippled.

Interesting are the sleighs in Rose Sprig, which were made in more than one size, including a salt. Lately a collector wrote me that she has found one bearing a date of 1888. The large-sized sleighs are attractive for flowers, in a table setting or even for general use.

Classification

ROSE SPRIG

PATTERN 146

(See Plates 86, 124, 125)

Form Number.
  1. Cake plate, on standard.
  2. Celery vase.
  3. Compote, open. Deep, on low foot.
  4. Creamer.
  5. Dishes.
      a. Boat-shaped, rose on each side.
      b. Oblong, deep, 9 x 6 inches.
      c. Square, with handle, 6 inches.

PLATE 122

1. ROSE in SNOW (square) creamer, sugar bowl, butter dish.
2. ROSE in SNOW (round) sugar bowl, creamer, mug, covered compote on high standard.
3. OPEN ROSE sugar bowl, creamer, egg cup.
4. CABBAGE ROSE goblet, covered compote, cordial.

PLATE 123—GOBLETS

Open Rose
Lily of the Valley

Wildflower
Bleeding Heart

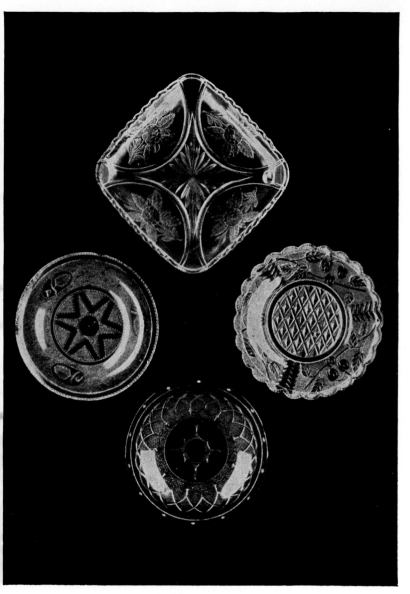

PLATE 124—SIX INCH PLATES

Rose Sprig, Beaded Acorn, Stippled Cherry, Loop and Dart with
Diamond Ornaments

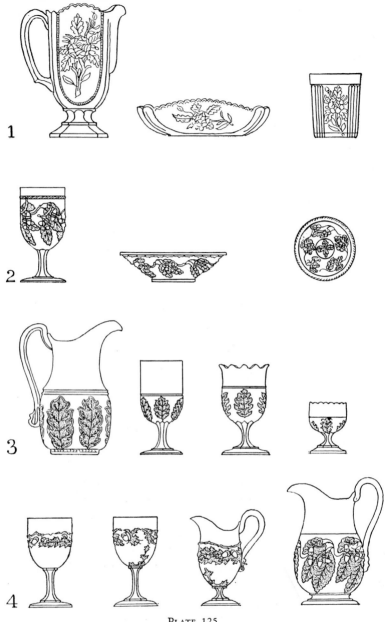

PLATE 125

1. ROSE SPRIG water pitcher, relish dish, tumbler.
2. ACORN goblet, butter dish (cover missing), sauce dish.
3. PRESSED LEAF water pitcher, goblet, spoonholder, footed salt.
4. ACORN VARIANTS goblet, goblet with leaf panel, creamer, water pitcher.

Form Number.

6. Goblets.
7. Pickle dish.
8. Pitcher, water. Two sizes.
9. Plate, square, 6½ and 10½ inch.
10. Sauce dish, footed.
11. Sleigh. Patent mark, 1888.
   a. Sleigh salt.
12. Spoonholder.
13. Tumbler.
   a. Same size, with handle added.
14. Tray, square, large; for water pitcher and goblets.

Colors: Amber; blue; yellow; clear.

WILDFLOWER

In an old and, unfortunately, undated catalogue of Adams & Co. of Pittsburgh, I found one of the best known of the more popular patterns collected to-day. We now call it Wildflower. In the Adams & Co. lists it is called "No. 140 Pattern." Wildflower scarcely needs describing. It has been collected assiduously for years, particularly in colors. I can remember when this glass was openly derided and people were advised not to waste their money on what was scoffingly referred to as "late Woolworth," or "baking powder glass." It is quite true that it dates from the late seventies, but it has its practical use and the design and colors are charming. The appeal of this pattern for collectors must be great, for it has become quite scarce and prices have materially advanced. The apple green particularly is in constant demand, and the price of the goblets is much higher than the average. Lucky the person who picked up a set of them years ago, before the demand had raised costs to their present level. One pays well for the yellow, blue and apple green. Some pieces are, comparatively, just as scarce as the early Beliflower. On Plate 126 is shown a number of pieces, including a champagne which is rare. Cordials are also to be had and are quite as difficult to find. One of the most appealing of the

Wildflower pieces is the little turtle salt. The turtle has a small boat-shaped dish on his back, which carries the Wildflower design. It comes in all colors, but one must be prepared for a long search. The salt may be seen on Plate 127.

Wildflower is another one of the popular patterns in which a few pieces have been reproduced since this book was revised in 1933. The fakes are adequately treated in my book on reproductions. The items copied are marked in this classification.

Classification

WILDFLOWER

PATTERN 147

(See Plates 123, 126, 127)

Form Number.

1. Bowls.
   a. Small, round, size of finger bowls.
   b. Square, flat fruit bowls. 6, 7 and 8 inch.
   c. Round. 6 inch.
2. Butter dish, covered, round. Two styles, flat and on a collared base.
3. Cake plate on standard, two sizes.
4. Celery vase.
4A. Champagnes.
5. Compotes.
   a. Covered, on high standards.
   b. Covered, on low standards.
   c. Open.
   d. Oblong, on high standard. Rare.
   e. Square, with rounded, flared top; on high standard. Very rare.
6. Cordials.
7. Creamer.
8. Dish, square, flat, 5¾, 6¼, and 7¾ inch.
*9. Goblets. Two types in reproductions. The latest appears in clear glass and in colors.
10. Pitchers.
    a. Syrup, with tin top.
    b. Water.

Form Number.

*11. Plates, square with cut-off corners, 10 inch. Originally termed cake plate. Reproductions in clear glass and in colors.

12. Platter, oblong, 10 inch.

13. Relish dish, oblong.

14. Salts, turtle-shaped.

15. Salt and pepper shakers, metal tops.

16. Sauce dishes.
>   *a.* Flat.
>   >   (1) Round. 4 inch.
>   >   (2) Square. 4½ inch.
>   *b.* Footed, round, 3½ and 4 inch.

17. Spoonholder.

18. Sugar bowl.

19. Trays.
>   *a.* Large, oval; for water pitcher and goblets.

20. Tumblers, water.

Colors: Apple green; dark amber; blue; light amber; clear; yellow.

STIPPLED FORGET-ME-NOT

Enjoying a well-deserved vogue at the present time, is the Stippled Forget-Me-Not. There are a number of designs featuring this flower, though not quite so prominently as in the one I am describing. This has a stippled background with three panels divided by small delicate, diamond-shaped ornaments. There are sprays of flowers and leaves in each of the panels, with a double band of the diamond ornaments above and below it. It is dainty and lovely, and the demand grows daily as it becomes better known. A few dealers used to refer to this pattern as "Forget-Me-Not-In-Snow."

The goblets are slightly smaller than the average, though this does not detract from their appearance. An attraction for collectors of this design is the existence of cups and saucers. These are not often found in glass but they have many valuable uses in a table service. Plates come with varied center designs, three of which are illustrated. While this pattern is not plentiful, sets of it may be assembled without too much effort. Having all the lacy appearance of the earlier Sandwich, it gives the impression of being much older than it actually is. In colors, the only pieces I have found are an amber tumbler and an oval opalescent salt.

Classification

STIPPLED FORGET-ME-NOT

PATTERN 148
(See Plates 74, 128, 129, 130, 138)

Form Number.
1. Butter dish.
2. Cake plate, on standard. Two sizes.
3. Celery vase.
4. Cordials.
5. Compotes, covered, 6, 7 and 8 inch. Covers generally missing.
6. Creamer.
7. Cups and saucers.
     a. Odd cup with collared base.
8. Goblets.
9. Hat. Toothpick holder. Rare.
10. Pitcher, water. Two sizes.
11. Plates.
     a. Seven-inch, baby center.
     b. Seven-inch, star center.
     c. Nine-inch, kitten center, with handles.
     d. Nine-inch, star center.
12. Relish dish, oval. Base matches salts.
13. Salts, large, oval. Lovely interlaced design in base.
14. Sauce dish.
     a. Round, flat.
     b. Round, footed.
15. Spoonholder.
16. Sugar bowl.
17. Syrup jug, metal top.

Form Number.

18. Tray, large, for water set.
19. Tumblers, water.

Colors: Clear glass; amber and opal are rare.

BARRED FORGET-ME-NOT

The second of the Forget-Me-Not series is another most attractive pattern. The background is stippled and the flowers and leaves twine in and out of narrow bars, which are placed in a conventional manner and suggest broken lattice. The goblet is formed of two panels, a clear double band dividing the two. About the base of the bowl is a band, over a half inch wide, of a design somewhat resembling herringbone. The stem is rather short, with a few small rings at the top and a small knob close to the base. It is altogether dainty and unlike any other. My interest was first aroused by finding one small cordial in this pattern and it led to finding the set. A later "find" in this pattern was a huge cake plate on a standard. The top is twelve inches in diameter, and the base is like a large inverted bowl, with a short stem in the center. The design is the same with the addition of four daisy-like flowers. It is the most effective dish of this sort one could find.

Barred Forget-Me-Not is also found in colors, including the popular "apple green." The stippling on the colored pieces is coarser than on the clear, particularly on the round cake plates. It is evidently a pattern of the 1870's.

Classification

BARRED FORGET-ME-NOT

Pattern 149

(See Plates 131, 132)

Form Number.

1. Butter dish.
2. Cake plates.
   a. Nine-inch, with closed handles.
   b. Extra large on standard.

Form Number.

   3. Cordials.

   4. Compotes.

      a. Covered, on high foot.
      b. Covered, on low foot. 8 inch.
      c. Open, small, on high foot.

   5. Creamer.

   6. Goblets.

   7. Pickle dish, square handles at each end.

   8. Spoonholder.

   9. Sugar bowl, square handles.

Colors: Apple green, blue, clear, golden amber.

PANELLED FORGET-ME-NOT

From all appearances the third one of the Forget-Me-Not group is of approximately the same date, and is not better known than the others. This one small flower must have inspired many glass designers to have been used so much. In this instance the flower is simply in a panel with a lightly stippled background. The goblet has three such panels, a narrow clear one on each side, and three panels of a simple block pattern. The stem is clear and round, the base being clear also but having an odd crimped effect. It is not like the crimped foot of a piece of early blown glass but, nevertheless, it is plainly marked with narrow flutings. The platters are ovoid, with square ends, the handles being stippled and having a spray of forget-me-nots. The center has an X-shaped ornament of little squares and dewdrops. The pickle dishes are the same shape as the platter. The covered butter dish has a square base on a standard and a round cover. The platter is shown on Plate 133, the goblet on Plate 130 and the butter dish on Plate 79.

I find that this pattern was made originally by the old firm of Bryce Bros. of Pittsburgh, Pa., during the Seventies and was listed by them as their "Regal." The catalogue in my possession is not complete and illustrates only the goblets and cordials. The items listed I have found in my travels.

Classification

PANELLED FORGET-ME-NOT

PATTERN 150

(See Plates 79, 130, 133)

Form Number.
1. Butter dish.
2. Cake plate on standard.
3. Celery vase.
4. Compote, covered, on high standard. **Several sizes.**
5. Cordials.
6. Creamer.
7. Goblets.
8. Jam jar.
9. Pickle dish, oval.
10. Pitcher, water. Two sizes.
11. Platter, oval.
12. Relish dish, small, rounded at one end.
13. Sauce dish.
    a. Footed.
    b. Round, flat.
14. Spoonholder.
15. Sugar bowl.

Colors: Amber; blue; clear; yellow.

FORGET-ME-NOT IN SCROLL

In Pennsylvania I found another pattern which may or may not be a native of that state, but I have not seen it anywhere else. It is a good clear glass having a stippled band about an inch wide through the center, containing a conventional flower motif with a scroll of fine leaves. The base of the bowl of each piece is stippled with a conventional design of leaves. The handle of the creamer is applied and crimped at the base. All these pieces are footed. Later on, during the Eighties, we find that most of the footed pieces are dispensed with. Such articles as sugar bowls, spoonholders, etc., were made to rest flat and squarely on the table. They thereby lost a certain dignity and daintiness and their appearance is more modern. This pattern appears to be a product of the late Seventies or Eighties. The open sugar, creamer and spoonholder may be seen on Plate 77.

Classification

FORGET-ME-NOT IN SCROLL

PATTERN 151

(See Plates 77, 86)

Form Number.
   1. Butter dish.
   2. Creamer.
   3. Goblet.
   4. Honey dish.
   5. Spoonholder.
   6. Sugar bowl.
Color: Clear glass.

RIBBED FORGET-ME-NOT

A dainty pattern both in point of the size of the pieces as well as the design, is known as Ribbed Forget-Me-Not. The existence of so many varieties of Forget-Me-Not patterns makes it imperative to have some distinguishing adjective in the title as a means of identification. The curious part of this particular or Ribbed Forget-Me-Not pattern is that all the pieces are diminutive in comparison with the other dishes of the same period, particularly sugars and creamers which, as a rule, were made double the size found in a modern service, doubtless because large families were not so unpopular in those days. One could not imagine a more attractive set of old glass for a breakfast tray than the one shown on Plate 137, consisting of a sugar bowl, butter dish and creamer. The little butter dish with its saucer-like base is charmingly adapted for marmalade. All the background of this glass is stippled in a

PLATE 126

1. DAHLIA creamer, water pitcher, champagne, footed sauce dish.
2. LILY of the VALLEY sugar bowl, goblet, creamer, plain footed creamer.
3. WILDFLOWER water pitcher, creamer, champagne, footed sauce dish.
4. WILDFLOWER celery vase, sugar bowl, tumbler, bowl.

1

2

3

4

PLATE 127

1. Elephant match holder, saddle match holder, covered salt with rooster medallion, dog's head as knob of cover.
2. Bird salt with cherry in beak, turtle WILDFLOWER salt, frog match holder.
3. Squirrel salt, Swan mustard jar, Bear jar, 4½ inch.
4. Owl creamer, rabbit covered dish, dog salt.

(See page 626)

PLATE 128

1. BLEEDING HEART compote on high standard, creamer, butter dish.
2. BLEEDING HEART spoonholder, footed tumbler, tumbler, egg cup.
3. STIPPLED FORGET-ME-NOT cup and saucer, tumbler, oval salt, sauce dish.
4. STIPPLED FORGET-ME-NOT compote on high standard, water pitcher, celery vase.

PLATE 129—LARGE PLATES

Palmette Variant
Dahlia

Willow Oak
Stippled Forget-Me-Not

PLATE 130—GOBLETS

Stippled Forget-Me-Not   Panelled Forget-Me-Not
Dahlia   Horseshoe or Good Luck

PLATE 131—LARGE PLATES

Horseshoe or Good Luck
Frosted Circle

Star Rosetted
Barred Forget-Me-Not

PLATE 132

1. BARRED FORGET-ME-NOT goblet, pickle dish, cordial.
2. CANE water pitcher, relish dish, spoonholder.
3. DOUBLE SPEAR sugar bowl, creamer, butter dish.
4. CHAIN footed sauce dish, goblet. CHAIN with STAR cordial, plate, 7 inch.

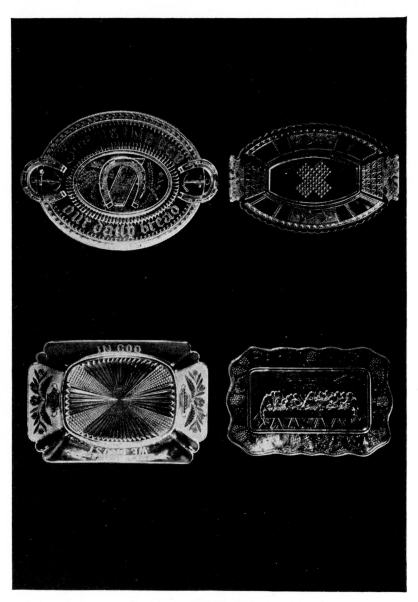

PLATE 133—BREAD PLATES

Horseshoe or Good Luck
Flower Pot

Panelled Forget-Me-Not
The Lord's Supper

sparkling frosted effect, the scroll design of forget-me-nots and leaves standing out in clear relief. Above and below the band carrying this design is a narrow band of fine ribbing.

Originally named the "Pert Set" by Bryce Bros. of Pittsburgh, Pa., the name seems most appropriate. Their old catalogue illustrates and lists only six pieces, so collectors of this design must be contented with a small set of it.

It is a mistake to believe that the same pieces were made in all patterns after 1850. A considerably larger number of pieces and variants were produced in those patterns which proved successful commercially. Moreover, the forms varied with the years.

This ware which belongs to the late Seventies, I have seen only in clear glass.

Classification

RIBBED FORGET-ME-NOT

PATTERN 152

(See Plate 137)

Form Number.
1. Butter dish.
2. Creamer.
3. Cups, handled.
4. Mustard jar, with cover. One found with spoon of wood.
5. Spoonholder.
6. Sugar bowl.

Color: Clear glass.

BEADED TULIP

Still not very well known to-day is a pattern that I am told was once called "Tulip" in Ohio. As an earlier pattern is so well known as Tulip and the old trade name for this was lost for so many years, I am calling it Beaded Tulip. The greater part of the pieces I have seen in this design came from Ohio, and later I learned it was made originally by the Lancaster Glass Co. of Lancaster, Ohio.

The design has a three-petalled flower not unlike a tulip, alternating with conventionalized leaves. The whole effect is most attractive, as though the pattern were beaded. The stem of the goblet is in narrow panels, having a knob at the top and base. It is almost more of a turning than a knob, with a tiny scalloped cut-out edge, giving the same beaded effect. The footed sauce dishes are among the most striking found in any pattern. The edge of the bowl is cut out in points, the same shape as the petals of the flowers. This is an unusual pattern of merit, which is not as well known as it deserves to be. The old trade name for it was Andes. Collectors would do well to give this pattern the attention it deserves, rather than to follow the line of least resistance, and collect the designs their neighbors or friends may have assembled.

Classification

BEADED TULIP

Pattern 153

(See Plates 44, 116)

Form Number.
  1. Butter dish.
  1A. Cake plate, on standard.
  2. Cordials.
  3. Compote, open, on high foot, 8 inch.
  4. Creamer.
  4A. Dish, oblong. Two sizes.
  5. Goblet.
  6. Pitcher, water.
  7. Plate, 6 inch.
  8. Sauce dish, footed, 4 inch.
      a. Flat, 4 inch.
  9. Spoonholder.
  10. Sugar bowl.
  11. Tray, round, for water set.
Color: Clear glass.

BLEEDING HEART

This is one of the few patterns which could have only one name and therefore no confusion has occurred over the proper title. It is plainly a Bleeding Heart taken from an old-fashioned garden. There are variants in the types of goblets, as many collectors have already learned. One is barrel shaped with a fairly heavy design and stippled leaves; another has a very thin design placed lower on the bowl and a third has straight sides to the bowl. The barrel-shaped bowl draws in noticeably at the top. The stems are hexagonal, forming a knob close to the base, which is clear. A most unusual piece in the Bleeding Heart is the relish dish, which is divided into four parts.

If the number of variations in any one pattern establishes anything it is the number of different factories that copied the original design. I have an old, illustrated catalogue of the King Glass Company of Pittsburgh, Pa., which was one of eighteen glass factories comprising the so-called "old Pittsburgh glass district" absorbed by the United States Glass Company, also of Pittsburgh, in 1891. The King catalogue illustrates the Bleeding Heart goblet and wine glass. Apparently the earliest goblet made was the one illustrated in this book on Plate 123. It corresponds exactly with that shown in the old catalogue, which was called "No. 85 Pattern." After the King Glass Company became a part of the United States Glass Company, it would appear that the latter designed another goblet which they called their "85 New Floral." It has the Bleeding Heart design on the bowl but the stem is different. It is plain and fluted, without any knob. The earliest one of this series was made during the Seventies. Fragments from the site of the old Sandwich factory reveal a Bleeding Heart pattern. The type they made has a cable cord at the edge where the cover joins, on covered dishes. Another typical Sandwich decorative idea, is a row of dots on the outer underside of the thick rim where the cover joins, on such pieces as compotes, sugar bowls and butter dishes.

Classification

BLEEDING HEART

PATTERN 154

(See Plates 123, 128)

Form Number.
1. Bowls, waste.
2. Butter dish.
3. Cake plate on standard.
4. Compotes, covered.
    a. On high foot.
    b. On low foot.
    c. Oval.
5. Cordial.
6. Creamer.
7. Dish, large, oval.
8. Egg cups.
    a. Barrel shape.
    b. Straight sides.
9. Goblets.
    a. Barrel shape, heavy design.
    b. Bowl with straight sides.
    c. Thin design low on the bowl.
10. Mugs, handled.
11. Pickle dish, oval.
12. Pitcher, water. Two sizes.
13. Plates. Very scarce.
14. Platter, oval.
15. Relish dish, with four divisions.
16. Salt, oval.
    a. Round, footed.
17. Sauce dish.
    a. Flat, round.
    b. Oval.
    c. Honey, or preserve dish. 3½ inch.
18. Spoonholder.
19. Sugar bowl.

Form Number.
  20. Tumbler, footed.
        a. Water tumbler.
  21. Wine glass.
Color: Clear glass.

PRIMROSE

One of the popular patterns to-day among many collectors is called Primrose. There is one variant which is alike in all the details except the flower. Because the flower in the variation closely resembles an English Daisy, many call it "Stippled Daisy," though this title must not be confused with the design treated in this book under that name. One reason for the popularity of the Primrose is that it is not only found in colors but the ever popular plates come in four sizes.

The Primrose design consists of three panels, each of them having a delicate spray of flowers and leaves. The background appears to be stippled, but on close examination one will find that it is made up of rows upon rows of fine cable cord. The bases of the bowls are fluted and the bands around the top edges have little vertical rows of dewdrops. All the pieces are footed. Goblets are very scarce in one section of New York State, but are plentiful in some localities. The covered pieces are attractive, the knob being in the form of a flower. On the best known pieces the small flower consists of ten pointed petals, five petals having one rib in the center and the other five being clear. In the variant the flower is made up of very fine clear petals that stand out in brilliant relief.

A satisfying number of pieces may be had in this lovely pattern, which are listed below. It was probably made in the late Seventies or possibly as late as 1880. A group, showing the elusive goblet, is pictured on Plate 136. Incidentally, the goblet is rather disappointing in comparison to the beauty of other pieces in this pattern. Usually the quality of the glass is poor and a wide clear marginal band leaves the design fairly low about the bowl. Goblets are more attractive in any style, when the bowl is fairly well covered with a pattern.

Classification

PRIMROSE

PATTERN 155

(See Plates 114, 136)

Form Number.

1. Bowl, round, similar to finger bowl but slightly deeper.
2. Berry bowl. Round, deep.
3. Butter dish, flat.
4. Cake plate, 8¾ inch, closed handles.
5. Cake plate, on standard.
6. Compotes, covered, on high foot, 6, 7½ and 8 inch.
7. Cordials.
8. Creamer.
9. Egg cups.
10. Goblets.
11. Pickle dish.
12. Pitcher, water. See *Tray,* for water set.
13. Plates, 4½ inch (known as Toddy plate), 6 and 7 inch. Also cake plate.
14. Platter, oval, conventional handles.
15. Sauce, footed, 4 and 5½ inch.
    a. Round, flat.
16. Spoonholder.
17. Sugar bowl.
18. Tray, round, for water pitcher and goblets.

Colors: Amber, blue, yellow, clear glass. Apple green pieces are exceedingly scarce. Clear glass found most readily. Colored pieces confined largely to plates. Yellow is the rarest shade.

DAHLIA

Very similar in character to the Primrose pattern, is one now called Dahlia. There has been considerable confusion among both dealers and collectors over the proper title of each of these patterns and it will be a matter of interest to have them properly named and identified. These two flower designs have sprung into sudden popularity during the past few years.

The Dahlia appears to have a stippled background to enhance the effectiveness of its clear flower and leaf design, but close scrutiny reveals a very fine mesh or screen, rather than a stipple. The effect is silvery and sparkling. The large clear flowers look cool and inviting against this charming surface. The goblets are particularly dainty and appealing. Cake plates may be had with closed handles. The seven-inch plate is rare and always in considerable demand. Clear glass pieces may be found without great difficulty. I presume most of this ware was made in color also. A water pitcher in amber and one in blue attracted my attention, as well as a plate in blue, and I have been told of blue and amber Dahlia goblets. This ware has every appearance of being a product of the late 1870's. It is found in many interesting forms. Most of them may be seen in the illustrations.

Classification

DAHLIA

PATTERN 156

(See Plates 105, 126, 129, 130, 138)

Form Number.
1. Butter dish.
2. Cake plate, closed handles, 9 inch.
3. Cake plate on standard.
4. Champagne.
5. Compote, large, covered on high standard.
6. Cordial.
7. Creamer.
8. Egg cup (double end).
   a. Rare type, with design weaving about the bowl, instead of straight around.
9. Goblet.
10. Mugs, with handles. Two sizes.
11. Pitcher, water.

Form Number.
   12. Plate, 7 inch.
   13. Platter, oval, grape handles.
   14. Salt.
   15. Sauce, 4 inch, flat, scalloped rim.
        a. Footed sauce.
   16. Spoonholder.
   17. Sugar bowl.
   18. Wine.
Colors: Clear; blue. Amber and yellow are scarce.

STIPPLED DAISY

   Found largely in Pennsylvania to-day is a pattern not particularly well known, which has no name so far as I know. The flower resembles an English daisy more closely than any other and the background is stippled, so I am calling it Stippled Daisy. Combined with the flower is a large conventionalized scroll, as one may see by examining the group shown on Plate 101. The scroll and the flowers stand out in rather heavy, clear relief against the stippled background. The glass has all the earmarks of the later ware and was made probably in the Eighties. I have encountered many sauce dishes in this design, but to date no goblet, though it may exist. The edges of the dishes are beaded, which rather adds to their attractiveness. The design is interesting and unusual and will probably be widely collected some day.

Classification
STIPPLED DAISY

PATTERN 157
(See Plate 101)

Form Number.
   1. Berry bowl, large and deep.
   2. Compote, open, with beaded edge. $8\frac{1}{4}$ diameter, 8 inches high.
   3. Creamer.

Form Number.

4. Dish, oblong, deep, 7 x 4⅜ inches. Several other sizes.
5. Sauce, flat, 4¼ inch.
6. Spoonholder.
7. Sugar bowl.
8. Tumbler.
9. Tray, oblong. Probably relish dish.

Color: Clear glass.

WINDFLOWER

The eagerness and zest displayed of late by collectors of pressed glass have brought to light at an astonishing rate patterns hitherto ignored. As a rule, homemade descriptive titles are given to them, each locality having its favorite name, thus increasing the confusion. A Connecticut collector asserts that some years ago the pattern shown on Plate 139 was called Windflower, but I doubt whether it was ever the original trade name. The flower in question really resembles a chestnut burr, but the old name is quaint and it is retained here because so many people in New England use it.

The decoration consists of large veined and stippled leaves, not unlike a chestnut leaf and a small flower. The design covers a good portion of the object, the heavily stippled leaves giving a decidedly attractive frosted effect. The general characteristics of this pattern in the shapes and types of pieces made are similar to those of the Palmette and Princess Feather. They were all a popular product of the late Sixties or early Seventies.

Classification
WINDFLOWER

PATTERN 158
(See Plates 120, 139)

Form Number.

1. Butter dish, flat, covered.
2. Celery vase.

Form Number.

3. Compotes, covered.
   a. On high standards.
   b. On low standards.
4. Cordials.
5. Creamer.
6. Egg cups.
7. Goblets.
8. Pickle dish, tapered at one end.
   a. Oval.
9. Pitcher, water.
10. Salts, footed.
11. Sauce dish, 4 inch.
12. Spoonholder.
13. Sugar bowl.
14. Tumbler, water.
15. Wine glass.

Color: Clear glass.

STIPPLED WOODFLOWER

From New Jersey came a sugar bowl and creamer of a lovely stippled pattern of which I have been unable to find any other pieces. Because it is unusually appealing and as a means of identification for collectors who may find other items, these two dishes are shown on Plate 136. It is reasonable to suppose that since these two pieces were made there must be others. After this book was revised in 1933, only one report came in to me on this pattern, which bears out my opinion expressed previously, that it was probably produced by some small factory which was not in operation very long, so that only a comparatively small amount of it was made. For some reason it was not copied to the extent that the majority of other patterns were. It is rather different in appearance, the entire background being stippled, the design consisting of many odd little flowers and fern-like leaves, suggesting wood flowers. It was probably made during the late Sixties or early Seventies.

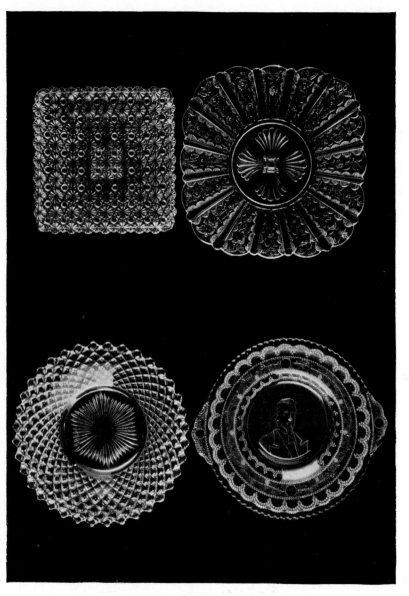

PLATE 134—PLATES

Daisy and Button
English Hobnail

Paneled Daisy
Odd seven inch plate

PLATE 135—SIX AND SEVEN INCH PLATES

Roman Rosette   Princess Feather   Overshot Glass

PLATE 136

1. FLOWER POT sugar bowl, creamer, water pitcher.
2. STIPPLED WOODFLOWER sugar bowl, creamer.
3. PRIMROSE covered compote, creamer, goblet, footed sauce.
4. PANELLED DAISY celery vase, compote on high standard, goblet.

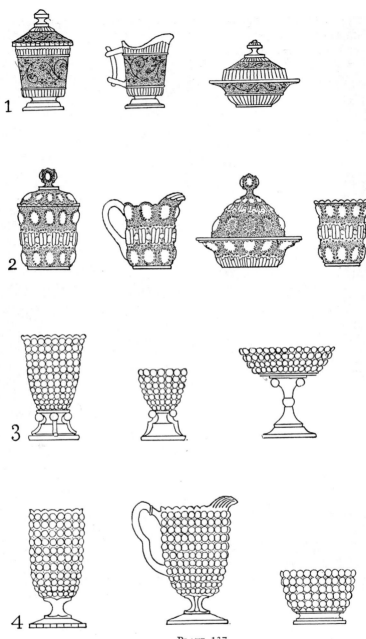

PLATE 137

1. RIBBED FORGET-ME-NOT sugar bowl, creamer, butter dish.
2. HEAVY JEWEL sugar bowl, creamer, butter dish, spoonholder.
3. THOUSAND EYE (three knob) celery vase, egg cup, compote.
4. THOUSAND EYE (plain) celery vase, water pitcher, bowl.

PLATE 138—SEVEN-INCH PLATES

Fine Cut
Diamond Cut with Leaf

Stippled Forget-Me-Not
Dahlia

PLATE 139

1. BARBERRY sugar bowl, pickle dish, spoonholder.
2. BARBERRY covered bowl, covered compote, footed sauce dish.
3. CURRANT sugar bowl, creamer, celery vase.
4. WINDFLOWER creamer, tumbler, spoonholder, egg cup, footed salt.

PLATE 140

1. SCROLL covered compote, sugar bowl, goblet, spoonholder.
2. THISTLE goblet, tumbler, spoonholder, egg cup.
3. SCROLL with FLOWERS creamer, goblet, egg cup.
4. DIAGONAL BAND creamer, goblet, water pitcher.

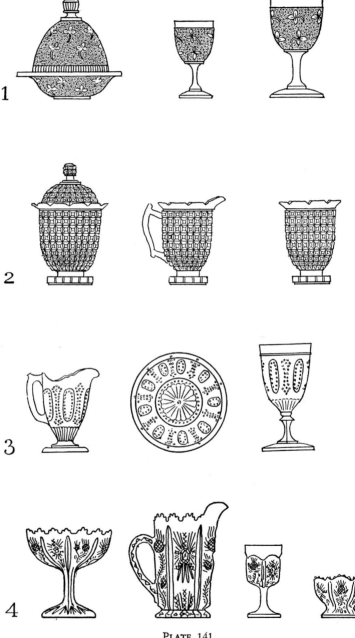

PLATE 141

1. STIPPLED CLOVER butter dish, cordial, goblet.
2. MILK-WHITE WAFFLE sugar bowl, creamer, spoonholder.
3. "101" creamer, plate, goblet.
4. PANELED THISTLE compote, water pitcher, cordial, salt.

Classification

STIPPLED WOODFLOWER

PATTERN 159

(See Plate 136)

Form Number.
  1. Creamer.
  2. Sugar bowl.
Color: Clear glass.

LILY OF THE VALLEY

Similar in character to the Barberry and Bleeding Heart and of the same period, is the Lily of the Valley. It is a dainty design, different in form from the other patterns. The glass is all clear but the bowls are well covered with the leaves and sprays of flowers. The footed pieces may be had with the plain stem or standing on three feet. Both forms are shown on Plate 126. The type with three feet is different and much more unusual. The design of the flowers is the same and each collector should decide which style he prefers. The Lily of the Valley not being as well known, has not been collected to any great extent but it deserves mention, for it is as attractive as any of the other flower patterns. A goblet is shown on Plate 123.

Classification

LILY OF THE VALLEY

PATTERN 160

(See Plates 123, 126)

Form Number.
  1. Butter dish.
      a. Footed.
      b. On three feet.
  2. Celery vase.
  3. Cordial.

Form Number.

  4. Creamer.
     a. Footed.
     b. On three feet.

  5. Cruet, tall stopper.

  6. Goblets.

  7. Pickle dish, tapered at one end.

  8. Relish dish, oval, deep.

  9. Salts, footed.

  10. Sauce dish, 4 inch, flat with cable edge.

  11. Spoonholder.
     a. On three feet.

  12. Sugar bowl.
     a. Footed.
     b. On three feet.

Color: Clear glass.

PANELED DAISY

A very attractive pattern of this period is the Paneled Daisy. The plates are found both round and square. The round ones, which measure about 7¼ inches, have a panel formed of a flower and leaves, with a stippled, scalloped band on each side, alternating with a fairly heavy bar. In the center of the plate is a conventional ornament. The edge is scalloped, as may be seen in the photograph on Plate 135. The square ones measure 9½ inches and these have rounded corners, as shown on Plate 134. The stem of the goblet is round and plain, the base being the same. The sauce dishes have a square rim though the dish is round in the center. The same is true of bowls and other pieces not footed.

This is one of the most charming of the flower patterns. It has not been collected extensively because it is not as well known as others. It is to be had in the usual number of forms.

While people may wonder at some of the curious "home-made" descriptive titles of pattern glass, I might point out that some of the original trade names also were curious. Most of the designs went under simple "line numbers," but a few had names which are in no way descriptive and apparently have no connection with the particular pattern. Paneled Daisy was originally christened "Brazil" by Bryce Bros. of Pittsburgh, who were the makers. No variations having been found, it would appear that they had a monopoly on the "Brazil," which was made over a period of years, starting with the Seventies.

Classification

PANELED DAISY

PATTERN 161
(See Plates 95, 134, 135, 136)

Form Number.

1. Bowls. Open, flared. 6, 7 and 8 inch.
2. Butter dish. Two styles, flat and footed.
3. Cake plates, on standard. 8, 9, 10 and 11 inch.
4. Celery vase.
5. Compotes.
   a. Covered, on high standard. 5, 6, 7 and 8 inch.
   b. Open, on high standard. Scalloped edge. 5, 7, 9, 10 and 11 inch.
6. Creamer.
7. Dishes. Oval, 7, 8, 9 and 10 inch.
8. Goblet.
9. Mug, large.
10. Pickle dish.
11. Pitcher, water, ½ gallon. See *Water set.*
12. Plates.
   a. Bread. 9½ inch, square.
   b. Seven inch. Round.
13. Salt and pepper.
14. Sauce dishes.
   a. Flared. 4½ inch.
   b. Footed. 4 inch.
15. Spoonholder.
16. Sugar bowl.
17. Sugar shaker.

Form Number.
   18. Syrup jug. Tin top.
   19. Tumbler.
   20. Water set, with tray and bowl.
Color: Clear glass.

FLOWER POT

It is curious how a collector of pressed glass will find one piece in a pattern that has never claimed his attention before and invariably other articles will follow. The first piece I found in this design was an oblong bread plate, which is shown on Plate 133. Water pitchers followed in two sizes. That the goblet exists I do not doubt, but continued searching has not revealed a single one so far. It is a dainty pattern with a heavily stippled background and an urn ribbed in relief, containing a pretty but utterly absurd spray of flowers. There are two large leaves and a flower closely resembling a wild rose. Springing from the petals of the rose are two tulips with leaves and two sprays of a flower I do not recognize. A verbal description of this design is not as satisfactory as a glance at the group illustrated on Plate 136. The larger pieces all stand on four little feet. The sauce dishes are unusual, being oblong, with a small handle at each end. Most of the pieces in this pattern are square. The Flower Pot was made, as nearly I can tell, during the Eighties.

Classification

FLOWER POT

Pattern 162

(See Plates 133, 136)

Form Number.
   1. Cake plate on standard.
   2. Bread tray, oblong.
   3. Butter dish, covered, on four feet.
   4. Compote. Open, 7 inches high.

Form Number.
  5. Creamer.
  6. Pitcher, water. Two sizes.
  7. Sauce dish, oblong, with handle at each end.
        a. Square, on feet.
  8. Spoonholder.
  9. Sugar bowl.
Color: Clear glass.

CLEMATIS

Little can be said about this pattern, as it belongs to the later period when attributions are impossible without any trade catalogue or available records to establish when and where it was made. It appears to be of the Seventies, though it may be later. The design is more effective in the glass than it appears to be in the group on Plate 75. I doubt if any botanist could identify this flower, which hangs downward on a vine-like stem. The stem and leaves are stippled, making them stand out in relief against the clear background. The stem of the flowers is almost like a rope and the leaves are not tulip leaves, so I believe this design came from the inner consciousness of its creator. It resembles a variety of clematis more closely than any other vine, so I am giving it that name. The forms follow closely those of the Cherry and others of this same period. It evidently was not a particularly popular pattern, as little of it is seen to-day.

Classification

CLEMATIS

PATTERN 163

(See Plate 75)

Form Number.
  1. Creamer.
  2. Goblet.
  3. Pitcher, water.

Form Number.

    4. Sauce, flat, 4 inch.

    5. Sugar bowl.

    6. Spoonholder.

Color: Clear glass.

THISTLE

A pattern somewhat in demand at this time is the Thistle. It is a simple but attractive design, consisting of a band of thistle flowers and leaves. The glass shows every indication of being of the Seventies. It may be found in many forms though I have never seen any plates. The design runs quite low about the bowl of the goblet, the balance being clear and leaving a wide band at the top. The tumblers are fairly heavy, and with a row of thumbprints indented near the base. A few fragments in this design were found at Sandwich, so it may have been made there, as well as by other factories, though it is not plentiful to-day.

Classification

THISTLE

PATTERN 164

(See Plate 140)

Form Number.

    1. Berry bowl, round and deep.

    2. Cake plate on standard.

    3. Compote, open, on low foot, 8 inch.

    4. Cordial.

    5. Creamer.

    6. Egg cup.

    7. Goblet.

    8. Pickle dish, tapered at one end.

    9. Pitcher, water.

   10. Sauce, flat and deep, 4 inch.

   11. Spoonholder.

Form Number.
  12. Sugar bowl.
  13. Tumbler.
     a. Tumbler, footed.
  14. Wine.
Color: Clear glass.

SCROLL WITH FLOWERS

Of the patterns using a scroll design as the important motif, the one called Scroll with Flowers is probably the best known. The old trade name having been lost and no new one agreed upon by collectors and dealers, the inability to designate it undoubtedly curtailed the demand for this glass. The design covers the objects fairly well. Among the features to be noted are the odd, quaint, old square handles used on all the pieces, even the egg cup. One of these may be seen in the group on Plate 140. The goblet has the stippled scroll, all of the backgrounds being clear, with a pretty, narrow conventional band both above and below. A wide variety of pieces were made, including the large cake plate with handles and a fascinating little mustard pot with cover.

This ware was presumably made in the late Seventies or early Eighties, though I find no record of it.

Classification

SCROLL WITH FLOWERS

Pattern 165

(See Plates 118, 140)

Form Number.
  1. Butter dish.
  2. Cake plate, with handles.
  3. Compote, covered, on low foot.
  4. Cordial.
  5. Creamer.

Form Number.

6. Egg cup.
7. Goblet.
8. Mustard pot, small, covered.
9. Pickle dish, oval, square handles.
10. Pitcher, water.
11. Salt.
12. Spoonholder.
13. Sugar bowl.

Color: Clear glass; blue; amber. Colored pieces are scarce.

PANELED FLOWER, STIPPLED

Every veteran collector knows that certain patterns are found more abundantly in some states than in others. Most of the popular pressed glass was widely distributed, but I find some designs in Pennsylvania that are rarely ever seen in New York State and vice versa. While touring in Pennsylvania lately I found a rather elaborate stippled and beaded pattern having panels containing flowers in relief. One panel shows a flower resembling a Fuchsia and in the alternating panel a flower not unlike a primrose. I saw a piece or two in almost every shop there, though I have rarely seen any of it outside of Pennsylvania. Several pieces are shown on Plate 77. The glass is brilliant and clear and would make an effective table decoration. None of the pieces is footed, but all have small ribbed panels extending part way up from the base, which add materially to their attractiveness. A variation of this same design came to my attention lately, having a flower similar to a Fuchsia in every panel. Later I found the original old catalogue illustrating and listing this pattern. It was made by the United States Glass Company of Pittsburgh early in the Nineties, and was originally called "Maine" or "No. 15066 Pattern." The goblet, as illustrated in the catalogue, is most attractive, and so are the tumblers. Apparently some of this ware was made in color, as I have found bowls in emerald green. In *Victorian Glass* this pattern is referred to by its original name of "Maine."

Classification
PANELED FLOWER, STIPPLED
or
"MAINE"

PATTERN 166
(See Plate 77)

Form Number.

1. Bowls, 6, 7 and 8 inch.
2. Bread plate, oval.
3. Butter dish. Flanged, with dome lid.
4. Cake plate on standard, 9, 10 and 11 inch.
5. Celery vase.
6. Compotes, open, on high foot, deep bowl, 5, 6, 7 and 8 inch.
   a. Compotes, open, on high foot, flaring bowl, 8, 9 and 10 inch.
7. Creamer.
8. Cruet.
9. Goblet.
10. Jelly compote, open, on high foot, 5 inch.
    a. Same as above, covered.
11. Mug, handled.
12. Pickle dish. 2 styles. 8 inch.
13. Pitcher, water. 2 sizes.
14. Preserve dish, 8 inch.
15. Salt and pepper shakers.
16. Spoonholder.
17. Sugar bowl.
18. Syrup jug.
19. Toothpick or match holder.
20. Tumbler.
21. Wine.

Color: Emerald green; clear.

SUNFLOWER

A different pattern which would appear to date from the Eighties, is the Sunflower. Each piece is divided into twelve squares that are fairly large. The top row of six squares contains in each block a sunflower with other lacy little flowers in the background. The lower row has in each block three fairly large leaves surmounted by some enticing posies that no botanist could ever name. They are purely fanciful but make a pretty showing. This design I have seen in clear, amber, milk-white and blue, though it is very scarce. I hope collectors may be able to add many more forms to my classification.

Classification

SUNFLOWER

PATTERN 167

(See Plate 108)

Form Number.
  1. Butter dish.
  2. Creamer.
  3. Spoonholder.
  4. Sugar bowl.
Colors: Clear; amber; milk-white; blue.

PANELED THISTLE

There is no denying the fact that the Paneled Thistle is a late pattern, but it is also true that it is attractive enough to be what might be termed highly collectible. It has been exhibited by a number of dealers who have shown pressed glass and it always proved to be popular. It is just as well, therefore, to forget the date of manufacture and enjoy it for what it is.

Paneled Thistle is an imitation of cut glass. It was first produced by the Higbee Glass Co., who used as their trade-mark a tiny bumble-bee. Some pieces, such as the plates, may be found to-day bearing the bee in the center of the dish. Later on this firm was absorbed by the United States Glass Company, of Pittsburgh, who naturally discontinued the use of the trade-mark. Collectors have often written me about the bumble-bee and asked why some of the glassware is marked and some other unmarked. The explanation is simple when the facts are known.

Unfortunately, the popularity of this pattern caught the notice of a certain factory producing reproductions, so that the country has been flooded with copies of the goblet with the flaring edge, as well as the small square plate and the large round one. The time will come when it will be possible to restrain this practice.

A large number of forms were made in this design, and I doubt if anyone can see and list them all. It is possible, however, to name enough to give the collector a comprehensive idea of what may be done with it. The goblets are attractive, being formed of panels that arch at the top, a thistle in one panel alternating with a conventional ornament in the other. One type of goblet flares out considerably at the top and the base is rayed. The panels on the bowl follow on to the top of the base, standing out in relief. The other type goblet has straight sides. Plates are most attractive and are found in several sizes. Many of the pieces, such as the sauce dish, a creamer and berry bowl, stand on little knobs that form feet. In fact, there seems to be no limit to what may be had in this Paneled Thistle. The market must once have been flooded with it and undoubtedly it was widely distributed. A group is shown on Plate 141.

Classification
PANELED THISTLE

PATTERN 168
(See Plates 114, 141)

Form Number.

1. Bowl, berry, knob feet. Large number of sizes.
2. Butter dish.
3. Cake plate, on standard.
4. Celery vase.
5. Cheese dish, flat, on foot.
6. Compotes, open, on high standards. Many sizes from 5¼, 7½ inches, etc., with scalloped edge.

Form Number.

    7. Cordials.
    8. Creamer, knob feet.
    9. Cruet.
    10. Dishes.
        a. Oblong.
        b. Oval, curled over edges, large.
        c. Fern dish. Square, with metal containers for plants. 7 inches.
        d. Square covered honey dish.
11. Goblet. Two styles, one with straight bowl and the other flared.
    12. Pitcher, water. Two sizes.
13. Plates, 7¼ square.
        a. Round, 8¼, 9¼* and 10¼ inch.
    14. Relish dishes.
        a. Long, oval, 8¼ inch.
        b. Wide, oval, 7½ inch.
    15. Salt, footed.
        a. Shaker salts.
        b. Individual size.
    16. Sauce dishes, several styles and sizes. Some have knob feet and others are flat.
    17. Sherbet cup, handled.
        a. On foot, flared.
    18. Spoonholder.
    19. Sugar bowl, with two handles.
    20. Vase, tall.
        a. Small vase.
    21. Tumblers, water.
    22. Wine glass. Two styles, as in the goblets.
Color: Clear glass.

Chapter XV

LEAF PATTERNS

BARBERRY

A pattern widely collected to-day is known as Barberry. The decoration is a long cluster of leaves and elongated berries. There are three variants of the goblets, one having clusters of berries that are round instead of elongated. In the other two types the leaves are fairly heavy and veined and the berries stand out clearly in low relief. The design partly covers the goblet, though it leaves a wide marginal band at the top. The third variant has a very thin design which is lower on the bowl of the goblet. It is the least attractive of the three.

I have been told that one type of barberry shrub grew prolifically near the seashore, which was the reason why the knob of the covered dishes in this pattern was made in the form of a seashell. This is only one of those legends about pressed glass patterns for the authenticity of which no one can vouch. A collector informs me that this ware was made in Fostoria, Ohio, but judging by the number of variants, it also must have been made elsewhere. There are many covered compotes and bowls of different sizes, and they are lovely and cool-looking in the clear glass. A few pieces of this design may be found in color, notably the six-inch plates. I have seen these in both amber and blue.

Some confusion in connection with the Barberry and the Currant designs may be avoided if the collector will note that the Currant pattern always carries the cable cord, while the Barberry does not. The decorative motif of these two is so similar that I have noticed, in sets assembled by collectors, specimens of both kinds. The differences may be clearly noted in Plate 139. This is one of the few pressed glass patterns having cup plates to match.

For the most part, these little dishes in our later tableware had passed the stage of being utilized to hold handleless cups but were designed as individual butters.

The Barberry must have been produced in large quantities by various factories, as it is not difficult to find to-day. At least one variation is known to have been produced at Sandwich. It would appear to be a ware of the Seventies.

Classification

BARBERRY

PATTERN 169

(See Plates 135, 139, 142)

Form Number.

1. Butter dish.
    a. Large and flat with extra wide rim, design around rim. Rare.
    b. Plain, round without broad rim, 6 inch.
2. Celery vase.
3. Compotes, covered.
    a. On high standards, various sizes.
    b. On low standards, various sizes.
4. Cordials.
5. Creamer.
6. Cup plates.
7. Dishes.
    a. Oval, 8 x 5½ inches (probably may be found in various sizes).
    b. Round, flat, covered, 8 inch.
8. Egg cups.
9. Goblets.
    a. Elongated berries.
    b. Round berries.
    c. Thin design, smaller.
10. Honey dish, 3½ inch.
11. Pickle dish, oval, tapering at one end.
12. Pitcher, water.
13. Plate, 6 inch.
14. Salt, footed.

Form Number.
  15. Sauce dish.
        a. Flat, round.
        b. Footed, round.
  16. Spoonholder.
  17. Syrup pitcher, applied handle. Pewter lid.
  18. Sugar bowl, covered, shell knob.

Colors: Amber; blue; clear. Colored pieces rare.

MAPLE LEAF

A heavily frosted and stippled pattern, similar in many respects to the Cabbage Leaf, is called Maple Leaf. This glass has been known to collectors for years, and why it is not more in demand to-day is a mystery. The only explanation is that collectors are not certain that it may be acquired in sets. They do know the charming ten-inch round plates that come in colors, and the same style of plate known as the "Grant Peace Plate" (Plate 144) showing General Grant's head in the center. Not so many are familiar with the unusual deep oval bowls on stippled feet, or the large covered compotes, also on stippled feet. Tumblers may be had in colors, but the goblets are exceedingly scarce.

This glass was made originally by Gillinder & Sons, of Greensburg, Pa. They called it simply "Leaf" pattern. It is obviously a grape leaf, but since I have usually heard both dealers and collectors refer to it as Maple Leaf, I have not attempted to change it. This pattern was made during the Seventies. The U. S. Grant Peace plates in colors with the leaf border have been quite popular. They were made by Adams & Company, of Pittsburgh, about 1885.

A charming feature of the Maple Leaf is the range of colors that one may find. Besides the heavily stippled, frosted glass it may be had in yellow, blue, emerald green, apple green, amber and clear. The emerald green is particularly handsome and unusual. All the pieces do not come in the same colors. The Peace plates for example, are not found in emerald green or frosted, but may be had in all the other colors named. The ten-inch round plates with conventional diamond center are found in all the colors except emerald green. I have seen the platters, footed dishes, etc., in all colors except apple green. They may have been made in this shade but not to my knowledge. The classification names the color range of the various articles. This glass was probably a product of the Seventies, except the Grant plates, which followed later.

Classification

MAPLE LEAF

PATTERN 170

(See Plates 143, 144)

Form Number.

1. Butter dish, oval, on stippled feet. Knob with cluster of grapes and leaves.
2. Creamer, oval on stippled feet.
3. Compote, round, on feet. Extra large, 9 inch diameter, 10½ inches to top of cover.
4. Compote, covered, various sizes.
5. Cup plate, or individual butter. Not exact match.
6. Dish, oval, covered, on stippled feet. Grape handles.
   a. Same, without handles, 10 inches long, 6 inches wide, 4¼ inches high.
7. Dish, oval, open, on stippled feet. Two sizes.
   a. Same, without feet.
8. Goblets. Rare.
9. Pitcher, water. Ovoid. Two sizes.
10. Plates. Maple Leaf border, conventional diamond pattern in center. 10 inch.
11. Plates. Wide Maple Leaf border inscribed, "Let us have peace. U. S. Grant." Center shows head of Grant, inscribed above semi-circle, "Born April 27, 1822, died July 23, 1885." Outside measurement, 10½ inches.
12. Platter, oval, diamond pattern in center. 13 inch.
13. Sauce. Form of maple leaves, on three feet. 5 and 6 inch.

PLATE 142—GOBLETS

Blackberry   Currant
Strawberry   Barberry

PLATE 143
Dolphin compote and Petticoat Dolphin candlesticks
Maple Leaf oval bowl, tumbler and platter

PLATE 144—LARGE PLATES

Diamond Cut with Leaf
Grant Peace plate

Odd Daisy bread plate
Maple Leaf plate

PLATE 145—LARGE PLATES

Teasel   Stippled Cherry
Festoon   Ivy in Snow

Form Number.

14. Spoonholder, oval, on stippled feet.
15. Sugar bowl, oval, on stippled feet.
16. Tumbler.

Colors; Clear; frosted; emerald green; apple green; blue; yellow; amber.

Peace Plates	*Dishes*	*Plates, 10 inch*
Apple green	Frosted	Clear
Blue	Clear	Frosted
Yellow	Emerald green	Yellow
Amber	Amber	Amber
Clear	Yellow	Blue
	Blue (deep shade).	

CABBAGE LEAF

A most amusing and unique pattern is one which is quite properly called Cabbage Leaf. The nursery tales concerning Farmer Brown and his trouble with Peter Rabbit in the cabbage patch could not have been known at the time this glass was produced, but nevertheless, the little sauce dishes composed of three cabbage leaves have Peter Rabbit's face in the base as clear as life. The cover of such dishes as require one, is formed of the stippled leaves, with a rabbit's head forming the knob. Three smaller rabbits' heads are peeping out from the leaves. On the under rim of the cover I note a cable cord of the type so often associated with the Sandwich product. The celery holder (now usually termed celery vase) has three large stippled cabbage leaves which roll out toward the top, leaving the top of the glass straight and clear. A group including a covered butter dish and the celery vase is shown on Plate 65. Generally this interesting pattern will be found in a heavily stippled, frosted glass, though I have seen a few pieces in amber. No goblets or tumblers have been encountered in my travels, but I presume they were made in a similar style to the celery holder; that is, partly frosted and partly clear.

This glass was probably made during the Seventies, or possibly later. An item of interest is a butter dish, exactly like the one illustrated, in green majolica, the rabbits' heads being colored brown.

Classification

CABBAGE LEAF

PATTERN 171

(See Plate 65)

Form Number.
1. Butter dish.
2. Celery vase.
3. Compote, covered, on high standard.
4. Creamer.
5. Pickle dish. Flat, in form of large single leaf.
6. Sauce dish, $3\frac{1}{2}$ inch.
7. Sugar bowl. Cover same as butter dish, illustrated.
8. Spoonholder.

Colors: Amber, clear glass, heavily stippled and frosted.

HOLLY

The Holly pattern is of the same period as the Barberry and the Currant. The goblet carries the small cable cord above the design, as is used in the Currant. The little round holly berries stand out in clear relief and the leaves are lightly stippled. It is altogether likely that all the usual forms were made though I have not seen many of them. The Holly probably was not so widely copied and did not enjoy the popularity that the Barberry did. There is every reason why it should be popular, when one thinks of its function during the Christmas holidays.

The classification lists only those few pieces I have seen. Many others must exist. A few fragments in this pattern have been excavated at Sandwich but not enough pieces were found to justify the belief it was produced there in large quantities.

Classification

HOLLY

PATTERN 172
(See Plate 116)

Form Number.
1. Compote, on low foot, 8½ inch.
2. Creamer.
3. Egg cups.
4. Goblets.
5. Pitcher, water.
6. Sauce dish, flat, 4 inch.
7. Spoon holder.
8. Tumbler.

Color: Clear glass.

BEADED ACORN

Belonging to the same period as the group of Beaded Grape Medallion patterns, or about 1870, is a slight variation known as the Beaded Acorn. The background of these pieces is stippled, the border of all dishes having three clear oval medallions which are beaded on the edge and contain an Acorn and Oak leaf. The six-inch plates have a plain edge with a single row of fine beading or dewdrops. The center of the plate has a six-pointed star outlined in the little dewdrops, as one may see on Plate 124. A series of these patterns, which are quite similar, were produced during the Seventies. Some have stippled backgrounds and clear stripes running horizontally and on others the stripes run vertically, dividing the stippled background into panels. These designs all use the acorns as knobs for the covered pieces. The forms run about the same in all this series. The Boston & Sandwich Glass Company produced Beaded Acorn. It is not known whether it was copied by any other factory.

Classification

BEADED ACORN

Pattern 173

(See Plates 65, 124)

Form Number.
1. Butter dish.
2. Champagne.
3. Compotes.
   - *a.* Covered, on low foot.
   - *b.* Open, on high foot.
4. Creamer.
5. Egg cup.
6. Goblet.
7. Honey dish, 3½ inch.
8. Plate, 6 inch.
9. Relish dish, oval, deep.
   - *a.* Small, oval, relish dish.
10. Salt, footed.
11. Sauce dish, flat, 4 inch.
12. Spoonholder.
13. Sugar bowl.

Color: Clear glass.

ACORN PATTERN VARIANTS

Apparently so many Acorn patterns were made during the late Seventies and Eighties, that they are difficult to classify. On Plate 125 are shown two lines of these, nearly all variants. The goblet in the upper row is the most attractive, showing large clusters of the acorns with stippled oak leaves. A cable cord runs around the top forming the marginal band. The base of the butter dish in the center of this row and the sauce dish, appear to match the goblet. Whether the water pitcher on the bottom line is supposed to match the goblet above, as some collectors claim, cannot be told definitely. For one thing, it lacks the cable cord. As a rule, if one piece shows the cable cord, all the others of the set do. The goblet alone is worth while in this pattern for anyone needing such a design. The first goblet in the lower line does not match any other pieces I have found. The next goblet and creamer match, both showing the odd little leaves running to the base of the bowls, forming panels. No doubt a full set of this might be acquired, as I have also found a footed salt, covered sugar bowl and butter dish. The classification of these two patterns will be listed separately.

Classification
ACORN PATTERN VARIANTS
PATTERN 174
Large Cluster of Leaves
(See Plate 125)

Form Number.
1. Butter dish.
2. Creamer.
3. Goblet.
4. Pitcher, water.
5. Sauce dish, flat, 4 inch.

Classification
ACORN PATTERN VARIANTS
PATTERN 174A
Panelled with Leaves
(See Plate 125)

Form Number.
1. Butter dish.
2. Cordial.
3. Creamer.
4. Egg cup.
5. Goblet.

Form Number.
  6. Salt, footed.
  7. Spoon holder.
  8. Sugar bowl.
Color: Clear glass.

SPRIG

It is difficult to name or describe a design having as its decorative motif a sprig of an unrecognizable shrub or flower. This pattern which is being named Sprig belongs to this class. I have heard it called "Barley" and "Indian Tree," but it is certain that these titles are both misnomers of recent origin. The dainty, fern-like sprig is not a piece of barley nor an Indian tree.

This glass is obviously of the Eighties; probably the very late Eighties. It is quaint, however, and deserves mention for that reason. All the pieces have a panelled effect, with a single sprig consisting of two tiny leaves with flowers running vinelike in every other division, the one alternating being left clear. It is not very well known at the present time, but probably will be in the future. Undoubtedly a wide range of pieces were made in this pattern, but I have only found those listed. Somewhere a butter dish must exist, since all the other tableware has been found.

Classification

SPRIG

PATTERN 175

(See Plates 78, 153)

Form Number.
  1. Bowl. Round, flat. 6 inches.
  2. Cake plate, on standard.
  3. Celery vase.
  4. Compotes, open. Various sizes, on either a high standard or low standard, from 7 inch.
  5. Cordial.

Form Number.

6. Creamer.
7. Dish, oval, deep.
8. Goblet.
9. Pickle dish.
10. Pitcher, water.
11. Platter, oval.
12. Sauce dish, flat, 4 inch.
    a. Footed sauce dish.
13. Spoonholder.
14. Sugar bowl.

Color: Clear glass.

Chapter XVI

STIPPLED IVY PATTERNS

IVY IN SNOW

Of the Ivy patterns which appeared during the late Sixties, one of the most attractive is the Ivy in Snow. The background of the pieces is stippled, like the Rose in Snow, and has three attractive sprays of bright ivy leaves and buds, in fairly high relief. The clear, veined leaves stand out brilliantly and effectively. The stems of goblets, wines, celery holders, compotes, etc., all match and are unusual, too. There is a knob fairly close to the bowl, the balance of the stem being delicately fluted. It is graceful and appealing. The stippling is particularly soft and fine, and has a lovely luster. This pattern is not so well known as many others, though fairly plentiful in some sections. It may be had in all the needed forms in the clear, as well as in a deep, rich amber. If it comes in other colors, I have not seen it. The amber pieces are exceedingly scarce. A few items may be had in milk-white, as well as some in crystal with the leaves decorated in ruby red.

Practically all of this set has been reproduced. The copies have been flooding the country for the past few years, in clear glass, as well as in milk-white. It will be necessary for collectors to study the differences between the old and the new, if they begin accumulating Ivy in Snow. The new items will be adequately treated in my revised and enlarged volume on reproductions.

It is not known who patented this design but it was produced for a number of years by the Cooperative Flint Glass Company, of Beaver Falls, Pa.

My suggestion to beginners is to avoid any of the three patterns which have been widely reproduced, and Ivy In Snow is one of them.

Classification
IVY IN SNOW

PATTERN 176
(See Plates 103, 119, 145)

Form Number.
*1. Butter dish, flat.
  2. Bowl, flat, 8 inch.
  3. Cake plate, on standard.
*4. Celery vase.
*5. Compote, covered, on high standard. Several sizes, from 6 inch.
  6. Cordial.
*7. Creamer (not footed).
  8. Cups, handled.
*9. Goblets.
10. Jam jar.
11. Pitcher, water.
*12. Plate, round. 7 and 10 inch sizes.
*13. Sauce, round and flat, 4 inch.
       a. Deep sauce, 6 inch.
*14. Spoonholder.
*15. Sugar bowl.

Colors: Clear*; milk-white*; amber; clear with leaves in ruby.

BUDDED IVY

The Budded Ivy is so styled because exactly the same pieces are found with vine alone, and at the first glance one would not notice the difference. The stippling is coarse on this design and the leaves of the vine which winds its way around the bowls of the objects, do not stand out in such high relief. They are similar in that they are lightly veined. The handles of the water pitcher and creamer are crimped at the base. It is a quaint pattern and fairly well known because it is quite plentiful, especially in New York

State. It may be found in all the needed pieces for general table use.

Classification

BUDDED IVY

PATTERN 177

(See Plate 119)

Form Number.

1. Butter dish, flat.
2. Compote on high standard.
3. Compote on low standard.
4. Creamer.
5. Goblets.
6. Salt, footed.
7. Sauce, 4 inch.
8. Spoonholder.
9. Sugar.
10. Syrup pitcher. Metal top.

Color: Clear glass.

STIPPLED IVY

This pattern is like the Budded Ivy, except that the vine is plain, without any flowers or buds. The leaves seem to be brighter, possibly because they stand out in slightly higher relief against the stippled background. The stems of all the footed pieces are formed of nine very narrow panels, and the bases are clear. I have never seen any of this Ivy pattern in color.

Classification

STIPPLED IVY

PATTERN 178

(See Plates 119, 146)

Form Number.

1. Butter dish, flat.
2. Compote, open, on high foot.

PLATE 146—GOBLETS

Thousand Eye   Cathedral
Swirl   Stippled Ivy

PLATE 147

1. RIBBED OPAL berry bowl, sauce dish, mug.
2. RIBBED OPAL creamer, pitcher, tall tumbler.
3. SPIRALLED IVY sugar bowl, spoonholder, water pitcher, tumbler.
4. STIPPLED STAR celery vase, sugar bowl, goblet.

PLATE 148—GOBLETS

Loop and Dart, diamond ornaments
Double Loop and Dart

Loop and Dart, round ornaments
Loop and Dart

PLATE 149

1. LEAF and DART celery vase, footed tumbler, creamer, footed salt.
2. LOOP and DART (round ornaments) creamer, celery vase, spoonholder, cordial.
3. LOOP and DART creamer, goblet, cordial, egg cup.
4. LOOP and DART (diamond ornaments) sugar bowl, butter dish, tumbler, water pitcher.

Form Number.
- 3. Compote, open, on low foot.
- 4. Creamer.
- 5. Egg cup.
- 6. Goblets.
- 7. Salt, footed.
- 8. Sauce, 4 inch.
- 9. Spoonholder.
- 10. Sugar bowl.
- 11. Syrup pitcher.

Color: Clear glass.

SPIRALLED IVY

An unusual Ivy pattern is called the Spiralled Ivy. I can learn very little about it and have only seen a few pieces. Possibly this design was not made in many other forms though my experience has been that when I find one or two pieces, the others usually follow. Very few people appear to be acquainted with this glass at all, though it is most attractive. The tumblers were sent to me from the West and then a water pitcher came from Richfield Springs, New York. The rest I found in Pennsylvania. The glass is fairly heavy, the tumblers having a wide band made up of five smaller rounded ribs alternating with a wide stippled band containing five-pointed Ivy leaves and small buds. There do not seem to be any footed dishes, so I judge this may be a pattern of the 1880's. It is an interesting as well as attractive glass and it is to be hoped that other pieces may be found.

Classification

SPIRALLED IVY

PATTERN 179
(See Plate 147)

Form Number.
- 1. Butter dish.
- 2. Creamer.

Form Number.
- 3. Sauce dish.
- 4. Pitcher, water. Quart and pint.
- 5. Spoonholder.
- 6. Sugar bowl.
- 7. Tumblers.

Color: Clear glass.

Chapter XVII

LOOP AND DART GROUP

LOOP AND DART

The group of grape patterns took much time to untangle, but the Loop and Dart series have been even more of a puzzle, for just when they all seemed to be rightly placed, an utterly unknown piece would make its appearance and disarrange the order. They are now classified so that both dealers and collectors should have little difficulty in identifying the wanted piece in this group.

The first I wish to describe is the plain Loop and Dart. As may be noted from the photographs on Plate 148 the design extends nearer to the top of the glass than on any of the others. The background is rather heavily stippled, the design standing out in clear relief. The goblet stem joins the base of the bowl in little points, like those seen where it joins the base. The creamer is footed, as may be seen on Plate 149. Another interesting feature of this glass is that the lids of all the covered pieces fit over the top edge, a small band closing over the outside. It would seem that one factory must have had a monopoly on this design, but just why so many similar variants were made is a question that cannot be readily answered. The same style of pieces appears to have been made in each group. The handle of the water pitcher and of the creamer is crimped at the base, together with other features suggestive of the patterns of the late 1860's. This group has been attributed to the Portland Glass Company, of Portland, Maine, a factory which was in operation only from 1863 to 1873. I do not know of any documented evidence to prove that all the variations originated there. The Loop and Dart design is illustrated in a catalogue in my possession of Richards & Hartley, of Tarentum, Pa. Fragments were also unearthed at the site of the Boston & Sandwich Glass Company.

It is strange a pattern of such obvious merit should not have become more popular during the past decade. Since it has not been in active demand, prices still remain exceedingly reasonable.

Classification

LOOP AND DART

PATTERN 180
(See Plates 148, 149)

Form Number.
1. Butter dish.
2. Celery holder.
3. Compote, low foot, 8 inch.
4. Cordial.
5. Creamer.
6. Egg cups.
7. Goblets.
8. Pitcher, water.
9. Plate, 6 inch. Scarce.
10. Salt, footed.
11. Spoonholder.
12. Sugar bowl.
13. Tumbler, water.
14. Tumbler, footed.
Color: Clear glass.

LOOP AND DART WITH DIAMOND ORNAMENTS

As may be seen on Plate 148 the Loop and Dart with diamond ornaments above the design, has really a double loop and dart. All the pieces in this series which have the diamond ornaments, also have the double loop. The goblet has a very wide marginal band at the top, with a fine double line just above the ornaments. The glass is stippled only as a background for the double Loop and Dart pattern. The stem is hexagonal, following the lines of the stem in the design on the base which is plain. The glass is bright and clear, particularly the covered pieces, which have the design in relief on the inside of the cover. The six-inch plate is interesting, and is shown on Plate 124.

This pattern has not been very widely known or collected, but it is bound to be popular when its charm is recognized. I have never seen any colored pieces in this ware. It has been definitely established as a Sandwich product, though it may have been produced by another factory as well.

Classification
LOOP AND DART WITH DIAMOND ORNAMENTS
PATTERN 181
(See Plates 124, 148, 149)

Form Number.
1. Butter dish.
2. Celery holder.
3. Compotes.
4. Cordials.
5. Creamer.
6. Egg cups.
7. Goblets.
8. Pitcher, water.
9. Plate, 6 inch. Scarce.
10. Salt, footed.
11. Spoonholder.
12. Sugar bowl.
13. Tumblers, footed.
14. Tumblers, water.
Color: Clear glass.

LOOP AND DART WITH ROUND ORNAMENTS

The third one of the Loop and Dart series has round ornaments, instead of diamond shaped. As will be noted in the photograph on Plate 148 the background has a finer, heavier stipple, to the extent that a first glance would make one think it pitted. The dart varies, being open instead of solid, and it meets a tiny point which reaches up from the base of the bowl. The stem is a plain hexagonal and rather prim looking. One fact is apparent in all the pieces in this group, and that is that they were nicely executed and the quality of the glass is good. The goblet has a nice ring to it.

All the forms are similar to the others in this series, and may be seen on Plate 149. Some pieces, such as a compote, may have a double design, but this only occurs when there is a wide space to cover.

After this book was revised the first time, in 1933, a patent was discovered, proving the Loop and Dart with round ornaments was produced by the Portland Glass Company of Portland, Maine. They were in business from the fall of 1863 until 1873—a brief ten years. A history of the factory may be found in my book, *Victorian Glass*. This particular Loop and Dart was designed by William O. Davis, who was superintendent of the factory from 1865. It is known that he was formerly associated with the old O'Hara Glass Company of Pittsburgh, during the 1850's. The patent date on the Loop and Dart with round ornament, is May 11, 1869. Some fragments in this design were unearthed at Sandwich, so whether it was carried on there after the Portland factory closed, or whether the pieces that were discovered were purchased to use as cullet, is not known at present.

Classification

LOOP AND DART WITH ROUND ORNAMENTS

PATTERN 182

(See Plates 148, 149)

Form Number.
1. Butter dish.
2. Celery vase.
3. Compotes, covered. 4 sizes.
      a. Compotes, open. 2 sizes.
4. Cordials.
5. Creamer.

Form Number.

6. Cup plates, possibly designed as individual butters.
7. Egg cups.
8. Goblets.
9. Lamp. Rare.
10. Pickle dishes, oval. **2 sizes.**
11. Pitcher, water.
12. Plate, 6 inch. Scarce.
13. Salt, footed.
14. Sauce dish, flat. 3¾ inches. Star in base.
     a. Sauce, 4 inch. Loop and Dart in base.
15. Spoonholder.
16. Sugar bowl. 2 styles, one having cover fitting over outside, the other with cover fitting inside.
17. Tumblers, footed.
18. Tumblers, water.

Color: Clear glass.

DOUBLE LOOP AND DART

Very similar to the Loop and Dart with diamond-shaped ornaments, is the Double Loop and Dart. The goblet has a wide marginal band with a stippled background as a basis of the double loop and dart motif. The loop forms an inverted heart with the dart pointing upwards from the base of the bowl. It is unusual and perhaps not as decorative as the others in this series. It is found in the usual forms though it is much more scarce in this particular variation.

Classification
DOUBLE LOOP AND DART
PATTERN 183
(See Plate 148)

Form Number.

1. Butter dish.
2. Celery holder.

Form Number.
3. Compotes.
4. Cordial.
5. Creamer.
6. Egg cups.
7. Goblets.
8. Pitcher, water.
9. Plate, 6 inch. Rare.
10. Salt, footed.
11. Spoonholder.
12. Sugar bowl.
13. Tumblers, footed.

Color: Clear glass.

LEAF AND DART

The Loop and Dart design and its different variants have now become familiar to both dealers and collectors. A design quite similar though not so well known, has been called by a few "Loop and Leaf." The leaf part is quite correct, but the dart should really not be called a "loop." It corresponds exactly with the dart of the Loop and Dart design. The background of this glass is stippled, the design standing out in relief. The band at the top has a border of tiny star-shaped ornaments. The stems of the footed pieces are a plain hexagonal and the glass is bright and clear. There is no ring, of course, for we have now passed the days of the lead-flint age in the popular pattern glass, which gave the glass the clear bell tone when tapped.

One of the most interesting discoveries in this glass was a covered salt. These covered salts appear to have been made in the earliest patterns of pressed glass, but it is extremely difficult to find them now with the covers. Salt did not attract the flies like sugar, therefore the futile task of covering these small dishes to keep out the moisture soon became irksome and the tops were discarded many years ago. A covered salt in the ribbed Ivy pattern is shown on Plate 39. They were made in the Bellflower, but I could not find one in time to have it photographed for this book.

The Leaf and Dart is a dainty, attractive pattern, probably produced in the early 1870's. I find it shown in an old catalogue of Richards & Hartley, of Tarentum, Pa., who called it their "Pride Pattern." Fragments were also discovered at the site of the Boston & Sandwich Glass Company.

Classification

LEAF AND DART

PATTERN 184

(See Plates 95, 149)

Form Number.
1. Butter dish.
2. Celery vase.
3. Cordial.
4. Creamer.
5. Egg cups.
6. Goblets.
7. Pitcher, water.
8. Salt, on foot.
9. Salt on foot, covered.
10. Sauce dish, flat, 4 inch.
11. Spoonholder.
12. Sugar bowl.
13. Tumblers, footed.

Color: Clear glass.

DOUBLE LOOP

Somewhat similar to the Loop and Dart patterns is another design known as Double Loop. This glass has a stippled background with an interlaced effect of narrow clear stripes in relief, dainty and silvery in appearance. Between each of the larger interlaced spaces is a teardrop. The glass is clear, brilliant and sparkling.

During the Seventies and Eighties these frosted and stippled effects were in vogue and they are equally popular to-day. The Double Loop is not very well known, but I predict greater popularity for it in the future. Originally called May Pole design, it was made by one of the factories in the old Pittsburgh glass district.

Classification

DOUBLE LOOP

PATTERN 185

(See Plate 101)

Form Number.

1. Berry bowls, round. 6 and 8 inch.
2. Butter dish.
3. Cake plate, on standard. 10 inch.
4. Compote, open, on high foot. 7 inch.
    a. Jelly compote. 4½ inch, open, on high foot.
5. Creamer.
6. Cruet, oil or vinegar.
7. Dishes, preserve. Oval. 7 and 8 inch.
8. Goblet.
9. Pickle dish.
10. Pitcher, water.
    a. Syrup pitcher, metal top.
11. Salt and pepper shakers.
12. Sauce dish. Flat. 4 and 4½ inch.
13. Spoonholder.
14. Sugar bowl.
15. Sugar sifter.
16. Tumbler, water.

Color: Clear glass.

DOUBLE SPEAR

During the mass production of pressed glass for cheap commercial purposes in the 1880's, many dainty and attractive patterns were made in the quaint old forms which are desirable to-day for decorative schemes. One little known design is called the Double Spear. The forms are similar to many earlier ones except for the absence of those few telltale signs that we learn to associate with earlier glass. The handle of the footed creamer is obviously pressed instead of applied. The butter dish is flat with a clear glass knob shaped with petals like a flower. The sugar bowl is also footed like the creamer. The glass is light in weight and has no ring. The design is made up of spear-like ornaments with some criss-crosses in between them.

It has considerable brilliance for such a late ware and doubtless many collectors will find merit in it. A group is shown on Plate 132. Listed are the only pieces I have seen.

Classificatioı

DOUBLE SPEAR

PATTERN 186

(See Plate 132)

Form Number.
1. Butter dish.
2. Celery vase.
3. Compote, covered, on high foot, knob in form of flower petals.
4. Creamer.
5. Egg cup.
6. Goblet.
7. Pitcher, water.
8. Spoonholder.
9. Sauce dish.
10. Sugar bowl.

Color: Clear glass.

Chapter XVIII

FRUIT GROUP

BLACKBERRY

It is quite possible for anyone to become enthusiastic over the Blackberry pattern. If a vote were taken I believe this would be adjudged the most popular pattern in milk-white glass. The goblets are a thing of beauty, many of them showing their opaline quality when held to the light. This pattern is probably slightly older than the Strawberry. Of the milk-white patterns collectible in sets, I believe the Sawtooth pattern to be the earliest, followed by the Blackberry, Strawberry and Paneled Wheat.

It has become possible to be able to date the beginnings of the popular Blackberry pattern. It was made of the best quality of milk-white glass and, together with Sawtooth, it ranks to-day as the finest to be had of the old patterns in white. Mr. Guy van Doren of Detroit, Mich., found a dated piece, wrote to the United States Patent Office in Washington and learned that the patent read:

To William Leighton, Jr., of Wheeling, West Va.
Design No. 3,829, dated February 1, 1870.
Design for ornamenting glass-ware.

Be it known that I, William Leighton, Jr., of Wheeling, in the County of Ohio, and State of West Virginia, have invented and produced a new and original Design for glass-ware and hot-cast porcelain, of which the following is a specification:

The nature of my design is fully represented in the accompanying drawings, to which reference is herein made; and

It consists of a wreath or band of blackberries, leaves, and stems, intended to be placed upon the bowls of the various articles or around the sides of dishes or upon the covers of dishes, in any manner that shall appear most ornamental.

I claim as my invention—

The design for glass-ware or hot-cast porcelain, consisting of a wreath of blackberries, leaves, and stems, as shown. In testimony whereof, I have signed my name to this specification, in the presence of two subscribing witnesses.

WILLIAM LEIGHTON, JR.

Witnesses:

H. HAZLETT.

CHAS. N. BRADY.

The design accompanying this document is exactly like the pattern shown in this book under Blackberry. It was produced in crystal, as well as in the milk-white, apparently from the same molds.

What may be said of the Strawberry cannot be said of the Blackberry, that the same molds were used for both the milk-white and the clear glass. By comparing the group of milk-white pieces on Plate 150 with those of the clear glass on Plate 151, it will be noted that the celery vase in milk-white has a short round stem while the clear glass is hexagonal and longer. The marginal band of the clear glass is much wider and the top does not flare quite so much. In the footed salts the milk-white one is noticeably more round in the bowl and has a foot but no stem. The clear glass one has a short round stem. While it is entirely possible that these may have been produced at the same time it is also more likely that this pattern may have been copied more widely. Of the group of milk-white pieces, the water pitcher and celery vase are exceedingly scarce. Note the crimped, applied handle on the water pitcher. Any of it is elusive enough, especially when one hopes to accumulate a set in a short time.

Fragments of a milk-white Blackberry have been found at Sandwich, but the design is not exactly the same. The Wheeling product is much finer in texture and the design is more compact and clear.

Classification
BLACKBERRY

PATTERN 187

(See Plates 142, 150, 151)

Form Number.
1. Butter dish.
2. Celery vase. Rare.
3. Compotes, covered.
   a. High foot.
   b. Low foot.
4. Creamer.
5. Dish, oval, deep. 8¼ x 5½. Rare.
6. Egg cup, double. Also found single.
*7. Goblet. Some may be found dated 1870, under the foot. Rare.
8. Honey dish.
9. Pitcher, water. Extremely rare.
10. Relish dish, flat.
11. Salt, footed. Two styles, which vary in size.
12. Sauce dish.
13. Spoonholder.
14. Sugar bowl.
   a. Bowl, oval. 3½ inches high, by 4½ x 5½. Very rare.
Colors: Clear glass; milk-white. Two types of knobs to covers. One is in shape of a blackberry and the other is a round medallion with a blackberry in the center. Latter appears to be of a later date.

STRAWBERRY

The Strawberry pattern is well known, particularly in milk-white. It has been in demand and collected for a number of years. It is found only in the clear glass and in the milk-white. Apparently the same molds were used for both. The quality of the milk-white glass is particularly fine in most of the pieces, especially in

PLATE 150—MILK-WHITE BLACKBERRY

Water pitcher   Celery vase   Butter dish   Egg cup   Salt, footed

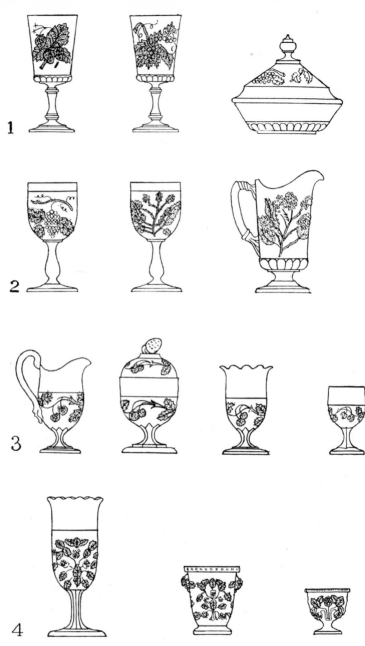

PLATE 151

1. STRAWBERRY and CURRANT goblet (showing both sides of bowl), butter dish
2. LOGANBERRY and GRAPE goblet (showing both sides of bowl), water pitcher.
3. STRAWBERRY creamer, sugar bowl, spoonholder, egg cup.
4. BLACKBERRY celery vase, spoonholder, footed salt.

PLATE 152—MILK-WHITE STRAWBERRY

Covered compote   Sugar bowl   Egg cup   Butter dish

PLATE 153—GOBLETS

Including many odd patterns not collectible in other forms.

(See page 628)

1 2 3 4 5

6 7 8 9 10

11 12 13 14 15

16 17 18 19 20

PLATE 154—GOBLETS
Including many odd patterns not collectible in other forms.
(See page 637)

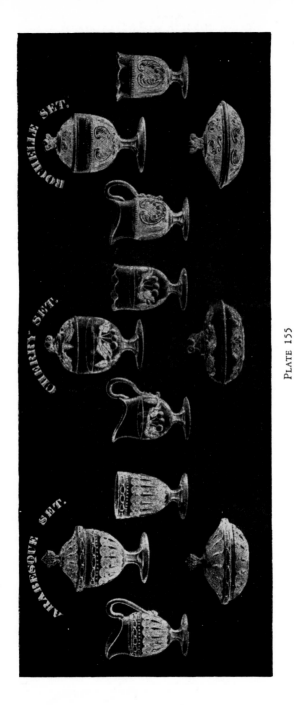

PLATE 155

Arabesque, Cherry and Rochelle (now termed Princess Feather) "sets," as taken from page of an old trade catalogue of Bakewell, Pears & Co.

the goblets. Many of these show an opal coloring when held to the light, and the texture of the glass is better than in most of the white that is found later on. A very interesting group of the milk-white Strawberry may be seen on Plate 152. Several line drawings taken from clear glass pieces are shown on Plate 151, and the goblet on Plate 142. I have carefully compared the clear glass and milk-white pieces and so far I have found them to be exactly alike in every detail. The design is delicate and attractive. Unfortunately no records are available to tell us where it was made, but judging by the forms it appears to be a product of the Seventies. The classification of the milk-white will be found in that chapter. I have never seen a water pitcher, celery or wines in this pattern though it is possible that they may exist.

Classification

STRAWBERRY

Pattern 188

(See Plates 142, 151, 152)

Form Number.

1. Butter dish.
2. Compotes, covered.
    a. High foot, 8 inch is usual size.
    b. Low foot, 8 inch is usual size.
3. Creamer.
4. Egg cup.
5. Goblet.
6. Honey dish.
7. Pickle dish, tapers at one end.
8. Salt, footed.
9. Sauce dish, flat.
10. Spoonholder.
11. Sugar bowl.

Colors: Clear glass; milk-white.

CURRANT

Very similar to the Barberry, which has been described in the foregoing pages, is the Currant. The two chief points of difference are that the currants are always round and there is always the small cable cord above the design. It is true that the leaves bear a suspiciously close resemblance to grape leaves, but this pattern is now very generally known as Currant. It is obviously of the same period as the Barberry. More variants appear of the Barberry than of the Currant but I believe that at least one factory must have produced both. These patterns might possibly date in the late 1860's but there is greater evidence of their being a product of the Seventies.

There is a wide range of pieces for the collector though I have never seen plates of any size in the Currant. They may exist but several collectors who have assembled sets tell me they have never seen any. There are many other attractive conventional designs in old pressed glass plates which will combine nicely with the stippled leaves and clusters of clear currants that make up this pattern. Almost all pieces have four clusters of fruit on each object though one rather showy variant has five bunches.

A few fragments of Currant have been found at Sandwich, but not enough to justify the belief that this design was produced there in quantity.

Classification

CURRANT

PATTERN 189

(See Plates 139, 142)

Form Number.
1. Butter dish.
    a. Flanged, center of base has currant design. Flanged rim covered with fine diamond pattern. Cover shows clusters of currants and has round stippled knob.

Form Number.

2. Cake plates, on standard.

    a. 9½ inch diameter, 5 inches tall, plain standard.
    b. 10½ inch diameter, 6½ inches high, hexagonal standard.

3. Celery vase, scalloped edge, flaring.

4. Compotes, covered.

    a. On high foot, 8 inch.
    b. On low foot, 8 inch.
    c. 6 inch, scallop and point design around edge of dish, collared base.

5. Cordials.

6. Creamer.

7. Dish, oval.

    a. 6 x 9 inches.
    b. 5 x 7 inches.

8. Egg cups.

9. Goblets, two sizes, 5½ and 6 inch.

10. Pitcher, water, crimped handle.

11. Sauce dishes.

    a. Flat.

        (1) Heavy, with cable edge.
        (2) Heavy, without cable edge.
        (3) Thin design, without cable edge.
        (4) Large, 4¾ inch.

    b. Footed.

12. Spoonholder.

13. Sugar bowl.

14. Tumblers, footed.

15. Wines.

Color: Clear glass.

BALTIMORE PEAR

One pattern that has been collected and popular for a number of years is known as Baltimore Pear. It has also been called "Maryland Pear," "Double Pear" and "Twin Pear." It has a large pear in relief on one side against a cluster of leaves, and on the reverse two pears, one overlapping the other with the leaves as a background. The sugar bowl has an ornament on each side simulating knobs and the base is clear and octagonal. The attractive feature is the clear pear which stands out in unusually high relief, thereby being rendered doubly effective. Some of the pieces, such as the water pitcher, have a double pear on both sides. The goblet is rather small with an unusual octagonal base.

Numerous stories regarding some of the various patterns circulate around among dealers and collectors, most of them being interesting but apocryphal. I was assured that this glass was made in Maryland. There is no particular variety of pear especially well known in Maryland nor any that is called either "Baltimore" or "Maryland." I expect it might more accurately be called a Bartlett! As a matter of fact, the design resembles a fig more than anything else. Fortunately, in time, fate led me to an old trade catalogue, illustrating and listing this glass. It was made by Adams & Company of Pittsburgh, where it was known as their "Fig" line. Later, for some unknown reason, the name was changed to "Gipsy." It came out first in 1888. In my article entitled "Pittsburgh vs. Sandwich, Adams & Company," published in *Antiques Magazine* for August, 1933, the best-known patterns made by the Adams Company are fully illustrated and described. It seems best to retain the name by which this glass has become so well known, and so it remains Baltimore Pear.

The cake plate has a star in the center of the base, with eight panels radiating from the corners of the star. Four of these panels are plain and four have the double pear and stippled leaf. This glass is found in two styles, one being round and the other paneled.

On Plate 153, number 4, is shown a goblet which has a small cluster of leaves and little pear. This design should in no way be confused with the Baltimore Pear. Still another goblet bears a single pear. This is a crude glass showing two mold-marks. It is of poor quality and very late. This does not belong to the Baltimore Pear group either. These are mentioned here to make the collecting of this pattern less confusing for both dealers and collectors.

Classification

BALTIMORE PEAR

PATTERN 190

(See Plates 66, 154, Number 10)

Form Number.
1. Bowls.
   a. Open, on collared base. 6, 7 and 8 inch.
   b. Berry bowl. Octagonal, panelled to match sauce dishes.
   c. Covered bowls. Various sizes.
2. Butter dish. Two styles, covered and open.
3. Cake plate, on standard. 9¼ and 10 inch.
4. Celery vase.
5. Compotes.
   a. Covered.
      (1) On high foot. Various sizes, 5, 6, 7 and 8 inch.
      (2) On low foot (collared bases). 5, 6, 7 and 8 inch.
   b. Open.
      (1) On collared bases. 5, 6, 7 and 8 inch.
      (2) On high foot. 5, 6, 7 and 8 inch.
6. Creamer.
*7. Goblet.
8. Pickle dish.
9. Pitcher, water.
*10. Plate. 10 inch.
11. Sauce dishes.
   a. Flat, octagonal. 3½ and 4 inch.
   *b. Footed.
   c. Collared base. 5 inch.
12. Spoonholder.
*13. Sugar bowl.
Color: Clear glass.

CHERRY

There is more than one Cherry pattern, but one of the most attractive is that which was produced in Pittsburgh by Bakewell, Pears & Co. in the Seventies. It was made in milk-white as well as in clear glass. Sets are shown as taken from the original catalogue, on Plate 155. A few pieces are also shown in line drawings on Plate 66. It is a most attractive pattern for anyone needing this sort of design. The cherries stand out in bright relief and the leaves are stippled. The knob of the covered pieces is formed of a leaf and two cherries. The handle is crimped on the pitchers and the footed pieces have all the ear-marks of an earlier ware. A number of forms are to be had, as listed in the following classification. The old catalogue only showed the "set" in milk-white, but doubtless the same pieces were made in clear as well.

Classification

CHERRY

PATTERN 191

(See Plates 66, 155)

Form Number.
1. Butter dish.
2. Compotes.
   a. Covered, on high foot, 8 inch.
   b. Open, on high foot, 8 inch.
   c. Open, on low foot, 8 inch.
3. Creamer.
*4. Goblet.
5. Sauce dish, flat, 4 inch.
6. Spoonholder.
7. Sugar bowl.
Colors: Clear glass; milk-white. It is encountered more frequently in clear glass.

PANELED CHERRY

Of the later period a very attractive pattern will be found in the Paneled Cherry. Undoubtedly a ware of the 1880's, it has considerable charm. The goblet has twelve panels and the bowl is well covered by three large clusters of cherries and leaves. The base is rayed and the knob stem has fairly large thumbprints in it.

The butter dish is the later style with saucer-like base and dome-shaped cover. The cover is paneled and the wide rim of the base carries a single row of large thumbprints. There is a star-shaped ornament in the base. The cherries stand out in bright relief and the leaves are veined and stippled. For anyone whose purpose requires glass with fruit, this has much to recommend it.

Classification

PANELED CHERRY

PATTERN 192

(See Plate 79)

Form Number.
1. Bowl, covered.
2. Butter dish.
3. Creamer.
4. Goblets.
5. Mug, marked "Sweetheart" in the base.
6. Pitcher, water.
7. Sauce dish, flat, deep.
8. Syrup jug, with glass cover.
9. Toothpick or match holder.
10. Tumbler.
Color: Clear glass.

STIPPLED CHERRY

Glass with a stippled background seems to have been a favorite with the early factories, and its popularity endured over many years. A well-liked pattern is the Stippled Cherry. The dishes all have three panels dividing the bright clusters of cherries and leaves and these panels are wide and consist of a double row of horizontal ribbing, slightly tilted in a way suggestive of a herringbone stripe. The cluster of three cherries and large cluster of leaves stand out in vivid relief against the snowy background. Plates are found in two sizes, one of which is shown on Plate 145. This is the large size, designed originally as a bread plate, with the inscription in the center: "Our daily bread." The centre of all the plates, sauce dishes, etc., have a most attractive diamond design. While I have not seen a great many forms in the Stippled Cherry, they undoubtedly exist. It is difficult to tell the exact date of this glass without records, but judging by appearances, it belongs to the late Eighties. This same design was used with roses in the panels, instead of cherries. Doubtless both patterns were produced by the same factory, though I only find a record of the cherry, which was made by the Lancaster Glass Company, of Lancaster, Ohio.

Classification

STIPPLED CHERRY

PATTERN 193

(See Plates 124, 145, 156)

Form Number.
1. Berry bowl, large, flat, round. 6 and 8 inch.
2. Butter dish.
3. Celery vase.
4. Creamer.
5. Mug.
6. Pitcher, water.
7. Plates.
    a. 6 inch.
    b. Bread, 9¼ inch.
8. Sauce dish, flat, 4 inch.
9. Spoonholder.
10. Sugar bowl.
11. Tumbler, water.
Color: Clear glass.

GOOSEBERRY

There is no mistaking the Gooseberry pattern, unless one has never seen a gooseberry! The design is clearly defined, the large gooseberries and leaves being in relief and stippled against a clear background. The goblet has a fairly wide marginal band at the top with a single row of dewdrops below that are no larger than the head of a pin. The design covers the rest of the bowl and the stem is plain. The water tumbler has the same tiny row of dewdrops both above and below the design, and another row around the foot of the base.

This glass is also found as readily in milk-white as in the clear. If it comes in colors, I have never seen it. It was presumably made during the Seventies. The milk-white classification of the gooseberry is given in Chapter 24.

From fragment findings, it would appear that this design was produced by the Boston & Sandwich Glass Company. Pieces were found both in clear glass and in milk-white.

Classification

GOOSEBERRY

PATTERN 194

(See Plates 103, 166)

Form Number.
1. Butter dish.
2. Compote, covered, on high foot.
   a. Sweetmeat, or 6-inch covered compote on high foot.
3. Creamer.
4. Goblets.
5. Honey dish.
6. Lemonade glass (tumbler with applied handle).
7. Pitcher, water.
8. Sauce dish.
9. Spoonholder.
10. Sugar bowl.
11. Tumbler, water.

Colors: Milk-white; clear.

STRAWBERRY AND CURRANT

On Plate 151 will be seen two pieces of this ware decorated with fruit. The goblet has strawberries on one side, in high relief, and a cluster of currants on the reverse. Both sides of the goblet are shown, that there may be no mistake about the design. It was a little difficult to judge what pieces bearing fruit are meant to match this goblet, as there are many odd fruit designs. A water pitcher was known to exist and then a butter dish was discovered, showing the same border about the base as on the bowl of the goblet, though the fruit design varies. The strawberries are in the base and the currant and pear on the cover. The glass in this fruited goblet is bright and clear, and has been in demand during the past year. The tumbler is well liked also, with the heavy design in relief. A number of other forms of this interesting ware, which probably dates no earlier than the Eighties, is listed below.

Classification

STRAWBERRY AND CURRANT

Pattern 195

(See Plate 151)

Form Number.
1. Butter dish.
2. Compotes.
    a. Open, on standard.
    b. Covered, on standard.
3. Creamer.
4. Goblet.
5. Pitcher, water. Two sizes.
6. Sauce dish, footed.
7. Sugar bowl.
8. Tumbler.

Color: Clear glass.

LOGANBERRY AND GRAPE

Later than the Strawberry and Currant is another goblet with a fruit design. The glass is obviously not as old and the base of the goblet shows only two mold-marks. The design is attractive, having a large cluster of loganberries (or possibly raspberries) on one side, and a large cluster of grapes on the reverse. In both cases the fruit stands out in high relief and the leaves are stippled. The glass is quite heavy. The only other piece I have seen to match is a water pitcher. These are shown here as a means of identification as fruit patterns are popular, though the glass is later than I like to include in this book.

Classification

LOGANBERRY AND GRAPE

PATTERN 196

(See Plate 151)

Form Number.
1. Goblet.
2. Pitcher, water.
Color: Clear glass.

Chapter XiX

LATER PERIOD. STIPPLED GROUP

PRINCESS FEATHER

The title of Princess Feather has come into general use for this pattern, though it is a name of comparatively recent origin. For a time a few dealers referred to it as "Lacy Medallion." It resembles closely the so-called "lace" glass of the earlier Sandwich period, though the quality of the glass is not the same and the ware is not nearly so heavy. In other respects it is just as lovely, for the stippled background is very fine. The three ornaments, each made up of two feather-shaped figures encompassing fine diamond points, are graceful and effective. Though one other pattern may resemble more closely in design some of the typical Sandwich, the Princess Feather retains more of the well-known sparkle and life. The flat rim, where the cover joins on some of the covered pieces, has a delicate design of leaves that greatly enhances its beauty.

One could scarcely choose a lovelier pattern to collect than this glass, which was made by Bakewell, Pears & Co., the well-known flint glass factory of Pittsburgh, Pa. For the first time I find in their old catalogue (undated, but presumed to be 1875-80) mention of glass "sets." As a matter of interest I am showing a page of sets taken from this catalogue. A set consisted of a sugar bowl, butter dish, creamer and spoonholder. Princess Feather, as may be noted from the illustration on Plate 155, was originally "Rochelle." It was made in clear glass and opaque white. The forms were many and interesting and apparently not all illustrated in the catalogue, as I have in the opaque a large plate with two small handles which is not shown. It is, of course, possible that this unlisted plate was made earlier or later than the date of the catalogue or perhaps by another factory. The classification is largely taken directly from the Bakewell, Pears & Co. catalogue.

Classification

PRINCESS FEATHER

PATTERN 197

(See Plates 23, 109, 112, 135, 155)

Form Number.
1. Bowl, on high foot. 7 and 8 inch.
2. Butter dish.
3. Cake plate, small closed handles, 9 inch.
4. Celery vase.
5. Compotes.
    a. Covered.
        (1) On high foot, 7 and 8 inch.
        (2) On high foot, 6 inch, sweetmeat jar.
        (3) On low foot, 6, 7 and 8 inch.
    b. Open, on low foot, 8 inch.
6. Creamer.
7. Dishes.
    a. Covered, with 8 inch plate.
    b. Oval, 7, 8 and 9 inch.
8. Egg cup.
9. Goblet.
10. Honey dish, flat, 3 inch.
11. Pitcher, water.
    a. Half-gallon.
    b. Quart.
12. Plates, 6, 7, 8 and 9 inch.
13. Salt, footed.
14. Sauce dish, flat, 4 inch.
15. Spoonholder.
16. Sugar bowl.

Colors: Clear glass, opaque-white.

ANTHEMION

An interesting pattern which has been overlooked because it is not better known, is one which has been called by the few collectors who know it, Anthemion. Wherever this interesting glass was made, it was well executed for a late ware. The background is entirely stippled with a fine, even stipple, like some of the earlier glass made at Sandwich. The clear leaf, reminding one of a palmette, stands out in clear relief. There is one long leaf alterating with a shorter one around each article. If goblets were ever made they must be lovely. So far none has been encountered in my travels though I have found a water pitcher and tumblers. The tumblers are most atractive, the design covering it with only an inch clear marginal band at the top. The Anthemion plate in the ten-inch size is charming. A cake plate may be found with edges that curl up slightly toward the center. The sauce dish is large with a clear rim and oak leaf in the base. This glass is reminiscent of the beautiful early "lace" glass of Sandwich fame, and will be more in demand when it is better known. No doubt many other forms were made which collectors can add to my classification.

Classification

ANTHEMION

PATTERN 198
(See Plate 58)

Form Number.
1. Berry bowl. Square with fan top edge, 7 inch.
2. Cake plate. Edges curl toward center, 9¼ inch.
3. Pitcher, water.
4. Plate, 10 inch.
5. Sauce dish, round, 4½ inch.
6. Spoonholder.
7. Tumbler.
Color: Clear glass.

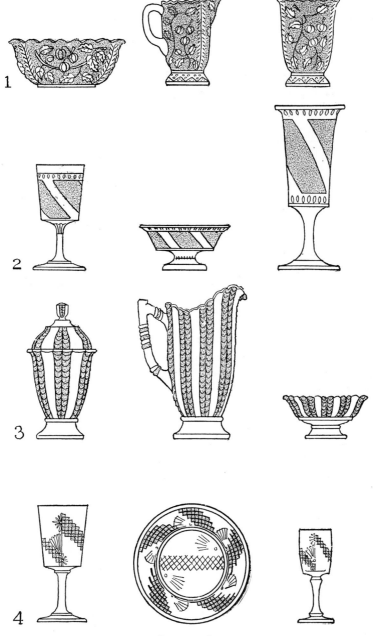

PLATE 156

1. STIPPLED CHERRY berry bowl, creamer, celery vase.
2. CLEAR DIAGONAL BAND goblet, footed sauce, celery vase.
3. FISH SCALE sugar bowl, water pitcher, footed sauce.
4. DIAGONAL BAND with FAN goblet, plate, cordial.

PLATE 157

1. SHELL and TASSEL (square) tray, cake plate on standard, covered compote, footed sauce dish.
2. SHELL and TASSEL (round) sugar bowl, butter dish, celery vase.
3. PLEAT and PANEL sugar bowl, creamer, spoonholder, footed sauce dish.
4. ROMAN ROSETTE sugar bowl, creamer, spoonholder, butter dish.

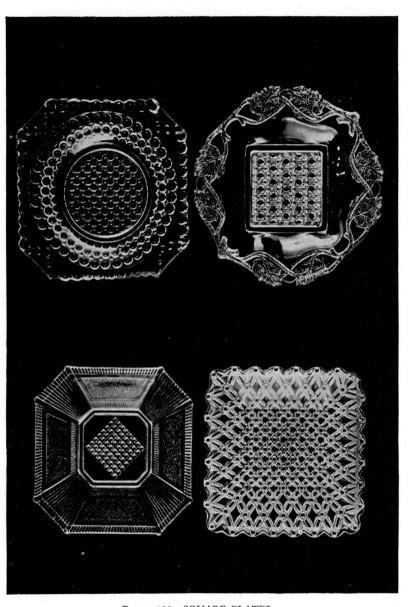

PLATE 158—SQUARE PLATES

Thousand-Eye   Maple Leaf, variant
Pleat and Panel   Nailhead

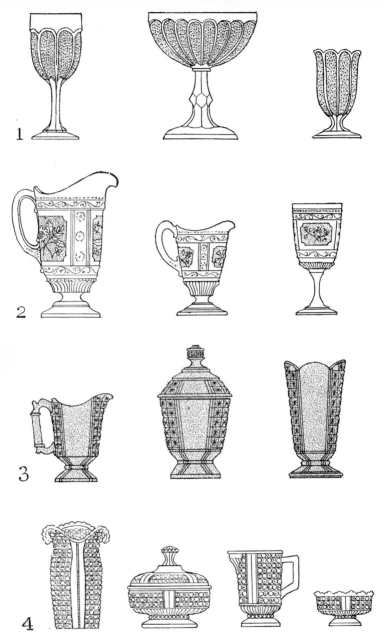

PLATE 159

1. MARQUISETTE goblet, compote on high foot, spoonholder.
2. WILLOW OAK water pitcher, creamer, goblet.
3. TWO-PANEL creamer, sugar bowl, celery vase.
4. THREE-PANEL celery vase, butter dish, creamer, footed sauce dish.

ARABESQUE

Arabesque is the name given by Bakewell, Pears & Co. to one of their most attractive patterns. It was made during the Seventies, when stippled and frosted effects had caught the popular fancy. The goblet shown in the photograph on Plate 121 shows, in careful detail, the lacy effectiveness of this glass. The background has a fine stipple and the spear-shaped ornaments which stand out in relief are outlined with beads heavier than the stippled background. This pattern is not well known to-day, but one may easily predict popularity for it when collectors realize the charm of the design.

The set as shown in the old catalogue is on Plate 155. Covered compotes may be had on a high or low foot. No plates are mentioned; in fact, the forms are few unless others were made at a later date, not given in this catalogue.

Classification

ARABESQUE

PATTERN 199
(See Plates 121, 155)

Form Number.
1. Butter dish.
2. Compotes, covered.
   a. On high foot, 6 and 8 inch.
   b. On low foot, 8 inch.
3. Creamer.
4. Goblet.
5. Sauce dish, flat, 4 inch.
6. Spoonholder.
7. Sugar bowl.
Color: Clear glass.

PLEAT AND PANEL

A homemade descriptive title has served its purpose and clung to this design, though it was not until this nomenclature was established that this pattern came to be known. It has many attractive features, one of them being the much sought-for plates. These were made in five sizes, square in form with "pleated" (fluted) corners and an attractive diamond-shaped ornament in the center. The goblet has three stippled squares which are divided by three wide, fluted, clear panels. The stem is round and stippled, the base being clear. There are two styles, one in which the panels reach only to the edge of the marginal band, and the other showing the tops of the heaviest panels above the marginal band, making an uneven edge. One platter is oblong with closed handles, the lovely frosted and stippled panels giving a brilliant effect. There is an unusual oblong covered dish and a square covered compote in a small size. The celery vase is square and mostly stippled. It is the contrast of the sparkling square plates, oblong platter and round goblets, that arrests attention in this distinctive glassware. The quality of the glass is clear and bright. A few colored pieces may be had, but they are few. I have seen the oblong platter in amethyst and yellow, and I am told it was also made in blue. A large clear platter has open handles. That Pleat and Panel was made in more than one factory may be assumed from the number of variations. However, the only printed record of it I find is in a Bryce Bros. catalogue. It was called the "Derby" pattern by them, and was made in Pittsburgh during the 1870's. The catalogue does not give a full list of the items produced, but the classification given below will prove to be nearly complete.

Classification

PLEAT AND PANEL

PATTERN 200

(See Plates 105, 111, 157, 158)

Form Number.
1. Butter dish.
2. Cake plate, square, on standard.
3. Celery vase.

Form Number.
- 4. Compotes.
  - *a.* Open, low.
  - *b.* Covered, on foot. 8 inches square, 12 inches high. Various sizes from small to large.
- 5. Creamer.
- 6. Dishes.
  - *a.* Covered, oblong, flat, 8 x 5 inches.
  - *b.* Covered, square on standard, 6 inch.
  - *c.* Deep, oblong.
  - *d.* Large, horsehoe in base.
- *7. Goblets.
  - *a.* Plain marginal band.
  - *b.* Heavy panels projecting slightly into marginal band.
- 8. Pickle dishes, oblong, 9½ inch.
- 9. Pickle jar, with cover. Also found with pair of jars on tray.
- 10. Pitcher, water.
- *11. Plates, square. Five sizes. 3½ inch were for butter. 7 inch size reproduced.
- 12. Platters, oblong. Two styles, open and closed handles.
- 13. Salt and pepper shakers, metal top.
- 14. Sauce dishes.
  - *a.* Flat, with handle, 3½, 4 and 5 inch.
  - *b.* On standard, 3½ and 4 inch. (The latter size is found with covers.)
- 15. Spoonholder.
- 16. Sugar bowl.

Colors: Clear. Amethyst, blue and yellow are rare.

SHELL AND TASSEL; SQUARE

The square Shell and Tassel has rounded corners, which are frosted, with a crackled effect, similar to the Tree of Life made by the Portland Glass Company, Portland, Me., and others. There are so many forms to choose from that it is a positive delight to the collector. The goblets are scarce, especially those with the knob stems. No plates have come to light so far, though there are oval platters in two sizes and oblong trays and oval deep dishes in any number of different sizes. The small covered dishes are another added attraction, to say nothing of the footed sauce dishes and flat handled desserts. The goblets are rather surprising in that they do not carry as much of the pattern as do the rest of the set. The spoonholder, celery vase, water pitcher, etc., are almost entirely frosted with the crackled effect. The goblet has a wide clear band at the top and three large shell-shaped figures with a tiny ornament between them. The rest of the pieces have four shell-shaped corners with clear panels in between, bearing a stippled drapery that has a tassel at the end of it. The bases of these pieces have two shells, and two lightly stippled ornaments without the tassel in between. The knobs of the covered pieces are shell-shaped, as shown on Plate 157. It is an altogether satisfying pattern to collect, with the large range of pieces to select from. This should not be confused with the round Shell and Tassel, which is treated separately.

The only authentic record I have found about this glass is a catalogue of the 1870's of George Duncan & Sons, Pittsburgh. It contains illustrations of the goblet, oval platter and deep-fruit dishes as well as the oblong dishes. It was referred to as their "No. 155 Pattern." The goblets are so extremely scarce to-day that I doubt if they were ever made by any other firm. Unfortunately, they have now been reproduced and they are excellent copies. The fakes may be detected quite readily by an expert.

Classification
SHELL AND TASSEL; SQUARE
PATTERN 201
(See Plates 97, 105, 157)

Form Number.
1. Butter dish.
2. Cake dish, on standard, large.
   a. Unusual small one on standard, 6½ inches in diameter, 4½ inches high.
3. Celery vase.

4. Compotes.
    a. Covered, 6 inch, on high stem. Various other sizes.
    b. Open, 4½ inch.
    c. Tall, open. Various sizes.
5. Dishes.
    a. Oval, deep, flaring sides, 11½ inches long, 6½ inches wide, 2¾ inches deep.
    b. Oval, straight sides, deep.
    c. Oval, deep, 10 x 9¾ inches.
    d. Small, shell-shaped, about size of a large salt.
*6. Goblets.
    a. Knob stem.
    b. Plain, round stem.
7. Jam jar.
8. Pitcher, water.
9. Platters.
    a. Oblong, with rounded corners.
    b. Oval, large and small size.
10. Sauce dishes.
    a. Footed, 3, 4 and 5 inch.
    b. Handled, flat, 3¼ and 4¼ inch.
11. Salt and pepper shakers. Rare.
    a. Shell-shaped, individual.
12. Spoonholder.
13. Sugar bowl.
14. Trays, oblong, two sizes.

Colors: Blue; amber; clear; yellow. Any colored piece is rare. As a set, this was made only in clear glass.

SHELL AND TASSEL; ROUND

It came as a surprise to some collectors of this pattern to find they had confused the square with the round Shell and Tassel. The round pieces are not quite so decorative as the square, since they are nearly all of clear glass. Possibly some may like it better, as the pieces are handled and have a recumbent dog as the knob of all the covers. The design is nearly the same but reduced in size. The sugar bowl is round with a broad clear expanse of glass. The shells are close to the base of the bowls and the round clear base has the design well up on the standard or collared part. The handles are square, with a small shell at the two corners. This style may come in as complete a number of forms, but if so, I have not seen them. It is possible that the goblets, platters and trays did double duty for both sets. The butter dish, sugar bowl, celery vase and spoonholder are shown on Plate 157, where one may readily see, by comparison, how different they are from the more elaborate form.

Classification

SHELL AND TASSEL; ROUND

PATTERN 202

(See Plate 157)

Form Number.
1. Butter dish, covered, knob in form of dog.
2. Creamer.
3. Celery vase.
4. Sauce dish, round, footed, handle on each side.
5. Spoonholder.
6. Sugar bowl, covered, knob in form of dog.

Color: Clear glass.

LOG CABIN

Suggestive of early pioneer days is a clear stippled glass made in the form of quaint little log cabins. The well-known West-ward-Ho glass, with its frosted design depicting the cabin of the early settler, the bison charging across the plains and the fleeing deer, has a sophiisticated air which is not found in the odd and unique glass called Log Cabin. The compote has a standard shaped like a tree trunk, and on top of it rests the cabin, with two windows in front and a chimney on the roof forming the knob for the cover. The creamer is built of logs with a branch-like handle and small stippled feet. All the pieces are similar, some having a door as well as windows. It has not been my good fortune to find a goblet or tumbler, but unquestionably they exist, as I have had the water pitcher. So far as I know this pattern was made only in clear glass. The little log cabin covered dishes which originally contained prepared mustard, do not match this design. It appears to be a ware of the 1870's.

Classification

LOG CABIN

PATTERN 203

(See Plate 106)

Form Number.
1. Butter dish.
2. Compote on standard, covered. Various sizes.
3. Creamer.
4. Pitcher, water.
5. Spoonholder.
6. Sauce dish.
7. Sugar bowl.

Color: Clear glass.

POWDER AND SHOT

Of the same era as the Beaded Acorn and many of the grape designs with stippled backgrounds, is one which was dubbed in the West "Powder and Shot." A few have called this Horn of Plenty, but an earlier pattern has been known for some years by that title. Powder and Shot is not an inappropriate name, as the clear horn-shaped ornament is not unlike a powderhorn and the heavier dewdrops which appear to be rolling from it are suggestive of shot. It was probably made in the early Seventies, like most of this series.

There is something dainty and appealing about this ware. The pieces are all footed and follow the forms of most of the earlier patterns. The bases of the footed pieces are stippled, and have a row of small dewdrops around the rim and a chain effect of dewdrops, clear in the center of the loops, forming the design on the base. Each bowl is divided into three panels by a narrow clear band, each panel having the powderhorn and shot. The covers have the three large powderhorns but are not divided by the panels. The knobs are of clear glass and in the shape of a seven-petaled ornament. This design is scarce but prices for it have not soared as yet.

According to fragments discovered at Sandwich, Powder and Shot was produced by the factory on the Cape. It is found in such a limited quantity that it is unlikely any other company produced it.

Classification

POWDER AND SHOT

PATTERN 204

(See Plate 79)

Form Number.

1. Butter dish.
2. Castor set.
3. Celery vase.
4. Compotes, covered.
    a. On low foot.
    b. On high foot.
5. Creamer, crimped handle.
6. Egg cups.
7. Goblet.
8. Salt, footed.
9. Spoonholder.
10. Sugar bowl.

Color: Clear glass.

STIPPLED STAR

To differentiate this from other star patterns, it is called Stippled Star. The background is stippled in a frosted effect, as the title suggests, and the stars stand out in clear relief. It is an unusual design. Being rather difficult to find, it is not likely that it was made in as large quantities as those patterns which proved to be popular at the time they were produced. All the Stippled Star glass that has come to my notice was found in Pennsylvania. It appears to be a ware of the Seventies and it is now fairly popular. Such pieces as I have seen were in clear glass, and it is to be doubted if it was ever made in colors. A group is shown on Plate 147. In all likelihood the usual forms may be found in this pattern, but the following are all that I can vouch for. A goblet of a very late copy of the Stippled Star came to my attention lately and I mention it here that collectors may not confuse it with the earlier ware. The stars on the copy are flat, the stippling is very light and the base shows only two mold-marks. Another variation was noticed in a compote, which had a clear background instead of stippled, with large stars in relief.

It is interesting to note how much glass was made in anticipation of the Centennial in 1876. Gillinder & Sons of Greensburg, Pa., and Philadelphia, contributed a large amount of it. Most of the patterns bearing stars or a bust of Washington, etc., were made for this event. I find the Stippled Star was produced by Gillinders. It is illustrated in an early, but, unfortunately, undated catalogue in my possession. I believe it is quite possible that this glass was made earlier than 1876.

Classification

STIPPLED STAR

PATTERN 205

(See Plate 147)

Form Number.

1. Butter dish.
2. Celery vase.
3. Compotes.
    a. Open, on high foot. Deep bowl. 7 and 8 inch.
    b. Open, on high foot. Shallow bowl. 7 and 8 inch.
4. Creamer.
5. Egg cup.

Form Number.
   6. Goblet.
   7. Preserve dish. Oval. 8 inch.
   8. Sauce dishes. Flat. 4, 5 and 6 inch.
   9. Spoonholder.
  10. Sugar bowl.
Color: Clear glass.

MARQUISETTE

Marquisette is not the old trade name for this pattern. So little of it is seen to-day, it probably was one of those patterns that did not prove to be commercially popular and therefore was neither extensively made nor produced over a period of time. The design consists of panels arched at the top. The background appears from a distance to be frosted and stippled, but upon closer examination it proves to be like a very fine screen or mesh. The outlines of the panels themselves are of clear glass and stand out in bright relief. The goblets are especially attractive. It is to be regretted that my classification of this appealing pattern is not more complete, but I have seldom encountered any pieces other than the goblets in my travels. From all appearances I judge this was made in the early 1870's. A few fragments in this glass were discovered at Sandwich but not in sufficient quantity to definitely establish it as one of their designs, at present. For a time, it was also produced by the Cooperative Flint Glass Company, of Beaver Falls, Pa., who may have purchased the molds from an earlier Pittsburgh concern.

Classification

MARQUISETTE

PATTERN 206
(See Plate 159)

Form Number.
   1. Butter dish.
   2. Champagne.

Form Number.
  3. Compote, open, on high foot.
  4. Cordials.
  5. Creamer.
  6. Goblets.
  7. Sauce dish, flat. 4 inch.
  8. Spoonholder.
  9. Sugar bowl.
Color: Clear glass.

FISH SCALE

A pattern which apparently named itself is the Fish Scale. It has been known for so long a time to dealers and collectors by this title, that it would cause much confusion to adhere to the original trade name, which was "Coral." It was made for many years by the old Bryce Bros. Company of Pittsburgh. It first came out in the Eighties and was carried through the Nineties. I regret to say that toward the end of its career it was among the assortments sold by the ten-cent stores for the holiday trade.

The goblet has a fairly long slender bowl, plain clear rounded stem, with a band of fish-scale pattern where it joins the clear base. It is a pretty goblet, with a double row of stippled fish scales, alternating with a rounded clear panel. It has a plain marginal band around the top. Many plates are found, which is always welcome news to collectors. They may be found both square and round. It is fairly plentiful though there are times when all glass patterns which are not usually scarce, develop an exasperating elusiveness particularly if the collector is in a hurry to complete sets.

Classification

FISH SCALE

PATTERN 207
(See Plates 120, 156)

Form Number.
  1. Bowls. Open, like flared sauce dishes. 6, 7 and 8 inch.
  2. Butter dish.

Form Number.

   3. Cake plates, on standard. 9, 10 and 11 inch.

   4. Celery vase.

   5. Compotes.

       a. Covered, on high standards. 6, 7 and 8 inch.
       b. Open, on high standard. 7, 8, 9 and 10 inch.

   6. Creamer.

   7. Goblet.

   8. Jelly dish. Footed. 4½ inch.

   9. Mug, large.

  10. Pickle dish. Tapered at one end, with handle.

  11. Pitchers, water. Quart and ½ gallon.

  12. Plates. 7 and 8 inch, round.

       a. Bread, square, with rounded corners. 9 inch.

  13. Salt and pepper shakers. Rare.

  14. Sauce dishes.

       a. Flared. 4 inch.
       b. Footed. 4 inch.

  15. Spoonholder.

  16. Sugar bowl.

  17. Tumbler.

  18. Tray. Oblong, with scalloped edge for salt and pepper.

  19. Water set, with tray and bowl.

Color: Clear glass.

ROMAN ROSETTE

This glass did not become well known until after *Early American Pressed Glass* was written, when the vogue for hunting old-time patterns brought out from cuboard shelves numbers of designs that had not been seen for many years.

The background of Roman Rosette is lightly stippled, with not so much of the silvery appearance noted in most of the other stippled patterns. The plates are scalloped, with one fairly large rosette in the center and a border of slightly smaller rosettes. The butter dish is saucer-like and deep, with a dome lid. The knob is round and flat with a rosette impressed in both sides. This ware was made by the United States Glass Company of Pittsburgh, where is was simply known as "15030 Pattern." It probably came out during the 1880's but it was still being produced during the early 1900's. The classification is taken directly from the old catalogue listing.

Classification

ROMAN ROSETTE

PATTERN 208

(See Plates 109, 135, 157)

Form Number.

1. Bowls. 5, 6, 7 and 8 inch.
2. Butter dish. Two styles.
3. Cake plate, on standard. 9 and 10 inch.
4. Castor set. Salt, pepper and mustard in glass frame.
5. Celery vase.
6. Compotes. 5, 6, 7 and 8 inch. High foot. Open and covered.
7. Cordial.
8. Creamer, one pint.
*9. Goblet.
10. Honey dish. Square, covered.
11. Jelly dish. Footed. 4½ inch.
12. Jugs. 5 and 7 ounce.
13. Molasses jars. Two sizes.
    a. With tin top.
    b. With nickel top.
14. Mugs. Two sizes.
    a. Large.
    b. Medium.
15. Pickle dish.
16. Pitcher, water. Quart. ½ gallon.
17. Plates.
    a. Large, bread.
    b. Seven inch.
18. Preserve dishes. Oval. 7, 8 and 9 inch.

Form Number.

19. Salt and pepper shakers.
20. Sauce dishes.
    a. Flat. 4 and 4½ inch.
    b. Footed. 4 inch.
21. Spoonholder.
22. Sugar bowl.
23. Tumbler.
24. Wine.

Color: Clear glass, with stippled background. A few pieces may be found decorated in red.

STIPPLED CLOVER

Very little can be said about this pattern, as it has not been my good fortune to find more than a few pieces of it. It is shown on Plate 141, as a means of identification. The first piece was a cordial, which was found in the basement of an old house that was torn down. Later I discovered a butter dish with a high domed cover, from which I believe this to be a pattern of the Eighties or even later. For those looking for good luck, this design should carry it to them. The background is entirely stippled, and the three-leaf clovers stand out in relief against it. In the base of the saucer-like butter dish are four three-leaved clovers, with one four-leaf clover directly in the center! Without doubt this glass must be fairly plentiful in some localities, but I have been unable to find any more four-leaf clovers.

Classification

STIPPLED CLOVER

PATTERN 209

(See Plate 141)

Form Number.

1. Butter dish.
2. Cordial.

Form Number.
   3. Goblet.
   4. Plate, large.
Color: Clear glass.

PICKET

An interesting ware that has escaped the attention of many is called Picket. The reason for this title is obvious, the only decoration on the glass being what looks like a quaint old picket fence. The entire fence is stippled again a clear background, the large square-headed nails in the rails showing bright and clear. The effect is quite unusual. This is believed to be the only pressed glass pattern using this particular decoration. The goblets are round. Such pieces as the celery vase are square and the open compote is square with mitered corners.

This ware was made by the King Glass Company of Pittsburgh, late in the Eighties or about 1890. It was known as the "London" pattern. Like many other designs, it is likely to be in greater de-. mand as it becomes better known.

Classification

PICKET

PATTERN 210

(See Plate 107)

Form Number.
   1. Butter dish.
   2. Celery vase.
   3. Compote, open, on high foot.
   4. Creamer.
   5. Finger bowl. Originally used with water set.
   6. Goblets.
   7. Pickle jar, with cover.
   8. Pitcher, water.
   9. Match holder.

Form Number.
   10. Salt, flat, oblong.
   11. Sauce dish.
   12. Spoonholder.
   13. Sugar bowl.
   14. Tray for water set.

Color: Clear glass, stippled.

Chapter XX

COLOR GROUP

THOUSAND-EYE

An outstanding popular pattern of the moment is called Thousand-Eye. In the beginning considerable confusion arose from the use of this title, there being such a quantity of patterns using different sizes of hobnails, flattened hobnails and dewdrops as the basis of the design. Most collectors and dealers are now familar with the six-, eight- and ten-inch plates with folded corners. They know the pieces that come with three knobs which curve out from the stems of the footed pieces to support the bowls bracket-wise, and the other type which has a plain stem and tiny scallops around the edge of the base of the footed dishes. Some prefer to collect only the three-knobbed pieces, while others are not so fastidious. The design on the bowls is the same in either case, consisting of large circular discs that graduate smaller in size toward the base and—this is important!—there is a small but pronounced diamond-shaped point in a row below each row of circles. It should be remembered that the goblet is found in only one form in the true Thousand-Eye, as illustrated. An accurate description is difficult. It is better to study Plate 137. There, also, may be distinguished the difference between the plain standards and those having the three knobs previously described. It is to be regretted that a covered dish in the three-knob style was found too late to be included in the illustrations. The cover has a knob corresponding with the design of the stem. The two styles are classified separately, though the reader should note that there are many individual pieces that are plain, which are only included under Pattern No. 211A. The style with three knobs as well as the six-, eight- and ten-inch plates, pickle dish and honey dish, were made by Adams & Company, of Pittsburgh, during the 1870's. Other items may have been produced by them also, but I name those illustrated in their catalogue. The pattern proved to be popular and so it was carried over a period of years.

The classification of this pattern is practically impossible to establish with absolute accuracy by reason of the vast number of forms designed and sold but the appended list gives more than a fair, general idea of what has been found.

Most of the pieces listed in 211A were made by Richards & Hartley, of Tarentum, Pa. They produced the lovely opalescent colored pieces which are so scarce and sought after to-day. This glass came out late in the Seventies and was continued for many years.

Classification

THOUSAND-EYE

PATTERN 211
(Style showing three knobs on standard)
(See Plates 137, 146, 158)

Form Number.
  1. Butter dish.
  2. Cake plate, on standard.
  3. Celery vase.
  4. Compotes.
      a. Covered, on low standard. Various sizes from 6 inches. Covers usually missing.
          (1) Shallow bowl, flaring.
          (2) Deep bowl, with less flare.
      b. Covered, on high standard. Various sizes from 6 inches. Covers usually missing.
          (1) Shallow bowl, flaring.
          (2) Deep bowl, with less flare.
      c. Open, on high and low standards. Various sizes.
      d. Shallow rounded bowl, square-faced at top.
  5. Creamer.
  6. Cruet.
  7. Egg cup.

Form Number.

8. Honey dish. Oblong, with cover.

9. Pitcher, water. Two sizes. Larger is 9 inches. Smaller is 7 inches and is often found blown. The latter are sometimes referred to as milk pitchers.

10. Sauce dish, footed.
    a. Round, flat.

11. Spoonholder.

12. Sugar bowl.

Classification

THOUSAND-EYE

PATTERN 211A

(Style with plain standard, together with all additional pieces to be used with both forms)

(See Plates 137, 146, 158)

Form Number.

1. Bowls.
   a. Size of large finger bowl.
   b. Berry, large and deep, without foot.

2. Butter dish. Footed, scalloped base.

3. Cake plate on standard.

4. Celery vase.

5. Cologne bottles.

6. Cordials. 4 inches.

7. Compotes; both open and covered. Some have deep rounded bowls and others are shallow, flaring more at the edge. It is difficult to find compotes with covers, especially in the smallest size. One style has top edge tilted, somewhat like later banana stands.

8. Creamer. Two sizes, one small.

9. Cruet.

10. Dish, small oblong with rounded corners. Two sizes.

11. Glass container with handle, having space for sugar bowl on one side and creamer on the other.

Form Number.

*12. Goblets.

  13. Hats (toothpick holders).

  14. Lamps. Several styles, usually with blown bowls.

  15. Match holder.

  16. Mugs. 3⅜ inches.

  17. Pickle dish. 9¼ inches.

  18. Pitcher, water, two sizes, scalloped edge on base.

*19. Plates.

     a. Square, folded corners, 6, 8* and 10 inch.

     b. Round, with clock face in center and alphabet border, 6 inch.

  20. Platter, oblong, rounded corners.

  21. Salt and pepper shakers.

     a. Tall, plain rounded band around center. Metal top.

     b. Covered with design to top edge. Metal top.

  22. Sauce dish, footed, 3½ inch, scalloped base and top.

     a. Round, flat.

  23. Spoonholder.

  24. Sugar bowl. Two sizes, one small.

  25. Syrup jug. Usually blown, and often with pewter cover.

  26. Toothpick holder, round.

  27. Trays.

     a. Large and round with low rim, for water pitcher and goblets, 12½ inch.

     b. Large, oval, for water pitcher and goblets. 14 inches long.

  28. Tumblers.

     a. Design only part way, with wide marginal band.

     b. Design nearly to top.

     c. Christmas tree light, or jelly tumbler. Found in several fine colors.

  29. Twine holder.

Colors: Yellow, blue, opalescent (scarce), apple green, amber, light amber, clear glass. Opaque blue (extremely scarce).

THREE-PANEL

A pattern which has earned itself an appropriate title is the Three-Panel. It had to be named, because collectors asked for a

PLATE 160—GOBLETS

Two Panel
Fine Cut

Fine Cut and Panel
Cane

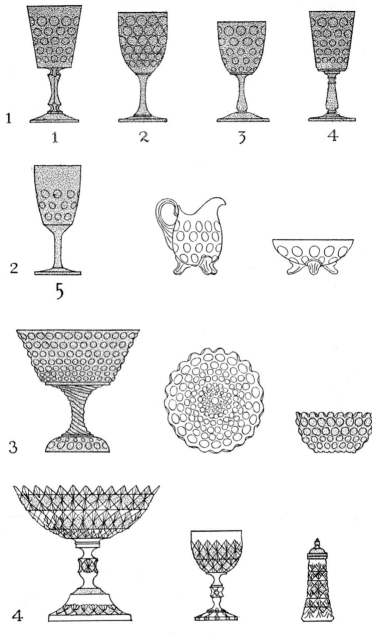

PLATE 161

1. INVERTED THUMBPRINT goblets. Variants.
2. INVERTED THUMBPRINT goblet, creamer, sauce dish.
3. RAINDROP compote, plate, finger bowl.
4. FINE CUT and BLOCK compote, goblet, salt shaker.

PLATE 162

1. CRANBERRY RED INVERTED THUMBPRINT celery vase, small celery holder, tumbler, wine, punch cup.
2. INVERTED THUMBPRINT. Three varieties of finger bowls; large, with base; medium and small.
3. RED BLOCK goblet, sugar bowl, cordial.
4. RUBY THUMBPRINT goblet, spoonholder, pint pitcher. celery vase.

PLATE 163—PLATES

Ray

Swirl

Maple Leaf, variant

Daisy and Button

designation for several years. The design is fairly elaborate, being made up of three panels divided into intersections by plain, heavy double bars. The panels contain numerous small raised circles, alternate ones having a tiny flower impressed in it. The bowl of the goblet is perfectly round and does not taper at the base. The base of the bowl is covered with a fine ribbing, and the stem is a plain hexagonal. It is a curious fact that this pattern comes in the usual range of colors, with the exception of apple green. Only a very small amount of any pressed table ware was ever made in amethyst.

Three-Panel has a noticeably dignified character to the forms. It is heavier than most of the popular colored glass and I suspect is earlier than most of the others. The weight, the quality of the glass, and the fewer number of forms would indicate it. It may date not later than 1870. It was produced by Richards & Hartley, of Tarentum, Pa., who referred to it simply as "No. 25 Ware."

Classification

THREE-PANEL

Pattern 212

(See Plates 96, 159)

Form Number.
1. Butter dish. Two styles, one having cover carrying the design and one having plainer cover.
2. Celery vase, flaring rim more like a flower vase.
    a. With straight sides.
3. Compotes.
    a. Open, on low standards, two sizes, 7 and 8½ inch. One flares more at top edge than other.
    b. Round bowl on low foot, flaring at top. Graceful and varying in form from the compotes with squared bases of bowls. Four sizes, 7, 8, 9 and 10 inch. Called cracker bowls.
4. Creamer.
5. Goblets.
6. Mugs, handled. Large and small.
7. Pitcher, water. ½ gallon, quart. Also milk pitcher.

8. Sauce dish, footed. 4 inch.
9. Spoonholder.
10. Sugar bowl.
11. Tumblers.

Colors: Clear; light amber; amber; blue; yellow.

TWO-PANEL

Two-Panel glass is an attractive design, much sought because it may be had in several colors. It was produced in large quantities during the period when colored glass was exceedingly popular. It is a simple pattern, consisting of two plain panels and two of an all-over pressed design of small squares, each one being impressed with a star-like motif. A few dealers used to know this design as "Daisy in the Square" or "Daisy in Panel." All of the pieces are ovoid, the clear panels being on the sides and the ornamental panels on each end. Around the pretty knob stem of the goblet is seen a row of small squares of the same design as on the pressed panels.

The glass christened "Two-Panel" in the first edition of *Early American Pressed Glass* was originally designated as "No. 25" ware by Richards and Hartley, of Tarentum, Pa., who were making it during the 1880's, and possibly earlier. The colors to be had are all of the popular shades, with the exception of amethyst. Apple green is now difficult to find in Two-Panel. It may be had in nice shades of blue, yellow and amber. The forms are numerous and attractive in shape.

Classification

TWO-PANEL

PATTERN 213

(See Plates 159, 160)

Form Number.
1. Bowl, oval, large and deep, collared base. Bowl has four panels, having all-over pressed design; 8⅝ x 10½ inches.
1A. Butter dish.

Form Number.

2. Celery dips.

3. Celery vase.

4. Compotes.
    a. Covered, on high foot.
    b. Open.
        (1) High foot.
        (2) Low foot, 5¾ inch.

5. Cordials.

6. Creamer.

7. Dishes, oval.
    a. Footed, 9 inch.
    b. Deep, 5 x 3 inches. Several other sizes.
    c. Flat; very unusual. (Made up of four panels, with all-over pressed design.) Four large scallops, 10½ x 8¾ inches.

8. Fruit bowl, 10 inch. Several sizes.

9. Goblets.

10. Jam jar, oval, flat base.

11. Lamps, kerosene type. Tall, all glass.

11A. Mugs. Two sizes.

12. Pickle dish, handles at each end.

13. Pitcher, water.

14. Salts, oval.
    a. Salt and pepper shakers.

15. Sauce dishes.
    a. Flat.
    b. Footed, 2 sizes.

16. Tray, large oval for water pitcher and goblets, handle at each end.

17. Tumblers, round, and show three panels.

18. Wines.

Colors: Blue, apple green, light yellowish green, yellow, amber, clear glass.

DIAMOND QUILTED

One of the loveliest and coolest looking of the colored glass designs is the Diamond Quilted. It is found in a charming array of pastel shades, pale and shimmering. There is a delightful yellow, a delicate light amethyst, a deep distinct amethyst, light blue, apple green, pale amber and dark amber. It may also be had in clear glass. Though this is one of the late wares, probably dating from about 1880, it is particularly appealing. It has a rather sophisticated air, but it may be used to advantage in highly decorative table schemes. It is one of the few patterns which may be had in amethyst. On Plate 104 is shown a group of forms. One may also find a lovely tall champagne glass, a cordial, and an unusual short-stemmed goblet. A few collectors I know have used one each of several of the colors in combination and the effect was unusual and pleasing. One collected six pieces of green and six of blue and combined them. Another used yellow and blue.

Being a fairly late pattern, produced in large quantities, the classification of it becomes a rather perilous undertaking. However, the forms listed will give a very fair idea of what one may do with this pattern. It has become so popular during the past decade, that it is more difficult to find to-day.

Classification

DIAMOND QUILTED

Pattern 214

(See Plate 104)

Form Number.
1. Butter dish, footed.
2. Celery vase.
3. Champagnes, 6¼ inches high.
4. Compotes, covered, on high and low standards, various sizes.
5. Compotes, open, on high standard, various sizes.
6. Cordials.
7. Creamer.
8. Goblet; usual stem.
   a. Short stemmed.
9. Pitcher, water.

10. Sauce, footed. 2 sizes.
    a. Round, flat, pressed design in base.
11. Spoonholder.
12. Sugar bowl, footed.
13. Tray, round, for water pitcher and goblets.
    a. Clover leaf-shaped tray for water set.
14. Tumbler.
Colors: Yellow, pale amethyst, deep amethyst, light blue, apple green, pale amber, dark amber, clear glass.

WHEAT AND BARLEY

This pattern has been popular for several years and it is particularly lovely in colors. Though it appears to date from the late seventies or, possibly, the Eighties, it is not found as readily as one might expect. All the pieces are paneled, with the exception of the plates. The goblet has twelve panels and a round clear base. The delicate design consists of a large spray of wheat and barley which hangs downward on the glass. This description does not do it justice, but one may see a group of it on Plate 50. It is found in blue, amber and yellow as well as in clear glass. The amber is particularly appealing in this design. Its original trade name was "Duquesne" and it was produced by the old firm of Bryce Bros., of Pittsburgh.

Classification
WHEAT AND BARLEY
PATTERN 215
(See Plate 50, 114)

Form Number.
1. Bowls.
    a. Fruit. Flat, open. 6, 7 and 8 inch.
    b. Covered, 6, 7 and 8 inch.
2. Bread plate, with handle.
3. Butter dish.

4. Cake plates on standards. 8, 9 and 10 inch.
5. Compotes.
     a. On high standard, shallow bowl. 7, 8 and 10 inch.
     b. On high standard. Covered. 6, 7 and 8 inch.
     c. On high standard, with handle on each side of bowl of com-
        pote. (Sweetmeat dish, with cover.) 6 inch.
6. Creamer.
7. Goblet.
8. Jelly dish. Footed. 5 inch.
9. Molasses jug. ½ pint and pint. (Syrup pitcher.)
10. Mug, large.
11. Pitchers. Quart and ½ gallon.
12. Plate, round. 7 inch.
     a. 9 inch, with closed handles. (Bread plate.)
13. Salt and pepper shakers.
14. Sauce dishes.
     a. Footed. 4 inch.
     b. Flat, with handle. 4 inch.
15. Spoonholder.
16. Sugar bowl.
17. Tumblers, water.
     a. Footed. (Same type used with tin cap for jelly.)
Colors: Amber, blue, clear glass and yellow.

CATHEDRAL

Another pattern that is found in a satisfying number of colors
is the Cathedral. I have heard it so-called for several years and it
is fairly well-known by that name. It was produced, I believe,
about the same time as the Diamond Quilted pattern, or 1880. It
is also to be had in amethyst, though not as readily as the Diamond
Quilted. The two pieces of Cathedral in deep amethyst that I
have found oftenest of all the various forms are a covered compote
on high standard and a deep round berry bowl. One may also see
a number of other articles in this rare color, including goblets and
wines.

While pieces of the Cathedral are not too plentiful, still a collector may assemble a set if he is a diligent searcher. The odd pieces are attractive when used alone. The sugar bowl is often used as a candy jar. The glass is fairly heavy and a good quality. The shade of amber is particularly bright and clear.

Bryce Bros., of Pittsburgh, seem to have had a monopoly on this design which they apparently carried over a period of years. It was known as their "Orion" pattern. The classification is taken from the pieces illustrated in their catalogue, together with others I have seen in my travels.

Classification

CATHEDRAL

Pattern 216

(See Plates 58, 146)

Form Number.
1. Berry bowl, round. 5, 6, 7 and 8 inch.
2. Butter dish.
3. Cake plate on standard.
4. Compotes.
    a. Covered, large on high standard; 11 inches high, 8 inch diameter.
5. Creamer.
6. Dishes, round, footed; in various sizes with four top edges bent toward the center.
7. Goblets.
8. Pitcher, water. 3 quarts.
9. Sauce dish, round, footed; 4 and 4½ inch.
    a. Flat 4 inch.
10. Spoonholder.
11. Sugar bowl.
12. Tumbler, water.
13. Wine glass.

Colors: Amber, amethyst, blue, clear glass, yellow.

MEDALLION

The Medallion pattern is satisfying to collect because of the range of colors. The apple-green shade, so popular to-day, may be found without great difficulty and the amber has a particularly lovely tone. The dishes are rather unusual in shape, being oblong with rounded ends. On the center of each side is a medallion and in the base of the dishes a conventional pressed design. The goblets are particularly attractive, the shape differing so much from the usual form. A group of Medallion is shown on Plate 102.

Unfortunately, I can find no record of where this glass was made, but it would appear to date from the Seventies. It was just one of many patterns produced during a highly competitive era for commercial purposes. This fact should not deter collectors, who must remember that many other objects are eagerly collected to-day that belong to the same era. Currier and Ives prints, for example, were cheap lithographs, many of them selling for a few dollars per hundred. Any glass that has survived usage and time has something to be said for it.

Classification

MEDALLION

Pattern 217

(See Plate 102)

Form Number.
  1. Butter dish.
  2. Compote, on high standard.
  3. Creamer.
  4. Goblet.
  5. Sauce dishes.
      a. Flat.
      b. Footed, 2 sizes.
  6. Spoonholder.
  7. Sugar bowl.
  8. Water pitcher.
Colors: Amber, blue, clear, green, yellow.

INVERTED THUMBPRINT

One of the most puzzling patterns to treat in this book, is the Inverted Thumbprint. The reason for this is that it is a late pattern, produced by any number of factories in large quantities. It appears to have been made from 1880 onward. The variations are so numerous that to cover them all is out of the question. To show enough varieties to make collecting them a less hazardous task is the best anyone can hope to do.

This design is to be had in all the usual colors, with the exception of amethyst. It may have been made in that tint also, but I have never seen it. It is fairly abundant in apple green, which is an exception to the rule for this color. Green generally is in great demand and almost always proves to be quite elusive.

The round thumb marks which stand out in relief on the inside of the bowl, are sometimes found with dots five-eighths of an inch in diameter, but usually a little smaller. Generally the design on the goblets is carried practically to the top of the glass, though I have seen one variant in which it extends only a short way up. The usual types are like those found on Plate 161. It will be noticed in all cases that the marks run slightly smaller toward the base. Number one has a tapering bowl, flat at the base, with a very pretty knob stem. Number two has a tapered, rounding bowl with plain round stem. In this one the marks do not stand in quite as high relief and are so close together that the impression is almost blurred. It is more distinct toward the base as the dots stand out higher in the lower part. Number three is a smaller goblet with a rounded knob stem. The thumb marks are smaller and much farther apart in this one. They stand out in fairly high relief, so the pattern is distinct. Number four is a good deal on the order of number one, in general contours. The dots are slightly smaller and farther apart, and, as will be noted, the stem is entirely different. I believe these four goblets give a comprehensive idea of what may be expected in the Inverted Thumbprint.

A favorite of some discriminating collectors who have a flair for decoration, is this same pattern in cranberry red. The tumblers are most attractive in the rose pink, deep cranberry red and amberina, a color combining the amber and red. In the latter the amber is usually at the base fusing into a lovely red at the top.

The finger bowls are found in three styles. One is rounded on the base, another has a small raised base and the third is a much smaller size without the base. A large sized tumbler may be had which was probably intended as a celery holder originally, but now is often used for flowers. In the other pieces of tableware, aside from the goblets, the thumb marks are fairly large and placed very regularly. There are exceptions, of course, such as tumblers with quite small thumb marks. The pieces will be found to match without much difficulty, except in the goblets.

The cranberry red and amberina I am listing separately, as they are not found in the large variety of pieces of the other colors, such as amber, blue, green and yellow.

Many pieces of Inverted Thumbprint will be found in color, combined with crystal. For instance, the red water pitcher often has a clear glass applied handle. The punch cups are usually found this way also, as well as fruit bowls, which may have three feet of clear glass.

For the benefit of collectors who like to know as much about the history of pattern glass as possible, I add a list of those factories which produced Inverted Thumbprint, giving the original trade name, whenever one is found in the old catalogues in my possession. Of the firms making this ware in large quantities, Hobbs, Brocunier & Company, of Wheeling, W. Va., were leaders. Hobnails and thumbprints were popular designs in their plant for many years. An old-time glass worker told me that the workmen at the factory used to refer to the hobnail as the "Wart" and to the inverted thumbprint as the "Dot." Tumblers were made up in all shades of color and sold by the dozen or half-dozen, packed in fancy colored boxes. Boxes of twelve usually consisted of six color combinations. Tumblers with diagonal ribbing were also made by this firm and sold in the same way.

George Duncan & Sons made an even greater variety of pieces. The cranberry red square-mouthed pitchers with crystal handles came in six sizes. Their Rubena Crystal was the same line, only partly clear, the upper part of each piece shading to red. Their Rubena Verde consisted of a yellow lower part shading to red from the center of the bowl of each piece. Their name for all this ware was "Polka Dot." In addition there were countless pieces, such as finger bowls, cordials, wines, clarets, tall champagne glasses, cruets, salts and peppers, celery vases, footed sauce dishes, compotes open and covered, and "table sets," which included a sugar bowl, butter dish, creamer and spoonholder.

Bryce Bros., of Pittsburgh, contributed their quota. They manufactured chiefly pitchers, tumblers, custard cups and small objects. The Central Glass Company, of Wheeling, W. Va., created a few items and so did Doyle & Company, of Pittsburgh. The latter made compotes which they called "French Dot," though their goblets are listed as plain "Dot." The Bellaire Goblet Company, of Findlay, Ohio, show several variations of goblets. The list might be prolonged, but it is enough to show what a task it would be to attempt to determine where all the variants were manufactured. It is largely a midwestern pattern.

There are not many reproductions in amberina at this writing. It is fairly safe to assume that the color combination may have deterred the makers, since the few attempts to copy it have not been successful. In cranberry red, there are numerous new tumblers, finger bowls and a few novelties. The new tumblers and bowls are much heavier in weight than the old ones and the color is not complimentary to the originals.

Classification

INVERTED THUMBPRINT
Cranberry Red and Amberina

PATTERN 218

(See Plate 162)

Form Number.
*1. Bowls, finger.
 a. Three styles, one with plate to match. One type finger bowl has been reproduced in cranberry color.
 b. Fruit.

Form Number.

2. Carafe; water bottle and tumbler.
3. Celery vase.
4. Cheese dish. Plate with dome cover.
5. Compote, on foot. Rare.
6. Cruets.
7. Creamer.
8. Custard, or Punch cups, usually with clear handles.
9. Goblet. Rare.
10. Hats. Toothpick or match holders. Rare.
11. Jars. Pickle, with metal top.
    a. Tall, covered.
*12. Pitcher, water. A large number of variations, including six sizes with square mouth and crystal handles.
13. Salt and pepper shakers. Scarce.
14. Toothpick holders in various novelty forms.
*15. Tumblers, water.
16. Wines, tall; like tumblers, only smaller and taper toward base.

Colors: Cranberry red; amberina.

Classification

INVERTED THUMBPRINT
Yellow and Other Colors

PATTERN 218A
(See Plate 161)

Form Number.

1. Butter dish, on three feet. Also footed.
2. Celery vase. Several styles, one being footed.
3. Clarets.
4. Compote, round base, rayed.
    a. Covered. 7, 8 and 9 inch.
    b. Open. 5, 6, 7, 8 and 9 inch.
5. Cordials.
*6. Creamer.
    a. On three feet.
    b. Collared base, matching sugar bowl of same style.

Form Number.

7. Cruets. Some blown, with hollow blown stoppers.

8. Cups, sherbet.

*9. Finger bowls.

10. Goblets (illustrated, Plate 161).

*11. Pitcher, water. Quart and ½ gallon.

12. Plates, round, scalloped edge.

13. Salt and pepper shakers. Swirled collared base.

14. Sauce dishes, round, on three feet. Also footed and flat.

15. Spoonholder, on three feet. Also footed.

16. Sugar bowl, on three feet. Also footed.

17. Sugar bowl, collared base.

18. Syrup pitcher. Swirled collared base, metal cover.

19. Tumblers.

20. Wines, like small tumblers. Originally listed as champagne glasses.

Colors: Yellow, blue, amber, green, clear glass.

RAINDROP

Raindrop is practically the same as the Inverted Thumbprint, except that the raised marks occur on the *outside* of the glass, instead of on the inside. It is more distinctly a definite pattern, the thumb marks being larger and the graduation in size more pronounced. Some of the glass is quite brilliant and scintillating, especially the plates and finger bowls. Certain pieces of this ware must have been made fairly early, as I find plates with heavy pontil marks. It was a late ware for the most part and turned out in large quantities. The usual colors are amber, yellow, blue and clear. Occasionally it is found in apple green. The compote shown on Plate 161 is unusually attractive with its swirled stem. The larger pieces of Raindrop have larger dots, in comparison, than the smaller ones. This is the design so often confused with Thousand-Eye. Thousand-Eye has smaller dots with a distinct small diamond point at each intersection. This, it should be noted, is the chief point of difference and should differentiate it instantly. Side by side, the two patterns do not look at all alike.

Classification

RAINDROP

PATTERN 219

(See Plate 161)

Form Number.

1. Compotes, various sizes, on high and low standards.
2. Cups and saucers.
3. Egg cups, double.
4. Finger bowls.
    a. Round.
    b. Top edge in points, which are bent in toward center.
5. Pickle dish, oval.
6. Plates. Large, with handles.
    a. Round, matching finger bowls.
    b. Alphabet border.
7. Sauce dish.
    a. Footed.
    b. Flat.
8. Syrup pitcher.
9. Trays, large and flat.

Colors: Amber; blue; yellow; apple green; clear glass; milk-white. The blue is a dark shade.

WILLOW OAK

This ware has been christened many times, thereby causing no end of confusion. I have heard it called Acorn and Oakleaf, Stippled Daisy, Thistle and Sunflower. None of these names seemed appropriate and in view of the fact that one real Sunflower pattern is given in this book it will save future complication to give it another title.

The Willow Oak is not as well known as it deserves to be. It is a particularly appealing design, delicate and dainty. Doubtless it would have been more widely collected had there not been so much difficulty over its name. It may be found in colors as well as in clear glass. The English daisy medallion plays a prominent part in the design, being the same motif used in the Rosette, Barred Forget-me-not, etc. The oblong panel showing oak leaves of two different varieties of oak, gives rise to the unusual title. The background of this panel is stippled, the rest of the glass being clear. The plates, in two sizes, are especially attractive.

It is well that collectors do not always agree on the beauty of any one design, for if they did all would seek the same pieces. As it is, there is plenty for everyone—with a little diligent searching. Those who are looking for something different and not widely known might well consider the Willow Oak. This ware was probably made during the 1870's. At least, I find no record of it except in a Bryce Bros., Pittsburgh, catalogue of that period. There, it was designated as the "Wreath."

Classification

WILLOW OAK

PATTERN 220
(See Plates 45, 129, 159)

Form Number.
1. Bowls. 7 and 8 inch.
2. Butter dish.
3. Cake plate, on standard.
4. Celery vase.
5. Compote, covered, on high standard. Wide flange. 6, 7½ and 9 inch. Bowls are usually shallow.
6. Creamer.
7. Finger bowl.
8. Goblet.
9. Mug, large.
10. Pitchers, water. Quart and ½ gallon. Also milk pitcher.
11. Plates.
     a. Round. 7 inch.
     b. Bread plate, with closed handles. 9 inch.
12. Salt and pepper shakers.

Form Number.
13. Sauce dishes.
   a. Flat, with handle. 4 inch.
   b. Footed. 4 inch.
14. Spoonholder.
15. Sugar bowl.
16. Tumbler.
17. Water set, with pitcher and bowl.
Colors: Amber, blue, clear glass.

BASKET WEAVE

The Basket Weave is another pattern that is most often encountered in colors, particularly the water sets. These come in amber, blue or yellow. The tray to this set is round, with a raised rim showing the basket weave. The center has a rural scene, picturing a little house closely resembling a log cabin, hills, trees, a stream with a bridge and, last but not least, a boy with his dog! The Basket Weave pattern is what the name suggests, so the title is appropriate. Aside from the tray of the water set, the rest of the pieces are composed solely of the woven pattern. The records I have found do not mention this design, which appears to date from the Seventies.

Classification

BASKET WEAVE

PATTERN 221

(See Plate 104)

Form Number.
1. Berry bowl.
2. Bowl, larger than usual finger bowl.
3. Bowl, round and flat, with cover; handles.
4. Cake plate, small handles.
5. Compote, covered.
6. Cordials.

Form Number.
- 7. Egg cups, double.
- 8. Cups and Saucers.
- 9. Goblet.
- 10. Pitcher, water.
- 11. Sauce dish, round, flat.
- 12. Syrup pitcher, metal top.
- 13. Tray for water set, round, 12 inch.

Colors: Blue, amber, yellow, clear, milk-white, apple green.

CANE

There is no difficulty in identifying this pattern by name, even when one has never seen a piece of it before, since the effect is of the cane seat of a chair. It has been accumulated and known by collectors for a number of years chiefly because it is plentiful and because it comes in divers colors. The ever popular apple green may be found more easily in this pattern than in almost any other.

There is a wide range of forms in the Cane, including the much sought after toddy plates. These measure $4\frac{1}{2}$ inches in diameter. The goblet is shown on Plate 160 and a group on Plate 132. I believe this to be a ware of the Eighties. No factual record of where it was produced is known at present.

Classification

CANE

PATTERN 222

(See Plates 132, 160)

Form Number.
- 1. Bowl, size similar to finger bowl.
- 2. Butter dish.
- 3. Creamer.
- 4. Goblets.
- 5. Pickle dish, oval.
- 6. Pitcher, water.
- 7. Plates, toddy, $4\frac{1}{2}$ inch.

Form Number.

   8. Sauce dishes.

      a. Footed.

      b. Round, flat, 4 inch.

   9. Spoonholder.

  10. Sugar bowl.

  11. Tray, large round; for water pitcher and goblets.

  12. Tumblers, water.

Colors: Amber; apple green; blue; clear; yellow.

FINE CUT

It is not difficult to predict that a pattern as delightful as the Fine Cut is bound to become more popular when it is better known. It is a pleasure to know that the plates are found not only in three sizes, but also in several colors. The attractive goblet is shown on Plate 160. The design, which is rather difficult to describe, may be seen there in detail. Besides the crystal, there is a pale, shimmering, clear yellow, a medium deep blue and a fairly dark amber. I have been unable to find it in either green or amethyst. I believe this ware belongs to the Seventies, as it is illustrated in a Bryce Bros., Pittsburgh, catalogue of that period. It was known simply as "No. 720 Pattern." Collectors would do well to consider this pattern, in making a selection for a table-setting, because it is one of the most attractive included in this book, whether in color or clear glass.

Classification

FINE CUT

Pattern 223

(See Plates 138, 160)

Form Number.

   1. Bowls, small. Footed finger bowls.

   2. Butter dish.

   3. Compote, covered.

   4. Creamer.

   5. Dish. Oblong, deep, open vegetable.

Form Number.
  6. Goblets.
  7. Pitcher, water.
  8. Plate, 6¼, 7¼, 10¼ inch.
  9. Sauce dish.
  10. Spoonholder.
  11. Sugar bowl.
Colors: Dark amber; deep blue; clear glass; pale yellow.

FINE CUT AND PANEL

During the Eighties, when colored pressed glass tableware was greatly in vogue, many interesting conventional designs were evolved by competitive factories to attract trade. Among these is one called Fine Cut and Panel. A few dealers used to refer to it as "Nailhead and Panel." The old trade name being long since lost, it matters little what these designs are christened so long as there is a means of identifying them. I have found the plate illustrated in an old Bryce Bros., of Pittsburgh, catalogue, but strangely enough, there is no pattern number or trade name given. It merely lists the plates in two sizes.

The attractive goblet in this glass may be seen on Plate 160. It is found in colors as well as in clear glass. The plates are an added feature, and the oblong platters are practical and useful in dinner table schemes. The sauce dishes are square and footed, as may be seen on Plate 61. While not as many forms have been noted in this glass as in many others of the period, industrious collectors may be able to find more to add to my list.

Classification
FINE CUT AND PANEL
PATTERN 224
(See Plates 61, 160)

Form Number.
  1. Bowl, size of finger bowl, originally used with water set.
  2. Butter dish, square.

Form Number.

3. Compote, on high standard.
4. Cordial.
5. Creamer.
6. Dish. Oblong, deep, open vegetable.
7. Goblet.
8. Pitcher, water. Two sizes.
9. Plates, round. 6¼ and 7¼ inch.
10. Platter, oblong.
11. Relish dish, oblong.
12. Sauce, footed, square.
13. Spoonholder.
14. Sugar bowl.
15. Tray; oblong, for water set.

Colors: Amber; yellow; blue; clear glass.

SWIRL

Of the later period of patterns closely related to the Daisy and Button group is one generally known as the Swirl. The design, as the title suggests, is a swirl; then a band of quilting similar to the English hobnail; then the swirl again around the base of the object. The goblet has an odd knob in the stem. It is round, with heavy ribs and the base is filled in with the daisy and button design. Goblets are found in two sizes, one being unusually large with a barrel-shaped bowl. This may be seen on Plate 146. The large goblet has a narrower marginal band at the top than the smaller one. Plates are collectible in three sizes, and all pieces are found in colors as well as in crystal. The amber is seen in two shades, and the blue is somewhat darker than is usual in the pressed glass of this later period; that is, of the Eighties. Goblets are scarce in color.

In fact, pattern glass has been collected so assiduously in recent years, especially those designs which are popular in their various colors, that any of it will challenge the most inveterate collector today.

Classification

SWIRL

PATTERN 225

(See Plates 69, 146, 163)

Form Number.

1. Butter dish.
2. Cake plate, on standard.
3. Celery vase, large, round.
4. Compotes, in various sizes.
5. Goblets, two sizes.
6. Plates, 6¼, 8 and 10 inch.
7. Salts, large and small.
    a. Large.
    b. Flat.
    c. Round.
    d. Celery dips.
8. Sauce dish. Round, collared base.
9. Sherbet cup.
10. Spoonholder.
11. Sugar bowl.
12. Tumblers, water.
13. Wines.

Colors: Amber; blue; clear; yellow.

SWAN

It is not often that one encounters pieces of the Swan pattern while touring antique shops. Most of those I own came from Pennsylvania. The covered dishes are oval, with a collared base. The knob of the covers is in the form of a large swan with his neck twisted about as though he were preening his feathers. On the lower part of such dishes is a rather elaborate medallion on each side, showing a swan with his long neck in the same position as on the knob. The background about the medallion is not stippled but has fine squares that resemble a coarse mesh. The two panels are divided by a single line on each side, in clear diamond points. The covers are of clear glass with the swan-knob just described. The goblets are unusual-looking, especially in colors. The swan-medallion is on each side, as on the covered dishes, but on the goblet the bird is swimming about, instead of having the contorted neck. The knob stem consists of a single heavy, ring-like turning around the hexagonal stem. The base is clear. It will be noted in the group on Plate 77 that the creamer has an odd handle, having a round knob at the top and bottom, with a star-shaped ornament impressed in it.

The Swan appears to be of the 1880's though it might possibly date from the late Seventies. How many colors are available I cannot say as I have seen so little of it. The amber I have owned has been in a light shade and I have seen pieces in yellow and clear glass. That many forms may be had that are not listed here I do not doubt, but only those I have seen are given.

Classification

SWAN

PATTERN 226

(See Plate 77)

Form Number.
1. Butter dish.
2. Creamer.
3. Dish, oval, covered.
4. Goblet.
5. Pickle jar, covered.
6. Pitcher, water.
7. Sauce dish.
   - *a.* Footed.
   - *b.* Round, flat, 4 inch.
8. Spoonholder.
9. Sugar bowl.

Colors: Light amber; yellow; clear glass; deep blue.

JACOB'S COAT

There are many ridiculous names for pattern glass, especially of the late period, and this is one of them. An artist who had just finished drawing some of the Jacob's Ladder pieces said: "Jacob's Ladder is an appropriate name but this is like Jacob's Coat. It may not have every color but it certainly has everything else on it!" It is a ware of the Eighties and a particularly fussy one. The covers of the dishes are divided into panels by a short band of ribbing and the design in the panels looks like a crazy quilt. The only pieces of this late ware I have seen have been in a bright amber and in clear glass. The creamer is rather large with a heavy pressed handle. I have not see many forms but no doubt they exist.

Classification

JACOB'S COAT

PATTERN 227

(See Plate 115)

Form Number.
1. Butter dish.
2. Celery vase.
3. Creamer.
4. Goblet.
5. Sauce dish, 4½ inches.
6. Spoonholder.
7. Sugar bowl.

Colors: Amber; clear.

RIBBED OPAL GLASS

While this beautifully colored opal glass is usually seen only in the opalescent, a number of pieces may be found in the blue-opalescent. This is rather an unusual design, though simple. It has vertical ribs that stand out in rather high relief, reminding one of a cog wheel. Many interesting forms may be found though I have never seen a goblet to match. A group of this glass may be seen on Plate 147. The berry sets are pleasing, and an unusual tall tumbler or lemonade glass, is sometimes encountered. Small glass match holders are often seen. Originally designed for toothpicks they now grace many tables as holders for matches or cigarettes. Pitchers come in various sizes, but no liqueur glasses have been found so far.

In an old trade catalogue of A. J. Beatty & Company, of Tiffin, Ohio, I find this glass illustrated and listed simply as "No. 87 Opalescent Ware." It is shown both in the blue and the opalescent. Also produced by this same company is a similar glass having ribs forming squares, in relief. Unfortunately the catalogue is undated, but I judge all this ware probably dates from the early 1880's. The classification given is taken from their list.

Classification

RIBBED OPAL GLASS

Pattern 228

(See Plate 147)

Form Number.

1. Bowls.
   a. Berry, round. 8 and 9 inch.
   b. Small, similar to finger bowl, 4¾ inch.
   c. Oblong, deep salad bowl.
2. Butter dish.
3. Celery vase.
4. Cracker jar, covered.
5. Creamers.
   a. Large.
   b. Small.
6. Dishes. Oblong. 7 and 8 inch.
7. Finger bowl.
8. Lemonade glass.
9. Match holder.
10. Puff box.
11. Pitcher, water.

12. Salts.
>   *a.* Salt and pepper shakers.
>   *b.* Individual salts.
>   *c.* Large table salts.

13. Sauce dish, round, deep. $4\frac{1}{2}$ inch.
14. Spoonholder.
15. Sugar bowl.
16. Sugar shaker.
17. Sugar and creamer, individual.
18. Toothpick holder. Two styles.
19. Tumblers.
>   *a.* Tall, lemonade.
>   *b.* Water.

Colors: Blue-opal; opal.

SWIRLED OPAL GLASS

Similar to the Ribbed Opal glass is another style in which the ribs run around the glass giving a swirled effect instead of running vertically as in the ribbed type. The forms are very much the same. Not many pieces of this Swirled glass have come to my attention, but it is listed here for purposes of identification. Since it comes in opalescent and blue-opalescent, it was probably also made in yellow-opalescent.

Classification

SWIRLED OPAL GLASS

PATTERN 229

Form Number.
1. Butter dish.
2. Creamer.
3. Egg cup.
4. Salt and pepper shakers, in holder.
5. Spoonholder.
6. Sugar bowl.
7. Tumbler.

Colors: Opalescent; blue-opalescent.

EMERALD GREEN HERRINGBONE

Not many collectors have taken note of the interesting forms to be had in a pattern which is generally seen in emerald green. Exceptionally few of the old pressed glass designs used this color which has such a high decorative value. While this glass is of the late period, it is as old as many other patterns that are being widely collected to-day. Due to the dark shade of its color, how effective a group of this glass may be, cannot be conveyed by a photo· graph. A goblet is shown on the page of goblets, Number 1, Plate 164. The berry bowls are round with square-faced tops and the sauce dishes match. The cordials are most interesting and scarce. It appears to be a ware of the 1880's. One collector asserted that this design creates a surpringly sophisticated table set, which must be seen assembled to be fully appreciated. It is a pleasing pattern when combined with milk-white glass.

Classification

EMERALD GREEN HERRINGBONE

PATTERN 230

(See Plate 164)

Form Number.
1. Berry bowl, large, deep.
2. Butter dish.
3. Cordials.
4. Creamer.
5. Goblets.
6. Pickle dish, oval.
7. Pitcher, water.
8. Plates, square. $7\frac{1}{4}$ and $9\frac{1}{4}$ inch.
9. Sauce dish, round, square-faced top, deep.
10. Spoonholder.
11. Sugar bowl.
12. Tumbler, water.

Colors: Emerald green; clear glass.

PLATE 164—GOBLETS

Including some patterns not collectible in other forms.

(See page 638)

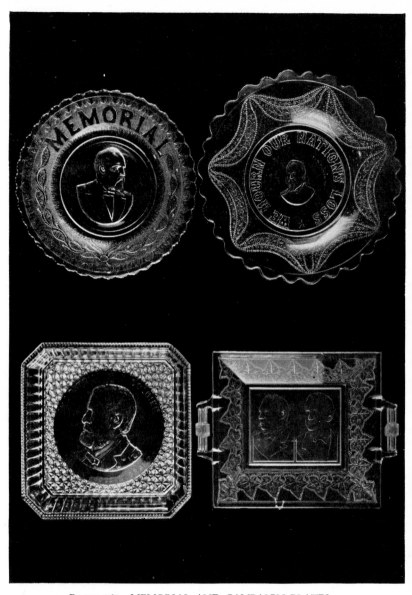

PLATE 165—MEMORIAL AND CAMPAIGN PLATES

Garfield Memorial   Garfield Drape
Grant   Cleveland and Hendricks

(See page 639)

PLATE 166

1. SOUTHERN IVY water pitcher, sauce dish, berry bowl.
2. BUCKLE with STAR goblet, sauce dish, pickle dish.
3. FESTOON spoonholder, sauce dish, creamer.
4. GOOSEBERRY goblet, tumbler, spoonholder.

RUBY THUMBPRINT

During the time of the World's Fair in Chicago there were two pressed glass patterns on the market which are collected to-day largely because of the decorative value of their color. On account of their present popularity and to insure identification, they are included in this book.

The Ruby Thumbprint, as it is largely called to-day, has a wide ruby red band above with a heavy thick, clear glass lower band impressed with large, round indentations. A great variety of forms were made, with the exception of plates, and the glass is fairly plentiful, as it was made over a period of years. A day's tour of antique shops is sure to reveal at least a few pieces. Ruby Thumbprint was also produced in all clear glass, but it is not much in demand, lacking the charm of vivid color.

Originally this glass was made by both Adams & Company, of Pittsburgh, and Doyle & Company, of the same city. It was known as "Excelsior," and was listed in all catalogues as the X L C R pattern. It was sold both plain or engraved, as the customer desired. Judging by the number of pieces produced, it must have had a wide sale and for many years. It was not made before 1890. The classification given is taken directly from the old catalogue price list.

Reproductions have appeared with the red band and in clear glass, the latter known to some collectors as "Kings Crown." Pieces that have been copied are marked with an asterisk, in the classification.

Classification

RUBY THUMBPRINT

PATTERN 231

(See Plate 162)

Form Number.

1. Bowls, collared base. 5, 6, 7, 8 and 9 inch.
    a. Berry bowl, round. 8 inch.
    b. Berry bowl (boat-shaped), pointed. 8 inch.

Form Number.

> c. Bowl, flared. 5 inch.
> d. Bowls, belled. 5, 6, 7, 8 and 9 inch.
> e. Bowls, open, flared with Sawtooth edge. 6, 7 and 8½ inch.

2. Butter dish.
3. Cake plate, on standard. 9 and 10 inch.
4. Castor set.
5. Celery vase.
*6. Champagne.
7. Custard cup.
8. Cups and saucers.
9. Compotes.

> a. Covered, on high standard. 5, 6, 7, 8 and 9 inch.
> b. Open, on high standard, with Sawtooth edge, belled. 5, 6, 7, 8 and 9 inch.
> c. Open, on high standard, with Sawtooth edge, flared. 6½, 7½, 9, 10 and 11½ inch.

10. Creamer.

> a. Individual sugar and creamer.

11. Cheese plate with cover.
12. Dish, dessert, square. 8 inch.

> a. Olive dish, handled.
> b. Preserve, oval. 6 and 10 inch.

13. Fruit basket, on high standard.
*14. Goblet.
15. Honey dish with cover. Square.
16. Mustard dish, with cover.
17. Orange bowl. Extra large compote, on standard.
18. Pickle jar, with cover.
19. Pickle dish.
20. Pitcher, water. Quart and ½ gallon.
21. Salts, oblong, individual.

> a. Large, oblong.
> b. Salt and pepper shakers.

22. Sauce dish.

> a. Pointed at each end. (Boat shape.) 4 inch.
> b. Round, belled. 4 and 4½ inch.
> c. Round. 5 and 6 inch.
> d. Round, not belled. 4 inch.

Form Number.

23. Sugar bowl.
24. Spoonholder.
25. Tankard (pitcher). ½ gallon.
    a. Tankard, pint size.
26. Toothpick holders.
27. Tumbler, water.
*28. Wines.

Colors: Red and white; clear glass. Made plain and engraved.
Also in clear glass, with gilt decoration and in amethyst with gilt.

RED BLOCK

Almost a twin of the Ruby Thumbprint, so far as color and period are concerned, is the Red Block. The design is coarser and consists of an unusually heavy pressing of hexagonal blocks, faceted, with a round flat surface which is painted red. One piece of this glass on a table is far from being impressive, but collectively, it at least has the merit of its cheerful color. Care should be taken by the collector to select pieces in good condition, as those dishes which have undergone rough usage are usually so worn that the red blocks look dingy. It is still possible to find this glass with the brilliant ruby band and the red blocks, in perfect condition. The goblet is highly decorative, with the wide ruby band at the top of the bowl and the bright colorful faceted blocks below, on a clear bowl. The stemware has a knob stem that is very pretty. Many forms are to be found, plates being the exception. Doyle & Company, of Pittsburgh, who made the Ruby Thumbprint, are also responsible for this ware. The design was carried on by the United States Glass Company after Doyle & Company merged with them. It was called "Eva" originally.

Several red and white combinations in pressed patterns were made at this period (the gay Nineties!) but they were discovered too late to be included in this book. Mention might be made of a particularly dainty and attractive one, the goblet being shown on Plate 164, Number 3. This was made in all-clear glass as well as with the red touches where the depressions are indicated in the panels. A large variety of pieces may be found in this pattern. A variant of the Red Block may be seen in a tumbler having a square block instead of the usual hexagonal block. These patterns are covered in my later volume, *Victorian Glass.*

Classification

RED BLOCK

PATTERN 232

(See Plate 162)

Form Number.
1. Bowls, berry. 6, 8 and 9 inch.
     a. Finger bowls.
2. Butter dish.
3. Celery vase.
4. Cheese dish. Plate, with large cover.
5. Cordials.
6. Creamer, large and individual.
7. Dishes, oblong. 8, 9 and 10 inch.
8. Goblets.
9. Mug, handled.
10. Pitcher, water.
11. Sauce.
     a. Round and deep. 5 inch.
12. Salt and pepper shakers, metal tops.
     a. Individual.
     b. Heavy table salt, round.
13. Sugar bowl.
14. Spoonholder.
Colors: Clear glass; red and white. A few pieces may be seen in yellow and white.

FINE CUT AND BLOCK

During the 1880's, the era of the well-known Daisy and Button design that proved so popular. the market was flooded with many all-over pressed patterns. Among these is one called Fine Cut and Block. It is possible I may not have seen all the color combinations that were used to decorate this ware but for the most part it is clear glass in a fine-cut, pressed effect similar to the more expensive cut glass, the larger blocks being decorated in color. One goblet has a yellow colored block, producing a most charming effect particularly when combined with colored linens. Another has a pink block and still another a deeper yellow bordering on orange. Though this is a late glass it could not have been produced on the same scale as the Daisy and Button, since it is difficult to find many pieces. Compotes and goblets are seen more frequently than other articles in this pattern. Known originally to the trade as No. 25 Pattern, this glass was made by the King Glass Company of Pittsburgh, which was absorbed by the United States Glass Company in 1891. The classification is taken from an original old catalogue.

Classification

FINE CUT AND BLOCK

PATTERN 233

(See Plate 161)

Form Number.

1. Bowls.
    a. Berry, handled. 6, 7, 8, 9 and 10 inch.
    b. Flaring.
    c. Round. 6, 8 and 10 inch.
    d. Orange. 8 and 10 inch.
2. Butter dish. Individual.
3. Cake plate, on standard. From 8 to 12 inch.
4. Champagne.
    a. Usual size.
    b. Saucer bowl.
5. Claret.
6. Compotes, open, on high standards. Various sizes, including 5 inch.
7. Cordial.
8. Custard cup.

Form **Number.**

9. Egg cup.
10. Finger bowl.
11. Goblet.
12. Lamp, handled.
13. Orange bowl and tray, combination. 10 inch.
14. Perfume bottles. Five sizes.
15. Pickle jar.
16. Pitchers, water. 3 pint and ½ gallon.
17. Plates. 6, 7 and 12 inch sizes.
18. Salts.
    a. Table.
    b. Individual, or celery dips.
    c. Footed.
19. Sauce dishes.
    a. Handled, flat. 4 and 5 inch.
    b. Round, footed. 3¾ inch.
20. Sugar bowl.
21. Wines.

Colors: Yellow and white; pink and white; deep yellow, bordering on orange; amber; blue and white; clear glass; light green and clear.

Chapter XXI

CLEAR CONVENTIONAL PATTERNS

HORSESHOE OR "GOOD LUCK"

A design which is at once decorative and something of a novelty, is called Horseshoe or "Good Luck." The covered dishes have knobs and handles in the form of horseshoes. The oval platter has handles in the form of horseshoes, a large horseshoe in the center, with stippled leaves and a conventional ornament around it. The border has an effective double row of heavy beading. The surprise comes in the goblets, which are exceptionally dainty and attractive. They have long bowls and short stems. One style has a plain round, rather thick stem and the other a more ornate one, ribbed, with a stippled band in the center showing round clear flattened hobnails. The unusual part is that the goblets do not show any horseshoe at all but only the flower motif. One is shown on Plate 130 and the other on the Plate of line drawings, Number 112. The bases of both are clear. The round plate is pictured on Plate 131 and the oval platter on Plate 133. This pattern must date from the early Seventies. It was once known to a few as "Prayer Rug," due to the ornament on the goblet which is without the good luck symbol. Probably it gained its pious title before collectors realized that this goblet really belonged to the Horseshoe pattern of glass.

Classification

HORSESHOE OR "GOOD LUCK"

PATTERN 234

(See Plates 112, 130, 131, 133)

Form Number.

   1. Bowls, oval, 5 x 8 inches; 5¾ x 9¼ ; 6½ x 10¼.

   1A. Butter dish.

Form Number.

2. Cake plate, on standard, 8, 9 and 10 inch.
3. Celery dips, like salts only much smaller, in shape of tiny horseshoes.
4. Celery vase, stems in two styles, like the goblets.
5. Cheese dish. Large, with horseshoe knob. Base frosted, with scene showing woman with churn.
6. Compotes.
    a. Covered, low, footed, 7½ inch.
    b. Open.
    c. Covered, on high foot.
7. Cordials. Rare.
8. Creamer.
9. Dishes, oblong.
    a. Covered, 8½ inch, flat, no standard; knob of cover has large horseshoe and smaller on each side.
    b. Open, 9 x 6 inches, 2½ inches deep.
10. Finger bowl.
11. Goblets.
    a. Knob stem.
    b. Plain, round stem.
12. Pickle dish.
13. Pickle jar, covered.
14. Pitcher, water, two sizes.
15. Plates, 7¼, 8¼ and 10 inch. Scarce.
16. Platters.
    a. Large, 10 x 14 inches, double horseshoe handles; horseshoe in center of platter.
    b. Oval, smaller.
17. Salts, large, in form of horseshoe. Also individual, small
18. Sauce dish.
    a. Flat, 4¼ inch.
    b. Footed, 4 inch.
    c. Flat, deep, 3¾ inches.
19. Spoonholder.
20. Sugar bowl.

Color: Clear glass.

STAR ROSETTED

For some years I have heard this glass referred to as Star Rosetted, and as there are other Star patterns to confuse the collector, it seems wise to retain the name by which it has been known.

Nearly everyone who has been interested in old pressed glass knows the popular Star and Feather seven-inch plates. The under surface of the border of this plate is entirely covered with tiny fine pointed stars, in relief. The outside surface of the Star Rosetted glass is likewise entirely covered with stars of the same size. The goblet, which is quite beautiful, may be seen on Plate 98. The cake plate (or it may originally have been intended for bread) has inscribed on the border, "A Good Mother Makes a Happy Home." All the articles of this tableware seem to be quite scarce, especially the goblets. Whether or not the Star and Feather plates were originally intended to match or to be used with this pattern, is debatable. I have seen the Star Rosetted in clear glass only, while the other plates may be had in yellow, green, blue, amber and clear glass. They combine nicely, being a convenient size for any number of dinner table uses.

This ware was probably made during the late 1870's or early 1880's, though I find no record of it in old trade catalogues.

Classification

STAR ROSETTED

Pattern 235

(See Plates 98, 131)

Form Number.
1. Butter dish.
2. Compotes, on high standard, open. 2 sizes.
3. Compotes, on low standard. 2 sizes.
4. Creamer.
5. Goblets.
6. Pickle dish.

Form Number.

7. Pitcher, water.
8. Plates. Inscribed, "A Good Mother makes a happy home." 10 inch.
9. Sauce dish.
   a. Clear scalloped rim, flat.
   b. Footed, round. 2 sizes, 4 and $4\frac{5}{8}$ inches.
10. Spoonholder.
11. Sugar bowl.

Color: Clear glass.

Star and Feather 7 inch plates. Colors: Amber; blue; yellow; apple green; clear glass.

GARFIELD DRAPE

Though much fiction is sold with glass to-day and we wonder what to believe of the stories that are handed down in regard to some of the patterns, it is undoubtedly true that many designs were inspired by events that took place. I am strongly inclined to believe that the Lincoln Drape pattern actually was made when the nation mourned Lincoln's death. In the Garfield Drape, the eleven-inch memorial plate tells the whole story. In the center is a bust of Garfield surrounded by a border of small stars. In small lettering in this circle is "Born Nov. 19, 1831. Shot July 2, 1881. Died Sept. 19, 1881." In larger lettering are these words: "We Mourn Our Nation's Loss." The border of this plate carries a festoon beaded with dewdrops. In the center of the festoons are sprays of flowers with a stippled background. The edge of the plate has a fairly large scallop. The other dishes in this pattern carry no other suggestion of matching this memorial plate than the lovely festoon of flowers. It is an attractive pattern, probably produced shortly after Garfield's death in 1881. Each of the smaller pieces, such as the footed sauce dish or goblet, has three festoons. The goblet has a fairly wide marginal band at the top. An old glassmaker, long associated with the trade, asserted that this pattern was made by Adams & Company, of Pittsburgh.

Classification

GARFIELD DRAPE

PATTERN 236

(See Plates 98, 104, 165)

Form Number.
1. Bowl.
2. Butter dish.
3. Cake plate on standard.
4. Compotes, covered, on high and low standards.
5. Creamer.
6. Goblet.
7. Honey dish.
8. Pickle dish, oval.
9. Pitcher, water, two sizes.
10. Plate, Memorial, scalloped edge, 11 inch.
    a. Same plate, center having a large star.
11. Sauce dish, footed, round.
12. Spoonholder.
13. Sugar bowl.
Color: Clear glass.

CORD AND TASSEL

Much confusion has been derived over the many "Drape" patterns. The earliest of all is the Lincoln Drape, assumed to have been made as a memorial at the time of Lincoln's death. This is a heavy, brilliant glass, and one of the last of the flint glass patterns made that kept the old bell tone. It is shown on Plate 46. The Shell and Tassel is another pattern having this ornament, though really without drapery. This is shown on Plate 97, as well as with the platters. Following, or very close to the same period, is the Cord and Tassel. It was "invented," or designed, by Andrew H. Baggs of Wheeling, West Va., who patented it on July 23, 1872. As is usually the case, the pattern carried only the patent number and that is the reason why so many home-made descriptive titles are necessary today. The glass is clear and has a band formed of two rows of fine cable, while in between a wide cable coils up and down, interspersed with tassels. Below the bottom cable which forms the band is another one that parallels it. An adequate verbal description is difficult to give and the group shown on Plate 116 will explain the pattern better than words. This glass is scarce in New York State. Indeed, so little of it is to be found in other sections that probably it never was a particularly popular pattern. Such patterns of pressed glass that proved popular were manufactured over a number of years so that most of them are not difficult to find to-day. Many forms of Cord and Tassel glass probably were made, but my classification covers only those I have seen.

Since a few fragments in this design were discovered at Sandwich, it has been suggested that possibly some of the glass was produced there. Goblets and cordials are fairly plentiful in New England.

Classification

CORD AND TASSEL

Pattern 237

(See Plate 116)

Form Number.
1. Butter dish.
2. Celery vase.
3. Compote, covered, on high foot.
4. Cordial.
5. Creamer.
6. Egg cup.
7. Goblet.
8. Pitcher, water.
9. Sauce dish.
10. Spoonholder.
11. Sugar bowl.
Color: Clear glass.

CARDINAL BIRD

A popular bird pattern is that called the Cardinal Bird. Some collectors call this Blue Jay, but a prominent ornithologist assures me, after viewing a piece of the glass, that no Blue Jay ever carried such a bill. Assuming this to be a fact, it seems proper to use the name by which many collectors already know it.

This glass is of the same period and similar in quality to that of the Liberty Bell. It is essentially a clear glass pattern and if it was ever made in color I have never seen it. The goblet, which is shown on Plate 98 shows the bird on a branch. On different pieces of this glass the cardinal is seen in different positions. The butter dish is amusing as it shows three birds, all looking very much alike. One is labeled "Red Bird" (which bears out the opinion that this is a cardinal), one "Pewit" and one "Titmouse." It is an interesting glass and in considerable demand to-day. It was probably made during the 1870's, though no record of it has been found.

Classification

CARDINAL BIRD

PATTERN 238

(See Plates 98, 100)

Form Number.

1. Butter dish.
2. Creamer.
3. Goblets.
4. Pitcher, water.
5. Sauce dish.
    a. Flat, round.
    b. Footed, two sizes, 4 and 5½ inches.
6. Spoonholder.
7. Sugar bowl.

Color: Clear glass.

SQUIRREL

Another unusual pattern, similar to the Owl and 'Possum, is the Squirrel. The stem of the goblet is also in the shape of a tree trunk though embellished with a few oak leaves. On one side of the bowl the squirrel is sitting up eating an acorn and on the reverse it is resting on a branch. The footed sauce dish has a plain scalloped rim and shows the squirrel in the same posture on both sides. These are shown on Plate 100. What an ideal design for residents of Squirrel Island, Maine!

Odd designs of this sort have a certain decorative value, and can be entertaining when used in certain settings. The Squirrel probably dates from the very late Seventies. I believe it was made by the same factory that produced the Owl and 'Possum. I have seen a creamer in another variation of this type of glass, in which a bird is seen among the branches of the trees. This piece is shown on Plate 190.

Classification

SQUIRREL

PATTERN 239

(See Plate 100)

Form Number.

1. Butter dish, squirrel knob.
2. Creamer.
3. Goblets.
4. Pitcher, water.
5. Sauce. Footed and round, flat.
6. Sugar bowl.

Color: Clear glass.

OWL AND 'POSSUM

An amusing design, also of the late Seventies, is called the Owl and 'Possum. The stem of the goblet represents the trunk of a tree and the bowl depicts the limbs with all small branches sawed off tree-surgeon fashion and sans foliage. Perched on a limb on one side is a sedate looking owl. On the reverse side, apparently asleep, is a 'possum. There is a marginal band at the top of the goblet, with a row of pointed ornaments, pointing down. Some of these have tiny stars imprinted on them. For a woodland home this would be an interesting ware.

While I have only been able to find a few pieces of this unusual pattern, I do not doubt that it was made in a number of forms.

Classification

OWL AND 'POSSUM

PATTERN 240

(See Plate 100)

Form Number.
1. Goblets.
2. Pitcher, water.
3. Sauce, footed.
Color: Clear glass.

BUCKLE WITH STAR

Many collectors will find in the Buckle with Star pattern a glass exactly suited to their needs. It is not well known at present but it undoubtedly will become more popular in time. It was produced at the same period as the Late Buckle pattern, and at the same factory. Bryce Bros., of Pittsburgh, called this their "Orient" pattern and produced it during the Eighties. The goblet has three of the pointed buckle-shaped ornaments, all of which are divided by seven petal-like blades that fill the vacant spaces in between. This large design covers all the bowl of the goblet, with the exception of the plain marginal band at the top. The pointed buckle is formed of a wide band, which is divided into small squares, each square having a conventional star-shaped figure that fills the space.

In the bright pointed oval in the center is impressed a larger star-like ornament. The stem of the goblet is hexagonal and has a knob close to the base of the bowl. Altogether the design is bold and elaborate. The knobs of the covered pieces are in the form of a Maltese cross. In the sauce dish, the design is necessarily so much smaller that it gives a lacy appearance. Not many pieces of this ware have come to my attention but no doubt they exist. The design is shown here as a means of identification. It was probably produced about 1880. The classification given is taken from Bryce Bros.' catalogue.

Classification

BUCKLE WITH STAR

PATTERN 241

(See Plate 166)

Form Number.
1. Bowl, covered. 6 inch.
2. Butter dish.
3. Compote. Covered, on high foot.
4. Cordial.
5. Creamer.
6. Dishes, oval. 7, 8, 9 and 10 inch.
7. Goblet.
8. Mustard jar.
9. Pickle dish. Oval, handle at each end.
10. Salt, footed.
11. Sauce. Flat, star center. 4 inch.
    a. Footed, round. 4½ inch.
12. Spoonholder.
13. Sugar bowl.
14. Syrup pitcher.
15. Tumbler, water.
    a. Tumbler, handled.

Color: Clear glass.

MOON AND STAR

A late pattern, heavy and effective for table decoration, has been called "Moon and Star." The pieces are made up of circular discs in relief, one row being impressed with a star-shaped figure and the one above being clear. The glass is particularly bright and shining, and the heavy circles glisten from every angle. The collared base of the butter dish is low and each circle carries the star. The cover has a larger circle, also impressed with the stars.

There are many interesting bowls and covered dishes. The goblet is particularly graceful with its tapering bowl, short stem and base impressed with the star-like ornaments. This glass belongs to that large group which constitutes the late period included in this book, but it is quite popular to-day. The "Moon and Star" is sometimes found partly frosted. It was made by Adams & Company, of Pittsburgh, whose trade name for it was "Palace." It was never produced by any other factory. An old-time glassworker in Pittsburgh assured me that it came out first in 1888 and was discontinued later due to its weight, which made the transportation expense too costly for the stores who handled it.

Classification

MOON AND STAR

PATTERN 242

(See Plates 69, 103)

Form Number.

1. Berry bowl, deep. 8 inch.
   - *a.* Open, flared. 6, 7, 8 and 10 inch.
   - *b.* Covered, flared. 6, 7, 8 and 10 inch.
   - *c.* Salad or fruit. Flared edge. 12½ inch.
2. Bread tray. Oblong.
3. Butter dish.
4. Cake plate, on standard. 9 and 10 inch.
5. Celery vase.
6. Champagne. Flared.

Form Number.

   7. Cheese dish. Plate, deep in center.

   8. Claret.

   9. Compotes.
>   *a.* Covered, on high standard. 8 and 10 inch.
>   *b.* Covered, on collared base. (Star pattern around base.) 6, 7, 8 and 10 inch.
>   *c.* Open, on high standard. Scalloped top. 6, 7, 8 and 10 inch.
>   *d.* Open, on high standard. More shallow, flaring bowl.
>   *e.* Open, footed. On collared base, with star design around base. 6, 7, 8 and 10 inch.
>   *f.* Open, fruit. More shallow, flaring bowl. Collared standard base with star pattern around base. 5½, 7½, 8½, 10½ and 12½ inch.

   10. Creamer.

*11. Egg cup, large.

*12. Goblet.

   13. Pickle dish, oval.

   14. Pitcher, water. ½ gallon.

   15. Preserve dish. Oblong. 8 inch.

   16. Salts, individual.
>   *a.* Salt and pepper shakers.

17. Sauce dish, footed.
>   *a.* Sauce, flat.

   18. Spoonholder.

   19. Sugar bowl.

   20. Syrup jug.

   21. Tray, oblong, large.

   22. Tumbler, footed.

   23. Vinegar or oil cruet.

   24. Water sets. Large round tray, pitcher, goblets and bowl.

Colors: Clear; clear, partly frosted. Goblets may be found with the moons frosted, or decorated in red.

LATE BUCKLE

The early 1880's would appear to be the date of this pattern, which I have christened the Late Buckle. It has a design that looks

* Reproduced.

like a buckle though quite different from the earlier Buckle pattern. The ovals are larger and the design bolder. The goblet bowl is fairly well covered by these ovals, which are closely joined. The banded part of the buckle is filled with a design similar to that employed by the "Two Panel" pattern, referred to by a few dealers as "Daisy in Square." It is a late type of pressing but nevertheless effective. It was produced by Bryce Bros., of Pittsburgh, who called it "Jasper" pattern. The classification is taken from their illustrated catalogue.

Classification

LATE BUCKLE

PATTERN 243

(See Plate 72)

Form Number.
1. Butter dish.
2. Cake plate, on standard. 8, 9, 11 and 12 inch.
3. Compotes, covered, on high standard. Knob of cover in form of Maltese Cross. 6, 7, 8 and 9 inch.
   a. Open, scalloped edge. 7, 8, 10 and 12 inch.
   b. Sweetmeat. 6 inch, covered, on high standard.
4. Creamer.
5. Dishes, oval, deep.
6. Goblet.
7. Pickle dish.
8. Pitcher, water. 3 quart.
9. Salt, footed.
10. Sauce dish.
    a. Flat. 4, 5 and 6 inch.
    b. Footed. 4½ inch.
11. Spoonholder.
12. Sugar bowl, footed.
13. Wines.

Color: Clear glass.

NAILHEAD

A glass which appears to be older than it actually is has been called by the few who know it Nailhead. It is really an appropriate name, as each intersection of the small lattice effect has a round clear disc about the size of the ordinary nailhead. The glass is brilliant and clear and heavy in weight. Were it not for the deep saucer-like butter dish with dome lid, which did not come into vogue until the 1880's, one might well believe it to be an earlier ware. The plates are very attractive, being found in both round and square styles. Both have scalloped edges, the square one having a nailhead in the center of each scallop.

These patterns of the Eighties are for the most part impossible to identify with any one factory, as glass making at that late date was on such a highly competitive commercial basis.

Classification

NAILHEAD

PATTERN 244

(See Plates 108, 158)

Form Number.

1. Butter dish.
2. Cake plate on standard.
3. Celery vase.
4. Cordial.
5. Compotes, open, on high foot.
    a. Open, 7 inch.
6. Creamer.
7. Goblet.
8. Pitcher, water.
9. Plates.
    a. Round, deep scalloped edge, star center, 9 inch.
    b. Square, 7 inch.
10. Sauce dish, flat, star center, scalloped edge. 4 inch.
11. Spoonholder.

Form Number.
 12. Sugar bowl.
 13. Tumbler.
Color: Clear glass.

SCROLL

Many collectors have doubtless seen pieces of the Scroll pattern here and there, while on "antiquing" trips, but little attention has been paid it due to the lack of demand. During the late Seventies and Eighties many patterns with a scroll-like motif were used, which are in many cases so similar as to make them confusing.

The Scroll pattern consists of a stippled band showing a conventional design of scrolls, with an oval dividing each one. The covers also have the band and the knobs are in the form of large acorns. The goblet is attractive, having arched panels below the band which follow the stem down to the base. There is no record of this glass and the old trade name has been lost, but it was probably produced in the late Seventies or early Eighties. It is found only in clear glass.

Classification

SCROLL

PATTERN 245

(See Plate 140)

Form Number.
 1. Butter dish.
 2. Compotes, covered.
     a. On high foot.
     b. On low foot.
 3. Cordials.
 4. Creamer.
 5. Egg cup.
 6. Goblet.
 7. Salt, footed.

Form Number.
8. Spoonholder.
9. Sugar bowl.
Color: Clear glass.

FAN WITH DIAMOND

An odd pattern not so well known to collectors to-day is called
Fan and Diamond. It appears to be a ware of the Seventies though
I do not find a record of it in any of the old glass catalogues that
are available. The design is rather striking. The fan-shaped ornament has every other petal stippled, and the diamond-shaped figure
has four small dots in relief with a larger one in the center. The
creamer is rather curious as one may see by examining the group
on Plate 76. The goblet has three fan-shaped ornaments and three
of the diamonds around the bowl. It was evidently produced in a
large variety of pieces in clear glass. So far I have not seen it in
color.

Classification

FAN WITH DIAMOND

PATTERN 246

(See Plate 76)

Form Number.
1. Butter dish.
2. Cordials.
3. Compotes.
    a. Covered, on high foot.
    b. On low foot, design on base.
4. Creamer.
5. Dish, oval, deep, 9 x 6¾ inch.
6. Egg cup.
7. Goblet.
8. Pitcher, water.
9. Sauce, flat, 4 inch.

Form Number.
   10. Spoonholder.
   11. Sugar bowl.
Color: Clear glass.

LATTICE

While roaming through antique shops, particularly in small towns, one will often encounter a piece or two of this pattern, called Lattice. The design is very simple, especially on the covered pieces. The plates, which come in three sizes, are attractive, as the pattern covers more of the space. The center of the plate is made up of small squares, with an ornament suggesting a four-petaled flower, in each intersection. While this same block effect with flowers is also used in the base of the covered pieces, very little of it shows on account of their size, and the covers.

This pattern is so little known that it may be picked up in shops at very modest prices. It is a late ware, probably of the 1880's.

Classification

LATTICE

PATTERN 247

(See Plate 78)

Form Number.
   1. Butter dish.
   2. Compotes.
   3. Cordial.
   4. Creamer.
   5. Egg cup.
   6. Goblets.
   7. Pitcher, water.
   8. Plates, 6¼, 7¼, 10 inch.
       a. Bread plate, oblong. Inscribed: "Waste not want not."
   9. Sauce dish, footed.
       a. Oblong, with handles in each end.

Form Number.
    10. Spoonholder.
    11. Sugar bowl.
Color: Clear glass.

HERRINGBONE

A wealth of pressed pattern glass was turned out during the Eighties, in designs so numerous that to classify them all is impossible. The most anyone can hope to do is to sort out those which are found in enough pieces to be collectible in sets, as we use that term to-day.

A design, not known to many and obviously of this period though the forms follow those of an earlier era, is now called Herringbone as a means of identification. Below the panels of herringbone is a chain-like effect, the loops of which are filled with little dewdrops. Below the chain is a row of shield-shaped ornaments, which will be found used in various ways on several patterns of the same period. The design covers the bowls of the various objects and is rather pleasing. The sugar bowl is footed and the knob of the cover is distinctly odd, having two little upright supports, holding a diamond-shaped piece. The butter dish is flat, with a pagoda-style of cover. The absence of an active demand is probably the reason why more of this glass is not seen in shops. It should not be confused with the Emerald Green Herringbone listed in this book, which also comes in clear glass.

Classification

HERRINGBONE

PATTERN 248

(See Plates 115, 121)

Form Number.
    1. Butter dish.
    2. Creamer.
    3. Goblets.

Form Number.
4. Pitcher, water.
5. Spoonholder.
6. Sugar bowl.
Color: Clear glass.

ROSETTE

The Rosette is a design which is neither widely known nor collected to-day. No one has ever mentioned it to me, but having found a number of pieces it is shown on Plate 106 as a means of identification. The principal decorative motif is a daisy-like flower, a number of these adorning each panel. There is a large one in the center with smaller ones beside it. The glass is not as brilliant as in the Willow Oak or any of the other pressed patterns having a flower practically identical with this one. For comparison of these I might mention the Primrose variant, sometimes called "Stippled Daisy" and the "Barred Forget-me-not," which shows a larger flower on the cake plate than on any of the other pieces. The explanation of the inferior quality of the glass may well be that it was made at a later period or that it is a cheaper copy produced by another factory. Judging by the forms and quality of the glass it should date from the late Seventies. It is attractive enough to interest many collectors. More than once I have seen someone who never before was interested in acquiring antiques of any sort, come across a not generally known pressed glass pattern and exclaim, "I remember that my grandmother had a set of this. I believe I will collect it because it reminds me of her."

The Rosette is found in a satisfying number of forms, judging by those I have seen. It is not possible for one person to see every piece of pattern glass ever made, but it is my experience that when one or two are found others usually follow. It was produced by Bryce Bros., of Pittsburgh, who also made the Willow Oak, a pattern which is very similar. The Rosette was originally known as "Magic." The classification is taken from one of their old catalogues.

Classification

ROSETTE

PATTERN 249

(See Plate 106)

Form Number.

1. Butter dish.
2. Cake plates, on standards. 9, 10 and 11 inch.
3. Celery vase.
4. Compotes.
   - *a.* Covered, on high standards. 6, 7 and 8 inch.
   - *b.* Open, on high standards. 6, 7, 8 and 10 inch.
5. Creamer.
6. Goblet.
7. Jelly dish, footed. 4½ inch.
8. Pickle dish. Odd shape; tapered with square end.
9. Pitchers, water. Quart and ½ gallon.
10. Plates. 7 inch.
    - *a.* Bread. 9 inch, with closed handles.
11. Salt and pepper shakers.
12. Sauce dish. 4 inch.
13. Spoonholder.
14. Sugar bowl.
15. Water set, with tray and bowl.

Color: Clear glass.

PEACOCK FEATHER

An early pattern of the heavy, so-called "lace" glass, made chiefly by the Boston & Sandwich Glass Company, is called to-day "Peacock Feather" or "Peacock Eye." A late pressed pattern has also come to be known as Peacock Feather. I do not feel that any confusion will result from their being called by the same name, as the glass referred to here is late and totally different in character.

There is something about the design of this glass that suggests a peacock feather. The pointed eye is beaded with fine dewdrops and a feather-like ornament follows to the base of the bowl. The handle of the creamer has a feather-like design pressed over the length of it. A group may be seen on Plate 106. An odd handled lamp of the kerosene period is shown on the same Plate. This ware was first produced about 1898 by the United States Glass Company of Pittsburgh. The classification is taken from their catalogue.

Classification

PEACOCK FEATHER

PATTERN 250

(See Plate 106)

Form Number.

1. Bowls. 6, 7 and 8 inch.
2. Butter dishes. Two sizes.
3. Cake plates, on standard. 9, 10 and 11 inch.
4. Castor set, with salt and pepper.
5. Celery boat.
6. Compotes.
    - *a.* Shallow, on high foot. 8, 9 and 10 inch.
    - *b.* Deep, covered, on high foot. 6, 7 and 8 inch.
7. Condiment set, with vinegar cruet.
8. Creamer.
9. Decanter.
10. Jelly dishes.
    - *a.* Covered, footed. 5 inch.
    - *b.* Open, footed. 5 inch.
11. Lamp, handled.
12. Molasses jar.
13. Oil cruet.
14. Pickle dish.
15. Pitcher, water. ½ gallon.
16. Preserve dish. 8 inch.
17. Salt and pepper shakers.
18. Sauce dishes. 4 and 4½ inches.
19. Spoonholder.

Form Number.
20. Sugar bowl.
21. Sweetmeat, deep bowl; with or without cover. Footed, 5 inch.
22. Tumbler.
Color: Clear glass.

PLAID

Very little can be said about this late pattern of which I have seen only a few pieces. It evidently was not a success commercially or else was produced by one of those factories the existence of which was short lived. The glass is light in weight, and appears to be a product of the late Eighties. The design is of large squares, each filled with many tiny squares. The effect is like a plaid. There is a clear scalloped rim on most of the pieces. It is mentioned in this book as a means of identification. A group consisting of a pickle dish, celery vase and base of sugar bowl is shown on Plate 76. These were the only pieces I found in time for the illustrations, though doubtless others exist for any interested collector.

Classification

PLAID

PATTERN 251

(See Plate 76)

Form Number.
1. Celery vase.
2. Pickle dish, spray of roses in base.
3. Sauce dish, 4 inch.
4. Sugar bowl.
Color: Clear glass.

FESTOON

A heavily ornamented glass that appears to be a product of the Eighties, is called Festoon. The background is finely stippled, the wide band in the center showing a festoon which consists of large dewdrops and oblong bead-shaped pieces. A narrower band at the top and bottom has heavy fan-shaped ornaments, both upright and inverted, which are divided by a row of dewdrops. Heavy circles with a cross in the center also enter into the design. The sauce dish has a row of the dewdrops on the top edge. In the base is a star-shaped ornament with dewdrops around it. The large plates are brilliant and attractive.

While this glass is not well known or in demand to-day, it is sure to be widely collected at some future time. Not much of it is seen in antique shops, but more pieces will undoubtedly come to light when the search begins.

Classification

FESTOON

PATTERN 252

(See Plates 145, 166)

Form Number.

1. Berry bowls, 9 and 10 inch.
2. Butter dish.
3. Cake plate, on standard.
4. Compote, on high foot.
5. Creamer.
6. Dishes, oblong. 2 sizes.
7. Finger bowl.
8. Pickle jar.
9. Pitcher, water.
10. Plates, plain rim. 8 and 9 inch.
11. Relish dish, 7¼ x 4½ inches.
12. Sauce dish, flat. 4½ inch.
13. Spoonholder.
14. Sugar bowl.
15. Tumbler, water.
16. Tray for water set. 10 inch.

Color: Clear glass.

HEAVY JEWEL

This is one of those designs seen so infrequently that dealers are unfamiliar with it. It belongs to an unknown and unnamed class. It is heavily jewelled. No other description fits it. It is brilliant and sparkling and no photograph can reproduce all the scintillating lights that are reflected from these pieces. The glass is very heavy in weight, as one might expect from the way it is laden. The entire background is stippled and there are large ovals of glass in heavy relief surrounded by dewdrops. The surface is fairly covered with these glistening mounds of glass, circled by smaller ones. It inevitably suggests the heavily bejewelled fat lady of the circus. But the glass is really highly decorative for certain purposes. To date I have been unable to find a goblet to match though one may exist. In some patterns tumblers were made but not goblets. In the more popular patterns, there are usually both.

Classification

HEAVY JEWEL

PATTERN 253

(See Plate 137)

Form Number.
  1. Butter dish.
  2. Creamer.
  3. Spoonholder.
  4. Sugar bowl.
  5. Tumbler, water.
Color: Clear glass.

DRAPERY

A pattern probably produced in the late Seventies, or possibly the Eighties, may as well be designated the "Drapery." It consists of a band of little dots below which is a row of stippled points from each one of which is suspended a cord and tassel. Below this is a wider pointed drapery, which drips tassels from all sides. The creamer and spoonholder have a very coarse stipple, while the goblet is dainty, with an almost frosted effect. One may be seen on Plate 121. The creamer is footed, with a fairly heavy pressed handle that is not crimped at the base.

I can find no record of this glass beyond the fact that it was made by Doyle & Company, of Pittsburgh, who called it their "Lace" pattern. Some fragments of it were found at Sandwich but not in sufficient quantity to be certain they produced it.

Classification

DRAPERY

Pattern 254

(See Plates 108, 121)

Form Number.
1. Butter dish.
2. Creamer.
3. Egg cup.
4. Goblet.
5. Plate, 6 inch.
6. Sauce dish, flat, 4 inch.
7. Spoonholder.
8. Sugar bowl.

Color: Clear glass.

HONEYCOMB AND STAR

The design of this glass is similar to the honeycomb patterns or that which was known in different factories by the old trade names of "New York," "Vernon," or "Cincinnati." The entire background is faceted, with every other thumbprint having a star-like ornament impressed in it. Every other row is left clear, without the ornaments. The glass is heavy in weight and the forms indicate that this ware is of a more recent origin than almost any other in the book. The butter dish has a scalloped rim, the star being in every other scallop. The base is the saucer type, with a large star in the bottom, and the cover has the high dome lid with knob resembling a large crystal-clear marble. The creamer, spoonholder and sugar bowl are not footed, another indication of their late origin. This glass is too recent to attribute to any one factory, but I am listing it for the benefit of those who may wish to identify the pattern. Only a few pieces of this design have come to my attention and these are listed below. I have never seen a goblet to match, though there are tumblers. They are very scarce.

Classification

HONEYCOMB AND STAR

PATTERN 255

(See Plate 102)

Form Number.
1. Butter dish.
2. Cake plate on standard.
3. Celery vase.
4. Compote, covered.
5. Creamer.
6. Spoonholder.
7. Sugar bowl.
8. Tumbler.
Color: Clear glass.

CHAIN

A late conventional pattern which should not be overlooked is called Chain. It has as its decoration, an interesting band containing a chain-like motif filled with a small diamond quilting. Large half-circles on either side of the chain complete the design in a pleasing manner. It is not a well-known pattern at this time but is described here as a means of identification. In the illustration of the Chain on Plate 132, is another pattern so very similar as to be quite confusing. The two patterns are placed on one line so that collectors interested in either one may note the differences. The quality of the glass and the forms found in each are so much alike as to make close observation necessary when collecting either one. The cordial and 7-inch plate are known as "Chain with Star" and will be treated separately. This glass apparently dates in the Eighties.

Classification

CHAIN

PATTERN 256

(See Plate 132)

Form Number.

1. Butter dish.
2. Cordial.
3. Creamer.
4. Goblet.
5. Pickle dish.
6. Plate. 7 and 11 inch.
7. Sauce dish.
    a. Footed, round.
    b. Round, flat.
8. Spoonholder.
9. Sugar bowl.
10. Water pitcher.
11. Wines.

Color: Clear glass.

CHAIN WITH STAR

Little can be said of this clear conventional pattern, beyond what has been said about the Chain in the preceding pages. It has a marked similarity to the Chain but when placed together these differences are quickly noted. While matching either one the collector should be on his guard not to confuse the two. The plates are dainty and have attracted some attention. This glass appears to be of the 1880's.

Classification

CHAIN WITH STAR

PATTERN 257

(See Plate 132)

Form Number.

1. Butter dish.
2. Cordial.
3. Creamer.
4. Goblet.
5. Pickle dish.
6. Pitcher, water.
7. Plate. 7 and 10 inch.
8. Sauce dish.
   a. Footed, round.
   b. Round, flat.
9. Spoonholder.
10. Sugar bowl.

Color: Clear glass.

Chapter XXII

BANDED PATTERNS

STIPPLED BAND

During the period when the various Grape and Acorn patterns were at the height of their popularity, which would be from 1869 through the Seventies, a pretty stippled ware was made, the panels of the frosted effects being divided by clear bands. On the lower part of the sugar bowl these are vertical with a plain marginal band above. On the cover they run horizontally. The knob is in the form of a large acorn, partly frosted and partly clear, which rests on two oak leaves. There is a small line of cable where the rim of the lid fits on to the bowl.

This is a pretty and effective pattern, though not well known at present. The glass is clear and bright, and it is presumed that all the usual forms found in the Grape patterns, may be had. It is safe to assume that it was produced by the Boston & Sandwich Glass Company, since a number of fragments were found there. Another point is the acorn knobs to the covers, which were widely used at Sandwich, though they had no monopoly on this design.

Classification

STIPPLED BAND

PATTERN 258

(See Plate 107)

Form Number.
1. Butter dish.
2. Creamer.
3. Goblet.
4. Salt, footed.

Form Number.
5. Spoonholder.
6. Sugar bowl.
Color: Clear glass.

DIAGONAL BAND

The Diagonal Band is a pattern of the Eighties, judging by the glass and its general characteristics. It is fairly heavy in weight and the design is dainty and unusual. The goblet has a plain marginal band and directly beneath it, a chain effect with a tiny flower-like ornament in each link. The diagonal band is conventional but attractive, being stippled through the center. The creamer is footed, with a simple pattern under the base. This is a pleasing pattern that is little known. It is usually found only in clear glass, though I have seen one platter in apple green

Classification
DIAGONAL BAND

PATTERN 259

(See Plate 140)

Form Number.
1. Cake plate on standard.
2. Compote.
3. Creamer.
4. Goblet.
5. Pickle dish, oval.
6. Pitcher, water.
7. Platter, oblong.
8. Spoonholder.
9. Sugar bowl.
Colors: Clear glass; apple green (scarce).

DIAGONAL BAND WITH FAN

The Diagonal Band with Fan is a pattern which is not well known to-day and has not been collected to any extent. One reason may be on account of its not having had a name. In rechristening patterns like these of which the old trade name has been lost, a short descriptive title has been chosen, chiefly to afford a means of identification.

Apparently a pattern of the Eighties, this glass is both simple and pretty. No doubt a large variety of forms were made but since there has been no demand, little of it has come to light. Probably all the usual pieces were made, but I have only seen those listed.

Classification

DIAGONAL BAND WITH FAN

Pattern 260

(See Plate 156)

Form Number.
1. Butter dish.
2. Compote, covered.
    a. Open, on low foot.
    b. Open, high foot, shallow bowl.
3. Cordial.
4. Creamer.
5. Champagne.
6. Celery vase.
7. Goblet.
8. Pitcher, water.
9. Plates, round. 6, 7 and 8 inch.
10. Sauce dish, footed. 2 sizes. 4 and 4½ inch.
11. Spoonholder.
12. Sugar bowl.
Color: Clear glass.

FLOWER BAND

During the era of the flower patterns, several were produced that used designs of bands of flowers or fruit in relief, both clear and frosted, around the center of the bowls. One goblet has a band (Plate 109) 1¼ inches wide, of roses, flowers and foliage, all in clear glass. The stem has sprays of Lily-of-the-Valley, lightly stippled and tied with a ribbon. The base of the compote is heavily ribbed. A footed sauce has a narrow band of roses, frosted. The glass in these pieces is bright and clear, though they probably date from the late Seventies. An odd feature of the flower band pattern is that each piece bearing a flower or fruit band of varying widths, has the same design on the clear base, to-wit, an acorn with oak leaves. Some of the pieces look a bit clumsy, having large handles. Among the most attractive are the round and oval dishes on collared bases, as these all have two frosted birds, usually with their bills together, forming a knob for the cover.

Classification

FLOWER BAND

PATTERN 261

(See Plates 107, 109)

Form Number.
1. Butter dish.
2. Celery vase.
3. Compote, round, on high standard. 8 inch.
   a. Round, on collared base. Several sizes.
   b. Oval, on collared base. Several sizes.
4. Creamer.
5. Goblet. 2 styles. Clear glass, or clear with band frosted.
6. Sauce dish; footed.
7. Spoonholder.
8. Sugar bowl.

Color: Clear; clear with frosted band.

DIAMOND AND SUNBURST

During the Eighties many conventionalized bands of a very simple character were used for purposes of decoration on clear glass. Few of these patterns are found in color. On Plate 78 may be seen a group of such a pattern, which for lack of any name at all, is here christened Diamond and Sunburst. The band of diamond-shaped ornaments has a little fan-shaped figure between each one. Little can be said of the design as it was placed on the market at a period when all the glass factories were on a highly competitive basis, each striving to turn out a ware to meet the popular demand at a popular price. I am convinced that this glassware was made in an unusually large number of forms but it has not been in active demand. So-called "cup plates," when found in late patterns, were designed as individual butters and therefore cannot be considered as indicative of the age of the glass.

Classification

DIAMOND AND SUNBURST

Pattern 262

(See Plate 78)

Form Number.
1. Butter dish.
2. Cake plate, on standard.
3. Celery vase.
4. Compote, covered, large, on high foot.
5. Creamer.
6. Cup plate, or individual butter.
7. Decanter.
8. Goblet.
9. Pickle dish.
10. Pitcher, water.
11. Salt, footed.
12. Sauce dish.
13. Sugar bowl.
14. Syrup jug, large, metal top.
15. Tumbler, paneled, with star in base.
16. Wine.
Color: Clear glass.

CLEAR DIAGONAL BAND

A pattern which dates from the late Eighties is the Clear Diagonal Band. It is a striking design, each piece having three wide, clear bands running diagonally about the bowl of the object, alternating with a wide band of coarse stipple. It really is not a stipple but rather more like a fine mesh of tiny little circles in a lightly frosted effect. This ware is later than I like to include in this book but it is given as a means of identification to those who may decide to collect it. It was made at a period when glass was turned out in such enormous quantities all over the country that it is imprudent to attribute it to any one factory.

Classification
CLEAR DIAGONAL BAND
PATTERN 263
(See Plate 156)

Form Number.
1. Butter dish.
2. Celery vase.
3. Compotes.
4. Cordial.
5. Creamer.
6. Goblet.
7. Pitcher, water.
8. Plates. 7¼ inch.
9. Platter. Inscribed through the center diagonally, "Eureka."
10. Sauce dish, footed.
11. Spoonholder.
12. Sugar bowl.

Color: Clear glass.

Chapter XXIII

DAISY AND BUTTON GROUP

DAISY AND BUTTON

Nearly every collector of pressed glass is familiar with the popular Daisy and Button pattern but not many have noted the several variants in this design. The Daisy and Button pieces are so numerous as to provide almost enough material for a book by themselves. To list every known piece would require considerable work and time; and it may be doubted if one could ever feel sure that the inventory was complete. The range of articles made includes everything from hats and slippers of various sizes to bowls and sauce dishes in numerous shapes, sizes and color; in fact, the number is endless. The only practical solution is to list the best known variations, naming a representative group of articles in each one, together with the range of colors.

The Daisy and Button was made during the 1880's and for years was accredited to the Boston & Sandwich Glass Company, during the period of its decline or shortly before the plant was closed down, in 1888. I know of no record to support this claim though there is no reason to doubt that it may have been produced there, since it was made by so many other factories. It was one of the most popular patterns ever sold and was made in huge quantities and widely distributed.

Collectors have noticed two distinct Daisy and Button patterns, one having the so-called "daisy" with a smooth round button, and the other having the daisy with a button that has a star-like ornament impressed in it. These variations are adequately shown by the goblets in the lower row on Plate 167. It will also be noted that the two goblets in the upper row on this Plate are not both Daisy and Button. The one in the left-hand upper corner has a diamond-cut pattern somewhat similar to the daisy, though different. It has sometimes been sold by dealers who failed to detect the difference. The goblet with the V-shaped ornament was made in the Daisy and Button, as were also the water tumblers. The Daisy and Button in the plain style, which does not include those which are panelled or with the cross bar or V ornaments, is usually found with the clear button. That with the thumbprint band generally has the star-impressed button.

It has been definitely ascertained that practically every factory in this country producing tableware at the time when this design was in vogue, turned out at least some novelties in it. Among those concerning whose output I have authentic records is the firm of Hobbs, Brocunier & Company, of Wheeling, W. Va. The number of pieces of the tableware illustrated in their catalogue under the name of "Hobnail" (Daisy and Button), is astonishing. They made it not only in crystal, but in a wide range of colors, including the well-known Amberina. It will be of considerable interest to many collectors to know that this illustrated catalogue has solved the mystery of the uses to which the various sizes of glass hats were originally put. The smallest size was an individual salt; the second size was for toothpicks; the third size was a spoonholder and the largest did service as a celery holder. Similarly, the Daisy and Button canoes did duty in various ways. The smallest is called in this catalogue "Yacht salt," the next size "Yacht-pickle," and the largest size "Yacht celery." Round plates with an edge consisting of an alternating scallop and point, were made in six- and seven-inch sizes. Hanging canoes were utilized as flower baskets. A little receptacle on three feet, for matches, is listed as a "Toy Tumbler."

It is impossible to state definitely how one may distinguish the "Hobnail" (Daisy and Button) pieces made by Hobbs, Brocunier & Company from those of other factories. The Wheeling Daisy and Button is the variant with the large pressed flower and smooth button. Of the large number of pieces they made, the only variety which might not also have been a product of other factories is one having a wide clear panel fluted on each side, as illustrated in this book on Plate 171, upper row.

PLATE 167—GOBLETS

Variant of Daisy and Button
with V ornament

Daisy and Button

Daisy and Button with Crossbar

Daisy and Button with Thumbprint

PLATE 168—DAISY AND BUTTON TUMBLERS

With Thumbprint   With V ornament
Crossbar with Thumbprint   Crossbar with pointed ornaments

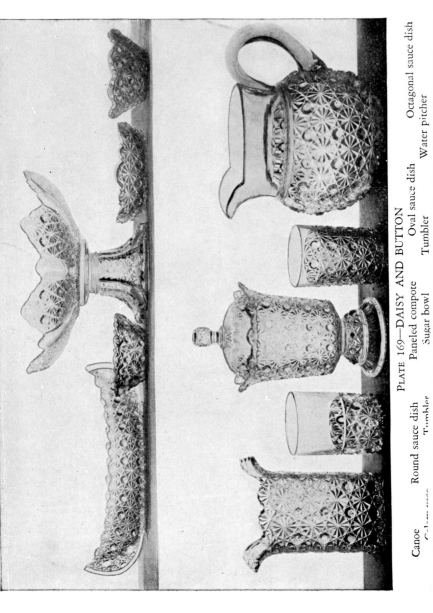

PLATE 169—DAISY AND BUTTON

Canoe   Round sauce dish   Paneled compote   Oval sauce dish   Octagonal sauce dish

    Tumbler   Sugar bowl   Tumbler   Water pitcher

PLATE 170—DAISY AND BUTTON

Crossbar celery vase   Butter dish   Creamer   Water pitcher
With Thumbprint, compote on high standard   Compote on low standard   Cake plate on standard

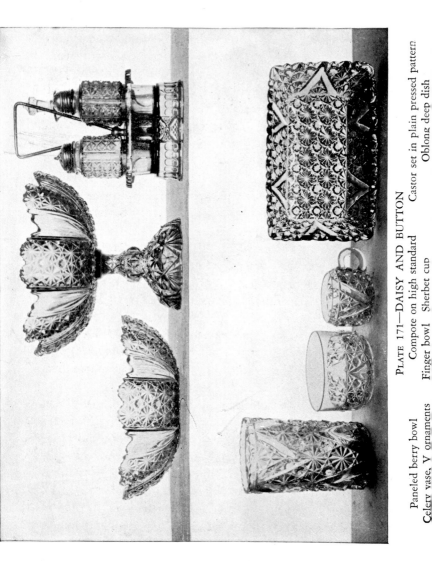

PLATE 171—DAISY AND BUTTON

Paneled berry bowl   Compote on high standard   Castor set in plain pressed pattern

Celery vase, V ornaments   Finger bowl   Sherbet cup   Oblong deep dish

George Duncan & Sons, of Pittsburgh, also made many novelties in this design, such as hats, slippers, cornucopias, umbrellas, etc. It corresponds to that of Hobbs, Brocunier & Company, and was also called "Hobnail." Their "Amberette" ware is listed in this book under a separate classification of Daisy and Button (Single Panel), because a full line of tableware was illustrated. The amber-colored panels combined with the clear Daisy and Button are most effective. The same dishes without an amber-colored panel were made in all-clear glass and in colors, under the name of "Ellrose Ware." The tall ale glass on a long slender stem in the Ellrose is most attractive.

Bryce Bros., of Pittsburgh, Pa., made quite a line of berry bowls in various shapes and sizes, as well as a large assortment of berry dishes, in a greater variety of shapes than any other factory. The well-known seven-inch square plates were made by them as well as a number of canoes in several sizes, which are listed in their catalogue as "Genesta," after the famous yacht. Their advertisement reads: "These Genesta Boats are for wall pockets for flowers, matches, etc." Incidentally, their name for Daisy and Button was "Fashion." The only egg cup in this pattern I have seen illustrated in the old catalogues in my possession was made by them and listed as "Star Egg." Their varied assortment of slippers are listed as "Puss Slipper," "Large Slipper," "Sandal," "Chinese Shoe," "Small Slipper," etc.

Challinor, Taylor & Company, or Tarentum, Pa., made several variations of the Daisy and Button pattern, very few of which are illustrated in this book. An elaborate one, with many short panels and thumbprints, is called "Ohio" ware. This was listed in crystal and colors. The round seven- and ten-inch plates, found with plain or with scalloped edge, are well-known among collectors and can now be definitely ascribed to this factory. It is interesting to note that these were advertised in crystal, old gold, blue and canary. Very few old ten-inch plates are encountered in color to-day as the market has been flooded with reproductions. The well-known emerald green Daisy and Button clover dishes came from Challinor, Taylor & Company, and were known as the "Clover" pattern.

Nearly all collectors are familiar with the berry bowls and dishes. A "Salt" was made to match such pieces as the creamer, sugar bowl, etc., having three panels to correspond to the clover-leaf shape of the bowls. Another variant by this same firm was called the Tremont, a rather plain set, with a narrow band of Daisy and Button running around each piece and narrow panels below it.

Richards & Hartley, of Tarentum, contributed to the Daisy and Button group a pattern designated as "Russian." Each dish consists of four large scallops, flaring outward at the top. An ice cream dish is oblong, with a clear fluted band around it and the pattern only in the bottom. A seven-inch "Cheese plate" is round with a plain edge. Their best-known Daisy and Button pattern was known as "Mikado" or "Pattern No. 99." It is illustrated in this book and listed as "Daisy and Button with Crossbar." A complete line of tableware was made.

In Ohio, A. J. Beatty & Sons, at Tiffin, were not to be outdone, and their "Van Dyke Pattern" is well known to-day as "Daisy and Button with V ornament." They manufactured a full line of it, in crystal as well as in colors. The plates do not have the V ornaments, but are round, with a scalloped edge and slightly deeper in the center.

Having described the best-known variants covering the items made by several of the largest tableware manufacturers known to have produced this design, collectors must determine for themselves which variety to select.

The classification below is for the plain Daisy and Button, as shown in the lower row on Plate 169. The other variations are classified separately.

Classification
DAISY AND BUTTON
Pattern 264
(See Plates 87, 163, 167, 169)

Form Number.
1. Ale glass. Long stem, tall. 2 sizes, medium and large.
2. Basket. Candy dish.

Form Number.

  3. Berry bowl, large, deep. All shapes and sizes. Some have collared base.

  4. Boats.
> *a.* Canoe, pointed at each end. Referred to as "Genesta."
> *b.* Canoe, rounded ends, bent over.
> *c.* Boat, pointed at one end, square at the other. Various sizes listed as "Yacht" salt, pickle dish and celery holder.

 *5. Butter chips.
> *a.* Round.
> *b.* Square.
> *c.* Square, with clover-cut corners.

  6. Butter dish.

  7. Castor sets.

  8. Celery vase. Many different shapes.

  9. Cheese dish. Plate, $7\frac{1}{4}$ inches, with high domed cover.

 10. Cologne bottles.

 11. Compotes, open, on standard.

 12. Creamer. Different shapes, from very small to large.

 13. Cruets. Various sizes.

 14. Dishes.
> *a.* Oblong, deep.
> *b.* Large, oblong, deep. Various sizes.

 15. Dish, oval, deep, paneled. Usually found in emerald green.
> *a.* Sauce to match, small. Composed of three sections, with small panel dividing. Sometimes referred to as clover-leaf.

 16. Egg cups. These are found only in a small size.

 17. Finger bowls.

 18. Goblets.
> *a.* Barrel shape.
> *b.* Divided in three panels by narrow panel.
> *c.* Straight sides.
> *d.* Paneled.
> *e.* Oval panel.

 19. Globes, for gas lights and lamps.

 *20. Hats. Four sizes, for individual salts, toothpicks, spoon-holders and celery holders.
> *a.* Toothpick size, with open fan top.
> *b.* Very small, called "Bandmaster's hat."

Form Number.

21. Match safe.

22. Mustard jar.

23. Pickle dish. Various shapes, including a fish.

24. Pickle jar, with cover.

25. Pitcher, water. Round, as illustrated. Various sizes and shapes, including tankard.

26. Plates.

> *a. Square. 7 inch, plain edge.
> b. Round. 6, 7, 7½ and 10 inch, plain edge.
> c. Round, scalloped edge. 6, 7, 7¼ and 10 inch.*
> d. Round, deep in center. Three sizes.
> e. Square, clover-cut corner, deep in center. Ice cream saucer.

27. Platters, oval, with handle at each end.

28. Sauce dishes.

> a. Round, scalloped edge.
> b. Boat-shaped.
> c. Octagonal.
> d. Triangle.
> *e. Square. Two sizes.
> f. Large and deep. Round bowl with four bent-in edges.
> g. Round, flared edge.
> h. Square, uneven top. Four larger scallops bent in, forming four points.
> i. Large, shallow, flaring bowl with scalloped edge. 6 inch.
> j. Basket-shaped, with two sides pressed inward.

29. Salts, individual. Triangular and other shapes.

30. Shoes, in form of flower holder.

*31. Slippers. Various sizes and colors, including Sandal, Chinese shoe, small and large slippers, puss slipper.

32. Spoonholder.

33. Sugar bowl. Several styles, including tall round, small round, and square on little feet.

34. Syrup jugs.

35. Toothpick holders, in various forms. Kettles, pails, animals, umbrellas, cornucopias,* etc.

36. Trays, various sizes and shapes, for water pitcher and goblets Clover leaf; round; oblong, with cut corners.

Form Number.
  37. Tumblers, water.
        a. Wide marginal band.
        b. Narrow marginal band.
        c. Finer design in low relief. Smaller than average.
        d. Whiskey tumbler. 2¾ inch.
Colors: Amethyst; light blue; fairly deep blue; yellow; apple green; dark green; light amber; dark amber; clear glass.

DAISY AND BUTTON (V Ornament)

This variation of the Daisy and Button pattern (clearly pictured on Plates 168, 171) was made originally by A. J. Beatty & Sons, of Tiffin, Ohio. The trade designation was "Vandyke Pattern." Their catalogue does not show a goblet to match, though the tumbler is pictured. Collectors who wish to match these pieces should note that there is a goblet with a V ornament (Plate 167) which is not the Daisy and Button design. The clear V ornaments are convex, heavy and shine vividly. There are at least two simple Daisy and Button goblets that combine nicely with this particular variant. Nearly all this ware was made during the Eighties and was in popular demand for a number of years.

Classification

DAISY AND BUTTON (V Ornament)

Pattern 265

(See Plates 167, 168, 171)

Form Number.
  1. Bowls, berry.
        a. Round, deep. 6, 7, 8 and 9 inch.
        b. Octagonal, deep. Scalloped edge in points. 8½ and 10 inch.
        c. Finger bowl.
  2. Butter dish.
  3. Celery vase.
        a. Straight sides.
        b. Flaring at top.
        c. Crimped top. (Four deep scallops.)

Form Number.

   4. Creamer.

   5. Dish, oblong, deep. Several sizes.

   6. Finger bowl.

   7. Goblet.

       a. Daisy and Button.

       b. Variant, with double V (Plate 157**).**

   8. Match or toothpick holder.

   9. Mug.

 10. Pickle jar with cover.

 11. Pitcher, water. Quart and $\frac{1}{2}$ gallon.

 12. Plates. (Sold with this pattern, but do not contain V ornament.)

       a. Round, flat, with scalloped edge. 6 and 7 inch.

       b. Same, deeper and with rim. 7, 8 and 9 inch.

 13. Sauce dishes.

       a. Round, shallow. 4 and 5 inch.

       b. Octagonal, pointed scallop. 5 inch.

 14. Shades. (Gas globes.) 4 inch.

 15. Spoonholder.

 16. Sugar bowl.

 17. Tray, oblong. For water sets.

 18. Tumblers, water.

Colors: Amber; yellow; blue; clear glass.

DAISY AND BUTTON (Cross Bar)

The Daisy and Button with Cross Bar ornamentation is seen more often than any of the other variations, aside from the plain and best known Daisy and Button design. A wide range of pieces was made and they are found quite readily to-day. Notice should be taken of the tumblers, which have two different bands at the top of the design. One band contains small round depressed circles and the other has a concave pointed decoration. These are shown in the lower row on Plate 168. The goblet is found ornamented with the circles like the water tumblers, but I have not seen them with the pointed design. They may come, but so far they have escaped me. A group of the tableware is pictured on Plate 170. The pattern is bolder in this variation than in any of the others. It may be found in the usual colors readily, though I have never seen a single piece with the cross bar in amethyst or apple green. The old trade catalogue of Richards & Hartley, of Tarentum, Pa., who apparently alone produced this particular variation of the Daisy and Button, lists only the colors named. It was known as their "Mikado" or "No. 99" pattern. It was made by them during the Eighties and possibly earlier.

Classification

DAISY AND BUTTON (Cross Bar)

Pattern 266

(See Plates 167, 168, 170)

Form Number.

1. Bowls, flat. 6 and 8 inch.
2. Bread tray, oblong.
3. Butter dishes.
    a. Flat, flanged.
    b. Footed.
4. Compotes.
    a. Open, on collared base. 7 and 8 inch.
    b. Open, footed, on high standard. 7 and 8 inch.
    c. Covered, on high standard. 7 and 8 inch.
    d. Covered, on low standard. 7 and 8 inch.
5. Creamers.
    a. Large.
    b. Small, individual.
6. Cruet. Various sizes to pint. Knob in form of Maltese Cross.
7. Finger bowl.
8. Goblet.
9. Ketchup bottle.
10. Lamps. Four sizes.
11. Molasses jug. (Syrup pitcher.)
12. Mugs, handled.
    a. Small.
    b. Large.

Form Number.

13. Pickle jars, covered.
14. Pickle tray, oblong, flat.
15. Pitchers, water.
    - *a.* Quart.
    - *b.* ½ gallon.
16. Preserve dishes, oval. 7, 8 and 9 inch.
17. Salt and pepper shakers.
18. Sauce dishes.
    - *a.* Flat, round. 4 inch.
    - *b.* Footed. 4 inch.
19. Spoonholder.
20. Sugar bowl.
21. Sugar dishes, individual.
22. Toothpick holder.
23. Tumbler.
24. Water set with tray and bowl.
25. Wines.

Colors: Light amber; dark amber; yellow; blue; clear glass.

DAISY AND BUTTON (Thumbprint)

The Daisy and Button with plain clear band containing thumbprints is to many the most attractive variation in this series. The tumblers and goblets have a panel, arched at the top, filled with the all-over pressed design. The compotes have square bowls with mitered corners, as may be seen in the group on Plate 170. This variant was made by Adams & Co., of Pittsburgh, and was known as "No. 86" pattern. It may have been produced during the Seventies, but most of this ware came out during the Eighties. Reproductions of the goblet in clear and in colors have flooded the countryside for a number of years. It is not difficult to detect the fakes, if one will take time to study the glass. So far, no other piece in this particular variation has been copied. It will be possible to restrain this unfortunate deception on the public, in the near future.

Classification

DAISY AND BUTTON (THUMBPRINT)

PATTERN 267

(See Plates 167, 168, 170)

Form Number.

1. Bowls.
   - *a.* Ice, finger bowl size.
   - *b.* Open. 6, 7 and 8 inch.
   - *c.* Covered. 6, 7 and 8 inch.
2. Cake plate, on standard.
   - *a.* Oblong bowl.
   - *b.* Square bowl.
3. Celery vase.
4. Clarets.
5. Compotes, with square bowls.
   - *a.* Open, on collared base. 6, 7 and 8 inch.
   - *b.* Covered, on low collared base. 6, 7 and 8 inch.
   - *c.* Covered, on high foot. 6, 7 and 8 inch.
*6. Goblet.
7. Jug. ½ gallon.
8. Pitcher, water.
9. Sauce dishes.
   - *a.* Square, shallow.
   - *b.* Round. 5 inch.
10. Tray, for water sets. Oblong, with handles.
11. Tumblers, water.

Colors: Yellow; blue; amber; clear glass.

DAISY AND BUTTON (PANELED)

The last of the variations of the Daisy and Button group is one having clear, fluted panels, as shown on Plates 169 and 171. The castor set, pictured on Plate 171, is sometimes used with the Daisy and Button, but that design is a plain, fine cut (pressed) similar to the goblet with the double V ornament. This particular castor set was the first of its kind ever made in all glass and was a product of the Adams & Company factory of Pittsburgh early in the Eighties.

Apparently a very small group of pieces with the wide panel was made by Hobbs, Brocunier & Company, of Wheeling, W. Va., as the classification given here covers all the items illustrated in their catalogue, together with those I have encountered in my travels. George Duncan & Sons, of Pittsburgh, made a large line of Daisy and Button with a single panel, which is listed in this book under a separate classification as "Daisy and Button, single panel." Their "Amberette Ware" was a most attractive clear daisy and button with plain amber panels, giving an interesting tone to the glass. Their "Ellrose" ware was exactly the same, except it did not have amber panels. It was advertised to be sold in crystal or colors.

Classification

DAISY AND BUTTON (Paneled)

Pattern 268

(See Plates 154, 169, 171)

Form Number.
1. Berry bowl, large round. 10 inch.
2. Compote, open on high foot.
    a. Deep bowl.
    b. Shallow, flaring bowl, two sizes.
3. Pitcher, water.
4. Sauce dish.
    a. Round, large.
    b. Smaller, shallow.
5. Tumbler.

Colors: Amber; blue; clear glass; clear with amber stripes. Goblet No. 3 on Plate 154 combines well with this variation. The tumblers and goblets are both scarce. So are any of the pieces in color combinations.

Classification
DAISY AND BUTTON (Single Panel)
Pattern 268A
(Not illustrated)

Form Number.

1. Bowls, berry.
   - *a.* Open, oval, collared base, shallow. 7, 8 and 9 inch.
   - *b.* Covered, round, on collared base. 7 and 8 inch.
   - *c.* Open, collared base, shallow. 7 and 8 inch.
   - *d.* Open, deep, no foot. Straight sides. 8 and 9 inch.
   - *e.* Open, deep, no foot. Flared at top. 8 and 9 inch.
   - *f.* Open, no foot, flaring berry bowl. 7, 8 and 9 inch.
2. Butter dish. 6 inch, collared base.
3. Cake plate, on standard. 10 inch.
4. Celery vase.
5. Celery boat. (Long, oblong dish.)
6. Compotes, covered, on collared base. 7 and 8 inch.
7. Cruets. Oil and vinegar bottles.
8. Goblet.
9. Pickle boat.
10. Pitcher, water. Quart and ½ gallon.
11. Plates.
    - *a.* Oval platter, originally termed Bread plate.
    - *b.* 7 inch, round.
12. Salt and pepper shakers.
13. Sauce dishes.
    - *a.* Round, flat. 4 and 4½ inch.
    - *b.* Round, footed. 4 and 4½ inch.
14. Spoonholder.
15. Sugar bowl.
16. Shades, for gas lights. 9 inch.
17. Tumbler, water.

Colors: Clear glass with amber stripe, called "Amberette Ware."
In clear glass or other colors, the same design is termed by the
same factory, "Ellrose Ware."

Chapter XXIV

MILK-WHITE GLASS

Collectors will find much to interest them in the study of what is generically known to-day as milk-white glass. At the very outset let it be stated that a more adequate terminology should be adopted than one usually hears from dealers and collectors who call it "milk glass." In the first place, there is no such thing and there never was. The various old-time trade names of the different classes of it were: White Enamel, Opaque White, Opaque, Opal, Opalescent and Alabaster. No serious objection can be found to the modern use of "milk-white" in referring to the plates and lace-edged bowls of divers patterns and sizes so popular during the Seventies and Eighties. In fact, this ware is so well known to-day as "milk-white" that it would be difficult to establish any other name in its place. The term was used in Ovington Brothers' catalogue of 1854-59, referring to "Milk White finger bowls, cut and plain." The chief objection has been and is to the misnomer of more or less recent origin: "Milk Glass."

Collectors have noticed certain differences in this opaque white glassware but only in a minority of cases have they seriously considered those differences. In the early days at Sandwich, as well as at other factories, this kind of glass was known and produced in divers forms. The Petal and Loop candlesticks, indissolubly associated in our minds with "Sandwich glass," were made, as well as early salts, cup plates, whale-oil lamps, vases and other small objects. Among these various articles even a novice will notice marked differences. A more logical classification to-day would be: milk-white, to designate that through which the light does not show at all; Opaque, which is not dead white but partly translucent; Opal, or a milk-white that shows "fire" when held against the light; and Opalescent, which is much more opalinely translucent than Opal. The quality varies according to the greater care taken by some makers in mixing as well as in the purity of the ingredients used and in the heating. The Petal and Loop candle-sticks were made, I believe, at the Sandwich factory between 1830 and 1850. They may be had in all-opaque or milk-white glass or in combination with colors, such as opaque base and opaque-blue top. Opaque-blue and opaque-green may also be had.

Much of the great difficulty found by students wishing to learn the history of this ware is due to the fact that one cannot be certain in reading the old records of the glass factories, whether the term "white" glass refers to opaque-white or to clear glass. In some old factories "white glass" always meant what we know to-day as milk-white. In others, "white" meant clear glass or crystal.

There is reason to believe that milk-white glass was made in the United States before the War of 1812. While further experiments were carried on by glass makers with milk-white in their efforts to develop a profitable trade in it, the evidence at hand would make it appear that it was not established on a paying commercial basis until about 1870, when it began to win popular favor. From that time on it must have been made in enormous quantities, to judge by the survivals.

One of the earliest pressed milk-white patterns is the "Saw-tooth," at one time referred to as "Pineapple." A group of this, in clear glass, may be seen on Plate 40. The forms in milk-white seem to be exactly like those of the crystal Sawtooth and it is therefore reasonable to assume that they must date at least from the early Sixties. Exceptional quality also may be found in the well-known and ever popular Blackberry design. The reader is referred to Chapter XVIII for an account of the patent granted in 1870 to the inventor of it. The Strawberry followed a little later. In all three of these patterns many pieces will be noted with a pronounced opalescent coloring.

The Paneled Wheat pattern, as seen on Plates 172 and 173, probably followed the earlier designs. After that there is no telling the chronological sequence of all the articles made and sold in different patterns and various sizes, such as plates, bowls, and compotes, as well as covered animal dishes without end. Most of this ware was made in Ohio and Pennsylvania.

During this same period, or, say, from 1870 on, other odd opaque combinations were produced, such as the Marble glass, so widely collected to-day, which is described on another page.

On Plates 182 and 189 may be seen the best known patterns in milk-white plates, which are also to be had in most cases in black and in opaque-blue. A very few have been found in opaque-jade-green. The large sized plates are shown on Plate 176. A group of covered dishes may be seen on Plates 178, 181 and 183.

That milk-white glass was not a commercially profitable product until the Seventies, seems certain, although a product acknowledged by the British to be superior to the European was made by several American factories prior to 1850. Many pieces may be found bearing the patent dates of 1870 and 1872. It will be noted that the majority carry the later date. The larger opaque white melon dish on Plate 181 is marked "Patented, Apr. 23, 1878,"* while the smaller is marked "Pat. applied for Nov. 8, 1870." Other novelties in milk-white that are popular to-day are the fish platters shown on Plate 174 and the small white plates (Plate 174). A double fish dish, not illustrated, and the platters are alike dated "June 4, '72."

Opaque white "hand" dishes, or, more accurately, those dishes in the shape of two hands with the palms upward and a cluster of grapes at the wrist, are finding uses to-day in table decorations, though originally intended for card trays. (Now reproduced.)

Much may be said for some of the "lace-edged" or "open-edged" bowls (Plate 175) of this same period. They are bound to become more popular as time goes on. The day will come when collectors will not be able to pick them up, one or two at a time, from farmers' wives in the rural districts as they do to-day. Often the lace-edged plates are found either with the centers covered with intricate designs in postage stamps, or embellished with bouquets of carnations or roses, heavily daubed on in oil paints. In such cases much patience is required to soak these decorations off, a lengthy bath in a strong sal soda solution being most helpful.

* Patent taken out by T. B. Atterbury, who designed it.

PLATE 172—MILK-WHITE PANELED WHEAT PATTERN COMPOTE AND BUTTER DISH

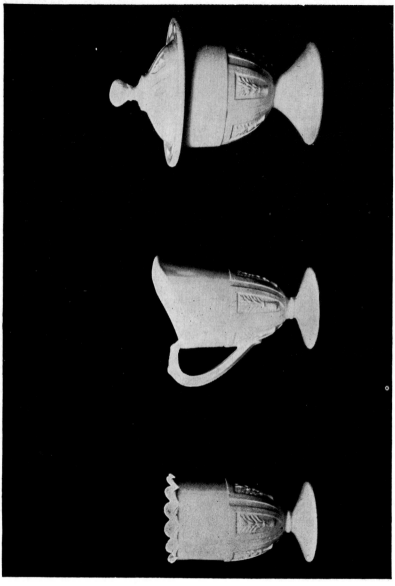

PLATE 173—MILK-WHITE PANELED WHEAT PATTERN SPOONHOLDER, CREAMER AND SUGAR BOWL

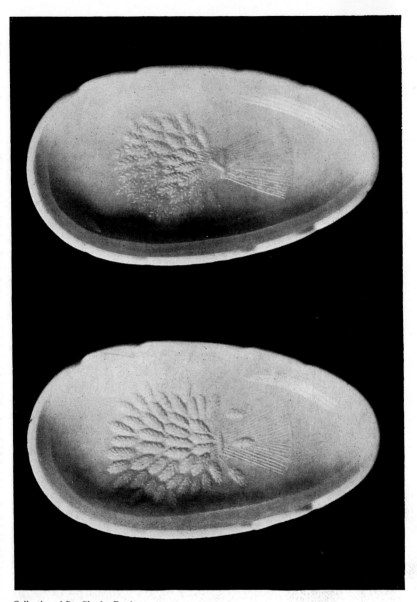

PLATE 173A—MILK-WHITE WHEAT RELISH DISH, SHOWING THE TWO
VARIATIONS

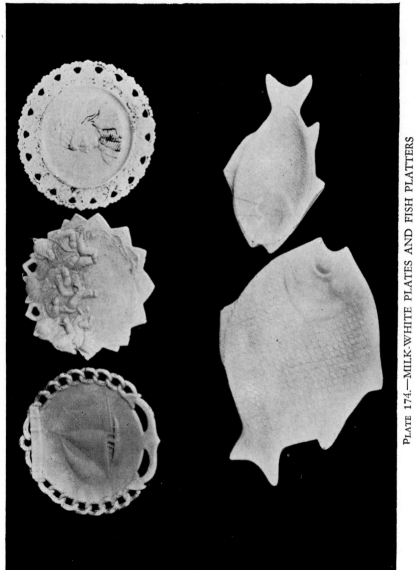

PLATE 174.—MILK-WHITE PLATES AND FISH PLATTERS

PLATE 175—MILK-WHITE "LACE EDGED" BOWLS

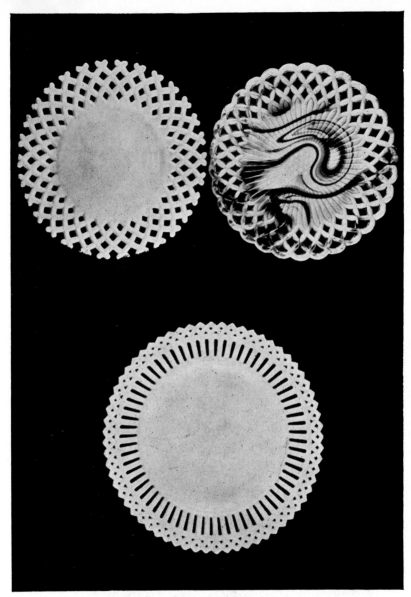

PLATE 176—LARGE PLATES

Lattice edge in milk-white   Open edge in Marble glass

Milk-white plate with Gothic border

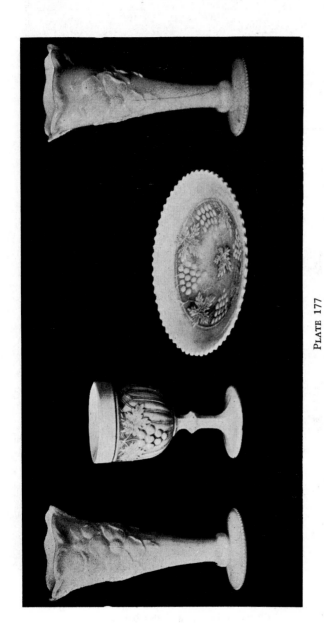

PLATE 177

MILK-WHITE VASES IN ROSE PATTERN   GOBLET AND PLATE IN OPAQUE CREAM COLOR

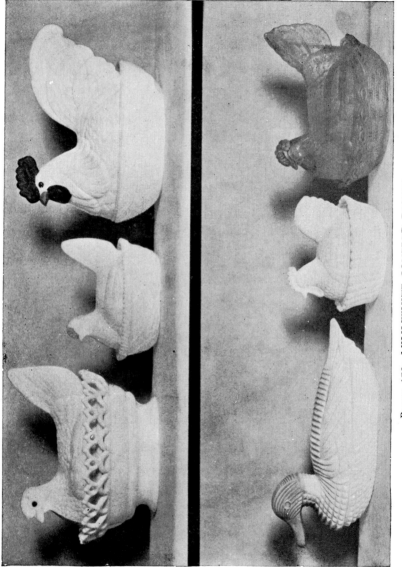

PLATE 178—MILK-WHITE COVERED DISHES

Of the three plates shown on Plate 189, the upper two were produced at Tarentum, Pa., by Challinor, Taylor & Company. They also made a specialty of Marble glass (known then as "Mosaic") and milk-white, open-edged plates (known as "Opal Ware"), besides compotes and covered animal dishes. Quantities of this ware were turned out by various factories from the Seventies on, culminating in the so-called "Stamp" plates and other novelties shown at the Pan-American Exposition in 1903.

The best-known patterns of plates made by Challinor, Taylor & Company are the Lattice Edge in ten-inch size, plain or with colored flower decoration in the center, Marble glass ten-inch open-edged plates (the latter being listed as a bread plate), the "Scroll with Eye" shown on Plate 189 and the "Arch," pictured on Plate 190. The last two were also made in "Fruit Nappies," which were plates with the open-work edge rolled up, forming a shallow bowl. After this company was absorbed by the United States Glass Co. of Pittsburgh, the latter used these designs to make fruit bowls, on high standards, in various colors. The Forget-me-not plate shown on Plate 182, an United States Glass Company product, came in "Opaque blue and colors," besides white. The company also made in the same pattern five-inch and nine-inch plates, as well as flat fruit bowls, card trays and other novelties.

Challinor, Taylor & Company had what they termed a "Farm Yard Assortment" of covered animal dishes, in opal, turquoise and olive-green. Their advertisement of this particular assortment ran as follows: "Farm Yard Assortment. How Packed. 6 Ducks and Eyes. 6 Roosters and Eyes. 6 Hens and Eyes. 6 Swans and Eyes. 6 Eagles and Eyes. 6 Fish and Eyes." The fish dish is on an oval base, the body being in a square checked or cube pattern and the back open to use as a relish dish. It is listed as "Opal Fish, Pickle, Eyed." It took time to glue the eyes in place and this added to the cost, so they were often sold without the inserted eyes.

Another assortment of large, milk-white, covered, animal dishes was also featured. They are decorated in color, as well as clear glass both plain and decorated. A turkey in reddish-brown on a green base was the largest. There seemed to be no end of color schemes, black included. Owl creamers came in several sizes and an open, flat fish dish in a cube or waffle pattern was listed as a pickle dish. Two of the most unusual of the eight-inch covered dishes are a Bull's head and a shaggy-haired dog. The former is listed as "Opal Bull's Head" and the cover only includes the bull's face. There is nothing about it to fire a collector with enthusiasm except for its oddity. The wild-eyed dog reclines on the cover, its long, wavy hair parted on the forehead so that it looks like a moustache and goatee. Altogether, it is a most curious-looking animal. The base is oblong and is formed of victorian braid and tassels. I have run across very few of these two dishes, but many of them must have survived. The largest number of five-inch covered hen dishes made in this country were manufactured by the Westmoreland Specialty Company of Grapeville, Pa. Its founder and president, Mr. Charles H. West, assured me that the prosperity of his concern was due to the very large sales of these little dishes in the old days, filled with prepared mustard, which sold in carload lots. Other factories produced them, too, but undoubtedly the largest number was supplied by his company. No end of other small dishes with covers showing lambs, cats, lions, battleships, lobsters, etc., were marketed by other firms, and are widely collected to-day for a variety of purposes, including candy, cigarette dishes, and even soup. (See Plates 178, 181 and 183.)

PANELED WHEAT (Milk-White)

Many collectors are familiar with a clear Wheat pattern, which shows a sheaf of wheat in a rather thin design on the surface of the dish. The goblet, for instance, has three of these bundles of wheat about the bowl. There is a much earlier Paneled Wheat pattern, most frequently seen in milk-white, that is an unusually fine, dignified design. In this latter pattern the wheat stands out in high relief in an indented panel.

Though my search for pressed glass patterns has taken me over many states, I have found the Paneled Wheat pattern to be the scarcest of the milk-white group. Goblets have turned up in clear glass but so far not in any color. They may exist but I have not seen them. There is no record, so far as I know, to shed any light on where the Paneled Wheat glass was made, but it is one of the most interesting of those designs produced in milk-white glass. A few fragments were discovered at the site of the Boston & Sandwich Glass Company, though not in sufficient quantity to establish it definitely as a Sandwich product.

Classification

PANELED WHEAT (Milk-white, Clear)

Pattern 269

(See Plates 172, 173, 173A)

Form Number.

1. Butter dish. Collared base. Removable drain. Lid 5½ inches diameter. Milk-white.
2. Butter dish, covered. Flat base. Flange rim. Removable drain. Lid. 5 inch diameter. Milk-white.
3. Compotes, covered.
   - *a.* Low. Flaring foot. 7¼ inches. Clear.
   - *b.* Low. Flaring foot. 8 inches. Milk-white. Clear.
   - *c.* Tall. Thick stem. 7 1/16 inches. Milk-white. Clear.
   - *d.* Tall. Tiered stem. 7½ inches. Milk-white. Clear.
   - *e.* Tall. Faceted stem. 8 inches. Milk-white. Clear.
4. Creamer, collared foot. Milk-white. Clear.
5. Creamer, ringed, collared foot. Milk-white.
6. Egg cup, footed. Milk-white. Clear.
7. Goblet. Clear.
8. Pitcher, water. Milk-white. Clear.
9. Relish dish. Tapered oval, 8 x 4½ inches. Alternating wide and narrow scallops.
   - *a.* Single large central sheaf inside (Schematic, high relief, no knot). Paneled sheaves outside. Clear.
   - *b.* Same center. Plain outside, no panels. Milk-white.
   - *c.* Single large central sheaf inside (more natural, lower relief, has a knot). Paneled sheaves outside. Clear.
   - *d.* Same center. Plain outside, no panels. Milk-white. Clear.

10. Sauce dish, flat. Milled rim. 4⅛ inches. Milk-white. Clear.
11. Sauce dish, flat. Plain rim 4 inch. Milk-white.
12. Spoonholder. Scalloped. Ringed waist. Milk-white. Clear.
13. Spoonholder. Milled rim. Ringed waist. Milk-white.
14. Spoonholder. Milled rim. Plain waist. Milk-white.
15. Sugar bowl. Plain rim. Ringed waist. Lid with inset collar. Milk-white.
16. Sugar bowl. Milled rim. Ringed waist. Milk-white.
17. Sugar bowl. Milled rim. Plain waist. Milk-white.
18. Sugar bowl. Spoon-rack rim. Ringed waist. Clear.
19. Sugar bowl. Spoon-rack rim. Plain waist. Milk-white.
20. Wine glass. Clear.
Color: Milk-white; clear.

Classification

MILK-WHITE PATTERNS
SAWTOOTH

PATTERN 270

(See Plate 40)

Form Number.
1. Butter dish.
2. Compotes.
   a. Covered, on high standard. Various sizes.
   b. Covered, on low standards.
   c. Open, on high and low standards. Various sizes.
3. Celery vase.
3A. Egg cup. Two styles, open and covered.
4. Salt, footed.
5. Creamer.
6. Sauce dish.
   a. Four-inch.
   b. Honey dish, 3½ inch.
7. Spoonholder.
8. Sugar bowl.

BLACKBERRY

PATTERN 271

(See Plate 150)

The milk-white Blackberry has been carefully classified, together with the story of the pattern, in Chapter XVIII, "Fruit Group." It is listed here again because a few pieces of the identical pattern occur in clear glass. The goblets may be found most readily, but they are rare. Other items also have been seen, though they are practically impossible to find to-day. Apparently very little Blackberry was made in clear glass. See page 462 for classification of this design in milk-white.

STRAWBERRY

PATTERN 272

(See Plate 152)

Form Number.
1. Butter dish.
2. Compotes, covered.
   a. High foot. Usual size, 8 inch.
   b. Low foot. Usual size, 8 inch.
3. Creamer.
4. Egg cup.
5. Goblet.
6. Pickle dish.
7. Salt, footed.
8. Sauce dish.
   a. Flat, 4 inch.
   b. Honey dish, 3½ inch.
9. Spoonholder.
10. Sugar bowl.

GRAPE

Opaque cream color, or "custard," often with touch of brown
decorating the design.

PATTERN 273
(See Plate 177)

Form Number.

1. Bowls, on collared base. Sides are flared.
2. Compotes.
3. Cups and saucers.
4. Goblet.
5. Jelly dish, with handles.
6. Plate, deep in center. 2 sizes.
7. Sauce dish, footed.
8. Sherbet cups.
9. Vase, small. Flared edge.

CHERRY

PATTERN 274
(See Plate 19)

Form Number.

1. Butter dish.
2. Compotes.
   - *a*. Covered, on high foot, 8 inch.
   - *b*. Open, on high foot, 8 inch.
   - *c*. Open, on low foot, 8 inch.
3. Creamer.
4. Goblet.
5. Sauce dish, flat, 4 inch.
6. Spoonholder.
7. Sugar bowl.

GOOSEBERRY

PATTERN 275
(See Plate 166)

Form Number.

1. Butter dish.
2. Compotes.

Form Number.
3. Creamer.
4. Goblet.
5. Mug, handled.
6. Sauce dish.
7. Spoonholder.
8. Sugar bowl.

PRINCESS FEATHER

PATTERN 276

(See Plates 19, 184)

Form Number.
1. Butter dish.
2. Celery vase.
3. Compotes on high standard, covered.
   a. Eight-inch.
   b. Seven-inch.
   c. Open, on low foot, 8 inch.
4. Creamer.
5. Dish, oval, 7, 8 and 9 inch.
6. Egg cup.
7. Pitcher, water.
8. Plate, 9 inch. Closed handles.
9. Sauce dish, 4 and 5 inch.
10. Spoonholder.
11. Sugar bowl.

ICICLE

PATTERN 277

(See Plate 19)

Form Number.
1. Butter dish.
   a. Flat.
   b. Deep base with flanged rim. Covered.

Form Number.

   2. Compotes.

      a. Covered, on high standard, 8 inch.
      b. Open, on high standard, 8 inch.
      c. Open, on low standard, 8 inch.

   3. Creamer.

   4. Dish, oval, deep, 7, 8 and 9 inch.

   5. Dish, individual butter, 3 inch.

   6. Egg cup, double.

   7. Pickle dish.

   8. Spoonholder.

   9. Sugar bowl.

MILK-WHITE WAFFLE

Pattern 278

(See Plate 141)

Form Number.

   1. Butter dish.

   2. Creamer.

   3. Spoonholder.

   4. Sugar bowl.

OPEN-EDGED PLATES

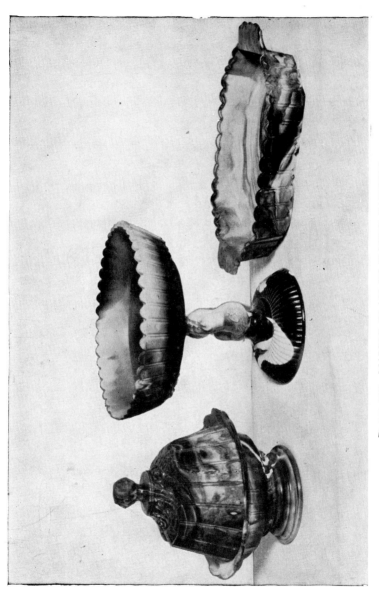

PLATE 179—MARBLE GLASS IN FLUTED PATTERN

Butter dish   Compote   Oblong deep dish

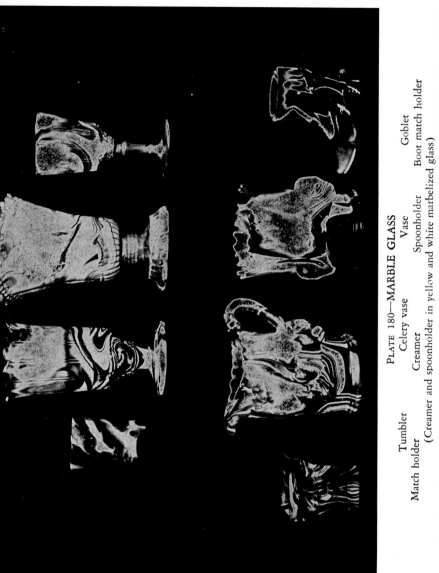

PLATE 180—**MARBLE GLASS**

Tumbler   Celery vase   Vase   Goblet

Match holder   Creamer   Spoonholder   Boot match holder

(Creamer and spoonholder in yellow and white marbelized glass)

Colors: Black, milk-white, opaque-blue, opaque-green, marble.

MARBLE GLASS

One of the most distinctive of all colored glass patterns is that generally known as Marble glass, because of its resemblance to the "marbling" on the inside of old book covers. It is also referred to as "slag," "onyx," "agate," "Connecticut glass" and "calico glass," but none of these is an appropriate name for so attractive a product. The original designation of the makers, Challinor, Taylor & Company, of Tarentum, Pa., was "Mosaic." This ware was manufactured by them in large quantities during the Seventies and Eighties. In one of their old catalogues in my possession is illustrated a complete line of Mosaic, which is shown in part on Plates 179 and 180. The glass itself is so unusual, so strikingly colorful, that the design seems of secondary importance. The delicately paneled lines, with the dainty pressed pattern underneath, are entirely adequate and suitable. There is a decided appeal to the tall slender goblets, so dignified and decorative. The open compote with its graceful stem in the form of a woman's head, is a distinct addition to any table scheme. There are covered compotes on low standards, oblong trays with a small handle at each end, a covered butter dish and small odd pieces that may be used for cigarettes or matches, as for example, a riding boot with spur, a small square dish with a loop on two sides and a tall square dish with four rounded posts. The goblets that match this particular set are exceedingly rare, and anyone who can assemble a dozen is to be congratulated. They are usually found one at a time. But plain tall tumblers also come in Marble glass and impatient collectors may use these in lieu of the much-sought-after goblets.

Clear amethyst or diamond quilted goblets are often combined with this marble pattern.

Challinor, Taylor & Company also made another design in Marble glass, as well as in crystal, opaque white and colors, which has an all-over small flower pattern. Their catalogue did not list many pieces, but they are classified here for the benefit of collectors. The ten-inch open-edged plates are an additional attraction. These were referred to, I find, by nearly all makers as "O. W. Plates"—meaning "Open Work." These vary greatly in shading, as do all of the Marble glass pieces. Specimens which show much white are not so pleasing as those that range from deep rose-pink to the richest purples. The rarest of all is a beautiful blue and white, streaked. Many of the most distinctive table schemes of decoration have been achieved through the use of this delightful glass, combined with colored linens and flowers or fruit that harmonize.

It is probably true that this Marble glass with its Whieldon effects was made at more than one factory, but out of scores of the old trade catalogues of factories operating at that period in Ohio, Pennsylvania, West Virginia, New York State and New England, the only reference I found was in the Challinor, Taylor & Company catalogue. Much space was devoted to it, as well as to other pieces of tableware in marble, opaque white, etc., especially the open-edged plates in various patterns. The firm also made some of the really superior covered dishes in the shape of swans, ducks, roosters, etc., as well as lattice-edged plates with colored flower decorations in the center.

While milk-white glass is known to have been made at Sandwich, I have not found documented evidence indicating Marble glass was ever a Sandwich product though there is no reason why it should not have been.

An old glass worker, a relative of Mr. Challinor of Challinor, Taylor & Company, told me that great difficulty was encountered in the making of Marble glass, in fusing the white of the mixture so that it would adhere to the colored part.

Much English Marble glass was exported to this country, most of which is marked with one or another of the British registry marks. The eight-inch lattice-edged plates are all English. There is no evidence that this size was ever produced in this country. Many of the English pieces are in the way of novelties. Their purple is usually deeper in shade than ours, and the coloring must have been mixed differently because it is possible for anyone who has handled any amount of Marble glass to spot an English piece across a room. There is practically no need to examine the base for their registry mark. Other English novelties will be found here in green and white mixtures, blue and white, as well as the purple. Other colors than purple are scarce.

Classification

MARBLE GLASS

PATTERN 279

(See Plates 176, 179, 180, 190)

Form Number.
1. Bowl. 8 inch. Peg bowl, to use in various standards.
2. Butter dish.
3. Celery vase. Two sizes.
4. Compotes.
    a. Covered, on high standard. Fluted stem. 7 and 8 inch.
    b. Covered, on low foot. 7 and 8 inch.
    c. Open, on low foot. 7 and 8 inch.
    d. Open, on high foot, woman's head in standard.
    e. On high standard, with open edge, matching plates.
5. Creamer.
6. Finger bowl. Originally used with water set.
7. Dishes. Oblong, deep, with handles at each end. 7, 8 and 9 inch.
8. Egg cup. Not fluted pattern.
9. Goblet.
10. Pickle dish. Handle at each end.
11. Pickle jar, with cover.
12. Pitcher, water.

Form Number.
13. Plates.
    a. Open edged. 10 inch.
    b. Open edged. 8 inch. Scarce. English.
14. Salt shaker.
15. Sauce dishes.
    a. Footed. 4 inch.
    b. Flat, round. 4 and 6 inch.
    c. Ice cream dish. Handle at each end.
16. Sherbet or ice cream tray. Similar to tray for water set, minus handles and scalloped edge.
17. Spoonholder.
18. Sugar bowl.
19. Water pitcher. ½ gallon.
20. Water set, complete with tray, goblets and bowl.
21. Water tray, oblong. Scalloped edge, handle at each end. Not as deep as usual trays.
22. Additional items in Marble glass, which are not fluted but may be used to advantage with this set, include candlesticks, flower vases, flaring at the top (Plate 180), boot match holders, and square match holders in two sizes. These may have been made by Challinor, Taylor & Company, although they do not appear in the one catalogue I possess.

Colors: Purple and white marble; yellow and white marble, ranging to deep brown; opaque blue; blue and white marble glass (very scarce). Other forms usually lighter in color, appear to be of a later period.

Classification

MARBLE GLASS (Flower Design)

Pattern 279A
(Not illustrated)

Form Number.
1. Butter dish.
2. Creamer.

Form Number.

3. Pitcher, water. Quart and ½ gallon.
4. Spoonholder.
5. Sugar bowl.
6. Tumbler.

Colors: Purple and white marble; crystal, opaque white and in colors. This pattern is illustrated in *Victorian Glass* as "Flower and Panel," as a further aid to collectors in identifying the design.

Chapter XXV

VICTORIAN GLASS MATCH HOLDERS
AND SALTS

On Plates 127 and 186 are shown a comprehensive group of those small receptacles made largely during the Seventies and Eighties, to do duty as salt dishes, toothpick containers, and match holders. To-day many of the salt dishes do double duty for either matches or cigarettes, while others are used for nuts and candies. You will find that old glass is apt to be put to uses which were undreamt of when the manufacturers first made it.

There is a fascination not to be denied in the study of any collection of these oddities of bygone days. Almost without fail every pressed glass pattern, from the earliest to the latest, had salts in one form or another. In fact, one of the earliest products of the Boston & Sandwich Glass Company, following their blown glass period, was the interesting pressed salts in the so-called "lace" glass. A large collection of the lacy salts are pictured in my book, *Sandwich Glass*. As pressed pattern glass became not only possible but profitable, odd pieces were added from time to time, in patterns in which entire "sets" were not made. Foremost among these were the toothpick holders, salts, mustard pots, and match holders. One of the early style of salts, following the lacier styles, is commonly known to-day as the Bird salt. These have been attributed to Sandwich. While this attribution may be justified, I have found no record to support the claim. One of these is shown on Plate 127. They are found in several colors, both with and without a seed or cherry in their beaks. They also come in two sizes, small and large. A rare specimen of the larger type is shown on Plate 186. This large bird with the cherry in its bill is a small mustard-jar, the acorn-knobbed cover having an opening for the spoon. This specimen happens to be of a clear, deep amber. Another scarce item on the same illustration is the toothpick or match holder supported by three tiny dolphins. This used to be accredited to Sandwich until it was positively identified with a midwestern factory. A replica of the tiny owl creamer may also be found in several sizes, including a water pitcher. They are also midwestern.

It is practically impossible to list every article of this sort manufactured over a period of years, but Plate 127 and Plate 186 give an accurate idea of what one may expect to find in these table accessories. They are interesting as useful additions to any table scheme. Being produced over a period of twenty years or more, it is not possible to state positively when or where each one was made. Factories copied from one another both processes and patterns, so that to hazard any guess to-day is futile. The pieces listed, I presume, may be found in various colors besides those I have actually seen and noted.

Classification

VICTORIAN GLASS MATCH HOLDERS AND SALTS
(See Plates 127, 186)

Form Number.
(Plate 186)

1. Dolphin match or toothpick holder, 4¼ inches high. Usually seen in amber, blue or clear glass.
2. Large turtle covered dish, or salt, 3½ inch. Milk-white.
3. Owl creamer, 3½ inch. Several colors, including milk-white and opaque blue.
4. Two cherubim supporting match or toothpick holder, 4 inch. Several colors.
5. Alligator, with holder on back for toothpicks or matches. 3 inch. Amber; clear glass.
6. Large open swan salt. Opalescent.
7. Small chick with broken egg on back. Salt, toothpick or matchholder. 2½ inch. White with frosted finish.
8. Rabbit with basket on back. Match or toothpick holder. Amber.

Form Number.

9. Cat reclining on cushion, supporting match or toothpick holder, 3½ inch. Clear; blue; amber; yellow.

10. Bird mustard jar, 3½ inches high. Acorn knob on cover. Amber, blue, clear.

11. Monkey. Originally intended for matches or toothpicks. 2¾ inch. Clear; amber; blue.

12. Rooster's head. Salt shaker, metal top. 3 inch. Clear.

13. Two roosters. Toothpick or matchholder. Blue.

14. Dog on oblong base, holding hat in mouth. Toothpick holder. Amber; clear.

*15. Dog drawing cart. Salt dish. Very small. Colors.

16. Swan drawing container. Probably salt. 4 inches long. (Plate 127)

17. Elephant. Match or toothpick holder. Amber.

18. Saddle. Match or toothpick holder. Amber; clear.

19. Covered salt with rooster medallion, dog's head as knob of cover. Clear.

*20. Bird salt with cherry in beak. Colors.

21. Wildflower pattern, turtle salt. Apple green; blue; amber; clear.

22. Frog matchholder. Clear.

23. Squirrel salt. Clear.

24. Swan mustard jar, covered. Amber; clear; blue.

25. Bear jar. Known to have been made at Sandwich. 4½ inch. Colors, mostly opaque.

26. Owl creamer, 3½ inch. Also made in several sizes, including a quart. Colors, including opaque glass.

27. Rabbit covered dish. Opaque brown; milk-white. 5 inch.

28. Dog salt, stippled. Clear glass.

* Reproduced.

Chapter XXVI

GOBLETS, ODD PLATES AND PLATTERS

While the purpose of this book is to list and classify only those pressed glass patterns which may be collected in sets, it was found advisable to illustrate certain goblets which by reason of similarity of design, size or contours or because they harmonize in other ways may be substituted for goblets known to match exactly but which are so scarce that it would take months of persistent hunting to complete a dozen. It has been the common experience of collectors everywhere that when one piece of an unknown pattern is found almost invariably other pieces of the same set follow in time. To enable collectors and dealers to identify some of the patterns of which only a few pieces are known it was decided to illustrate these goblets on Plates 153, 154, 164.

On Plate 190 are shown a few pieces other than goblets of patterns in which groups to illustrate them adequately could not be completed when this book went to press.

GOBLETS

GOBLETS

(See Plate 153)

1. Goblet with wide stippled band around the bowl, balance clear. No other pieces to match have been seen so far.
2. Stippled bowl with clear flowers. This is an odd goblet, a variant of number seven. (See below.)
3. Brilliantly clear goblet in a variant of the Waffle pattern This has three bars between the panels, instead of two as in the Waffle.
4. Pear pattern. Small design low on the bowl, with cluster of leaves. Collectible in sets. A few other pieces have been seen to match, including a creamer. This pattern should not be confused with the Baltimore Pear. See *Victorian Glass*.
5. Hobnail goblet. This is the Pointed Hobnail and may be used with any of that group dating from 1868. This particular style is preferred by many collectors. See Hobnail group.
6. Blackberry pattern. A very attractive odd goblet in clear glass with clusters of stippled leaves. This is sometimes mistaken for the well-known Blackberry pattern which is collectible in sets.
7. A stippled flower band pattern, in which no other pieces to match have been seen.
8. Goblet in an attractive flower pattern. Bowls, 6 inches. Butter dish. Celery tray, large. Compote 5 inches high by 4½ inches diameter. Creamer. Plates, 10 inch. Spoonholder. Sugar bowl. Water pitcher. Late pattern which was apparently produced in sets. Has been found most frequently in Illinois.
9. Odd goblet, in a variation of Horseshoe or Good Luck. This is alike in all details to the latter, except for the flower motif and shield bearing Odd Fellows emblem. Apparently made by same factory that produced Good Luck, possibly on special order.
10. Early flint glass goblet, of a style made during the late Sixties at Sandwich. Now known as Scarab.
11. Early flint glass Diamond Point with Panels goblet of a pattern produced by the New England Glass Co. and at Sandwich. Lower part of bowl has diamond points, panelled above the design. Many pieces were undoubtedly made to match this goblet, as a creamer and footed tumbler have been found. See *Victorian Glass*.
12. Goblet of a style made during the Eighties. Cable cord forms panels, and medallion contains open fan with head of a girl. Made by Bellaire Goblet Company, Findlay, Ohio.
13. Goblet of three panels, each containing a delicate spray of flowers.
14. Early flint glass goblet made by the McKee Brothers, of Pittsburgh, and named by them "Brilliant." Tumblers were made in the same pattern.
15. Loop and Fan goblet. Produced by U. S. Glass Company during 1890's. Collectible in sets.

1. MILK-WHITE covered melon dish, SWAN salt, covered melon dish.
2. MILK-WHITE eagle covered dish, hen lace-edged covered dish, GRAPE salt.
3. Cow mustard jar, hen covered dish, log cabin.
4. OPAQUE BLUE OWL, yellow and white MARBLE glass spoonholder, FISH covered dish.

1

2

3

4

5

6

7

8

PLATE 182—MILK-WHITE PLATES

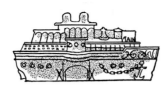

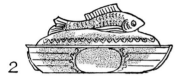

PLATE 183

1. MILK-WHITE tall eagle inscribed "E Pluribus Unum"; battleship Maine, small covered hen dish.
2. MILK-WHITE dish with fish on cover, dish with turtle on cover.
3. MILK-WHITE sleigh with hen on cover, dish with lion on cover.
4. MILK-WHITE battleship with Uncle Sam on cover, dish with head of Admiral Dewey on cover.

PLATE 184

Page from Bakewell, Pears & Co. catalogue illustrating their opaque "Rochelle" pattern.
This is now known as Princess Feather.

PLATE 185—KNIGHTS OF LABOR PLATTER
(See page 643)

1.

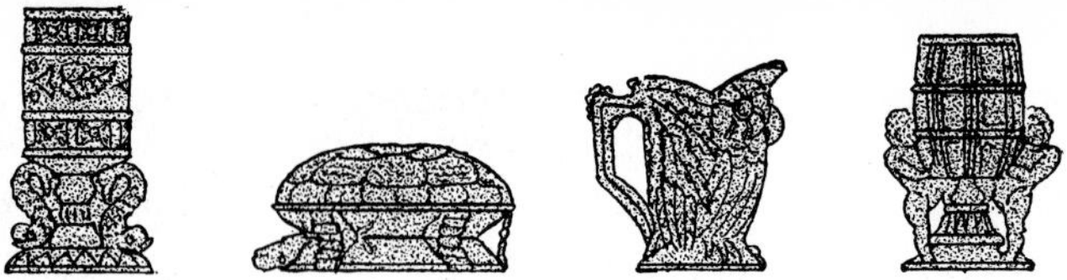

2.

3.

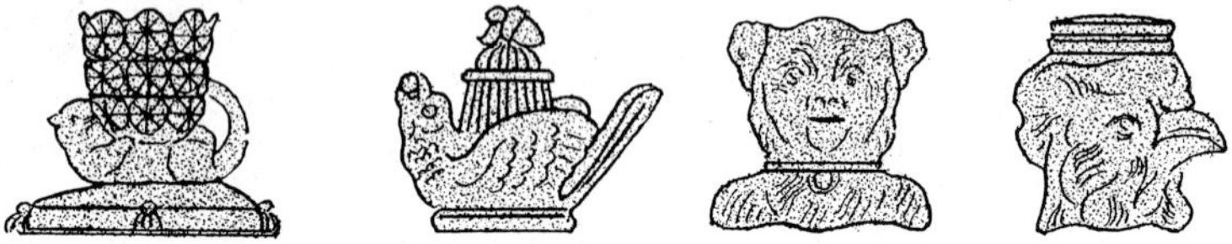

4

PLATE 186

1. DOLPHIN match holder, TURTLE salt, OWL creamer, CHERUB match holder.
2. ALLIGATOR match holder, SWAN salt, CHICKEN toothpick holder, RABBIT match holder.
3. KITTEN match holder, BIRD mustard jar, MONKEY toothpick holder, ROOSTER salt.
4. ROOSTER match holder, DOG match holder, DOG salt, SWAN salt.

PLATE 187—LARGE PLATES

Late Thistle   Block with fan border
Open edge, with basket weave center   Double vine

PLATE 188

DEEP DISH WITH SHEAF OF WHEAT IN CENTER
LARGE TRAY WITH SCENE DEPICTING NIAGARA FALLS

16. Attractive goblet having a stippled stem and leaves, with chain effect above. No other pieces to match have been found to date.
17. Goblet in a square block pattern, with square base. This is often found in colors, particularly in a shade of turquoise, or greenish-blue. Open and covered square compotes, sauce dishes, spoonholder, sugar and creamer have been found. Collectible in sets.
18. Sprig. Pattern described under that title in this book.
19. Wheat. This goblet is similar to number thirteen in that it is of clear glass and has three panels, each having a thin design. It should not be confused with the earlier Paneled Wheat pattern shown elsewhere in this book.
20. Variant of Currant pattern which appears to be later. This one has a thin pattern of larger leaves, with odd long cluster that might be grapes.

GOBLETS

(See Plate 154)

 *1. Lace Dewdrop goblet. Brilliant with many dewdrops of varied sizes. More attractive than illustration indicates. Base ornamented. Made in Pittsburgh by Duncan in clear, and later from the old molds by the Coöperative Flint Glass Company, Beaver Falls, Pa. It is still made in milk-white, as well as clear glass.
  2. Goblet having three elaborate medallions, each containing a head. This pattern sometimes confused with the Minerva and with Three-Face.
  3. Daisy and Button. Three clear oval panels, balance of the bowl covered with the pressed pattern.
  4. Odd goblet which may be combined well with any of the Dewdrop patterns. A large clear star in relief has a double circle of small dewrops forming a chain effect.
  5. Late Cable variant. Evidently a pattern of the Eighties, which may be found in colors.
  6. Early Sandwich glass spoonholder. These are found in clear glass, translucent white and yellow. It is possible other colors may be had also. It is interesting to know that these odd pieces were sold to hold cigars, tapers, etc.
  7. Spoon holder of type made at Sandwich, similar to Number 6 except that design varies slightly. Colors: Amethyst rare. Lamps were made to match this pattern.
  8. Heavy flint glass goblet similar in design and age to the one listed in this book under Eugenie.
  9. Pattern sometimes referred to as Honeysuckle. Background of design is stippled. Probably other forms exist.
*10. Baltimore Pear goblet. Pattern described under that title.
 11. Mioton. Pattern described under that title.

12. Brooklyn. This is the old trade name for this heavy flint glass. Compotes, goblets and ale glasses may be had, and no doubt other forms exist. It belongs to the late Fifties or early Sixties.

13. Pillar Ale glass. Pattern described under that title.

14. Almond Thumbprint. Many forms exist in this pattern which are described under that title. Milk-white; clear glass.

15. Daisy and Button. A variation of the pattern that is popular to-day and may be found in colors.

16. Grape pattern. Late period.

17. Paneled goblet, with small stars above and below panels, like on Star and Feather plates. Late period. Collectible in other forms.

18. Conventional pattern. Other forms are available, such as compotes, etc.

19. Loop Variant, as described under Petal and Loop.

20. Loop Variant, as decribed under Petal and Loop.

GOBLETS

(See Plate 164)

1. Pattern found in fine shade of emerald green or clear glass. Many pieces of this have been seen, including square berry bowls (round bowl), sauce dishes to match, sugar bowl and cordials. Listed as Emerald Green Herringbone and described under that title.

2. Goblet in a Cable pattern, later period than early cable shown in this book.

3. Broken Column goblet. Each panel has three cut-out spaces, like notches. This is found in all clear glass, and also in clear with the notches touched in bright red. The latter are both dainty and effective. Made by Richards & Hartley, Tarentum, Pa., in complete sets. See *Victorian Glass.*

4. Paneled Grape with Thumbprint. A pattern made fifty years ago. A full set may be collected, including many odd sized pitchers and syrup jugs.

5. Centennial goblet. Bowl has drapery design and Centennial dates. Knob stem. No other pieces to match are known.

6. Goblet showing a number of birds in flight, and one butterfly.

7. Goblet having six oval panels, three containing a single rose and three with two diamond-shaped ornaments. These alternate around the bowl. To date no other pieces to match have been found. This is a fairly heavy glass, probably dating from late Sixties.

8. Goblet of later period, having a band of diamond-shaped ornaments with oval impressed in center and lightly stippled background.

9. Odd goblet having two large crossed leaves lightly stippled and an ornament that looks like a cluster of four peppers. There are three such clusters of leaves and peppers around the bowl of each goblet.

10. Late goblet of period close to 1890, having alternating panels of clear glass and of a design of diamond-shaped ornaments.

11. Goblet of pattern which is collectible in a set. This is sometimes called "Actress" or "Jenny Lind." Jenny Lind is a misnomer as one panel shows a bust marked "Kate Claxton" and the reverse has a different bust marked "Lotta." A complete set may be found in this pattern, including covered compotes.

12. This goblet is called "Valentine." It has a background of small diamond points, and three large clear hearts outlined in dewdrops, showing a woman's face in each one. Stem has three little beaded hearts, stippled in the center. Water pitchers to match may be found. Made by United States Glass Company and originally called "Trilby."

13. This goblet is more attractive than it appears in the illustration. There is a wide stippled band with an irregular line in clear relief. The balance of the goblet is clear, with three clusters of grapes having stippled leaves.

14. This goblet is another which is much more attractive than the illustration might indicate. The bowl is largely covered with grape leaves, veined and stippled, with a few clusters of grapes between in bright relief. So far no other pieces to match have been seen.

15. Fruit goblet. This has three panels divided by single line of diamond points. One panel has strawberries, leaves and a flower; another contains a cluster of cherries and leaves, and the third a bunch of grapes, though the same leaves are used as with the cherry. This is apparently a pattern of the Eighties.

16. Late paneled goblet, having an odd four-petaled flower, leaves, and what might be apples hanging from some of the branches. There are two sprays on each goblet. The goblet is clear, with design lightly stippled. The stem has three turnings, forming a knob.

17. Deer pattern, apparently a glass dating about 1890. The goblet has three panels containing the deer, each in a different posture. Sprays of flowers divide the panels.

18. Early flint glass goblet with English registry mark on the inside of the bowl. This is illustrated here to show how easily we might mistake for American the glass made in England during the corresponding era.

19. Goblet in amber glass, showing a pattern collectible in many pieces. This is apparently a glass of the Eighties.

20. Simple conventional design of a goblet probably produced during the Eighties.

ODD PLATES AND PLATTERS

As political personages and events were pictured on the historical whiskey or campaign flasks, so were they shown in lesser numbers on plates and platters of the cheaper commercial glassware, such as the popular pressed glass of the later period. In certain instances, the deaths of well-known heroes were also commemorated, the earliest shown in pattern glass being the Lincoln Drape, said to have been inspired by the mourning after the assassination of Lincoln. The Cable pattern was suggested by the completion of the laying of the Atlantic cable. At a later date we have the well-known Grant Peace plates with the maple leaf border, in honor of Grant's victories which ended the Civil War. The Garfield Drape (Plate 165) mourns the death of President Garfield. This pattern may be collected in a complete set. None of the pieces is distinctly suggestive of Garfield with the exception of the large eleven-inch plate, the rest of the glassware having only the beaded festoon of flowers of the set. The six-inch plate on Plate 52 showing a bust surrounded by stars must have appeared at the time Benjamin Harrison was running for President in 1888. The other large plate marked "Memorial" was on the market shortly after Garfield's death. These two plates are odd pieces and may not be found in other shapes.

The Centennial naturally prompted the making of many historical and political pieces of glassware. The Liberty Bell pattern came out at this time as well as the other two platters and goblets pictured on Plate 117. The Washington platter is inscribed "First in war, first in peace and first in the hearts of his countrymen." This is in clear glass, though I have also seen it with the bust of Washington frosted. The trade name was "Washington Bread Plate." These platters were made by Gillinder & Sons, of Philadelphia, as well as others with the same borders, but different centers. One with Independence Hall in the center, had over it the inscription: "The Nation's Birthplace." Another showed Carpenters Hall, with the inscription: "The Continental Congress first assembled in Carpenters Hall, Sept. 5, 1776." Still another, in a smaller size, with a star in the center, was marked: "Centennial" on each handle. In the catalogue it was listed as "Centennial pickle." Some of these interesting trays and platters have been found in color. Another Centennial piece is the Prescott and Stark platter, "The heroes of Bunker Hill," which is clear glass, as is

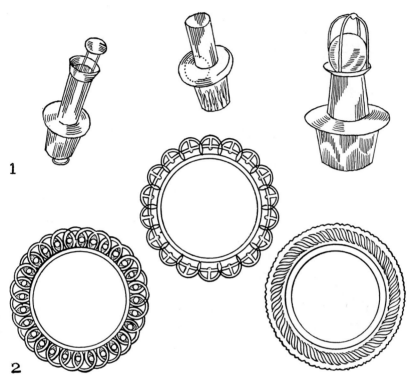

1

2

PLATE 189
PATENT CORKS
MILK-WHITE PLATES
(See page 616)

PLATE 190—ODDS AND ENDS

1. BIRD creamer, crossed fern sauce dish, swan salt.
2. PICKLE jar, double vine relish dish, shell spoonholder.
3. Bakewell, Pears & Co.'s "THISTLE" decanter and water pitcher, draped star sauce dish, butterfly salt.
4. MILK-WHITE plate, stippled chain salt, rare purple marble glass candlestick.

(See page 645)

also the goblet directly underneath showing the American shield. On the side of the bowl of the goblet is another shield bearing the dates 1776-1876. Still another Centennial goblet may be seen on Plate 164.

The square tray on Plate 165 (evidently designed for water pitcher and goblets) bears the inscription "The Patriot and Soldier," "Gen. Ulysses S. Grant." This is in clear glass and I have come across several of them. The oblong platter next to it with a handle at each end bears the busts of Cleveland and Hendricks and was probably inspired by the election of Cleveland and his running mate in 1884. These are the best known of this group, though undoubtedly many others may be found.

On Plate 185 is the interesting Knights of Labor platter, of which I have seen several in colors. This organization was the forerunner of the American Federation of Labor and played an important part in its day. Beer mugs, ale glasses and other pieces to match were made by the United States Glass Company, of Pittsburgh, Pa.

The Railroad platter on Plate 110 is not in commemoration of the founding of the Baltimore & Ohio Railroad as some collectors think. As a matter of fact, it is more plausibly believed to commemorate the opening of the Union Pacific Railroad in 1869, and shows the famous Engine No. 350. Americans have always been fond of the romance of our railroads. They developed this country and we have never forgotten it. The round tray on the same Plate was designed to hold a water pitcher and goblets. The makers, the Bellaire Goblet Company, of Findlay, Ohio, also made goblets, clarets, wines, cordials and all manner of tableware to match the design consisting only of the pressed pattern seen on the border of the tray. The scene in the center of the tray is most amusing and is said to have been taken from a "darky comic" by Currier & Ives. At any rate, we hope Rastus is able to move the mule and wagon over the track before the train comes much closer. I have seen these sets in clear glass as well as in yellow. Other "comics" exist. Gillinder & Sons made a series of them which they listed as "Puck" plates, such as the boys' wagon pulled by a dog that decided to chase a rabbit, and others. Some of the large plates that do not match collectible sets are shown as a means of identification, and also because large plates are always in demand for service plates, as well as for other purposes. The Niagara Falls tray was made by Adams & Co. of Pittsburgh, during the Seventies.

PLATES AND PLATTERS

ODDS AND ENDS

(Plate 190)

1. Bird creamer. Opaque-blue bowl in Crossed Fern pattern (a number of forms may be found, especially in milk-white, including footed sauce dishes in two sizes). Swan-footed salt dish in milk-white.
2. Frosted Deer jam jar (made by Duncans of Pittsburgh to be sold with Three-Face set). Double Vine pickle dish, Shell sugar bowl (cover missing).
3. Pillar and Bull's-Eye decanter and water pitcher. Odd bowl in dewdrop design with star motif (not Dewdrop with Star), Butterfly footed salt.
4. Milk-white plate in Arch pattern, footed salt in Stippled Chain (collectible in many forms). Marble glass fluted candlestick.

Chapter XXVII

PRESSED PATTERNS AND TABLE
DECORATIONS

It seems fitting, at the conclusion of a book devoted to the description and classification of old patterns of American pressed glass, to offer a few practical suggestions to those persons who do not collect glass and have no special fondness for old-fashioned things as such but are interested in the artistic possibilities of whatever may prove valuable in home decoration. To these, unfamiliar as they probably are with our pressed patterns, the charm and variety of the tableware illustrated in this book will be a revelation. No end of these old designs are so quaint and full of character, so overwhelmingly suggestive of bygone days and manners, that they help to produce "atmosphere" in the dining room as inevitably as the infinitely less subtle sideboard or chairs or panelling. Moreover, many are worthy of any artist's study, not alone for what they suggest, but as bits of pure design.

Of course, there will be the usual chuckle from alleged experts of antiques who still think it humorous to refer to all pressed glass as "early Woolworth," or "Mid-Victorian atrocities." But if it is undoubtedly true that scores of the patterns shown in this book may not have high artistic or historical merit, on the other hand, it is only fair to bear in mind that neither is every piece of furniture made from designs by Sheraton or Hepplewhite a masterpiece. At all times and in all places, master-craftsmen have had their off moments and the old American glassmakers were no exceptions. To condemn as inartistic many of our distinctively American pressed glass patterns is absurd. Study the illustrations and look not for the worst but for the best. There is beauty enough in them for all purposes, if you seek charm of line, dignity, quaintness and quality of material. You will find many excellent designs utterly free from European influences, which is more than can be said for most of our arts and crafts during our first century as a nation. Good designing is good designing and all the scoffing of the ignorant and the incompetent cannot make it anything else. That is why to-day it is not the poor who buy this "cheap" glass, but the wealthy, not the ignorant but the discriminating! You will not find it displayed on the kitchen tables of farmhouses but in the period dining rooms of fastidious collectors. And one does not have to be rich to collect it!

An entire volume could be written on the numberless ways in which early American pressed glass can be effectively used in home decoration. The reader might turn back to the chapter on Milk-White Glass, a ware with which nearly everyone is familiar whether or not they are collectors or hunters of antiques. The white Sawtooth, one of the earliest patterns, now exceedingly scarce, is one of the most desirable for those who are willing to search patiently—and to pay well! The Blackberry, another early pattern in this glass, is considered by many to be the handsomest. The glass is of fine quality, often showing the fiery lights of the opal, especially when held to the light. This ware is at its best when used with a linen of warm color, as for example, a peach-colored tablecloth with flesh-colored zinnias and heliotrope for flowers. Other colors for linen to be used with milk-white glass are a rich fuchsia shade of red or a primrose yellow.

White glass is not a success on a white tablecloth, but it is decidedly attractive on white mats or doilies where the mahogany, old cherry or walnut of the table is the principal contrasting color and deep purple grapes and leaves are used in lieu of the usual floral accessories. Another smart use of milk-white glass is in combination with dark-green linen, using small, compact, symmetrical bunches of snowberries instead of flowers. Colored goblets or tumblers can often be used successfully with the milk-white glass, if you avoid a conflict of colors in the linen or the flowers.

Crystal glass in the various patterns described and illustrated in this book offers a wide range of opportunities for combination with different china, linen, flowers and fruits. Your favorite pattern may harmonize beautifully with brown Staffordshire china on brown linen, bordered with beige and brown, using fruits instead of flowers; say black and pink-cheeked yellow plums. Dark blue Staffordshire china on natural colored linen bordered with deep sapphire blue is charming when set off, for example, by the brilliant crystal sawtooth. More color may be added if desired by using sapphire blue wine glasses. Sapphire-blue witchballs could be used in the compotes, with grapes arranged over them. Clear glass patterns are also interesting on lettuce-green linen with white zinnias and green grapes. Pewter plates would add much to this scheme.

For those who have specialized in collecting yellow or "canary" glass, it is suggested that they try a rich ecru-colored linen with chartreuse and lettuce-green border. Snowberries and white zinnias complete this picture unless one prefers fruits, in which event green grapes, purple-black grapes and plums are charming.

Amber glass is particularly lovely under artificial light, when the yellow or "canary" glass loses its tone. In the fall or winter what could be more inviting than a table in flame-colored linen, using single or miniature dahlias in shades of yellow, orange and flame red?

One of the most dignified patterns in an unusual glass, is the fluted purple Marble glass. Read the chapter that treats of it. When properly used it has more distinction than all other types. The forms and coloring are fascinating. Of the linens to use with this glass, the most attractive are mauve bordered with the deeper mauve shades of the glass; oyster-white linen bordered with mauves; gray-pink linen bordered with the deep mauves of the glass. White linen is excellent since it does not take away in the slightest any of the importance of the glass itself. Flowers should be in the proper shades of mauve and rose. The difficulty in securing these makes fruits easier to use with this striking glass, as for instance, when you combine deep reddish-purple plums and black grapes with apples of the right shades of deep red. Black open-edged plates fit in perfectly, although one may substitute old mauve

Staffordshire china. Amethyst goblets or tumblers are scarce but still obtainable. Find a new interest in life by looking for them. Think of how the table will look—and keep on searching!

Emerald-green glass is one of the most beautiful in color and combines attractively with ecru linen bordered with the green of the glass. Pewter plates fit finely, and, of course, black glass plates. Snowberries used with this glass never fail to please, though green and black grapes are nearly as effective.

Opaque blue glass, though it is scarce in many forms, is a favorite today because it can be combined most effectively with opal glass on peach-colored linen with peach-colored roses and white flowers. Another much admired combination is a soft mauve-blue linen with opal glass, light blue Staffordshire china and Chinese Forget-me-nots for flowers. One should always remember that, as a rule, the smartest schemes are those done practically in shades of either one color or closely related colors. The haphazard mixing of hues should be avoided as much as possible on your table as everywhere else. There must be contrast but that contrast must be created to help and not to upset the harmonizing unity of the entire color scheme. If you have the love and the knowledge and the patience, you will find the glass.

The temptation to continue is difficult to resist but a writer's duty is done when the attention of people of artistic tastes is called to the infinite possibilities of early American pressed glass. It talks for itself—if you will only listen!

INDEX

8 5